Modern Software Review:

Techniques and Technologies

Yuk Kuen Wong
Griffith University, Australia

IRM Press

**Publisher of innovative scholarly and professional
information technology titles in the cyberage**

Hershey • London • Melbourne • Singapore

Acquisitions Editor: Michelle Potter
Development Editor: Kristin Roth
Senior Managing Editor: Amanda Appicello
Managing Editor: Jennifer Neidig
Copy Editor: Larissa Vinei
Typesetter: Marko Primorac
Cover Design: Lisa Tosheff
Printed at: Yurchak Printing Inc.

Published in the United States of America by
        IRM Press (an imprint of Idea Group Inc.)
        701 E. Chocolate Avenue, Suite 200
        Hershey PA 17033-1240
        Tel: 717-533-8845
        Fax: 717-533-8661
        E-mail: cust@idea-group.com
        Web site: http://www.irm-press.com

and in the United Kingdom by
        IRM Press (an imprint of Idea Group Inc.)
        3 Henrietta Street
        Covent Garden
        London WC2E 8LU
        Tel: 44 20 7240 0856
        Fax: 44 20 7379 0609
        Web site: http://www.eurospanonline.com

Library of Congress Cataloging-in-Publication Data

Wong, Yuk Kuen, 1973-
    Modern software review : techniques and technologies / Yu Kuen Wong.
        p. cm.
    Summary: "This book provides an understanding of the critical factors affecting software review performance and to provide practical guidelines for software reviews"--Provided by publisher.
    Includes bibliographical references and index.
    ISBN 1-59904-013-1 (hardcover) -- ISBN 1-59904-014-X (softcover) -- ISBN 1-59904-015-8 (ebook)
    1. Computer software--Quality control. 2. Computer software--Evaluation. 3. Computer software--Development. I. Title.
    QA76.76.Q35W65 2006
    005.1--dc22
                                2006003561

British Cataloguing in Publication Data
A Cataloguing in Publication record for this book is available from the British Library.

To my father and mother.

Modern Software Review:
Techniques and Technologies

Table of Contents

Preface

An Introduction to the Subject Area

High quality software is of vital importance for the survival and success of companies where many manual tasks are now automated through software, which can provide increased speed, accuracy, assurance, reliability, robustness, and productivity. Software is often a key component of companies' strategic plans for gaining and sustaining competitive advantage. A single undetected error or omission during the software development process could have disastrous consequences during operation. Software errors and omissions can also lead to undesirable outcomes such as reduced customer satisfaction, increased maintenance costs and/ or decreased productivity and profits.

Although information technology can be considered a well-established discipline, software projects are still prone to failure. Even when a software project is not classified as a failure, the general level of software quality leaves much room for improvement. Software review or inspection is one of the important techniques for improving software quality.

In the last thirty years, software reviews have been recommended as one of the most cost effective quality assurance techniques in software process improvements and are widely used in industrial practice. The goal of software review is to improve the quality of the product by reviewing interim deliverables during design and development. It is defined as a "non-execution-based [technique] for scrutinizing software products for defects, deviations from development standards". Most researchers agree that software review is considered the most cost effective technique in cost saving, quality and productivity improvements in software engineering. More specifically, software review can 1) detect defects right through the software development life cycle from concept proposal to implementation to testing; the earlier defects are detected in development, then the easier and less costly they are to remove/correct; and 2) detect defects early in the software development life cycle that are difficult or impossible to detect in later stages; improve learning and communication in the software team, since software development is essentially a human activity.

Overall Objectives and Mission of This Book

The overall objective and mission the proposed book is to provide:

- An understanding of the critical factors affecting software review perfomance.
- Practical guidelines for software reviews.

Readers will gain a deep understanding of current software review literature and theoretical models for analysis software review performance. More specifically, this helps readers to understand the critical input and process factors that drive software review performance. Practical guidelines are drawn from the literature, theoretical models, methodologies, and the results from industry survey and cases studies.

The Scholarly Value of this Book and its Contributions to the Literature in the Information Technology Discipline:

- To increase the understanding of what inputs the typical review process uses in practice.
- To identify the key factors influencing software review performanceTheoretical models help to understand the important relationships between inputs, process, and performance perspective.
- The rigorous quantitative industry questionnaire survey and qualitative (case study: in-depth interviews) case studies are contributed to the software review literature.
- To provide useful and practical guidelines for organizing and conducting software reviews.

Abstract

Information Technology can be considered a well-established discipline, however, software development projects are still prone to failure. Even if a software project is not classified as a failure, the general level of software quality leaves room for improvement. One of the most prevalent and costly mistakes made in software projects today is deferring the activity of detecting and correcting software problems until the end of the project (Boehm & Basili, 2001). Hence, the cost of rework in the later stages of a project can be greater than 100 times that of the project costs (Fagan, 1976; Leffingwell & Widrig, 2000). About 80% of avoidable rework comes from 20% of defects (Boehm & Basili, 2001). As a result, techniques such as software review for improving software quality are important. The current software review literature lacks in empirical evidence on identifying critical inputs and process factors influencing review performance because there is little empirical manipulation of these variables. Where inputs are manipulated, the results are often conflicting and inconsistent. Hence, *what* inputs to use for effective software review in practice is still open to determination. Different input requirements directly affect how the software review is organized.

The overall objective of this book is to explore and understand the critical factors that significantly influence software review performance in practice. In other words, the aim of this book is to further empirically validate the important relationships between software review inputs, process, and performance. Thus, this study is interesting and important for both researchers and practitioners.

The main structures of the book include: literature review, review software, review tools, and technologies, understanding the relationships between inputs, process and software review performance, development of a theoretical model, development of the industry survey plan (instruments (questionnaire), design, pre-tests, sampling, data gathering, data analysis), case study (in-depth interviews of the real life cases), recommendations, and the final writing.

In this book, both quantitative and qualitative methods were employed when collecting and analysing empirical data in order to maximise the reliability and validity of the study. A questionnaire mail survey was arranged with 205 respondents from the software industry in Australia. A cross validation study using an in-depth interview with experts was conducted with five cases (companies). The rich qualitative data from the in-depth interviews and quantitative data (statistical analysis) from the questionnaire survey offers a comprehensive picture of the use of software review in practice. The final conclusion of the book is drawn from a comparative analysis of the quantitative and qualitative results. The empirical data obtained from surveys and in-depth interviews with experts is cross-examined and discussed. The main conclusion of the study is described below.

The current empirical software review studies focus heavily on the explicit inputs (e.g., supporting documents) rather than implicit inputs (reviewer characteristics). However, the survey results in this study suggest that the implicit inputs play a dominant role in software review performance. The findings suggest that the characteristics of the software artefact have no significant direct influence on software review performance and supporting documents have little direct impact on review performance. The results show that only the use of previously reviewed software documents has an effect on software review performance. Interesting results demonstrate that reading techniques and prescription documents have no impact on software review performance. It has previously been argued in the software review literature that reading techniques are considered the most effective explicit input for improving software review performance, however, the survey results show that previously reviewed software documents are more critical than reading techniques documents. Both survey and in-depth interview results suggest that current reading techniques in the software industry are not conclusively beneficial to software review performance. This suggests that reading techniques documents need to be carefully designed and used in practice.

To achieve a higher performance in the software review process, selection of reviewers becomes the most critical factor. These results confirm the theory by Sauer, Jeffery, Land, and Yetton, (2000) and in part, Laitenberger and DeBaud's model (2000). In relation to reviewer motivation, interesting results suggest that motivation, in particular, perceived contingency, is another important factor in the software review process and review performance according to the survey results. However, this variable is often ignored in the empirical software review literature. Although several researchers have recommended that reviewers' motivation should be important in software review performance, to our knowledge, no empirical study has been carried out to support this. The findings suggest that company support, encouragement and reviewer agreement for the way the company conducts software review helps to increase reviewers' motivation and effort and hence improve review performance.

Finally, teamwork is the dominant factor in the review meeting process. The survey results show that teamwork is the best indicator of a successful software review meeting. The more collaborative a review team, the higher the software review performance that can be achieved.

In summary, the key driver to software review performance is reviewers' experience, followed by previously reviewed software documents, perceived contingency (support, encouragement, and reviewer agreement with the company), and teamwork.

Structure of This Book

This book is organised into twelve chapters. Each chapter is briefly summarised as follows:

Chapter I discusses why study software review. The chapter identifies advantages of software review that include improving software quality, cost saving, and productivity. In particular, the chapter presents experts' opinions — the impact of software review on software engineering. In the final section of the chapter, the book addresses the aim of the book and the organization of the book.

Chapter II presents the software review literature including the history of software review, forms of software review structure, and informal review approaches. More specifically, in the literature review, the chapter reviews the six-step Fagan's Software Review (i.e., planning, overview, preparation, group meeting, reworks, and follow-up), form software review structure (i.e., Active Design Review, Two-Person Review, N-fold Review, Phased Review, Use of Review Meeting), IEEE standard for software review, informal review approaches (i.e., Walkthrough, Pair Programming, Peer Check, Pass-Around), and a comparison of formal and informal review approaches.

Chapter III describes tools and technologies for software review. The chapter starts with an explanation of the difference between paper-based and tool-based software reviews, as well as collaborative asynchronous vs. synchronous software review. Followed by an evaluation and comparison of software review tools' features. The chapter identifies the tools features for the group review process. The final section of the chapter reviews a framework for supporting tool-based software processes.

Chapter IV discusses software review tools and how they support the software review process. Tools including: Intelligent Code Inspection in "C" Language (CICLE), Scrutiny, Collaborate Software Inspection (CSI), InspeQ, CSRS, Requirement Traceability (RADIX), InspectA, Asynchronous Inspector of Software Artefacts (AISA), Web Inspection Prototype (WiP), HyperCode, Asynchronous/Synchronous Software Inspection Support Tool (AISSIT), Fine-Grained Software Inspection Tool, CORD, Agent-based Software Tool, Internet-based Inspection System (IBIS), and VisionQuest are discussed in the chapter.

Chapter V presents use of software review inputs, supporting process structure techniques, methods of measuring software review performance, and the limitations of the current software review literature. In particularly, the chapter reviews use of inputs (that include review task, supporting documents, reviewer characteristics), review process (team size, roles design, decision-making method during the review process, and process gain and losses), and qualitative and quantitative methods for performance measurement. The chapter also identifies limitations of the current software review literature.

Chapter VI proposes a theoretical model for analysing software review performance. The Explicit and Implicit Input-process-Output (EIIO) Model is developed for further analysis software review performance. The model includes three major components–inputs, process, and output. Inputs can be classified into explicit inputs and implicit inputs. Explicit inputs refer to software review task (artefact) characteristics and supporting documents. Supporting documents include reading techniques (e.g., checklist, scenarios readings), business reports, prescription documents, and previously reviewed software documents. Implicit inputs include reviewers' ability and their motivations. During the meeting process, the process factors can be classified into communication, teamwork, status effect, and discussion quality. Software review performance is often measured by the number of defects found. The chapter presents the important relationships between inputs, process, and performance. Five propositions between these relationships are discussed in the final section of the chapter.

Chapter VII presents the Industry survey design. In order to understand how practitioners conduct their software reviews in their development environment in software industry, an industry survey is conducted. The industry survey can also validate the theoretical EIIO model. The chapter mainly discusses the industry survey design. A survey plan (i.e., research method, survey design, questionnaire design, measurements of models and scales, sampling techniques, validation of questionnaire procedures, data collection methods, data analysis methods) is detailed described in the chapter.

Chapter VIII discusses industry survey results and findings. The overall survey results provide an understanding of software review in practice and a validation of the proposed EIIO model. This allows better understanding of the direct and indirect relationships between software review inputs, process, and performance. The survey includes four major procedures–response, preliminary analysis, exploratory analysis, and hypotheses tests. The response section discusses response rate, response characteristics, and response bias. The primary analysis focuses on descriptive and missing value analysis whereas, exploratory analysis focuses on reliability and validity of the survey results. The hypotheses tests analysis effects on software review inputs, process, and performance.

Chapter IX discusses the revised EIIO model. This presents interesting results from a comprehensive data analysis procedure. The chapter provides a simple review guide (four steps of conducting software review) after discussions of the revised EIIO model.

Chapter X presents an industry cases study. The case study provides qualitative results and rich information from industry experts' opinions. The method used in the case study is in-depth interview. The data collection procedures and the findings are discussed in the chapter. The findings include 1) issues of conducting software review, 2) common types of software review inputs, 3) discussions of inputs affect review process and performance, and 4) discussions of process affect performance (review outcome).

Chapter XI presents practical guidelines and recommendations for both practitioners and researchers. Useful recommendations of use of inputs, the need for team review meetings and selection measurement metrics (review performance) are provided in the chapter.

Chapter XII concludes contributions and future directions. Theoretical and methodological contributions are addressed. The chapter discusses limitations of the industry studies in this book and future software review directions.

References

Boehm, B. W. & Basili, B. R. (2001). Software defect reduction top 10 list. *IEEE Computer*, *34*(1), January.

Fagan, M. E. (1976). Design and code inspections to reduce errors in program development. *IBM System Journal*, *15*(3), 182-211.

Laitenberger, O. & Debaud, J. M. (2000). An encompassing life cycle centric survey of software inspection. *The Journal of Software and Systems*, *50*(1), 5-31.

Leffingwell, D. & Widrig, D. (2000). *Managing software requirements: A unified approach.* NJ: Addison Wesley.

Sauer, C., Jeffery, R., Land, L., & Yetton, P. (2000). Understanding and improving the effectiveness of software development technical reviews: A behaviourally motivated programme of research. *IEEE Transactions on Software Engineering*, *26*(1), 1-14.

Acknowledgment

In preparing this book, I received tremendous help from a number of individuals whom I would like to thank. I would like to thank many people for their help and support while I was carrying out my book.

Special thanks go to Professor Waynne Chin from The University of Houston for providing Structural Equation Modeling Partial Least Square (SEM-PLS) workshops and advising on the execution of statistical data analysis and methodology design.

I am extremely grateful for the work of a great team at Idea Group Inc. In particular, to Kristin Roth who continuously addressed all my questions and prodded for keeping the project on schedule and to Mehdi Khosrow-Pour and Jan Travers for the invitation. Thanks to various reviewers for their critical comments and feedback on this book. I would like to thank the volunteers participating in the industry survey and the case study. Thanks to the voluntary students that provided additional help.

Finally, I would like to thank a number of friends and colleagues, who in their own separate ways, kept me sane during this undertaking. And of course, thanks goes to my family for all their support.

Yuk Kuen Wong, PhD

Chapter I

Why Software Review?

Abstract

The aim of this chapter is to discuss the benefits of software review. The key benefits of software are improving software quality and providing cost saving and productivity improvement. It has been agreed that software review is one of the best influence on software engineering. This chapter describes the structure of the book and explains each chapter's focus. The overall objective of this book is to provide an understanding of the critical factors affecting software review performance and to provide practical guidelines for software reviews.

Introduction

High quality software is of vital importance for the survival and success of companies where many manual tasks are now automated through software, which can provide increased speed, accuracy, assurance, reliability, robustness, and productivity (Chen & Wei, 2002; Humphrey, 1995, 2002b; Will & Whobrey,

1992, 2003, 2004). Software is often a key component of companies' strategic plans for gaining and sustaining competitive advantage (Gilb & Graham, 1993; Humphrey, 2002a, 2002b). A single undetected error or omission (Will & Whobrey, 2004) during the software development process could have disastrous consequences during operation (Humphrey, 1995; Parnas & Lawford, 2003a, 2003b). Software errors and omissions can also lead to undesirable outcomes, such as reduced customer satisfaction, increased maintenance costs, and/or decreased productivity and profits (Schulmeyer & Mcmanus, 1999).

Although information technology can be considered a well-established discipline, software projects are still prone to failure (Humphrey, 2002b; Sommerville, 2001, 1995; Voas, 2003). Even when a software project is not classified as a failure, the general level of software quality leaves much room for improvement (Boehm & Basili, 2001; Chen, Kerre, & Vandenbulcke, 1995; Lyytinen & Hirschheim, 1987). Software review or inspection is one of the important techniques for improving software quality (Boehm & Basili, 2001; Fagan, 1986; Thelin, Runeson, & Wohlin, 2003).

The goal of software review is to improve the quality of the product by reviewing interim deliverables during design and development (Fagan, 1976, 1986; Porter & Votta, 1997, 1998). Defects are detected early and removed before the product is released (Sommerville, 2001; Xu, 2003; Zhu, Jin, Diaper, & Ganghong, 2002).

Software review or inspection is a widely recommended technique for improving software quality and increasing software developers' productivity (Fagan, 1976; Freedman & Weinberg, 1990; Gilb & Graham, 1993; Humphrey, 1995; Strauss & Ebenau, 1994). In particular, Fagan's review (or inspection) is recommended as one of the ten best influences on software development and engineering (Boehm & Basili, 2001; Biffl, 2001; Biffl & Halling, 2003; Briand, Freimut, & Vollei, 1999; Fagan, 1986; Gilb & Graham, 1993; McConnell, 1993; Wohlin, Aurum, Petersson, Shull, & Ciolkowski, 2002). Software review was originally proposed by Michael Fagan at IBM in early 1970's (Fagan, 1976).

Why Study Software Review?

Software review is an industry-proven process for eliminating defects. It has been defined as a "non-execution-based [technique] for scrutinizing software products for defects, and deviations from development standards" (Ciolkowski, Laitenberger, & Biffl, 2003). Most researchers agree that software review is considered the most cost effective technique in cost saving, quality, and productivity improvements in software engineering (Ackerman, Buchwald, &

Lewski, 1989; Basili, Laitenberger, Shull, & Rus, 2000; Biffl, 2001; Boehm & Basili, 2001; Fagan, 1986; Gilb & Graham, 1993; Russell, 1991). Studies show that 42% of defects result from a lack of traceability from the requirements or design to the code (O'Neill, 1997a, 1997b). More specifically, software review can (Briand, Freimut, & Vollei, 2000):

- Detect defects right through the software development life cycle from concept proposal to implementation to testing; the earlier defects are detected in development, then the easier and less costly they are to remove/ correct,
- Detect defects early in the software development life cycle that are difficult or impossible to detect in later stages, and;
- Improve learning and communication in the software team (Huang, 2003; Huang et al., 2001), since software development is essentially a human activity.

Improve Software Quality

A defect is an instance in which a requirement is not satisfied.

(Fagan, 1986)

One of the benefits of software review is to improve software quality in the early stages of the software development cycle (Basili & Selby, 1987; Basili et al., 2000; Biffl, 2001; Boehm & Basili, 2001; Calvin, 1983; Christenson, Steel, & Lamperez, 1990; Fagan, 1976, 1986; Freedman & Weinberg, 1990; Humphrey, 2000, 2002a, 2002b; Shull, Lanubile, & Biasili, 2000; Travassos, Shull, Fredericks, & Basili, 1999).

Experience reports also show that software review consistently improves software quality (Ackerman et al., 1989; Collofello & Woodfield, 1989; Fagan, 1976; Kitchenham, Kitchenham, & Fellows, 1986; Knight & Myers, 1993; Weller, 1993). Past studies have shown that software review is an effective technique that can catch between 31% and 93% of the defects, with a median of around 60% (Ackerman et al., 1989; Barnard & Price, 1994; Basili & Selby, 1987; Boehm & Basili, 2001; Collofello & Woodfield, 1989; Fagan, 1976, 1986; Kitchenham et al., 1986; Knight & Myers, 1993; Weller, 1993).

For example, Fagan (1976) reported that 38 defects had been detected in an application program of eight modules (4439 non-commentary source statements written in Cobol, by two programmers at Aetna Life and Casualty), yielding defect detection effectiveness for reviews of 82%. Kitchenham et al. (1986) found that 57.7% of defects were found by software reviews at ICL where the total proportion of development effort devoted to software reviews was only 6%. Conradi, Marjara, and Skatevik (1999) found at Ericsson in Oslo that around 70% of recorded defects, took 6% to 9% of the development effort, and yield an estimated saving of 21% to 34%.

In addition, Grady and Van-Slack (1994) reported defect detection effectiveness for code reviews varying from 30% to 75% whereas Barnard and Price (1994) reported an average of 60% to 70% of the defects were found via code review at Hewlett Packard. In a more recent study, it has been suggested that software reviews removed 35% to 90% of all defects during the development cycle (Boehm & Basili, 2001).

Cost Saving and Productivity Improvement

Another benefit of software review is to reduce development costs and improve productivity. One of the most prevalent and costly mistakes made in software projects today is deferring the activity of detecting and correcting software problems until the end of the project (Boehm & Basili, 2001). The cost of rework in the later stages of a project can be greater than 100 times the cost of correction in the early stages (Fagan, 1976; Leffingwell & Widrig, 2000). About 80% of avoidable rework seems to come from 20% of defects (Boehm & Basili, 2001).

A traditional defect detection activity, such as formal testing, only occurs in the later stages of the software development cycle when it is more costly to remove defects. Testing typically leads to quick fixes and ad-hoc corrections for removing defects; however, those measures reduce maintainability.

Most studies have claimed that the costs for identifying and removing defects in the earlier stages are much lower than in later phases of software development (Ackerman et al., 1989; Basili et al., 2000; Ciolkowski et al., 2003; Fagan, 1986; Weller, 1993). For instance, the Jet Propulsion Laboratory (JPL) found the ratio of the cost of fixing defects during software review to fixing them during testing between 1:10 and 1:34 (Kelly, Sherif, & Hops, 1992), the ratio was 1:20 at the IBM Santa Teresa Lab (Remus, 1984), and at the IBM Rochester Lab it was 1:13 (Kan, 1995). As a result, techniques such as software review for early defect detection are highly necessary.

Software review is a human-based activity to "verify" that software can meet its requirements (Fagan, 1986); where software review costs are directly determined by reviewers' efforts. Davis (1993) measured the cost of errors from various stages of the system development life cycle and reported that huge cost

Figure 1. Relative cost to repair a defect at different lifecycle phases (Adopted from Leffingwell & Widrig, 2000)

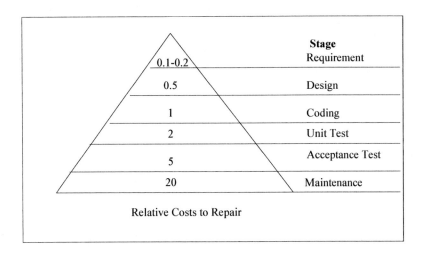

savings could be achieved from finding defects in early stages. Finding defects in the early stage of requirements versus finding errors during the final stage of maintenance leads to a ratio of cost savings of 200:1 (Davis, 1993) (see Figure 1).

Despite perceptions that software reviews are additional work that slow the development, there is ample evidence that software reviews actually reduce development time, as reviews are more efficient than other methods such as testing (Ackerman et al., 1989; Bourgeois, 1996; Collofello & Woodfield, 1989; Kitchenham et al., 1986; Weller, 1993). Software projects are often required to deliver high quality software in limited timeframes to tight deadlines.

Numerous experience reports have proved that software review techniques can significantly reduce costs and improve software development productivity (Ackerman et al., 1989; Bourgeois, 1996; Fagan, 1976, 1986; Gilb & Graham, 1993; Kitchenham et al., 1986; Musa & Ackerman, 1989; Weller, 1993; Wheeler, Brykczynski, & Meeson, 1996). For instance, Ackerman et al. (1989) reported that they took 4.5 hours to eliminate a defect by unit testing compared to 2.2 hours by software code review while Weller (1993) found that testing took about six hours to find each defect while software review took less then one hour per defect.

Further, Jet Propulsion Laboratory (JPL) took up to 17 hours to fix defects during formal testing, in a documented project. The average effort for 171 software reviews (five members) was 1.1 staff-hours per defect found and 1.4–1.8 staff hours per defect found and fixed (Bourgeois, 1996). Kitchenham et al. (1986) reported that the cost of detecting a defect in design inspections was 1.58 hours at ICL.

In summary, software review is the most cost effective technique for improving software quality by detecting and removing software defects during the early stages of the software development life cycle (Basili et al., 1996; Fagan, 1986; Gilb & Graham, 1993).

The Best Influences on Software Engineering

"One of the great breakthroughs in software engineering was Gerald Weinberg's concept of egoless programming–the idea that no matter how smart a programmer is, reviews will be beneficial. Michael Fagan formalized Weinberg's ideas into a well-defined review technique called Fagan inspections. The data in support of the quality, cost and schedule impact of inspections is overwhelming. They are an indispensable part of engineering high-quality software. I propose Fagan inspection (review) as one of the 10 best influences." (McConnell, 2000)

"Inspections (reviews) are surely a key topic, and with the right instrumentation and training they are one of the most powerful techniques for defect detection. They are both effective and efficient, especially for upfront activities. In addition to large scale applications, we are applying them to smaller applications and incremental development" (Chris Ebert, in McConnell, 2000).

"I think inspections (reviews) merit inclusion in this list. They work, they help foster broader understanding and learning, and for the most part they do lead to better code. They can also be abused–for instance, in cases where people become indifferent to the skill set of the review team, or when they don't bother with testing because they are so sure of their inspection process" (Terry Bollinger, in in McConnell, 2000).

"I would go more basic then this. Reviews of all types are a major positive influence. Yes, Fagan inspection (review) is one of the most useful members of this class, but I would put the class of inspections and reviews in the list rather than a specific example" (Robert Cochran, in McConnell, 2000).

After this overview of the benefits of software review, the aims and significance of this study are described in the next section.

Aims and Significance of This Book

The overall objective and mission the proposed book is to provide:

- An understanding of the critical factors affecting software review perfor-mance, and;
- Practical guidelines for software reviews.

Readers will gain a deep understanding of current software review literature and theoretical models for analysis software review performance. More specifically, this helps readers to understand the critical input and process factors that drive software review performance. Practical guidelines are drawn from the litera-ture, theoretical models, methodologies, and the results from industry surveys and cases studies.

Summary

This chapter outlines the benefits of software review and importance in software engineering discipline. History of software review, terminology used, and an overview of current literature will be discussed in next chapter.

References

Ackerman, F. A., Buchwald, L. S., & Lewski, F. H. (1989, May). Software inspection: An effective verification process. *IEEE Software*, 31-36.

Barnard, J., & Price A. (1994, March). Managing code inspection information. *IEEE Software*, 59-69.

Basili, V. R., & Selby, R. W. (1987). Comparing the effectiveness of software testing strategy. *IEEE Transaction on Software Engineering*, *13*(12), 1278-1296.

Basili, V. R., Green, S., Laitenberger, O., Lanubile, F., Sorumgard, S., & Zelkowitz, M. (1996). The empirical investigation of perspective-based reading. *International Journal on Empirical Software Engineering*, *1*(12), 133-144.

Basili, V. R., Laitenberger, O., Shull, F., & Rus, I. (2000). Improving software inspections by using reading techniques. *Proceedings of International Conference on Software Engineering* (pp. 727-836).

Biffl, S. (2001). *Software inspection techniques to support project and quality management: Lessons learned from a large-scale controlled experiment with two inspection cycles on the effect defect detection and defect estimation techniques.* Unpublished PhD Thesis. Department of Software Engineering, Vienna University of Technology, Australia.

Biffl, S., & Halling, M. (2003, May). Investigating the defect detection effectiveness and cost benefit of nominal inspection team. *IEEE Transaction on Software Engineering, 29*(5), 385-397.

Boehm, B. W., & Basili, B. R. (2001, January). Software defect reduction top 10 list. *IEEE Computer, 34*(1).

Bourgeois, K. V. (1996). Process insights from a large-scale software inspections data analysis, cross talk. *Journal Defence Software Engineering,* 17-23.

Briand, L. C., Freimut, B., & Vollei, F. (1999). *Assessing the cost-effectiveness of inspections by combining project data and expert opinion.* International Software Engineering Software Research Network, Fraunhofer Instituted for Empirical Software Engineering, Germany, ISERN Report No. 070-99/E.

Briand, L. C., Freimut, B., & Vollei, F. (2000). *Using multiple adaptive regression splines to understand trends in inspection data and identify optimal inspection rates,* International Software Engineering Software Research Network, Fraunhofer Instituted for Empirical Software Engineering, Germany, ISERN Tr 00-07.

Calvin, T. W. (1983, September). Quality control techniques for "zero defects". *IEEE Transactions on Components, Hybrids, and Manufactory Technology, 6*(3), 323-328.

Chen, G. Q., & Wei, Q. (2002). Fuzzy association rules and the extended algorithms. *Information Science, 147,* 201-228.

Chen, G. Q., Kerre, E. E., & Vandenbulcke, J. (1995). The dependency-preserving decomposition and a testing algorithm in a fuzzy relational data model. *Fuzzy Sets and Systems, 72,* 27-37.

Chen, G. Q., Vandenbulcke, J., & Kerre, E. E. (1992). A general treatment of data redundancy in a fuzzy relational data model. *Journal of the American Society for Information Science,* 304-311.

Christenson, D. A., Steel, H. T., & Lamperez, A. J. (1990). Statistical quality control applied to code inspections. *IEEE Journal, Selected Area Communications, 8*(2), 196-200.

Ciolkowski, M., Laitenberger, O., & Biffl, S. (2003). Software reviews: The state-of-the-practice. *IEEE Software*, 46-51.

Collofello, J. S., & Woodfield, S. N. (1989). Evaluating the effectiveness of reliability-assurance techniques. *Journal of Systems and Software*, (9), 191-195.

Conradi, R., Marjara, A. S., & Skatevik, B. (1999, December). Empirical study of inspection and testing data at Ericsson, Norway. *Proceedings of the 24th Annual Software Engineering Workshop*, Maryland.

Davis, A. M. (1993). *Software requirement: Objectives, functions, and states*. Englewood Cliffs, NJ: Prentice-Hall.

Fagan, M. E. (1976, July). Design and code inspections to reduce errors in program development. *IBM System Journal, 15*(3), 182-211.

Fagan, M. E. (1986). Advances in software inspections. *IEEE Transaction on Software Engineering, 12*(7).

Freedman, D. P., & Weinberg, G. M. (1990). *Handbook of walkthroughs, inspections, and technical review: Evaluating programs, projects, and products* (3rd ed.). Dorest House Publishing.

Gilb, T., & Graham, D. (1993). *Software inspection*. Harlow, UK: Addison-Wesley.

Grady, & Van Slack, T. (1994). Key lessons in achieving widespread inspection use. *IEEE Software, 11*(4), 46-47.

Humphrey, W. S. (1995). *A discipline for software engineering*. Boston: Addison-Wesley.

Humphrey, W. S. (2000). *Introduction to the team software process*. Boston: Addison-Wesley.

Humphrey, W. S. (2002a). *Introduction to personal software process*. Boston: Addison-Wesley.

Humphrey, W. S. (2002b). *Winning with software: An executive strategy, How to transform your software group into a competitive asset*. Boston: Addison-Wesley.

Kan, S. H. (1995). *Metrics and models in software quality engineering*. Boston: Addison-Wesley.

Kelly, J. C., Sherif, J. S., & Hops, J. (1992). An analysis of defect densities found during software inspection. *Journal on Systems Software*, (17), 111-117.

Kitchenham, B., Kitchenham, A., & Fellows, J. (1986). *The effects of inspections on software quality and productivity*. Technical Report, ICL Technical Journal.

Knight, J. C., & Myers A. E. (1993, November). An improved inspection technique. *Communications of ACM, 36*(11), 50-69.

Leffingwell, D., & Widrig, D. (2000). *Managing software requirements: A unified approach*. NJ: Addison Wesley.

Lyytinen, K., & Hirschheim, R. (1987). Information systems failure: A survey and classification of the empirical literature. *Oxford Surveys in Information Technology, 4,* 257-309.

McConnell, S. (1993). *Code complete: A practical handbook of software construction*. Redmond, WA: Microsoft.

McConnell, S. (2000, January/February). The best influences on software engineering. *IEEE Software*.

Musa, J. D., & Ackerman, A. F. (1989, May). Quantifying software validation: When to stop testing? *IEEE Software*, 19-27.

O'Neill, D. (1997a). Estimating the number of defects after inspection, software inspection. *Proceedings on 18th IEEE International Workshop on Software Technology and Engineering* (pp. 96-104).

O'Neill, D. (1997b, January). Issues in software inspection. *IEEE Software*, 18-19.

Parnas, D. L., & Lawford, M. (2003a). Inspection's role in software quality assurance. *IEEE Software*, 16-20.

Parnas, D. L., & Lawford, M. (2003b, August). The role of inspection in software quality assurance. *IEEE Transaction on Software Engineering, 29*(8), 674-675.

Porter, A. A., Mockus, A., & Votta, L. (1998, January). Understanding the sources of variation in software inspections. *ACM Transactions on Software Engineering and Methodology, 7*(1), 41-79.

Porter, A. A., & Votta, L. (1998). Comparing defection methods for software requirements inspection: A replication using professional subjects. *Journal of Empirical Software Engineering, 3,* 355-379.

Remus, H. (1984). Integrated software validation in the view of inspections/reviews. *Software Validation*, 57-65.

Russell, G. W. (1991, January). Experience with inspection in ultralarge-scale development. *IEEE Software, 8*(1).

Schulmeyer, G. G., & Mcmanus, J. I. (1999). *Handbook of software quality assurance* (3rd ed.). Upper Saddle River, NJ: Prentice Hall.

Shull, F., Lanubile, F., & Biasili, V. (2000, November). Investigating reading techniques for object-oriented framework learning. *IEEE Transaction on Software Engineering, 26*(11).

Sommerville, I. (1995). *Software engineering* (5th ed.). Harlow, UK: Addison-Wesley.

Sommerville, I. (2001). *Software engineering* (6th ed.). Harlow, UK: Addison-Wesley.

Strauss, S. H., & Ebenau, R. G. (1994). *Software inspection process.* McGraw-Hill.

Thelin, T., Runeson, P., & Wohlin, C. (2003, August). An experimental comparison of usage-based and checklist-based reading. *IEEE Transaction on Software Engineering, 29*(8), 687-704.

Travassos, G. H., Shull, F., Fredericks, M., & Basili, V. R. (1999, November). Detecting defects in object oriented design: Using readying techniques to increase software quality. *The Conference on Object-Oriented Programming, Systems, Languages, and Applications* (OOPSLA), Denver, Colorado.

Voas, J. (2003, May/June). Assuring software quality assurance. *IEEE Software*, 48-49.

Weller, E. F. (1993). Lessons from three years of inspection data. *IEEE Software, 10*(5), 38-45.

Wheeler, D. A., Brykczynski, B., & Meeson, R. N. (1996). *Software inspection: An industry best practice.* Los Alamitos, CA: IEEE Computer Society Press.

Will, H., & Whobrey, D. (2003). The assurance paradigm and organisational semiotics: A new application domain. *IWOS.*

Will, H., & Whobrey, D. (2004). The assurance paradigm: Organizational semiotics applied to governance issues. In K. Liu (Ed.), *Systems design with signs studies in organisational semiotics.* Dordrecht: Kluwer Academic Publishers.

Wohlin, C., Aurum, A., Petersson, H., Shull, F., & Ciolkowski, M. (2002). Software inspection benchmarking: A qualitative and quantitative comparative opportunity. *Proceedings of the 8th Symposium on Software Metrics (Metrics '02)* (pp. 118-127).

Xu, J. (2003, August). On inspection and verification of software with timing requirement. *IEEE Transaction on Software Engineering, 29*(8), 705-720.

Zhu H., Jin, L., Diaper, D., & Ganghong, B. (2002). Software requirements validation via task analysis. *The Journal of Systems and Software, 61*, 145-169.

Chapter II

Software Review History and Overview

Abstract

The aim of this chapter is to review software review literature. The literature is drawn from Fagan's software review and forms of review structures. Fagan's software review includes six-step review processes — planning, overview, preparation, group meeting, re-review, and follow up. The forms of review structures can be classified into Active Design Review, Two-Person Review, Phased Review, and Use of Review Meeting. The literature review also provides an understanding of the IEEE Standard for software reviews and informal software reviews. The common informal reviews include Walkthroughs, Pair Programming, Peer Check, and Pass-Around. It also compares and contrasts bring a comparison these review methods.

Introduction

In the last thirty years, software reviews have been recommended as one of the most cost effective quality assurance techniques in software process improvements and are widely used in industrial practice (Ackerman, Buchwald, & Lewski, 1989; Boehm & Basili, 2001; Fagan, 1976; 1986; Gilb & Graham, 1993; Parnas & Lawford, 2003a, 2003b; Schulmeyer & McManus, 1999; Tvedt & Gollofello, 1995; Weller, 1993). The primary goal of a software review is to find defects during the software development life cycle (Biffl & Grossmann, 2001; DeMarco, 1982; Gilb & Graham, 1993; Halling & Biffl, 2002). A defect is considered to be any deviation from predefined quality properties (Boehm, 1981; Fagan, 1986; Humphrey, 2002b; Mathiassen, 2000; Wallance & Fuji, 1989; Will & Whobrey, 2004). The current definition of a software review is broader in scope than the one originally provided by Fagan (1976). Each review variation will be discussed in detail in the following sections.

The software review approach involves a well-defined and disciplined process in which qualified reviewers analyse software for the purpose of finding defects (Parnas & Lawford, 2003b; Ciolkowski et al., 2002). Existing studies such as Fagan's software review (1976), Freedman and Weinberg's technical review (1990), and Yourdon's structured walkthrough (1989) have segmented the analytical framework according to the aims and benefits of reviews (Gluch & Brockway, 1999), the review process, and the outputs of review (Chatters, 1991). Even though some forms of software review (input process and output standard) are covered in IEEE standards, no single clear and consolidated solution that should be used has yet been provided for the software industry (ANSI/IEEE, 1998; Biffl, 2000; IEEE Standard 830, 1993; Johnson, 1998).

Since Fagan's incremental improvements to software review were first proposed and trailed at IBM in 1972 (Fagan, 1986), several variations of Fagan's review have been put forward to improve performance, including new methodologies that promise to leverage and strengthen the benefits of software review (Kosman & Restivo, 1992; Miller, 2000; Parnas & Lawford, 2003a, 2003b). Some distinctive structural differences among the review approaches have developed from Fagan's original proposal. These comprise changing activities or emphasizing different purposes at each stage (Bisant & Lyle, 1989; Knight & Myers, 1993; Martin & Tsai, 1990; Parnas & Weiss, 1985), changing the team number (single and multiple review teams) (Bisant & Lyle, 1989; Kelly, Sherif, & Hops, 1992; Owen, 1997; Porter, Siy, Toman, & Votta, 1997; Porter, Siy, & Votta, 1997), changing the use of review meetings (Biffl & Halling, 2003; Johnson & Tjahjono, 1998; Porter, Votta, & Basili, 1995; Votta, 1993), reducing the number of roles (D'Astous & Robillard, 2001; Porter & Votta, 1994; Russell, 1991), introducing other external supports such as reading techniques (Basili et al., 1996; Biffl & Halling, 2002; Fusaro et al., 1997; Gough et al., 1995; Shull et al., 2000a; Zhang & Basili, 1999), computer tools (Drake, & Riedl, 1993; Johnson & Tjahjono, 1997; MacDonald et al., 1996; Mashayekhi, Murphy & Miller, 1997; Vermunt et al., 1999), and decision making methods (Sauer, Jeffery, Land, & Yetton, 2000).

In particular, Anderson et al. (2003a, 2003b) and Vitharana and Ramamurthy (2003) illustrated the importance of computer-assisted review tools in improving review process, while Porter, Votta, Basili (1995), focused on structural aspects of teams, such as the team size or the number of sessions, to understand how these attributes influence the costs and benefits of software review. Wheeler et al., (1997) Yourdon (1989), and Freedman and Weinberg (1984) discuss other types of defect detection techniques such as walkthrough, a particular type of peer review. Evident in each of these studies is the difficulty practitioners face in determining *what* are the critical factors or key inputs influencing the software review performance (Ciolkowski, Laitenberger, & Biffl, 2003; Wohlin, Aurum, Petersson, Shull, & Ciolkowski, 2002).

This chapter presents the software review literature including: 1) software review terminology; 2) Fagan's review; 3) forms of review process, such as active design review; two-person review, N-fold review; phased review and uses of the review meeting; 4) IEEE Standard for software and the limitations of IEEE Standard; and 5) informal reviews, such as Walkthrough, Pair-programming, Peer-desk, and Pass-around.

Software Review

Software review is an industry-proven process for improving software product quality and reducing the software development life cycle time and costs (Biffl & Halling, 2002; Boehm & Basili, 2001; Calvin, 1983; Easterbrook, 1999; Fagan, 1986; Gilb & Graham, 1993; Kelly & Shepard, 2000; Kelly et al., 1992; Kitchenham, Pfleeger, & Fenton, 1995; Mays, Jones, Holloway, & Studiski, 1990; Pressman, 1996; Voas, 2003; Wheeler, Brykczynski, & Meeson, 1996). Software review can be categorized based on the degree of formality or according to relative levels of discipline and flexibility in the review process (Shepard & Kelly, 2001; Wiegers, 2002). Formal reviews usually have the most rigorous process structures (Fagan, 1976; Wohlin et al., 2002). They often require advance planning and support from organization infrastructure (Briand, Freimut, & Vollei, 1999). Informal reviews are unstructured processes arising to meet the needs of specific situations on demand (Wiegers, 2002). They often require less time and have lower costs.

Terminology

The terminology used to discuss the software review process is often imprecise, which leads to confusion and misunderstanding. Though the terminology is often misleading, all review processes share a common goal: to find defects in the software artefact (Humphrey, 2002b).

There is confusion in both the literature and the industry regarding management review, technical review, inspection, and walkthrough. In some cases, these terms are used interchangeably to describe the same activity and in other cases are differentiated to describe distinct activities. The IEEE 1028-1998 Standard, presents the following definitions for each type of review (IEEE Standard 1028, 1998):

- **Management Review:** A systematic evaluation of a software acquisition, supply, development, operation, or maintenance prose performed by or on behalf of management that monitors progress, determines the status of plans and schedules, confirms requirements and their system allocation, or evaluates the effectiveness of management approaches used to achieve fitness for purpose.

- **Review:** A process or meeting during which a software product is presented to project personnel, managers, users, customers, user representatives, or other interested parties for comment or approval.

- **Technical Review:** A systematic evaluation of a software product by a team of qualified personnel that examines the suitability the software product for its intended use, and identifies discrepancies from specifications and standards. Technical reviews may also provide recommendations of alternatives and examination of various alternatives.

- **Inspection:** A visual examination of a software product that detects and identifies software anomalies, including errors and deviations from standards and specifications. Inspections are peer examinations led by impartial facilitators who are trained in inspection techniques. Determination of remedial or investigative action for an anomaly is a mandatory element of a software inspection, although the solution should not be determined in the inspection meeting.

- **Walkthrough:** A static analysis technique in which a designer or programmer leads members of the development team and other interested parties through a software product, and the participants ask questions and make comments about the possible errors, violation of development standards and other problems.

In the context of this book, the generic term of "review" will be used to refer to all review techniques. The only exception to this is in the discussion of *management review.* Management review is distinguished by the fact that it deals with a higher level of software management and does not address the lower level technical issues common to most software review processes (ANSI/IEEE, 1998; Gilb & Graham, 1993; Ebenau & Strauss, 1994; Wieger, 2002).

In preparing this literature review it has been found that the terms software *review* and *inspection* are used interchangeably, and no clear difference exist between the terms. This book uses the term *review,* which is the predominant term for describing the process at the focus of this study. The term "defect" is defined as any issue or problem that does not meet the requirements (Leffingwell & Widrig, 2000), and is used interchangeably with "error" and "omission".

Fagan's Software Review

Software review was originally introduced by Fagan at IBM in Kingston, 1972 (Fagan, 1986) for two purposes: 1) improve software quality and 2) increase software developer productivity. Since that time, Fagan's software review process has been adopted as a method for best practice in the software industry, although some other less formal review approaches are still used (Boehm & Basili, 2001; Wiegers, 2002). Michael Fagan developed a formal procedure and well-structured review technique (presented in Figure 1). The review process

Figure 1. Fagan's six steps software review process

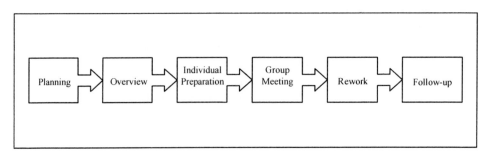

essentially includes six major steps: planning, overview, individual preparation, group review meeting, rework, and follow-up (Fagan, 1976, 1986).

Planning

The objective of planning is to organize and prepare the software review process. Typically this involves preparing the review materials and review procedures, scheduling the meeting, selecting appropriate review members, and assigning their roles (Ackerman, 1989; Aurum et al., 2002; Fagan, 1976; Gilb & Graham, 1993; Laitenberger & DeBaud, 2000).

Overview

The purposes of the process overview include educating reviewers about the artefact and the overall scope of the software review (Fagan, 1986). The software creator (author) explains the overall scope and the purpose of the software review to the team. This allows reviewers to understand and familiarise themselves with the artefact. Most software reviews conduct an overview meeting — also called the 'Kickoff Meeting' (Doolan, 1992; Fagan, 1976; Kelly et al., 1992). Gilb and Graham (1993) stated that the overview meeting is not necessary for all software artefacts, especially code review, as it can increase the overall time and effort of review, reducing the benefits that can be gained.

Supporters of the overview meeting suggest that it should be conducted only when the benefits can be justified (Laitenberger & DeBaud, 2000). First, when a software artefact is complex and difficult to understand, the overview meeting allows the author to explain the details of the software artefact to the team (Fagan, 1986; Porter & Votta, 1998). Second, reviewers will better understand the relationship between the artefact and the whole software system. In both scenarios, it will enhance review performance and save time in later review phases (Laitenberger & DeBaud, 2000).

Preparation

Preparation allows individual reviewers to learn about and analyse a software artefact and prepare to fulfil their assigned role (Ackerman et al., 1989; Wiegers, 2002). Fagan (1976) stated that the preparation stage allows individual reviewers to understand the software artefact before a group review meeting.

Reviewers should study the software artefact and should try hard to understand the intent and logic by consulting the support documentation, such as checklists

(Chernak, 1996; Fagan, 1976; Miller, Wood, & Roper, 1998; Thelin, Runeson, & Wohlin, 2003). It is also stated that no formal review activity should take place at this stage.

However, recent researchers often conduct the individual review task (i.e., performing individual defect detection) immediately rather than undertaking this preparation stage, it has argued that more benefits accrue from this process (Ackerman et al., 1989; Basili et al., 1996; Biffl, 2001; Johnson, 1999a, 1999b; Porter et al., 1998). Votta (1993), Bisant et al. (1989) and Johnson and Tjahjono (1998) pointed out that conducting individual preparation only to educate reviewers about the software artefact is costly. Evidence is shown in several publications that no preparation is needed for individual defect examination, which can attain better review results (Basili, 1997; Basili et al., 1999; Doolan, 1992; Fowler, 1986; Johnson; 1999b; Porter et al., 1995).

Group Meeting

The objectives of a group meeting (review meeting) are to find and collect defects (Fagan, 1976). Sometimes, group meetings are also called "logging meetings" (Gilb & Graham, 1993). Review teams meet and the reader summarizes the work.

Fagan (1976) found that group meetings could provide a "synergy effect" that result in a collective contribution that is more than the mere combination of individual results. Fagan referred to this type of effect as a "phantom" effect (Fagan, 1986). However recent research findings show that the synergy effect in the group meetings is relatively low (Johnson & Tjahjono, 1998; Votta, 1993). Research suggests that reviewers' expertise improves results in software review. (Basili et al., 1996, Porter & Votta, 1998; Sauer et al., 2000). Sauer et al. (2000) propose that the effectiveness of defect detection is driven by individual reviewers' experience, such as expertise in the domain knowledge area and experience in software review.

A major problem of group meetings is the relatively high cost (Boehm & Basili, 2001; Johnson, 1998). This is mainly people's time but also includes the difficulties associated with scheduling meetings and accessing people's time (Porter & Votta, 1997; Votta, 1993). Software review group meetings account for approximately 10% of development time (Votta, 1993). The software review process can slow development down by as much as 13% (Johnson, 1998; Votta, 1993). Since efficiency (use of time) is one of the critical factors in project success (Biffl, 2000; Boehm, 1981; Boehm & Papaccio, 1988; Briand, Eman, & Freimut, 1998; Briand et al., 1999; Wilson, Petocz, & Roiter, 1996; Wilson & Hall, 1998; Xu, 2003) the longer the time spent the higher the costs and the lower the efficiency. A typical software review group consists of a number of members including the author, a moderator, and a recorder (Fagan, 1976; Laitenberger & DeBaud, 2000). Votta (1993) stresses that the size of the group matters. Effective face-to-face meetings allow only two people to interact well (Votta, 1993). Where groups have been larger, Votta notes that participation decreases across time. This suggests that effective software reviews require only small groups with as high a level of expertise as can be achieved (for example, one author and one reviewer) (Bisant & Lyle, 1989; Porter & Votta, 1994).

Reworks

Rework, often called the "defect correction process" (Fagan, 1976; Porter & Votta, 1994), is that phase of review that allows the author to resolve problems by reviewing, revising, and correcting the identified defects of the software artefact.

Follow-Up

The objective of follow-up is to validate the quality of correction. At this stage the moderator decides if further review is required (Briand, 1999; Briand, Emam, Freimut, & Laitenberger, 1997; Doolan, 1992; Emam & Laitenberger, 2001; O'Neill, 1997a; Runeson & Wohlin, 1998). Some researchers have attempted to quantify this exercise by identifying review metrics that will allow the need for further review to be estimated (Ackerman et al., 1989; Barnard & Price, 1994; Ebenau & Strauss, 1994; Emam & Laitenberger, 2001; Gilb & Graham, 1993).

For instance, software review metrics including the total number of defects, elapsed time for individual preparation and group meeting, and the number of reviewers have been used to measure the process. Three major benefits of review metrics are to provide a benchmark that will allow: 1) assessment of the quality of the review, and a decision whether to re-review the document, 2) better understanding of the potential problems or issues within the development process, and 3) valuable feedback for the review process (Biffl & Grossmann, 2001; Gilb & Graham, 1993; Grunbacher, Halling, Biffl, Kitapci, & Boehm, 2002; Humphrey, 1995; Humphrey, Snyder, & Willis, 1991; O'Neill, 1997b; Wiegers, 2002).

Forms of Review Process Structures

Five major review process structures have been described: 1) Active Design Reviews (Parnas & Weiss, 1985), 2) Two-Person Review (Bisant & Lyle, 1989), 3) N-Fold Review (Martin & Tsai, 1992), 4) Phased Review (Knight & Myers, 1993), 5) Review without Meeting (Johnson & Tjahjono, 1998; Porter et al., 1995; Votta, 1993).

Active Design Review

Active Design review was introduced by Parnas and Weiss (1985). The rationale behind the idea is that 1) when reviewers are overloaded with information they are unable to find defects effectively, 2) reviewers are often not familiar with the objective of the design and they are often unable to understand detailed levels of the artefact, 3) large group review meetings often fall short of their objectives. Complex social interaction and the varying social status of individuals within the group can result in communication breakdown and individual apprehension fractures the process (Parnas & Weiss, 1987; Sauer et al., 2000).

The Active Design review process comprises three steps (Parnas & Weiss, 1985). In the first step the author presents an overview of the design artefact. In the second step (defect detection) the author provides an open-ended questionnaire to help reviewers find defects in the design artefact.

The final step is defect collection. Review meetings focus on small segments of the overall artefact, one aspect at a time. An example of this might be checking for consistency between documented requirements and design functions. This helps to ensure that functions are correctly designed and implemented.

This segmented meeting strategy allows reviewers to concentrate their efforts in small dimensions, minimising information overload and helping to achieve better results. The Active Design review only focuses on two roles (the role of the author and the role of the reviewer) in a review meeting to maximise efficiency. A reviewer is selected on the basis of his/her expertise and is assigned the task of ensuring thorough coverage of the design documents. A reviewer is responsible for finding defects, while the author is responsible for discussing the artefact with the reviewer. Parnas and Weiss (1985) successfully applied this approach to the design of military flight navigation systems, but did not provide any quantitative measurements. However, other empirical evidence has shown the effectiveness of variations of this approach. Examples include research into different reading techniques (Roper et al., 1997) and studies of team size (Knight & Myers, 1991; Porter, 1997).

Two-Person Review

The Two-Person review process was first introduced by Bisant and Lyle in 1989. This is a similar approach to Active Design review insofar as it also concentrates on role design and team size in a review meeting. This approach adopts Fagan's formal review method but removes the role of the moderator. Roles in the Two-Person review are the author and the reviewer.

The Two-Person review empirically validates that developers' productivity can be improved since it maximises the use of the resources of a review team and reduces the costs of having a large review team (Bisant & Lyle, 1989). However, one limitation is that it requires significant experience of reviewers in performing the review process.

N-Fold Review

The N-fold review was developed by Martin and Tsai in 1990. This process rests on the premise that a single review team may find only a small number of defects in an artefact, whereas multiple teams working in parallel sessions should find a large number of defects (Martin & Tsai, 1990).

By dividing tasks, it is possible to ensure that groups will not duplicate each other's efforts. Each team follows Fagan's six-step review process, and is comprised of three to four people. The roles can be classified into 1) the author, 2) a moderator, and 3) reviewers. The moderator is responsible for all the coordination activities. The defect examination time is about two hours for each team.

Studies show that increasing the number of teams resulted in finding more defects with a low defect redundancy (the overlap between defects found by each group) (Martin & Tsai, 1990). Research by Martin and Tsai (1990) found that 35% of defects were discovered by a single team compared to 78% found by all teams. There was no significant overlap between the defects found by the different teams.

However, achieving a successful N-fold review depends on two key factors 1) the availability of expertise in a team and 2) capacity to meet the additional costs involved in conducting the N-fold approach (Martin & Tsai, 1990).

Phased Review

Knight and Myers introduced the Phased review in 1993. As the name implies, the review process is carried out in a series of partial reviews or mini-reviews.

Phased review adopts a combination of ideas from the Active Design review, Fagan's software review and N-fold review methods. It follows Fagan's six-phase approach with each phase done in sequential order. During each phase, reviewers undertake a full examination of a specific property (e.g., portability, reusability, or maintainability) of the artefact.

A review cannot progress to the next phase until all work (including rework) is completed for the current phase of review. The reviews can be divided in two types: 1) single-reviewer approach, and 2) multiple-reviewer approach. In the single-reviewer approach a single person examines the artefact. In the multiple-reviewer approach, several reviewers individually examine the artefact using different checklists and then discuss the defects in a meeting. The key drawback of a phased review is that it is a more costly method than other more conventional reviews (Porter & Votta, 1997). This may explain why the phased review is not widely used in practice.

Use of Review Meeting

The review meeting has been the core of the software review process in the last decade. In Fagan's review, the key focus is on the review meeting phase where team members identify and discuss defects in a meeting. However, many studies have radically changed the structure of Fagan's review in two areas: 1) preparation and 2) collection (this can be with or without a review meeting) (Johnson & Tjahjono, 1998; Porter et al., 1995; Votta, 1993). In the preparation stage, the aim is to identify defects, whereas the aim of collection stage is to collect the defects from the reviewers (Fagan, 1986).

Fagan (1976) believes that the review meeting is crucial since most defects can be detected during the meeting. The main objective of a review meeting is to create a synergy effect. Synergy can be defined as the identification of additional gains (process gains) made because additional defects are found through the meeting discussion. By combining the different knowledge and skills of different reviewers a synergy is created in the group meeting that allows *group* expertise to be utilised in the review process (Humphrey, 2000; Sauer et al., 2000). The implicit assumption is that the interaction in a review meeting contributes more than the combination of individual results.

In other words, team members can find more defects in a group discussion than would be found if all the defects found by individuals working without a meeting are combined. Further, it has been suggested that review meetings give benefits such as: 1) education; there are knowledge gains for junior reviewers since they can learn from senior, more experienced reviewers; 2) empirical studies have confirmed that a meeting approach is significantly better at reducing the number of reviewers' mistakes and that reviewers actually prefer review meetings over a 'non-meeting' approach (Johnson, 1998; Mashayekhi, Drake, & Riedl, 1993; Porter & Votta, 1997; Stein, Riedl, Harner, & Mashayekhi, 1997).

Although there is a significant body of research presenting the advantages of group meetings to the software review process, this research is contradicted by work which suggests that holding a review meeting does not have a significant effect on the review performance (Johnson & Tjahjono, 1997; Votta, 1993).

Results from a study by Eick et al. (1992) showed that reviewers were able to identify 90% of defects during the preparation stage of software review, while only 10% of the defects found were found during the review meeting phase. Further, laboratory experiments at AT&T Bell Labs were unable to find any process gains from synergy effects in group meetings (Votta, 1993). Johnson (1998) also reported that individual reviews are more productive than software reviews that rely upon review meetings.

The face-to-face meetings required for a group review process can be labour intensive and as a result quite expensive to hold. Organising and conducting meetings can be very time consuming and requires significant amount of effort because it requires organizing several people into one meeting on a specific day and time (Porter et al., 1995). The costs of review meetings are not easily justified because the number of defects found is not significantly different to those found in non-meeting based methods (Johnson & Tjahjono, 1997; Mashayekhi, Drake, & Riedl, 1993; Mashayekhi, Feulner, & Riedl, 1994).

The benefits of holding a review meeting are still debated in the software review literature. The key issue in this debate is whether defect detection is improved through a focus on individual activity, or whether it is improved through group meetings. Current research presents no conclusive answer. For instance, the average net meeting gain is greater than the average net meeting loss by approximately 12% in Cheng and Jeffery's study (1996), whereas Porter et al. (1995) found that the average net meeting gain rates are not much different from zero: average net meeting gain was between –0.9 and +2.2. However, Cheng and Jeffery (1996) concluded that the experience of the subjects is a factor that could have biased their results of that experiment. Votta (1993) also argues that the major reason for not holding meetings is based on the availability of experts.

IEEE Standard for Software Reviews

As a result of efforts in software engineering to improve the software review process for defect detection, the IEEE committee has developed guidelines for best practice in software review. No discussion of the literature in this field would be complete without a discussion of those guidelines.

The IEEE Computer Society's standard for software reviews describes a systematic review process applicable to software artefacts. It considers seven steps (IEEE 1028 standard, 1998):

1.   **Introduction:** Describes the objective of the systematic review and provides an overview of the systematic review procedures.

2.   **Responsibilities:** Defines the roles and responsibilities needed for the systematic review.

3.   **Inputs:** Describes the requirements for inputs needed by the systematic review.

4.   **Entry Criteria:** Describes the criteria to be met before the systematic review can begin, including authorization and initiating events.

5.   **Procedures:** Details the procedures for the systematic review including planning the review, overview of procedures, preparation, examination/ evaluation/recoding of results, rework and follow-up.

6.   **Exit Criteria:** Describes the criteria to be met before the systematic review can be considered complete.

7.   **Output:** Describes the minimum set of deliverables to be produced by the systematic review.

The basic processes of the IEEE guidelines are very similar to Fagan's review except that different types of reviews and explicit inputs used in the software review process are described. However, there are three issues in adopting the IEEE guideline in practice. First, partitioners would find the difficulty to adopt a most sustainable review approach in their development environment since the guidelines do not provide explicit suggestions. Second, the important relationships between input, *process,* and output are missing in the guidelines because the guidelines only conceptualise the input-output relations. Third, the guidelines focus on the use of explicit inputs (documentation-based), while reviewers' characteristics (e.g., experience) are totally ignored. Software review is a human-based activity; and therefore, selection of reviewers is vital to the review performance.

A comparison of other informal review approaches and the discussion of the input-process-output relationship will be described in the following sections.

Informal Approaches to
Software Review

Other software review approaches including walkthroughs, pair programming, peer check, pass-around, and ad-hoc review have been presented as alternatives to formal software review and are discussed further in this chapter.

Walkthrough

Walkthrough has been presented as an alternative to software review. In this approach the author describes the artefact to a group of peers and seeks comments (Freedman & Weinberg, 1990; Mavin & Maiden, 2003; Rowley & Rhoades, 1992; Yourdon, 1989). Walkthrough is most appropriate where the primary review objective is to educate others about the product (Freedman & Weinberg, 1990). A typical walkthrough does not follow a defined procedure or, specify criteria; it requires no management reporting and generates no measurement metrics (Fagan, 1986). The number of participants in a walkthrough can be up to 20 people or more (Freedman & Weinberg, 1990). Further, there is no constraint on meeting time limits (Yourdon, 1989). This can be an efficient way to examine the artefact because the author can draw the reviewers' attention towards the product (Yourdon, 1989). However, the process is largely unstructured and the risk of overlooking defects is high.

Pair Programming

In a pair programming approach, two programmers work simultaneously on the same program at a single workstation (Beck, 2000; Cliburn, 2003; McDowell et al., 2003). This approach provides an informal review of the software artefact as the two programmers work continuously and incrementally on the working product (Katira et al., 2004). The rationale behind the pair programming paradigm is that "two heads are better than one" (Jeffries, Anderson & Hendrickson, 2001; McDowell et al., 2003; VanDeGrift, 2004; Williams & Kessler, 2000). As the pair works, typically with one partner coding while the other checks and reviews the software, they can identify defects and make corrections immediately (Katira et al., 2004; McDowell et al., 2003).

Peer Check

In a peer check, only one person besides the author examines the software artefact (Hayardeny, Fienblit, & Farchi, 2004; Wiegers, 2002). A peer check approach depends purely on the reviewer's knowledge and skills, and self-motivation (Hayardeny et al., 2004; Humphrey, 1995). Peer check usually is informal but it can be formalised by using checklists and establishing simple procedures and metrics for collection (Petry, 1996). At the completion of the defect detection, the author and reviewer will prepare and discuss the defects list. Although having many similarities to individual software review, a peer check is typically a local or informal process with no consistent set of practices (Petry, 1996; Wiegers, 2002). The peer check is often presented as the least expensive approach to software review. However, the defects found are only those identified by the reviewer as this approach does not extend to discussions with the author or other experts during the review process.

Pass-Around

A pass-around is another type of review method in which the author distributes multiple copies of the artefact to the reviewers for concurrent review (Wiegers, 2002). The pass-around approach combines the multiple efforts of reviewers and provides timely feedback. It permits each reviewer to see the comments that others have already written. This helps to reveal differences in interpretation and to minimize redundancy. At the completion of the review process, the author corrects the artefact using the feedback received. This approach is very useful where formal group meetings cannot be held. However, a pass-around lacks the synergy effect often attributed to group meetings since there is no interaction or discussion between reviewers in this review process.

Comparing Formal and Informal Software Review Approaches

The optimal goal of all review approaches is to find defects in the artefacts in a timely and effective manner. Table 1 indicates which review approaches are appropriate for achieving specific objectives (Wiegers, 1998, 2002). The best way to select a review approach to use in a given situation is to keep a record of review effectiveness and efficiency in the organization. This study is particularly interested in the process of finding defects. The use of inputs, process support and performance measurements are discussed in the next section.

Table 1. Suggested review methods for meeting various objectives (Wiegers, 2002, p. 43)

Objectives	Formal software review	Walkthrough	Pair programming	Peer check	Pass-around
Find product defects	X	X	X	X	X
Check conformance to specifications	X			X	X
Check conformance to standards	X			X	X
Verify product completeness and correctness	X	X			X
Assess understandably and maintainability	X		X		
Demonstrate quality of critical or hight-risk components	X				
Collect data for process improvement	X				
Measure document quality	X				
Educate other team members about the product		X	X		X
Reach consensus on approach		X	X		
Ensure that changes or defects fixes were made correctly		X		X	
Explore alternative approaches		X	X		
Simulate execution of a program		X			
Minimize review cost				X	

Summary

This chapter presented software reviews literature. Starting with history of software reviews, terminology used, structure of software reviews and different forms of review approaches. Tools and technologies for supporting software review process will be discussed in next chapter.

References

Ackerman, F. A., Buchwald, L. S., & Lewski F. H. (1989, May). Software inspection: An effective verification process. *IEEE Software*, 31-36.

ANSI/IEEE. (1989). An American national standard. *IEEE Standards for Software Reviews and Audits, ANSI/IEEE Standard 1028-1998.*

Aurum, A. (2003). Supporting structures for managing software engineering knowledge. In A. Aurum, R. Jeffery, R. Wohlin, & M. Handzic (Eds.), *Managing software engineering knowledge.* Berling, Heidelberg, New York: Springer.

Barnard, J., & Price, A. (1994, March). Managing code inspection information. *IEEE Software*, 59-69.

Basili, V. R. (1997). Evolving and packaging reading technologies, special issue. *The Journal of Systems and Software, 38*(1), 3-12.

Basili, V. R., Green, S., Laitenberger, O., Lanubile, F., Sorumgard, S., & Zelkowitz, M. (1996). The empirical investigation of perspective-based reading. *International Journal on Empirical Software Engineering, 1*(12), 133-144.

Basili, V. R., Shull, F., & Lanubile, F. (1999). Building knowledge through families of experiments. *IEEE Transactions on Software Engineering, 25*(4).

Beck, D. (2000). *Extreme programming explained: Embrace change.* Boston: Addison-Wesley.

Biffl, S. (2000). *Investing the defect detection effectiveness and cost-benefit of optimal nominal inspection team. Technical Report 00-36*, Dept. Software Engineering, Vienna University of Technology, Australia, August 2000. Submitted to IEEE Transactions on Software Engineering.

Biffl, S. (2001). *Software inspection techniques to support project and quality management: Lessons learned from a large-scale controlled experiment with two inspection cycles on the effect defect detection and defect estimation techniques.* Phd Thesis. Department of Software Engineering, Vienna University of Technology, Australia.

Biffl, S., & Grossmann, W. (2001). Evaluating the accuracy of defect estimation models based on inspection data from two inspection cycles. *Proceedings of International Conference on Software Engineering* (pp. 145-154).

Biffl, S., & Halling, M. (2002). Investigating the influence of inspector capability factors with four inspection techniques on inspection performance. *Proceedings of IEEE Symposium on Software Metrics, Metrics'02.*

Biffl, S., & Halling, M. (2003, May). Investigating the defect detection effectiveness and cost benefit of nominal inspection team. *IEEE Transaction on Software Engineering, 29*(5), 385-397.

Bisant, D. B., & Lyle, J. R. (1989). A two person inspection method to improve programming productivity. *IEEE Transactions on Software Engineering, 15*(10), 1294-1304.

Boehm, B. W. (1981). *Software engineering economics, advances in computing science and technology.* Englewood Cliffs, NJ: Prentice-Hall.

Boehm, B. W., & Basili, B. R. (2001, January). Software defect reduction top 10 list. *IEEE Computer, 34*(1).

Boehm, B. W., & Papaccio, P. H. (1988). Understanding and controlling software costs. *IEEE Transaction on Software Engineering, 14*(10), 1462-1473.

Briand, L.C., Eman, E. K., & Freimut, B. G. (1998). *A comparison and integration of capture-recapture methods and the defection profile method.* International Software Engineering Software Research Network, Fraunhofer Instituted for Empirical Software Engineering, Germany, ISERN Report No. 11-98.

Briand, L. C., Emam, K, Freimut, B. G., & Laitenberger, O. (1997). Quantitative evaluation of capture-recapture models to control software inspection. *Proceedings of the 8ᵗʰ International Symposium on Software Reliability Engineering* (pp. 234-244).

Briand, L. C., Freimut B., & Vollei, F. (1999). *Assessing the cost-effectiveness of inspections by combining project data and expert opinion.* International Software Engineering Software Research Network, Fraunhofer Instituted for Empirical Software Engineering, Germany, ISERN Report No. 070-99/E.

Calvin, T. W. (1983, September). Quality control techniques for "zero defects". *IEEE Transactions on Components, Hybrids, and Manufactory Technology, 6*(3), 323-328.

Chatters, B. (1991). *Software inspection, colloquium on software engineering: Producing better systems.*

Cheng, B., & Jeffery, R. (1996). Comparing inspection strategic for software requirement specifications. *Proceedings of the 1996 Australian Software Engineering Conference* (pp. 203-211).

Chernak, Y. (1996, December). A statistical approach to the inspection checklist formal syntheses and improvement. *IEEE Transactions on Software Engineering, 22*(12).

Ciolkowski, M., Laitenberger, O., & Biffl, S. (2003). Software reviews: The state-of-the-practice. *IEEE Software,* 46-51.

D'Astous, P., & Robillard, P. N. (2001). Quantitative measurements of the influence of participant roles during peer review meeting. *Journal of Empirical Software Engineering,* (6), 143-159.

Demarco, T. (1982). *Controlling software projects.* New York: Yourdon Press.

Doolan, E. P. (1992). Experience with Fagan's inspection method. *Software-Practice Experience, 22*(3), 173-182.

Easterbrook, S. (1999). Verification and validation of requirements for mission critical systems. *Proceedings of International Conference on Software Engineering* (pp. 673-674). Los Angeles.

Ebenau, R. G., & Strauss, S. H. (1994). *Software inspection process, system design and implementation series.* McGraw Hill.

Eick, S. G., Loader, C. R., Long, M. D., Votta, L. G., & Vander, Wiel, S. (1992). Estimating software fault content before coding. *Proceedings of the 14th Intentional Conference on Software Engineering* (pp. 49-65).

Emam, K. E., & Laitenberger, O. (2001). Evaluating capture-recapture models with two inspectors. *IEEE Transaction on Software Engineering, 27*(9), 851-864.

Emam, K. E., & Madhavaji, N. (1995, July). A field study of requirement engineering practices in information systems development. *IEEE CS Press* (pp. 68-80). Loss Amities, California.

Fagan, M. E. (1976). Design and code inspections to reduce errors in program development, *IBM System Journal, 15*(3), 182-211.

Fagan, M. E. (1986, July). Advances in software inspections. *IEEE Transaction on Software Engineering, 12*(7).

Fowler, P. J. (1986). In-process inspection software products at AT&T. *AT&T Technical Journal, 65*(2), 744-751.

Freedman, D. P., & Weinberg, G. M. (1990). *Handbook of walkthroughs, inspections, and technical review: evaluating programs, projects, and products* (3rd ed.). Dorest House Publishing.

Gilb, T., & Graham, D. (1993). *Software inspection.* Harlow, UK: Addison-Wesley.

Gluch, D. P., & Brockway, J. (1999, April). *An Introduction to Software Engineering Practices Using Model-Based Verification, Technical Report, CMU/SEI-99-TR-005.* ESC-TR-005.

Grunbacher, P., Halling, M., Biffl, S., Kitapci, H., & Boehm, B. W. (2002). Repeatable quality assurance techniques for requirements negotiations. *Proceedings of the 36th Hawaii International Conference on System Sciences (HICSS'03).*

Halling, M., & Biffl, S. (2002, October). Investigating the influence of software inspection process parameters on inspection meeting performance. *IEEE Proc-Software, 149*(5), 115-121.

Hayardeny, A., Fienblit, S., & Farchi, E. (2004, April). Concurrent and distributed desk checking. *Proceedings of 18ᵗʰ International Parallel and Distributed Processing Symposium* (pp. 26-30).

Humphrey, W. S. (1995). *A discipline for software engineering.* Boston: Addison-Wesley.

Humphrey, W. S. (2000). *Introduction to the team software process.* Boston: Addison-Wesley.

Humphrey, W. S. (2002a). *Introduction to personal software process.* Boston: Addison-Wesley.

Humphrey, W. S. (2002b). *Winning with software: An executive strategy, how to transform your software group into a competitive asset.* Boston: Addison-Wesley.

Humphrey, W. S., Snyder, T. R., & Willis, R. R. (1991). Software process improvement at Hughes Aircraft. *IEEE Software, 18*(4), 11-23.

IEEE Standard 830. (1993). *IEEE Recommended Practice for Software Requirements Specifications, IEEE Standard 830,* Institute of Electrical and Electronics Engineers Inc., New York.

IEEE Standard 1028. (1998). *Software Engineering Standard Committee of The IEEE Computer Society, IEEE Standard 1028.* IEEE Standard for Software Review, Institute of Electrical and Electronics Engineers Inc., New York.

Jeffries, R., Anderson A., & Hendrickson C. (2001). *Extreme programming installed.* Boston: Addison-Wesley.

Johnson, P. M. (1998, February). Reengineering Inspection. *Communication of ACM, 41*(2), 49-52.

Johnson, P. M. (1999a, February). A critical analysis of psp data quality: Result form a case study. *Journal of Empirical Software Engineering.*

Johnson, P. M. (1999b). Leap: A personal information environment for software engineers. *International Conference on Software Engineering* (pp. 654-657).

Johnson, P. M., & Tjahjono, D. (1998). Does every inspection really need a meeting? *Empirical Software Engineering,* (3), 3-35.

Katira, N., Williams, L., Wiebe, E., Miller, C., Balik, S., & Gehringer, E. (2004, March). Paired programming/ collaborative learning: On understanding compatibility of student pair programmers. *Proceedings of the 35ᵗʰ SIGCSE Technical Symposium on Computer Science Education.*

Kelly, D., & Shepard T. (2000). Task-directed software inspection technique: An experiment and case study. *Proceedings of the 2000 Conference of the Centre for Advanced Studies.* Mississauga, Canada.

Kelly, J. C., Sherif, J. S., & Hops, J. (1992). An analysis of defect densities found during software inspection. *Journal on Systems Software*, (17), 111-117.

Knight, J. C., & Myers A. E. (1993, November). An improved inspection technique. *Communications of ACM, 36*(11), 50-69.

Kitchenham, B., Pfleeger, S. L., & Fenton N. (1995). Toward a framework for measurement validation. *IEEE Transaction on Software Engineering, 21*(12), 929-944.

Kosman, R. J., & Restivo, T. J. (1992, November 9-12). Incorporating the inspection process into a software maintenance organization. *Proceedings of Conference on Software Maintenance* (pp. 51-56).

Laitenberger, O., & Debaud, J. M. (2000). An encompassing life cycle centric survey of software inspection. *The Journal of Software and Systems, 50*(1), 5-31.

Mashayekhi, V., Drake, J. W. T., & Riedl, J. (1993, September). Distributed collaborative software inspection. *IEEE Software*, 66-75.

Mashayekhi, V., Feulner, C., & Riedl, J. (1994). CAIS: Collaborative Asynchronous Inspection of Software. *Proceedings of the 2ⁿᵈ ACM SIGSOFT Symposium on Foundations of Software Engineering* (pp. 21-34). New York, *19*(5).

Martin, J., & Tsai, W. T. (1992, February). N-fold inspection: A requirements analysis technique. *Communications of ACM, 33*(2), 225-232.

Mathiassen, L., & Stage, J. (1990). Complexity and uncertainty in software design. *Proceedings of the 1990 IEEE Conference on Computer Systems and Software Engineering* (pp. 482-489). IEEE Computer Society Press.

Mavin, A., & Maiden, N. (2003, September). Determining socio-technical systems requirements: Experiences with generating and walking through scenarios. *Proceedings of 11ᵗʰ IEEE International Requirements Engineering Conference*.

Mays, R. G., Jones, C. L., Hollowa,y G. J., & Studiski, D. P. (1990). Experiences with defect prevention. *IBM Systems Journal, 29*(1), 4-32.

McDowell, C., Hanks, B., & Werner, L. (2003, June). Experimenting with pair programming in the classroom. ACM SIGCSE Bulletin. *Proceedings of the 8ᵗʰ Annual Conference on Innovation and Technology in Computer Science Education*, 35(3).

Miller, J. (2000). Applying mate-analytical procedures to software engineering experiments. *The Journal of Systems and Software, 54*, 29-39.

Miller, J., Wood, M., & Roper, M. (1998). Further experiences with scenarios and checklists. *Empirical Software Engineering, 3*, 37-64.

O'Neill, D. (1997a). Estimating the number of defects after inspection, software inspection. *Proceedings on 18th IEEE International Workshop on Software Technology and Engineering* (pp. 96-104).

O'Neill, D. (1997b, January). Issues in software inspection. *IEEE Software*, 18-19.

Owen, K. (1997). Software detailed technical reviews: Findings and using defects. *Wescon'97 Conference Proceedings* (pp. 128-133).

Parnas, D. L., & Lawford, M. (2003a). Inspection's role in software quality assurance. *IEEE Software*, 16-20.

Parnas, D. L., & Lawford, M. (2003b, , August). The role of inspection in software quality assurance. *IEEE Transaction on Software Engineering*, *29*(8), 674-675.

Parnas, D. L., & Weiss, D. M. (1985, August 28-30). Active design reviews: Principles and practices. *Proceeding of ICSE'85* (pp. 132-136). London: IEEE Computer Society.

Parnas, D. L., & Weiss, D. M. (1987). Active design review: Principles and practices. *The Journal of Systems and Software*, *7*, 259-265.

Petry, B. L. (1996, May). Getting the most out of legacy code: The uses of hypercode within a typical is organization. *Proceedings of the IEEE Aerospace and Electronics Conference, NAECON 1996* (pp. 20-23).

Porter, A. A., Mockus, A., & Votta, L. (1998, January). Understanding the sources of variation in software inspections. *ACM Transactions on Software Engineering and Methodology*, *7*(1), 41-79.

Porter, A. A., Siy, H. P., Toman, C. A., & Votta, L. G. (1997). An experiment to assess the cost-benefits of code inspections in large scale software development. *IEEE Transaction on Software Engineering*, *23*(6), 329-346.

Porter, A. A., Siy, H. P., & Votta L. G. (1997). Understanding the effects of developer activities on inspection interval. *Proceedings of International Conference on Software Engineering* (pp. 128-138).

Porter, A. A., & Votta, L. G. (1994). An experiment to asses different defect detection methods for software requirements inspections. *Proceedings of 16th International Conference on Software Engineering*, Icse-16 (pp. 103-112).

Porter, A. A., & Votta, L. G. (1997, November/December). What makes inspections work? *IEEE Software*, 99-102.

Porter, A. A., & Votta, L. (1998). Comparing defection methods for software requirements inspection: A replication using professional subjects. *Journal of Empirical Software Engineering*, *3*, 355-379.

Porter, A. A., Votta, L. G., & Basili, B. (1995). Comparing detection methods for software requirements inspection: A replicated experiment. *IEEE Transaction on Software Engineering, 21*(6), 563-575.

Pressman, R. (1996). *Software engineering: A practitioners approach.* McGraw Hill.

Rowley, D.E., & Rhoades, D.G. (1992, June). The cognitive jog-through: A fast-paced user interface evaluation procedure. *Proceedings of the SIGCHI Conference on Human Factors in Computing Systems.*

Runeson, R., & Wohlin, C. (1998). An experimental evaluation of an experience-based capture-recapture method in software code inspection. *Journal of Empirical Software Engineering, 3,* 381-406.

Russell, G. W. (1991, January). Experience with inspection in ultralarge-scale development. *IEEE Software, 8*(1).

Sauer, C., Jeffery, R., Land, L., & Yetton, P. (2000). Understanding and improving the effectiveness of software development technical reviews: A behaviourally motivated programme of research. *IEEE Transactions on Software Engineering, 26*(1), 1-14.

Schulmeyer, G. G., & Mcmanus, J. I. (1999). *Handbook of software quality assurance* (3rd ed.). Upper Saddle River, NJ: Prentice Hall.

Shepard, T., & Kelly, D. (2001). How to do inspection when there is no time. *Proceedings of International Conference on Software Engineering* (pp. 718-719).

Stein, M. V., Riedl, J., Harner, S. J., & Mashayekhi, V. (1997). A case study of distributed, asynchronous software inspection. *Proceedings of the 19th International Conference on Software Engineering* (pp. 107-117).

Thelin, T., Runeson, P., & Wohlin, C. (2003, Augus). An experimental comparison of usage-based and checklist-based reading. *IEEE Transaction on Software Engineering, 29*(8), 687-704t.

Tvedt, J. D., & Gollofello, J. S. (1995, August 9-11). Evaluating the effectiveness of process improvements on software development cycle time via system dynamics modelling, *Proceedings of the 19th Annual International Computer Software and Applications Conference* (pp. 318-325). Dallas.

VanDeGrift, T. (2004, March). Paired programming/ collaborative learning: Coupling pair programming and writing: Learning about students' perceptions and processes. *Proceedings of the 35th SIGCSE Technical Symposium on Computer Science Education.*

Voas, J. (2003). Assuring software quality assurance. *IEEE Software*, 48-49.

Votta, L. G. (1993, May/June). Does every inspection need a meeting? *ACM Software Engineering, 18*(5), 107-114.

Wallance, D. R., & Fuji, R. U. (1989). Software verification and validation: An overview. *IEEE Software*, 10-17.

Weller, E. F. (1993). Lessons from three years of inspection data. *IEEE Software, 10*(5), 38-45.

Wheeler, D. A., Brykczynski, B., & Meeson, R. N. (1996). *Software inspection: An industry best practice.* Los Alamitos, CA: IEEE Computer Society Press.

Wiegers, K. E. (1998, September-October). Read my lips: No new models! *IEEE Software, 15*(5).

Wiegers, K. E. (2002). *Peer reviews in software: A practical guide.* Boston: Addison-Wesley.

Will, H. (2004, July 19-20). Semiotic information systems: Cognitive, methodological, organizational, and technological criteria. *Proceedings of the 7th International Workshop on Organizational Semiotics.* Setúbal, Portugal.

Will, H., & Whobrey, D. (2004). The assurance paradigm: Organizational semiotics applied to governance issues. In K. Liu (Ed.), *Systems design with signs studies in organisational semiotics.* Dordrecht: Kluwer Academic Publishers.

Williams, L. A., & Kessler, R. R. (2000). All I really need to know about pair programming I learned in kindergarten. *Communication of the ACM, 43*(5), 108-114.

Wilson, D. N., & Hall, T. (1998, March). Perceptions of software quality: A pilot study. *Software Quality Journal, 7*(1), 67-75.

Wilson, D. N., Petocz, P., & Roiter, K. (1996). Software quality assurance in practice. *Software Quality Journal, 5*, 53-59.

Wohlin, C., Aurum, A., Petersson, H., Shull, F., & Ciolkowski, M. (2002). Software inspection benchmarking–a qualitative and quantitative comparative opportunity. *Proceedings of the 8th Symposium on Software Metrics (Metrics'02)* (pp. 118-127).

Xu, J. (2003, August). Inspection and verification of software with timing requirement. *IEEE Transaction on Software Engineering, 29*(8), 705-720.

Yourdon, E. (1989). *Structured walkthroughs* (4th ed.). Prentice Halls.

Yourdon, E. (1993, February). Quality: What it means and how to achieve it. *Management Information Systems*, 43-47.

Chapter III

Software Review Tools and Technologies

Abstract

This chapter presents software review tools and technologies which include: paper-based vs. tool-based software review, collaborative asynchronous vs. synchronous software reviews, applying software review tools in the software review process, paper-based and Web-based reviews tools, evaluation of asynchronous and synchronous design, and comparing software review tools features. This chapter also presents the software review tools can monitor and improve software review process, especially in a group review process. The final section of the chapter presents a knowledge centric software framework for building tools that perform software review, analysis, and transformations.

Introduction

A number of computer support tools have been developed to support the software review meeting process (Halling, Biffl, & Grunbacher, 2002). Many tools provide documentation facilities that allow software review documents to be shared across networks, browsed online, and edited by reviewers (Anderson, Reps, & Teitelbaum, 2003; Anderson, Reps, Teitelbaum, & Zarins, 2003; Chan, 2001; Gintell, Houde, & Mckenney, 1995; Harjumaa, Hedberg, & Tervonen, 2001; Johnson & Tjahjono, 1997; MacDonald & Miller, 1999; MacDonald, Miller, Brooks, Roper, & Wood, 1995; Miller & Macdonald, 1998, 2000; Perpich, Perry, Porter, Votta, & Wade, 1997; Stein, Heimdahl, & Riedl, 1999; Tyran & George, 2002; Van Genuchten, Cornelissen, & Van Dijk, 1997, 1998; Van Genuchten, Van Dijk, Scholten, & Vogel, 2001; Vermunt, Smits, & Van Der Pijl, 1998).

The current trend of software review is for using software review tools to support software review process. Past research has shown a spectrum of advantages of using software review tools supporting technical review. First, a computer-support tools review environment can reduce paper works and clerical costs, decrease error rates of recording review meeting and comments, and allow computerised data collection and data analysis.

Software review tools can integrate the review method with other components of the specific software development method such as asynchronous review and facilitating both metrics collection. Companies will adopt software review tools simply because of such potential benefits over manual software review techniques (Radice, 2002).

Paper-Based vs. Tool-Based Software Reviews

The traditional Fagan software review is a paper-based review. All of the information record and dissemination are relied on the paper. During every defined meeting, all members work together and discuss the defect they found in the same place, so that the tool support is not a major concern, even though there are some tools for paper-based review. On the other hand, some project teams can not find suitable tools to support their modern distributed software engineering projects so they have to either select whole paper-based review or construct tools with unique features for new software reviews (Hedberg & Harjumaa, 2002).

However, sometimes, software review must rely on cooperation and communication with tools-support system (i.e., collaborative asynchronous review system). For example, when a developer must review loose distributed systems, application of paper-base review is problematical.

In addition, even in the Fagan review, tool support may accelerate the software review and save cost of software review. But a study result gained opposite results (MacDonald & Miller, 1997) that effectiveness of tool-supported review has equal performance as effectiveness of paper-based review.

However, the data can be found on Bruce Hungerford's studies (Robert, 1999) showing that traditional software review meetings slow project progress by around two weeks because of coordination problems. On the other hand, some studies (Bianchi et al., 2001; Porter & Votta, 1997; Votta, 1993) argue that meeting may not provide real benefit for enhancing software review as team members expected so that review meetings should be minimized. For instance, major tool-supported reviews are capable of supporting flexible processes in various sizes of meeting during preparation and meeting. Therefore, we still can have certain confidence that tools-support review is better than the traditional manual Fagan review.

Collaborative Asynchronous vs. Synchronous Software Reviews

The typical synchronous review is Fagan software review. All activities in the synchronous software review happen in a linear fashion. And the meetings are located in same place at the same time (Li, 1995).

Asynchronous review is changing the linear-style process into a flexible process. Activity, especially on fault detecting, does not have a clear successor. The activities can be performed at the same time. The authors of the paper (Dunsmore, Roper, & Wood, 2003) believe that activities like fault detect can be separate processes in parallel so that the air time can be reduced significantly.

As a rule, asynchronous review must rely on the computer tools supported, namely e-mail, CASE tools, mosaic, BBS, lotus notes, and so on. Therefore, time spent training a user can be a limitation of Collaborative asynchronous review, but the computer-based communication may be good for knowledge management.

Applying Software Review Tools in the Software Review Process

Software review is efficient and effective for defect detection. However, most of the review was similar to Fagan's Review (Fagan, 1976), which was manual performing, paper-based review. Review team members have to take lots of time to follow the defined route, which reduces the efficiency of review. In order to overcome that, many researchers invent tools to support review.

The tools for software review are classified into two categories. One is tools for paper-based, another is tools for online review tools (Macdonald & Miller, 1999). It is no doubt that online review tools are more complex and flexible than paper-based tools.

Tools for Paper-Based Reviews

There are few tools for paper-based review. Two of them will be evaluated in this article: the first one is COMPAS (Barnard & Collicott, 1990), which is the first tool for paper-base reviews that allows the review to be scheduled. In fact, the original goal of the tool is for document management, which can auto-collect data for review.

Another is review process assistant (IPA), which totally models the stages of software review. It covers planning, preparation, meeting, and so on. It can collect and sort review info in database.

Compared to COMPAS, IPA provides more functionalities and supports. IPA provides the ability of supporting either individual or group. Moreover, the latest version IPA can operate online.

Web-Based Software Review Tools

There are about ten Web-based (online) software review tools. Some widely practiced will be discussed in this article. At first, ICICLE-intelligent code review in a C language environment (Bell, 1993; Brothers, Sembugamoorthy, & Muller, 1990) is designed for software reviewers with C or C++ background. Since it only supports review in C and C++, it is not suitable for general review. It can support both group and individual review as well. The second Web-based software review tool is Collaborative Asynchronous Review (CAIS), which is designed by Mashayekhi, Feulner, and Riedl (1994). The aim of the tool is to support asynchronously software review. It can meet online and share data and documents in flexible time, thus it may reduce time of review. The final tool is ASSIST (MacDonald, 1998). It has a user-friendly interface, which allows users to open multiple browsers. Users can select items from item lists, browse and view the code of the item on code browse simultaneously. It also can automatically collect review data.

Most of Web-based software review tools support some major function: document support, individual preparation, meeting support. ASSIST provides the most comprehensive support of the three tools. It supports linked annotations, cross-referencing, checklist, distributed meetings, decision support, and data collection. The only limitation is that it does not support automated analysis.

Evaluation of Asynchronous and Synchronous Designs

Most tools are either an asynchronous or synchronous design for supporting software review process. Murphy and Miller (1997) compared asynchronous and synchronous review tools (see Table 1).

Hedberg (2004) recently proposed that the next generation tool is to build "comprehensive tools". He suggested that the basic idea of the software review tool is to help reviewers to handle artefacts based on a predefined process that yield annotations and metrics as results. To meet the modern software development, two new aspects of software review tools should be flexibility and integration (Hedberg, 2004). In particular Hedberg (2004) claimed that the new model provides a number of benefits (see Figure 1).

- **Flexibility:** This covers both the process and supporting tools, to ensure tolerable levels of adoption effort and acceptance.

- **Process:** The process can be lightweight or all-inclusive, comparing both asynchronous and asynchronous phases. It will usually be carried out using network techniques, but traditional meetings can be included if necessary.

- **Distribution:** This carries out with tools that enable efficient running of the process. Independence of time and place, online recording of issues and data management can be achieved through networked tools.

Table 1. Comparing asynchronous and synchronous review tools (Murphy & Miller, 1997)

Features	Descriptions
Synergy	Votta (1993) statues that synergy makes no or little impact in the synchronous meeting, therefore holding up the review process until a meeting can be scheduled wastes time and may delay the development process. In the asynchronous design, meetings are removed and the findings of Porter, Votta, and Basili, (1995) and McCarthy, Porter, Siy, and Votta (1995) commented that no loss is incurred in the number of defects found.
Participation	The moderator can very easily see just how much each reviewer is contributing in the review meeting in both the synchronous and asynchronous designs. In the former, they can see which reviewers are speaking up regularly and which are not. In the asynchronous design, all communications are automatically copied to the moderator, who can build up a database of each reviewer's contributions, and so gauge their input over the whole software review.
Process Improvement	Following from the previous, the keeping of communications passed between reviewers can form a valuable record of review experiences, and can be used to improve the process in future. It is hard to imagine such a facility being built into a synchronous meeting, as this would involve recording or transcribing many hours of such software reviews.
Peer Review	In both designs the moderator can Jude how well a reviewer has performed by monitoring their communications, but the database message provides evidence for any formal assessment that would otherwise be based solely on opinion.
Conversations	Meetings are limited to strictly serial, one-on-one conversations. Asynchronous software review can have any number of parallel, n-way threads proceedings at any one time.
Automation	The traditional meeting can be automated, but usually takes the form of a paper-based design. The need for a communications mechanism in the asynchronous design may form the basis of tool support for the whole process.
Location	The asynchronous review can be distributed in space as well as in time. There is no need for the reviewers to be in the same room or the same site. In their study, Mashayekhi et al. (1994) described a software review team with members in the USA and Japan. In contract, any tools that have supported the synchronous software review process have still required the software review team to be in the same room.
Decision Making	Deciding whether a proposed defect is to be included or not is usually decided by asking each reviewer to vote on the issue. This can cause contention as the software review may be evenly divided on the matter, or a minority may refuse to agree with the consensus. The implicit voting associated with asynchronous reviews leaves such decisions to the moderator, who decides whether or not to include a defect on the basis of the reviewers' individual submissions. An initial attempt was made to gather quantitative data on the performance of both the design and the tool, using students from a practical software engineering class to perform a small software review. After completing the exercise, the participants completed a questionnaire, with answers on normal Likert scale. Due to the small number of participants, detailed analysis is inappropriate, but the responses provided encouragement by their highly positive nature.

- **Interoperability:** The interoperability of the processes and tools will be required to enable convenient everyday use of the method and to improve the effectiveness of software reviews.

These features should make software review easier to implement and less effort required (Hedberg, 2004).

Hedberg suggested that two questions should be asked when seeking quality tools for software review (Hedberg, 2004):

Figure 1. Interrelationships between the three basic aspects of software review tools and two new aspects (adopted from Hedberg, 2004)

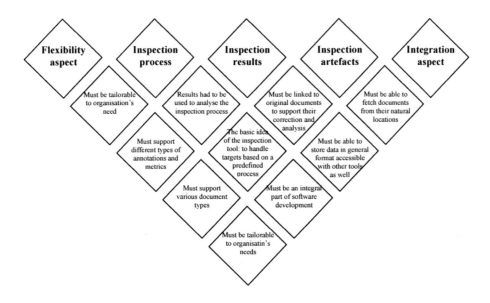

1. Are the virtual review process and tools supporting it as flexible as they should be? Especially, what changes should be made to the processes when using a tool, or what changes, should be made to the tool if following the original processes in the organisation?

2. Is the organisation able to make efficient use of the interoperability of the processes and tools? Especially, where are the bottlenecks when creating seamless operation between software review and other phases?

The two questions raise some critical factors or limitations in the deployment and usage of technology support software reviews. While software review is only one part of the larger software development cycle, as a well-defined software review process provides better direction to the research in the distributed software development (Hedberg, 2004).

Table 2. Features of the software review tools

Features	Descriptions
Comment-link	The tool allows user to create a link to part of documents
Cross-referencing	The tool allows user to travel different documents through references
Automated detection	The tool can automatically detect and mark defect on documents
Supporting material	The tool can handle different types of supporting documents
Distributed meeting	The tool allows user who in different places to meeting together via network
Decision support	The tool provides some suggestions for dealing with defects detected
Data statistics	The tool can collect the defect data and create a statistics for them

Comparing Software Review Tools Features

In this section, we have compared software review tools in the following features (Capers & Jones, 1991; Filippo & Mallardo, 2003; Lanubile & Mallardo, 2002):

- document and defect handling,
- individual reading support collaboration support, and
- data statistics.

These features can be divided into some more detailed features, namely comment-link, cross-referencing, automated detection, supporting material, asynchronous meeting support, decision support, and data statistics (Capers & Jones, 1991; Filippo & Mallardo, 2003; Lanubile & Mallardo, 2002). The entire sub-features list and comparison of synchronous and synchronous software review tools are summarized in Tables 2 and 3.

Groupware Supported Inspection Process

Groupware Supported Inspection Process (GRIP) (Halling, Grunbaher, & Biffl, 2001a, 2001b) was proposed by Halling and his team in 2001, and this idea was driven from Active Inspection Management (AIM) Process (see Figure 2). The AIM helps to collect, use accurate and timely data for monitoring and improving software review process. The main components of the AIM process-planning,

Table 3. Comparing synchronous and asynchronous software review tools (features X indicates that tools have the particular feature)

	Synchronous Software Review Tools						Asynchronous Software Review Tools						
	ASSIST	ICICLE	CSI	InspeQ	IBIS	Scrutiny	CSRS	CAIS	AISA	InspectA	CodeSurfer	HyperCode	Wip
Comment-Link	X	X	X		X	X	X	X	X	X	X	X	X
Cross-Referencing	X	X			X						X		
Auto-Detection	X	X		X						X	X		
Checklist	X	X	X	X			X	X		X	X	X	X
Supporting Material	X	X		X	X	X					X	X	X
Distributed Meeting	X		X		X							X	X
Decision Support	X					X	X	X	X	X			
Data Statistics	X	X	X		X	X	X	X					X

in-process monitoring, post-process evaluation, and process improvement — interacting with technical review process (Halling et al., 2001a). AIM provides "a cycle improvement" which includes planning for the software review process, measures is then used to adjust the planning techniques for the software review process and thus feedback into the next cycle of software review (Halling et al.,

Figure 2. GRIP framework

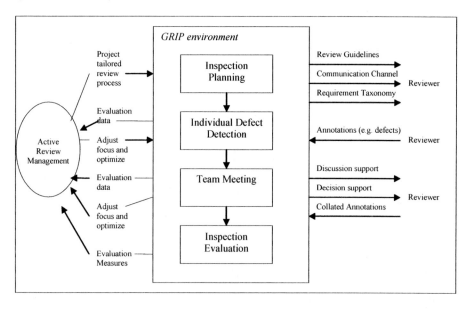

2001a). This review process represents cycles which include the following steps (Halling et al., 2001a):

1. Starts for each review with the planning activity
2. Monitors the software review execution
3. Evaluates the software review results afterwards in details
4. Derives suggestions for process adjustments and improvement

Figure 2 presents a GRIP environment that integrates the software review management process and the technical review process including Active Inspection Management Process.

The GRIP framework allows to standard the software review process, provide automatic data collection and software review management capabilities and it is fully integrated into the software review process and also provides detect detection support for software review (Halling et al., 2001a, 2001b). The GRIP can easily be tailored to different software review process designs (e.g., asynchronous, synchronous, with or without meeting) while many other software review tools are specifically develop support a special software review process

(Halling et al., 2001a, 2001b). In summary, the GRIP framework allows (Halling et al., 2002):

- To focus inspector (reviewer) attention on a specific part of the documents, inspection (review) (or project) manager simply changes the task assignment for the inspector (reviewer). The inspector (reviewer) is immediately informed whenever he logs on to the GSS (Group Support System) workspace.

- To support a new user perspective, an additional inspector (reviewer) is simply added to the current inspection (review) in the Group Support System. Whenever the new inspector (reviewer) enters the Group Support System he sees his assigned tasks, can read defects and comments of other inspectors (reviewers), or directly communicates with other inspectors (reviewers) (all these options are customizable to the specific inspection (review) design).

- To schedule a meeting, the meeting is simply added as a task to the current inspection (review) design. All inspectors (reviewers) are immediately informed, receives information on the meeting purpose, and can use the groupware support tools for synchronous team activities (e.g., for voting on defect severity).

- To its flexibility, GRIP collects the data necessary for improved inspection (review) management. In this context defect reporting is the most important aspect. As mentioned earlier it is important for later processing to describe a defect and specify its location precisely.

Knowledge Centric Software Framework

Knowledge Centric Software (KCS) is another software review framework that embodies the pattern-based approach and provides capabilities for addressing different language and different application domains (Kothari, Bishop & Sauceda, 2004) for code review. The aim of KCS framework is for building tools that perform software review, analysis, and transformations. According to Kothari et al. (2004), the KCS Framework provides:

- A pattern-based approach for creating customized tools for different application domains

- An eXtensible Common Intermediate Language (XCIL) to address many languages with a single toolset
- An eXtensible Pattern Specification Language (XPSL) to serve as an umbrella for multiple analysis/transformation technologies
- A core set of analysers to support queries and transformations that require global data and control flow analysis
- eXtensible Markup Lanagauge (XML-based) representation for leveraging XML tools and also provides interoperation ability with other tools
- Standardization and compliance of XCIL with MSIL, JVM, and UML action semantics

The major weaknesses of the KCS framework for developing and use of automation tools are the lack of usability and scalability (Kothari et al., 2004). For example, the problem of information explosion and this is important for a complex system.

Summary

In summary, the first three generations follow directly the degrees of freedom in the classification of groupware. The first transition is from early same-place, same-time tools to distributed but still same-time tools. Total independence of time and place was implemented in the third generation asynchronous tools. Web-based software review tools are still asynchronous, but are distinguished from the previous generations by their technological base.

However, no studies other than those (above authors) undertaken by the above software developers exist to have evaluated or verify verified the important role these tools may have to play in improving software review performance. While it is the consideration of this research that a comparative evaluation of the tools would be an important study to undertake, it is outside of the scope of this research. Types of software review tools and how they work will be further discussed in next chapter.

Acknowledgment

I would like to thank Yan for his kind assistance in completing this chapter.

References

Anderson, P., Reps, T., & Teitelbaum T. (2003a). Design and implementation of a fine-grained software inspection tool. *IEEE Transaction on Software Engineering*, 721733.

Anderson, P., Reps, T., Teitelbaum, T., & Zarins, M. (2003b). Tool support for fine-grained software inspection. *IEEE Software, 20*(4), 42-50.

Barnard, H. J., & Collicott, R. B. (1990). COMPAS: A development process support system. *AT&T Technical Journal, 62*(2), 52-64.

Bell, (1993, January). *Communications Research, ICICLE User's Guide.*

Brothers, L., Sembugamoorthy, V., & Muller, M. (1990, October). ICICLE: Groupware for code inspection. *Proceedings of the 1990 ACM Conference on Computer Supported Cooperative Work* (pp 169-181).

Capers & Jones. (1991). *Applied software measurement: Assuring productivity and quality* (2nd ed.). McGraw Hill.

Chan, K. (2001, August 27-28). An agent-based approach to computer assisted code inspections. *Proceedings of Australian Software Engineering Conference* (pp. 147-152).

Dunsmore, A., Roper, M., & Wood, M. (2003). The development and evaluation of three diverse techniques for object-oriented code inspection. *IEEE Transactions on Software Engineering, 29*(8).

Fagan, M. E. (1976). Design and code inspections to reduce errors in program development. *IBM System Journal, 15*(3), 182-211.

Filippo, L., & Mallardo, T. (2003). Tool support for distributed inspection. *Proceedings of the 26th Annual International Computer Software and Applications Conference (COMPSAC'02).*

Gintell, J. W., Houde, M. B., & Mckenney, R. F. (1995, July 10-14). Lessons learned by building and using scrutiny, a collaborative software inspection systems. *Proceedings of the 7th International Workshop on Computer-Aided Software Engineering* (pp. 350-357).

Halling, M., Biffl, S., & Grunbacher, P. (2002). A group-supported inspection process for active inspection management. *Proceedings of the 28th Euromicro Conference*.

Halling, M., Grenache, P., & Biffl S. (2001b, December). Tailoring a COTS group support system for software requirement inspection. *Proceedings of the Automated Software Engineering Conference*. San Diego, CA: IEEE Computer Society Press.

Halling, M., Grunbaher, P., & Biffl, S. (2001a, July). groupware support for software requirements inspection. *Proceedings of the Workshop on Inspection in Software Engineering (WISE'01)*.

Harjumaa, L., Hedberg, H., & Tervonen, I. (2001). A path to virtual software inspection. *Proceedings of the 2nd Asia Pacific Conference on Quality Software* (pp. 283-287).

Hedberg, H. (2004). Introducing the next generation of software inspection tools. *PROFES 2004*, LNCS 3009 (pp. 234-247). Berlin, Heidelberg: Springer-Verlag .

Hedberg, H., & Harjumaa, L. (2002). *Virtual software inspections, for distributed software engineering projects*. Oulu, Finland: Department of Information Processing Science, University of Oulu, Finland.

Johnson, P. M., & Tjahjono, D. (1997). *Assessing software review meetings: A controlled experimental study using CSRS*. New York: ACM Press.

Khoshgoftaar, T. M., & Munson, J. C. (1990). The lines of code metric as a predictor of program faults: A critical analysis. *Proceedings of Computer Software and Applications* (pp. 408-413).

Kothari, C. S., Bishop L., & Sauceda, J. (2004). A pattern-based framework for software anomaly detection. *Software Quality Journal, 12*, 99-120.

Lanubile, L., & Mallardo, T. (2002). Preliminary evaluation of tool-based support for distributed inspection. *Proceedings of ICSE International Workshop on Global Software Development*. Orlando, FL, USA.

Li, X. L. (1995). A comparison-based approach for software inspection. *Proceedings of the 1995 Conference of The Centre for Advanced Studies on Collaborative Research*.

MacDonald, F. (1998). *ASSIST V2.1 User Manual, Technical Report EFoCS-28-98*, Department of Computer Science, University of Strathclyde.

MacDonald, F., & Miller, J. (1997). A Software Inspection Process Definition Language and Prototype Support Tool. Software Testing, *Verification and Reliability*, 7(2), 99-128.

MacDonald, F., & Miller, J. (1999). ASSIST: A tool to support software inspection. *Information and Software Technology, 41*, 1045-1057.

MacDonald, F., Miller, J., Brooks, A., Roper, M., & Wood, M. (1995, July 10-14). A review of tool support for software inspection. *Proceedings of 7th International Workshop on Computer-Aided Software Engineering* (pp. 340-349). Toronto.

Mashayekhi, V., Feulner, C., & Riedl, J. (1994). CAIS: Collaborative Asynchronous Inspection of Software. *Proceedings of 2nd ACM SIGSOFT Symposium on Foundations of Software Engineering.* New York, *19*(5), 21-34.

McCarthy, P., Porter, A., Siy H., & Votta, L. (1995). *An experiment to assess cost-benefits of inspection meeting and their alternatives, Technical Report*, Computer Science Department University of Maryland.

Miller, J., & Macdonald, F. (1998, October 13-16). Assisting exit decision in software inspection. *Proceedings of 13th IEEE International Conference on Automated Software Engineering* (pp. 281-284).

Miller, J., & Macdonald, F. (2000). An empirical incremental approach to tool evaluation and improvement. *The Journal of Systems and Software, 51,* 19-35.

Murphy, P., & Miller, J. (1997). A process for asynchronous software inspection. *Proceedings of 18th IEEE International Workshop on Software Technology and Engineering* (pp. 96-104).

Perpich, J. M., Perry, E. D., Porter, A. A., Votta, L. G., & Wade, M. W. (1997). Anywhere, anytime code inspections: Using the Web to remove inspection bottlenecks in large-scale software development. *Proceedings of International Conference on Software Engineering, ICSE* (pp. 14-21).

Porter, A. A., & Votta, L. G. (1997, November/December). What makes inspections work? *IEEE Software*, 99-102.

Porter, A. A., Votta, L. G., & Basili, B. (1995). Comparing detection methods for software requirements inspection: A replicated experiment. *IEEE Transaction on Software Engineering, 21*(6), 563-575.

Radice, R.A. (2002). *High quality low cost software inspections.* Andover, MA: Paradoxicon Publishing.

Stein, M. V., Heimdahl, M. P. E., & Riedl, J. T. (1999, October). Enhancing annotation visibility for software inspection. *Proceedings of 14th IEEE International Conference on Automated Software Engineering* (pp. 243-246). Cococa Beach.

Tyran, C. K., & George J. F. (2002). Improving software inspection with group process support. *Communication of the ACM, 45*(9), 97-92.

Van Genuchten, M. V., Cornelissen, W., & Van Dijk., C. (1997, January 7-10). Supporting inspection with an electronic meeting systems. *Proceedings of* the Hawaii International Conference on System Sciences (pp. 405-411).

Van Genuchten, M. V., Cornellissen, W., & Van Dijk, C. (1998). Supporting inspections with an electronic meeting systems. *Journal of Management Information Systems, 14*(3), 16-178.

Van Genuchten, M. V., Van Dijk, C., Scholten, H., & Vogel, D. (2001, May/ June). Using group support systems for software inspections. *IEEE Software*.

Vermunt, A., Smits, M., & Van Der Pijl, G. (1998). Using GSS to support error detection in software specifications. *IEEE Proceedings of 31st Annual Hawaii International Conference on System Sciences* (pp. 566-574).

Votta, L. G. (1993). Does every inspection need a meeting? *ACM Software Engineering, 18*(5), 107-114.

Chapter IV

How Software Review Tools Work

Abstract

There are many software review tools for supporting the software review process, particularly in a group review. This chapter presents an overview of common software review tools and discussions on how these tools work in software review process. A number of software review tools will be discussed in this chapter. These include: Intelligent Code Inspection in a C Language Environment (ICICLE), Scrutiny, Collaborate Software Inspection (CSI), InspeQ, CSRS, Requirement Traceability tool (RADIX), InspectA, Asynchronous Inspection of Software Artefacts (AISA), Web Inspection Prototype (WiP), Asynchronous/Synchronous Software Inspection Support Tool (ASSIST), CORD, Agent-based Software Tool, Web-based Software Review System, Internet-Based Inspection System (IBIS) and VisionQuest.

Intelligent Code Inspection in a
C Language Environment (ICICLE)

The ICICLE (Intelligent Code Inspection in a C Language Environment) is the first published software review tool, which was developed at Bellcore (Brothers, Sembugamoorthy, & Muller, 1990). The ICICLE tool is designed to support code review and assists reviewers in both individual preparation and group meetings. ICICLE provides a synchronous communication support to group meetings. It has been argued that traditional code review meeting is manually documented (i.e., using paper and pen to record defects detected). This documentation procedure is very time consuming, tedious and could be inconsistent recording (Brothers et al., 1990). One of the aims of this tool helps software reviewers to find obvious defects.

Brothers and his team (1990) suggested that ICICLE provide several benefits to code review:

- To detect routine sorts of errors, with the goal of freeing the code inspector (reviewer) to concentrate on verifying the correct implementation of requirement, specifications, and designs.
- Offers various forms of knowledge about the code being inspected (reviewed), including domain and environment knowledge, and information from various forms of analysis such as cross-referencing.
- To allow code inspectors (reviewers) to easily traverse source code in a windowed environment instead of riffling thought hard copy from many different files.
- To render the code inspection (review) meeting paperless through a shared window interface which enables the code inspectors (reviewers) to fulfill their roles electronically.

The ICICLE tool consists of two phases in the review process, the individual review and group review meeting. The group review meeting takes in the same location/venue, usually a reviewers' seat at nearby computers. Individual reviewer allows entering comments on each line of code. According to MacDonald, Miller, Brooks, Roper, and Wood (1995), the researcher found that "the computer supported meeting format appeared to cause substantial changes in the dynamics of the code inspection (review) meeting." In other words, the procedures of the code review meeting using ICICLE can enable roles during the group meeting process (Brothers et al., 1990). For examples, addition duty of a moderator is to record statistics relating to coding defects discovered during code review. Reader can direct the attention of the other reviewers to areas of interest in the source code. Scribe records must to be agreed by the review team. Author should present in the code review meeting and answer the reviewers' question. Any additional reviewers can participate and share meeting discussions.

How It Works

In the document handling, ICICLE has a multi-window interface which is implemented in the software tool kit for the X window System (Brothers et al., 1990). The central disply window of the ICICLE interface is the window which "displays actual source code, with each line being numbered, annotations, and feedback from user activity" (Brothers et al., 1990). This split window feature allows reviewer to review two parts of code simultaneously (MacDonald et al., 1995). ICICLE also has a manipulation function that provides a set of controls for manipulation and status of the comment in the comment window. Reviewers can enter their comments into the comment window.

In the preparation stage, it is private to the reviewer and the comments are owned by individual reviewers. Individual reviewer can comment on each line of code by clicking on the line number's symbols. The first symbol indicates the status of the comments; this could be deferred (not comment yet), ignored (no comment) or transferred (should be discuss in the group review meeting). All comments can be modified, updated and deleted by reviewers. They can also to be accepted, modified and rejected by the review team. The second symbol indicates comment's classification; this could be defects, warnings, hazards, and standards violations (MacDonald et al., 1995). In additional, ICICLE provides cross-referencing and a hypertext knowledge browser features. The cross-referencing feature "provides information for objects such as variable" whereas a hypertext knowledge browser feature provides a hypertext knowledge browser to "assist the reviewer with domain specific knowledge, as well as in indexed browser to peruse pages such as those for UNIX" (MacDonald et al., 1995).

In the meeting support, there are three major instances of communications — sharing the window view, proposing comment and directing focus of attention (Brother et al., 1990).

The first instance of communication is sharing the window view. The reader guides all the reviewers thought the module being analysed. During this meeting process, all windows are locked synchronously with the reader's control the windows. As the reader scrolls or changes the window views for different files, the entire reviewers' windows will be changed accordingly by the reader. However, reviewers can choose the split window feature that allows them to have a combination view of both private and public in the window.

The second instance of communication is proposing comment. When a reviewer proposed a comment, a small window with the text of the comment pops up onto all reviewers' screens. This small window is called "scribe" and is the control window for "accept" or "reject" the comment. This scribe window is a public window which allows all reviewers to modify the proposed comments and produced a merged file output.

The final instance of communication is directing focus of attention feature. ICICLE allows any reviewer to "identify" or "point" something on other reviewer's screen by clicking the cursor movement which can create a "mark" on other reviewers' screens. Other reviewers can correspond accordingly.

Data collected by ICICLE system can generate a statistic defect report at the end of the group review meeting.

Scrutiny

Scrutiny is an online collaborative software review tool, which was developed at Bull HN Information Systems in conjunction with the University of Illinois (Gintell, Houde, & Mckenney, 1993). It is a synchronous meeting review tool. It is one of the early comprehensive collaborative process software review tool (MacDonald et al., 1995). Scrutiny currently supports text documents only. Scrutiny can be used in the formal review process and it supports for multi-users review but does not support for rules and checklists. It provides a "petri-net based process modelling language" that allows the system to implement alternative software review methods, such as a "shared preparation" phase in which reviewers have access to each other's preliminary findings (Gintell et al., 1993; MacDonald et al., 1995). However, in comparison with the ICICLE, the Scrutiny usage can depart radically from manual software review processes, such as geographically distributed software reviews (MacDonald et al., 1995).

How It Works

The overall software review process using Scrutiny can be divided into four stages (i.e., initiation, preparation, resolution, and completion) (Gintell & Menni, 1997).

In the first initiation phase, a software review team is selected and notified. A moderator loads a review document into the system and make available to all reviewers. The document is displayed in Scrutiny with the current focus (Gintell & Memmi, 1997).

In the second stage, preparation phase, this involves the reviewers enter their comments for review meeting. Reviewers can enter comment while reading through documents. There are a few control functions on the window. These functions allow reviewers to create, modify, and delete comments/annotations (Gintell & Memmi, 1997). The comment could be questions, potential defects, remark, or reply (MacDonald et al., 1995). The reviewers are guided by the moderator to read and enter comments. There is no checklist or supporting documents available in the preparation phase. During individual review process, the communication channel is asynchronous where each individual reviewer enters his/her comments without and any discussion or viewing other reviewers' comments (Gintell & Memmi, 1997). All entered comments will be discussed in next phase.

In the third stage, resolution phase, the moderator guides reviewers through the documents and defect collection (Gintell & Memmi, 1997). The moderator also has additional control on all Scrutiny windows. Each Scrutiny window contains a list of comments made on the current document. The reviewers' status display contains a list of the reviewers along with an indication of their current activities (MacDonald et al., 1995). This allows all reviewers focus on particular section of the document. The reviewers also can see each others' comments, make additional comments. The communication is synchronous where all reviewers review at the same time on the same document.

In the final stage is completion. Once each defect has been discussed and agreed by the review team. The system produces a summary of the defects that have been discussed (a poll is taken and recorded in the system every time during the review) (MacDonald et al., 1995). The recorder takes the final step of data collection of software review. These include classification of defects and generate reports containing the summary of defects as well as the appropriate statistics and metrics (Gintell & Memmi, 1997). Software review is completed when all defects are resolved.

Collaborate Software Inspection (CSI)

Collaborate Software Inspection (CSI) was built and used in a case study to compare online distributed computer-mediated software review meeting vs. face-to-face software review meetings at the University of Minnesota (Mashayekhi, Feulner, & Riedl, 1994). As with other software review tools, the CSI provides the similar process characteristics of Humphrey's Software review method with hypertext capability. CSI is developed for group review meeting in the 1) same time and place, 2) same time and place, 3) same time and different place, and 4) different time and same place. CIS supports both asynchronous and synchronous activities that include materials distribution, individual preparation/individual review, group review meeting, recording and reporting (Mashayekhi et al., 1994).

How It Works

In handling document, CSI provides a browser displays document under review, which automatically numbered each line. It contains hyperlinks from the reviewed document to a defect list, reviewer's comments, defect summary, and actions (Mashayekhi et al., 1994). This allows reviewers easy navigation between different areas of the documents, but the current system does not support preparation stage or for checklists.

In individual preparation, reviewer can select a line of document, a sub-window pops up and that allow reviewers make comments. Reviewers are free to create annotations in any line of the documents (MacDonald et al., 1995). All comments and defect lists are recorded and can be organised and available in an electronic form. For general comments about the documents, CSI provides notepad systems for general comments other than specific line of the documents. Upon completion of individual preparation, author can view all annotations that made by the reviewers. The author can sort defects in different category, integrate the annotations and create a summary defect list.

At the group review meeting, the review document can be viewed by all reviewers simultaneously. The author guides the group review team using the defect list. Defects or issues are discussed and agreed by the review team. The original comments are also available for reviewers to understand the nature of the fault. New comments can be added and recorded during the synchronous meeting discussions. CSI supports electronically facilitation to the meeting discussion and also controls access to information by established permission (MacDonald et al., 1995).

The meeting can be facilitated by audio-conferencing or teleconferencing when a review team members in a variety of disparate location.

At the final stage of the review process, the review summary indicates whether the review document is being accepted or it requires further review. In additional, the summary also indicates the meeting information such as number of reviewers, roles, history logs, defects statistics, time spent in the meeting, time taken to find defects, and other metrics (MacDonald et al., 1995).

InspeQ

InspeQ was developed to support the phased software review process (Knight & Myers, 1993). The InspeQ was executed on "Sun 3, Sun 4, and IBM RS/6000 computers running various forms of Unix and the X-window display system and the OSF/Motif widget set" (Knight & Myers, 1993). Although the InspeQ achieves the goals of efficiency and rigor in the phased review process, it is not viewed as essential to the "Phased Inspection" method (MacDonald et al., 1995). Similar to other software review tools, InspeQ provides numbers of facilities to support software review process. These include work product display (views the documents), checklist display (allows the status of each checklist to be displayed and modified), standard display (review rational and a detailed descriptions), highlight display (helps locating particular aspects of the documents) and comments display (comments on the documents) (Knight & Myers, 1991).

How It Works

InspeQ provide a browser simultaneously to view and to examine multiple separate parts of a document. Each reviewer allows to making comments on part of the text or line numbers of the documents. Each comment posts on the comment display window which allows author to view.

Table 1. InspeQ facilities (Source: Knight & Myers, 1991, p. 33)

Facilities	Descriptions
Work product display	• Permits display, scrolling, repositioning, and searching the text. • Multiple instances of display window can be used to permit inspection (review) of related but separate areas.
Checklist display	• To ensure that inspector (reviewer) is informed of exactly what checks are involved in a given phase. • The display also accepts inputs from the inspector (reviewer) indicating the status of the various required checks. • The permits InsepQ to check compliance.
Standards display	• A complete definition of the standards that the checklists are designed to check.
Highlight display	• Helps the inspector (reviewer) find and isolate specific product features quickly. • The highlighter allows features to be extracted and displayed in a separate window.
Comments display	• To record anything in the product with which he is not satisfied.

During the individual preparation stage, individual reviewer uses a display checklist to help his or her to find defects. The checklist provides a list of requirements that reviewers should look for and ensure reviewers know exactly what is required to do in the individual preparation stage. Reviewers use the checklist window as a guideline to inspect the review document, by making each item on the checklist window to determine whether each check item has been addressed or not. Using checklist in the review process, it provides a rigorous review. A completed check list is displayed in the "checklist window". Examples also support reviewers to complete the individual review task. In addition to the checklist display window, InspeQ also supports monitoring of personnel and file tracking (e.g., standard and highlight display windows) (MacDonald et al., 1995).

InspeQ is aimed for individual reviewer use, and as such has no provision for supporting a group meeting (MacDonald et al., 1995). As a result, the system generates a summary report and defects list for individual reviewer only. Then, all individual reports can be reconciliation.

CSRS

CSRS is developed to support computer-mediated communication formal software review process (Johnson, 1994). The CSRS is heavily used in academic research and laboratory experiments studies. The goals of CSRS is to reduce the human effort in review process, by conducting software review incrementally during the development and provide online capabilities to collect metrics (Stein, Riedl, Harner, & Mashayekhi, 1997). The CSRS is similar to Scrutiny, it provides an internal process modelling mechanism to support a variety of review methods. CSRS's primary method is FTArm, which "is unique among methods by being designed explicitly to support properties of computer-mediated communication and review" (Johnson, 1994).

CSRS automatically collect data (e.g., number of defects/issues found, comments made, time spent on software review, starting time, finishing time, event logs, etc.). Another feature of CSRS is that it supports variety of software review process and handling several types of documents and languages.

How It Works

CSRS supports Fagan's software review process (MacDonald et al., 1995). In the planning phase (set-up), the moderator selects review group members, assigns roles, uploads review documents and defect list, prepares checklist, schedules review process, develops instruction, and informs the review team regarding the software review.

In the overview phase, it is the orientation stage. An overview of the software review and the review document are presented by the author to the software team. The objective the overview is that it allows review team to familiarise with the review document and the overall software review process.

At the preparation stage, each reviewer reads the review document and finds defects. Any defects/issues/comments can be recorded in the defect form. There is no communication between reviewers and individual each reviewer works privately. When all reviewers complete the task, they can move on to next stages.

Next stage is group discussion, known as public review. All issues/comments are summarised into one list. All reviewers are able to view the combined list. The discussion of the review meeting is asynchronously. The system does not support group review meeting. So, the meeting is face-to-face approach. The reviewers can asynchronously vote on the status of each issue. New comments or issues can be added, modify or deleted. When all issues are resolved, the moderator will decide on the need for further discussions or declare the completion of the discussion.

Once the group discussion is completed, the fifth step is consolidation. CSRS does not support reporting facilities. The moderator needs to write the report and result details from both private and public phases (individual preparation and group discussion). If there are unresolved issues remaining, the moderator will determine whether the meeting is required.

In the final stage of the software review, additional group review meetings may be required if there are unresolved issues. If all issues have been resolved, the moderator signs off for the software review completion. The reviewers will also be notified.

Requirement Traceability Tool (RADIX)

Requirement traceability refers to the "ability to describe and follow the life of a requirement, in both a forwards and backward direction" (Gotel & Finkelstein, 1994). The requirement traceability tool (RADIX) is designed for verifying software requirements (Yu, 1994; Yu, Smith, & Huang, 1990). A requirement tracing method is a systematic method to assist 5ESS Switch scientist and engineers to delivery quality software (Yu, 1994).

How It Works

RADIX supports the author to develop feature specification documents according to requirement documents using RADIX macros. It is necessary to ensure that each requirement is labelled and bold and is addressed in developing feature specification documents. A list of feature requirements can be generated and the feature specification document can be facilitated to verify a client's requirements.

Upon completion of verification of requirements, a set of architecture development specifications and requirement development specification documents can be designed and generated using RADIX tool. RADIX tools can support authors to specify the architectural type of requirement feature and to label and highlight the internal development requirement for the features. The system also supports requirement mapping among feature specification documents, architectural development specification, and requirement development specification. During this process, a requirement checklist is automatically generated from the requirement development specification document and references to their source.

During design phase, a design development specification is developed using RADIX tool. Each design development specification item is labelled and assigned feature development requirement to the development units. RADIX provides traceability function for both backward and forward requirement tracing. Each requirement is performed to verify converge of requirements in the design development specification.

In the detailed design and coding stages, reviewers look up the development units to check whether all requirements have been addressed. Again, a summary list of all requirements related to design and coding will be generated from RADIX. The summary list provides verification purpose to requirements, design, and coding.

To ensure the test has a full coverage on all requirements, each test is assigned a test number. This allows reviewers to map between test identify numbers and requirement label numbers. RADIX produces a summary of review results, including which requirement numbers have not be reviewed. The mapping table can show which feature requirements are not tests and how tests and requirement are related (Yu, 1994).

One of the key features of RADIX is to provide backward and forward requirement tracing to ensure complete review of converge requirements in all stages of software development.

In addition, Yu (1994) claimed that RADIX has a number of advantages. This includes better quality, more requirement focus, improving test effectiveness,

Table 2. The advantages of RADIX (adopted from Yu, 1994)

Advantages	Descriptions
Better quality	Fewer defects errors found were related to requirement. By comparing the number error found during development before product devilry to customers, it has reduced by 20-30%.
Requirement focus	The tool supports heavily in the requirement review rather than the traditional in the design and coding reviews.
Improve testing effectiveness	Increase the test coverage (measured by tests/thousand lines of code) up to 100%.
Costs benefits	Reducing repairing costs since defects were found and correction in the early requirement phase and fewer defects found in the later stage of system development (e.g. coding and testing).
Popular tool for users	Since the RADIX tool was released to AT&T Bell Laboratories in 1989, the tool was being invoked by users on an average of 18,000 times a month
Standardisation	The use of the RADIX macros in the development documents has been standardized as part of the development methodology.
Requirement information shared with other tools	The enumerated requirement information can be used in conjunction with other requirement and testing tools.

cost benefits, popular tool for users, standardisation, and sharing requirements with other tools (see Table 2). However, the RADIX tool does not support for software review meeting process, but automated functions in software review and verification in the software development process.

Similar to RADIX, there are number of commercial tools for requirement traceability which can be classified into general-purpose tools (mainly cross-referencing), special-purpose tools (more implicit tool and limited guidance), workbenches (have features of general-purpose and special-purpose tools features and commonly provide realisation) and environments (integrated all aspects of development with powerful database management system) (Gotel & Finkelstein, 1994) (see Table 3).

However, there two problems of requirement traceability will need to resolve. These include (Gotel & Finkelstein, 1994):

1.   Lack of common definition: How can requirement traceability be coherent and consistent?

2.   Conflicting underlying problem: Individuals may have own understanding or view to each problem or requirement.

Table 3. Tools support for requirement traceability (adopted from Gotel & Finkelstein, 1994, p. 96)

Requirement Traceability (RT)	General-purpose Tools	Special-purpose Tools	Workbenches	Environments
Priority given to RT	Any general-purpose tool can potentially be configured for RT purposes; through RT is not a concern of the basic tool.	Those that support RE activities (e.g., analysis techniques), often provide some form of RT as a by-product of use, but RT is not focal.	Priority depends on the focal set of activist. Where is are RT and management (in RT workbenches), RT is the main concern. Where other RE activities are focal, RT is a side concern.	Typical a side concern, though the extent of this depends on whether or not there are dedicated tools for RT contained in the composite environment.
Support provide for RT	No explicit support is provided. RT must be hand-crafted and the resulting support provided depends on he initial effort expend in doing this. The focus can easily become configuring the tool to enable RT either than ensuring RT itself.	Support in implicit in the framework provided for carrying out the main activity of the tool. Mundane and repetitive tasks, which are usually necessary to provide basic RT, are typically automated as consequence of proper use the tool.	In RT workbenches, support is explicit (else as special-purpose tools). No need analytical ability is provide, but they offer: (1) guidance – through adherence to RE approach (typically top-down decomposition), type to establish (2) assistance – by parsing textual documents to tag requirements, establishing (syntactic) links between then, and through a repository which manages any bookkeeping and rudimentary checking.	Provide as a by-product of coordinated tool use and adherence to RE philosophy. Extent of support depends on the internal integration strategy and or repository structure. More guidance and assistance if it has dedicated RT tools, or if it is a main concern. RT maintenance is supported if the repository can manage quantise of information and reconfigure after change.
Requirement related information that can be made traceable	Ability to trace any information which can be input to the tool (be this textual, graphical, etc), so potentially able to trace all requirement-related information if sufficient effort and foresight are exercised.	Predefines the amount and type of information that can be input and made traceable. This typically restricted to that information necessary to carry out the activity the tool supports. Only a limited scope of requirement-related information can be traced.	Potential to race a diversity of requirement-related information. RT workbenches often impose arbitrary limits on the amount and type of information. They trace how an RS was produced, but usually only its derivation from a textual baseline, not its exploratory development, refinement, and context of production. Additional information (e.g. information notes) can often be recorded, but is of limited use for RT.	Potential to trace information related to requirements in all project phases. Tendency to focus on information derived from requirement in the RS in later phases, so less emphasis on production related information about individual requirement. Often support the RT of versions, variants, and user-defined items.
Task and job roles that RT can assist	Offer complete tailor ability. RT can be provided to support any task and job role, though it is problematic to meet different needs simultaneously without any RT infrastructure in place.	RT is provided to assist the activity to tool supports, so the role of the tool user is predefined. Their task specific frameworks constrain the domain of working, making them difficult to sue for other purposes.	Support for a breadth of activities within the concern of the tool's domain (e.g., able to assist requirements checking etc). Support specific jobs, but often configurable to support tasks for other project phases. RT workbenches tend to support managerial activities rather than the activities of RS producers.	RT can assist lifecycle-wide tasks and roles (e.g., those related to maintenance and management, such as impact analysis and progress reporting, etc). More support for activities related to the use of requirements rather than production and refinement.

Asynchronous Inspector of Software Artefacts (AISA)

Asynchronous Inspector of Software Artefacts (AISA) was the early Web-based software review tool (Stein et al., 1997). AISA supports asynchronous and distribution software review as well as reviewing both textual and graphical

Table 3. cont.

Requirement Traceability (RT)	General-purpose Tools	Special-purpose Tools	Workbenches	Environments
Longevity of RT support	Configured for immediate needs. RT can degrade with quantities of information and time, as not usually integrated with lifecycle-wide tools, and poor at handling change and evolution.	Provide RT at a snapshot in time to support a specific activity, so neglect requirement for on-going management. Longevity of support depends on both horizontal and vertical integration with other tools.	RT is provided for the duration of the activities supported. Predominantly forward-engineering tools, so RT can deteriorate with progression to later phases, as it can be difficult to reflect any work here and account for integration. Longevity of support depends on vertical integration with other tools.	Can provide RT for a project's life, though tends to start from a techniques to assist activity coordination and integration (e.g. workspaces). Often depends on agreed RS and strict project partitioning, so RT can deteriorate when requirements are unstable and overall control is lacking.
Support for the traceability of group activities	Promote individualistic working as provide no common or consistent framework for RT, so encourage immediate and ad hoc solutions. Typically used, by a single user, to record activities after they have happened.	Can provide tight RT for the immediate needs of particular requirements-related activities. Those supporting group activity, often provide traceability of it.	RT workbenches provide god RT from and back to information which is initially input to the tool, and through a breadth of related activities (i.e. fine-grained horizontal RT within requirement phases). Added value (e.g., RT checks, visibility).	Ability to provide on-going RT (i.e., depth of converge of vertical RT). Open environments (and meta-CASE), provide more flexibility in the choice of RE approach and in the RT of this.
Main strengths	Flexibility to provide customised RT to suit individual project and organisational needs. Often sufficient for the RT of small and short term projects.	Can provide tight RT for the immediate needs of particular requirements-related activities. Those supporting group activity, often provide traceability of it.	RT workbenches attempt to be holistic, but non support all activities. Typically enforce: a top-down approach; classification schemes; and pre-empt a relatively static baseline (without support for its development). As RT depends on correct use, the main concern can be RT rather than RS production. RT workbenches integrate poorly, so difficult to support the RT of early problem definition work, or to provide on-going RT with later changes (much manual intervention can be required to do so).	RT is typically coarse-gained and dependent on stop-wise development. As the tightness of RT varies, iteration and later requirements changes can prevent on-going RT (due to poor backwards RT, which rarely accounts for the occurrence of manual intervention or work-around). Increasing flexibility (with those tools open to external integration), is typically counterbalanced by poorer RT.

documents (e.g., entity-relationship diagram or class diagram) (Stein et al., 1997). The AISA Web-based tools can be built using existing structures and were reasonable easy to develop.

How It Works

At the initial stage, the moderator loads a review document to the AISA, schedules the starting date and completion date.

In the individual preparation phase, comments can be posted to AISA. For the graphical documents, AISA provides zoom operation–where reviewers can view the document in hierarchical style. There are number of features of AISA, such as annotation and listing and hypertext link. After the preparation phase, the author remove duplicates and the reviewers can then discuss possible solutions for the defects they have found (Stein et al., 1997).

During the group meeting, a distributed, asynchronous discussion meeting is conducted using the www client interface. All defects comments are available for all reviewers. Reviewers can vote to accept or reject defects. If issues can not be resolved during the meeting, the moderator marks the defects for next sessions analysis until all issues are resolved.

At the completion of software review, a defect summary and a metrics list are generated by ASIA. One of advantages of AISA is to collect useful metrics such as (Stein et al., 1997, 112):

- **Defect Duplication:** The ratio of defect collected to the combined defects from all reviewers. The higher ratio of a defect of found indicates that the defect is found by many reviewers
- **Defect Density:** The rate of merged faults per reviewer. A low density of defect may indicate a high quality of review document
- **Discussion Activity:** The number of discussion. A large number of discussions may indicate an active discussion
- **Fault Resolution:** Percentage of merged defects were fixed using the system. A high percentage of fault resolution may indicate the effectiveness of AISA

After the moderator checks and signs off the completed software review, a notification will be automatically sent to the author and reviewers (Stein et al., 1997).

Web Inspection Prototype (WiP)

Web Inspection Prototype (WiP) is another Web-based tool, which provides a set of functions for distributing the requirement documents to be reviewed (Harjumaa & Tervonen, 1998).

The WiP is developed to support distributed software review processes. It utilizes the WWW to distribute the review document, tailors the software review process model according to the development environment, can assign roles, adds or removes a checklist, allows reviewers to add, modify, and remove comments, has searching, cross-referencing, e-mail notification, combining comments/ annotations using hypertext and reporting capabilities, and generates metrics and statistics summary (Harjumaa & Tervonen, 1998).

How It Works

At the initial stage, a review document will be loaded to WiP. The moderator enters all reviewer information, roles, and loads related documents into the system. WiP automatically selects appropriate hyperlinks to the selected reviewers' personal pages.

During the individual preparation stage of software review, reviewers can log-in to the system via their browsers. All relevant documents such as checklists, source documents, and instructions are available for reviewers. WiP provides friendly user interface and hyperlinks for easy navigation within a document.

Another feature of WiP is HTML pages which allow reviewers to open multiple windows for cross-referencing and searching. To load and generate a new HTML page takes about a few seconds or up to 2 minutes depending on the network traffic and bandwidth. Individual reviewers can add, modify, and delete comments using annotation function. It is easy to access other supporting documents such as checklists by clicking the hypertext or hyperlink. Reviewers can view the specific checklist section related to the section of the reviewing document. References can also be added to the checklist items by reviewers as well.

After the individual preparation, each reviewer can generate a summary of the report. The window pops up a new dynamically HTML page with information about the number of comments made and total time used on software review. The report provides individual performance evaluation.

In the group meeting processes, all group members can view an automatic combined summary of issues/comments with the review document in a dynamically HTML page. Reviewers can view any detailed comments or statistic at any time of the group review process. All issues need to be agreed on and resolved in this process.

At the completion of the group review, a summary of report is produced which contains number of reviewers involved, total time spent on the software review, total time spent on individual review, number of issues found and resolved, etc.

InspectA

InspectA is a completed automation tool, which allows the whole software review process to be automated (Murphy & Miller, 1997), from planing such as selecting a moderator and communications between software review team, through follow-up stage where the moderator verified and finalised that all the defects raised during the software review have been resolved.

InspectA is an e-mail-based and asynchronous tool for software review (Murphy, Ferguson, & Miller, 1999). The tool is not based on world-wide-Web approach (all reviewers can view other individual reviewer comments). The argument is when reviewers can view other reviewers members defect lists during the individual preparation that they may discourage. (Murphy et al., 1999). Another reason is that reviewers may focus or discuss other reviewers' comments rather than focus their own individual reviews (Murphy et al., 1999). Miller and their team believed that e-mail-based tool provide a number of advantages. These include (Stein et al., 1997, p.108):

- **Sharing Information:** Allow exchange and sharing information via e-mail tool
- **Threads of Discussion:** Allow individual reviewers to contribute and free feel to comments during the individual preparation
- **Visual Cues:** Easy to format in the document such as bold or italics
- **Train of Through:** Offer other reviewers to response and reply
- **Reaching a Consensus:** Voting can be sent via e-mail tool
- **Co-Ordination:** Moderator can easily send information to all reviewers
- **History:** Allow reviewers to keep a record of their comments

How It Works

In the initial stage, the moderator creates a list of reviewers and documents using InspecA tool. Each reviewer will receive an e-mail and a review document as well as supporting documents (defect list, instructions, checklist, etc). InspecA provides users friendly interface to facilitate the review process.

At the individual preparation phase, InspecA provides four windows display review documents, checklist, defect entry list, source document. Reviewers can open multiple screens simultaneously for cross referencing purposes. For example, a checklist, a defect classification list, and a review document can be displayed in front of the reviewers' screen at the same time. InspecA also provides a notepad to reviewers to record and edit comments in the notepad. They also can work on the document in a number of sessions. InspecA provides an automatically "save" function when reviewers log-off the system each time.

Upon completion of individual preparation, all reviewers e-mail their private comments to the moderator via InspecA. All comments will be merged and circulated to all reviewers via e-mail.

During the group meeting phase, there is no synchronous meeting in InspecA software review. Group discussion is via e-mail only. New comments can be added to the merged list. The final defect list is collected by moderator and it will be e-mailed to author.

In the follow up phase, the moderator decides whether the updated document can be accepted or rejected.

HyperCode

HyperCode is another one of the earliest Web-based software review tools (Perpich, Perry, Porter, Votta, & Wade, 1997). It uses the common gateway interface (CGI), the HyperCode system allows software reviewers using WWW browsers for software review (Perpich et al., 1997). It is used for code review and very similar to the WiP. Reviewers can comments on the Web and material is delivered via the Web (Perpich et al., 1997). The process contains only asynchronous phases, and other reviewers are able to see the comments, so there is no software review meeting required when in HyperCode (Perpich et al., 1997). After individual review, the results are colleted together into a report containing links from the original material to the comments (Perpich et al., 1997).

Perry and his team (Perry, Porter, Wade, Votta, & Perpich, 2002) suggested that there are four primary different between paper-based and HyperCode software review processes. First, HyperCode provided automated approach to support software review process, this can reduce time and amount of review effort. Second, notification between software review team can be use e-mail tool. Third, all comments or annotations are visible to all participated software reviewers in the whole review process. Forth, there is no meeting requirement needed in the HyperCode process. In other words, the review discussion is asynchronous communication.

How It Works

HyperCode utilizes the www technology that allows reviewers to view and comments on the review document any time. Individual reviewer can add, modify and delete the comments via their own desktop (Perpich et al., 1997). It requires reviewers to log-in to the system each time. All reviewers can view the same documents simultaneously.

Communication and notifications between the moderator, the author and reviewers use e-mail facilities. All comments or issues made by reviewers are automatically recorded by HyperCode.

Similar to WiP, reviewers can open multiple windows and hyperlinks allow reviewers easily cross referencing and searching. The interface is very user friendly. The HyperCode interface is easily designed and developed. It can be similar to the paper-based layout. The HyperCode tool can produce summary of statistic report and metrics.

At end of software review, author rework the work product according the issues and comments made by the review team. The moderator will check and determine whether there is a need of re-review.

Recently, HyperCode has been extended to support a workflow system for better process of software review. The review process consists of (Perry et al., 2002):

1. Request for software review — additional code or enhancements to code

2. The moderator decides whether software review is needed

3. The Author distributed the code using HyperCode tool

4. The author can then select a review team and enter in the HyperCode form

5. A notification is sent to the review team and project management. Reviewers will also be notified the review schedule including the starting and closing date

6. At the preparation stage, further information about the review location, role assignment, instructions of the software review process

7. During the defect detection process, reviewers identify defects and enter comments into the system. All comments and annotations will be automatically update and summary the defect lists

8. Upon completion of the defect detection, HyperCode can generate a summary of defects list, as well consolidated all issues and comments that are reported by the reviewers

9.   Next, the author looks all comments and resolves all issues that are made by the review team

10. In the final step, the altered document will be checked by moderator to determine the need for re-review

Asynchronous/Synchronous Software Inspection Support Tool (ASSIST)

Asynchronous/Synchronous Software Inspection Support Tool (ASSIST) is built to provide both individual and group software review (MacDonald et al., 1995). It can perform both synchronously or asynchronously, with either different place or same place meeting. It uses a costumed designed modelling language (Review Process Definition Language (IPDL)) and a flexible document type system to allow support of any software review process (MacDonald & Miller, 1999). ASSIST is a client/server architecture, where the server is a central database to store documents and data. Table 4 shows details of four features of ASSIST tool.

Table 4. ASSIST features (Source: MacDonald & Miller, 1997, p. 5)

Features	Descriptions
Execute window	• Provides each participant with a list of the people involved in the inspection (review) and their status, along with a list of the documents available • Double-clicking on a document name opens the appropriate browser for that document
List browser	• Allows the user to manipulate lists of items, typically document annotations describing defects • Lists can be either read only or read-write • Each item with a list consists of a title, the name of the document which the item refers to, a position within that document, a classification and a free-form textual description • Items can be added, removed, edited and copied between lists • List browser allows participants to propose items from their personal copied to a master list of defects
Text browser	• Allows documents to be viewed and annotated via a list browser and the browser is based on the concept of current focus • The current focus can be annotated, or existing annotation read • The browser indicates the current lie number and the percentage of the documents inspected (reviewed) • A fine (search) facility is available
Simple browser	• This browser is used for all supporting documents, such as checklists and specifications

How It Works

ASSIST is a second-generation software review technology tool and it provides number of features to support software review process.

An active checklist browser can automatically display a relevant checklist item to a relevant section of code and support C++ software review environment; easily add specific documents and browsers; browser also automatically detect and remove duplicate items; a hypertext-link to help browsers; cross-referencing feature support a reviewer to work multiple documents and to navigate within a document; freely added and modify the defects, comments or annotations (MacDonald et al., 1997).

In the group meeting, ASSIST allows individual group member to post personal comments to the master list, allowing whole group members to discuss them. It also consolidates multiple lists of defects. This can automatically detect and delete duplicate items from the reviewers (MacDonald & Miller, 1999).

Fine-Grained Software Inspection Tool/CodeSurfer

The Fine-Grained Software Review Tool is designed for "exposing the results of sophisticated whole-program static analysis" (Anderson, Reps, & Teitelbaum, 2003) to the software review. This is also known as CodeSurfer. The idea was original developed from the "dependence graphs" which applications activities include parallelization (Burke & Cytron, 1986), optimization (Ferrante, Ottenstein, & Warren, 1987), program testing (Bates & Horwitz, 1993), and software assurance (Horwitz and Reps, 1992). A description of how this tool work is summaries as following section.

How It Works

The CodeSurfer has number of viewing features. These include (Anderson et al., 2003):

- **Project Viewer:** View the file hierarchically, then by function
- **File Viewer:** Displays source files
- **Call Graph Viewer:** Shows the program graph

- **Finder:** Searching capabilities allow reviewers to request variable declarations, occurrences, uses, and assignment, restricting attention to global, file statics, function statics, formal parameters, etc.

- **Set Calculator:** Allows manipulate the program

According to Anderson and his team, (2003) the tool: "computes many static-semantic representations of the program; including an accurate call graph and dependence graph. Whole-program pointer analysis is used to make sure that the representation is precise with respect to aliases induced by pointer usage. View on the dependence graph and related representations are supported. Queries on the dependence graph allow an inspector (reviewer) to answer detailed questions about the semantics of the program. Facilities for openness and extensibility permit the tool to be integrated with many software-development processes. There are two main thrusts in its development. The first is to improve the scalability of the system. This will be achieved partly by using demand-driven techniques to reduce the up-front cost of building the dependence graph. The other trust is to extend the domain of applications for the system."

CORD

The CORD is developed for increasing the consistency between requirements and a detailed design (Chechik & Gannon, 2001). The CORD creates a "finite-state abstraction" of a detailed design and checks it against a set of properties automatically generated from the requirements (Anderson et al., 2003). Its features are similar to other static analysis tools such as CodeSuper. The aim of CORD is to "simplify the verification of properties of program; this system abstract the forms of their formal specification notations or create abstract models from program that could be analysed with state-exploration" (Chechlik & Gannon, 2001, p. 669).

How It Works

CORD is an analysis technique to develop a design model, detailed design or data flow analysis of language construct. This tool allows verifying the consistency with requirements to detailed design.

"CORD is highly scalable and envision being used in a software development process in which requirement specifications are first written and checked for consistency and completeness. Then, a detailed design is automatically verified for consistency with the requirement. Afterwards, a real implementation is written code and design statement is assured through code a developer some assurance that code implements the system behaviour specified in the requirements. Finally, the implantation is thoroughly tested" (Adopted from Anderson et al., 2003).

Agent-Based Software Tool

Agent-based software tool in code review is designed by Chan (2001). Chan (2001) recently proposed the agent-based software tool that can help reduce the cost and increasing the number of defects detected in software review process. The main focus of the intelligent agent software tool (Chan, 2001):

- Automate as much of the paper work and administrative tasks as possible
- Enable the inspection (review) to perform inspection (review) according to their schedules. This aims to reduce the inspection (review) interval, and thus reducing the turn around time for obtaining inspection (review) results
- Provide as much assistance to the inspector (reviewer) as possible during preparation
- Maximise the number of major faults found while keeping the time costs of the process low

How It Works

Intelligent agent software tool support Fagan's software review process. At the initial stage, the author informs the moderator about the software review. The author can create a moderator agent to monitor the software review process. Information such as review document, checklist, and source materials are needed to provide to the moderator. Next, the moderator agent starts to select experienced software reviewer and assigning role for each review team.

During the preparation phase, individual reviewers conduct private defect detection. All issues and comments will need to record into the system. Each reviewer focuses different aspect of review documents. In other words, if a reviewer is assigned to look for coding rules, then he or she focuses on the coding rules only. There are other perspectives of reading the documents such as design patterns and common errors. Numbers of the agents also help reviewers look for defects. For example, an agent can highlight the specific document related to the checklist. The agents also learn the activities or preferences of a reviewer by learning the reviewer behaviour.

In the software review group meeting, the reviewer agents inform the moderator the completion of individual preparation. All issues and comments will be collected and consolidated into the list. The author or the moderator agents notify the reviewers about the review meeting. The reviewers can view, vote and add new comments during the meeting process. The author works with the review team to resolve all issues. The decision can be accept, contest or reject.

After the Web-based (virtual) meeting, a follow-up face-to-face meeting may conduct. The decision is based on the outcome of the virtual meeting. The moderator and author have the final decision to determine the need of the face-to-face meeting. Alternatively, the moderator may ask for another Web-based (virtual) meeting.

The next phase is follow-up. In this stage, the author removes or corrects defects and an altered document will be produced. If the author is not satisfied with the altered document, re-review may be conducted.

In the re-work stage, the author informs the moderator to arrange another software review. If the work is satisfaction, the moderator can announce the completion of software review. The key role of the moderator agent is actively collect, store and produce metrics to assistant software review process. After rework confirmation is received, the moderator agent can retire (Chan, 2001).

Internet-Based Inspection System (IBIS)

Internet-Based Inspection System (IBIS) is developed for support geographically distributed software review (Lanubile & Mallardo, 2002). IBIS was original designed by Cavivano, Lanubile and Visaggio (2001). This tool is another Web-based application which "based on a lightweight architecture to achieve the maximum of simplicity of use and deployment" (Lanubile & Mallardo, 2002). The IBIS can support Fagan's Software Review Process. There are a several advantages of deploying IBIS (Lanubile & Mallardo, 2002):

- IBIS is Web-based software review tool, it allows reviewers access from their desktop. This could improve the chance of reviewers participating in software review
- It allows software review perform in different place, even a software review is conducted in different countries

- Allow different experts participate in the software review process. Those experts could from outside the organisation or different department

How It Works

IBIS supports seven steps of software review process–planning, overview, discovery, collection, discrimination, rework, and follow-up.

During the planning stage, the moderator ensures all documents (e.g., review document, checklist, review goals, defects classification, defect form, and instruction, etc.) are loaded to the IBIS. Selecting reviewers and assigning roles are also required to be completed at the planning stage. Participated reviewers will be notified the review details via e-mail (Lanubile & Mallardo, 2002).

In the overview stage, reviewers accept the review task and access to IBIS system to get the relevant materials. At this stage, moderator overview the purpose of the software review and the review document is available to reviewers.

During the discovery stage, individual reviewers begin to inspect the documents. All annotations and comments can be recorded in the defect form. A checklist and a defect classification are also available for reviewers. Defect list is automatically saved when a reviewer logs-off each time. An e-mail notification will be sent to the moderator when reviewers complete their review task. The moderator can generate a discovery log which indicates how adequately the review performed.

Next stage is collection, all individual defect lists and discovery logs are consolidated into one list. Duplicate defects or issues would be deleted and merged. The moderator can produce a summary report of defects found from the individual preparation stage (discovery stage). Both moderator and author would determine which defects/issues should be discussed and which reviewers should be selected for the next stage. IBIS produces a statistics report to support the decisions made by the author and the moderator.

At the discrimination, the group review discussion is asynchronous communication. Each defect or issue in the discrimination list will be discussed, resolved, and agreed upon by the review team. New comments can be added, modified, and deleted during the discussion process. For the false positives defect, only the author or the moderator can remove them.

Upon completion of discrimination, the author starts to fix the defects. This stage refers to rework. The author checks and fixes all defects that are found from the discussion. An altered document will be uploaded and a notification will be sent to the moderator via e-mail.

In the final stage of software review — follow-up — the moderator checks the altered documents and decides the need for re-review according to author recommendation. A summary report is produced by the moderator who signs off on the completion of the software review. The reviewer team can then be notified via e-mail.

VisionQuest

VisionQuest aims to support experimentation formal anonymity technical review (Vitharana & Ramaurthy, 2003). The advantages of anonymity in-group collaboration are (Er & Ng, 1995):

- Each reviewers has equal weight
- Avoid the dominance group or status effect during the review process
- Since the comments are made by an anonymous person, criticisms are rather the issues than a person
- Voting is anonymous; the final decision is more likely to be objective and based on merit

How It Works

At the individual preparation phase — there is no communication in the individual. Each individual reviewer studies the program specification, identifies the defects and records them in a defect list. They all work on defect detection privately.

During group meeting process, all reviewers send the defect list to the moderator. Duplicate defects, issues, and comments are removed. A summary defect list will be generated and distributed to the review team. Each issue is discussed, agreed upon, and resolved by the review team.

The meeting discussion is supported by Group Support System (GSS) (Vitharana & Ramaurthy, 2003). No reviewers' comments and discussion are anonymous. Voting and agreement is also anonymous. Reviewers feel free to comment and vote without any concerns.

Summary

In summary, this chapter described modern software review tools and techniques. The different types of software review tools and how they work. To achieve better software review performance, it is important to understand use of inputs and software review process. The common types of software review inputs, process factors and performance measurements will be explained in next chapter.

References

Anderson, P., Reps, T., & Teitelbaum T. (2003). Design and implementation of a fine-grained software inspection tool. *IEEE Transaction on Software Engineering,* 721-733.

Bates, S., & Horwitz, S. (1993). Incremental program testing using program dependence graphs. *Proceedings of Symposium on Principles of Programming Language* (pp. 384-396).

Brothers, L., Sembugamoorthy, V., & Muller, M. (1990, October). ICICLE: Groupware for code inspection. *Proceedings of the 1990 ACM Conference on Computer Supported Cooperative Work* (pp. 169-181).

Burke, M., & Cytron, R. (1986). Inter-procedural dependence analysis and parallelization, *Proceeding SIGPLAN '86 Symposium Complier Construction* (pp. 162-175).

Cavivano, D., Lanubile F., & Visaggio, G. (2001). Scaling up distributed software inspections. *Proceedings of 4th ICSE Workshop on Software Engineering over the Internet,* Toronto, Canada.

Chan, K. (2001, August 27-28). An agent-based approach to computer assisted code inspections. *Proceedings of Australian Software Engineering Conference* (pp. 147-152).

Chechik, M., & Gannon, J. (2001, July). Automatic analysis of consistency between requirement and design. *IEEE Transaction on Software Engineering, 27*(7), 651-672.

Er, M., & Ng, A. (1995). The anonymity and proximity factors in group decision support systems. *Decision Support Systems, 14*(1), 75-83.

Ferrante, J., Ottenstein, K., & Warren J. (1987). The program dependence graph and its use in optimization. *Transaction Programming Languages and System, 3*(9), 319-349.

Gintell, J. W., Houde, M. B., & Mckenney, R. F. (1993, July 10-14). Lessons learned by building and using scrutiny, A collaborative software inspection systems. *Proceedings of the 7th International Workshop on Computer-Aided Software Engineering* (pp. 350-357).

Gintell, J. W., & Memmi, G. (1997, March). Lessons learned with ACME and environment integration experiment. *ACM SigSoft Software Engineering Notes, 22*(2), 77-81.

Gotel, O.C.Z, & Finkelstein, C. W. (1994, 18-22 April). An Analysis of the Requirements Traceability Problem, *Proceedings of the First International Conference on Requirement Engineering* (pp. 94-101).

Harjumaa, L., & Tervonen, I. (1998, January 6-9). A WWW-based tool for software inspection. *Proceedings of the 31st Hawaii International Conference on System Sciences* (pp. 379-388).

Horwitz, & Reps, T. (1992, May). The use of program dependence graphs in software engineering. *Proceedings of the 14th International Conference on Software Engineering* (pp. 392-411).

Johnson, P. M. (1994, May). An instrumented approach to improving software quality through formal technical review. *Proceedings of the 16th International Conference on Software Engineering*, Sorrento, Italy.

Knight, J. C., & Myers, A. E. (1993, November). An improved inspection technique. *Communications of ACM, 36*(11), 50-69.

Lanubile, L., & Mallardo, T. (2002). Preliminary evaluation of tool-based support for distributed inspection. *Proceedings of the ICSE International Workshop on Global Software Development*, Orlando, FL, USA.

MacDonald, F., & Miller, J. (1997). A comparison of tool-based and paper-based software inspection. *Empirical Foundations of Computer Science (EFoCS)*, Department of Computer Science, University of Strathclyde, EfoCS-25-97, RR/97/203.

MacDonald, F., & Miller, J. (1999). ASSIST–A tool to support software inspection. *Information and Software Technology, 41*, 1045-1057.

MacDonald, F., Miller, J., Brooks, A., Roper, M., & Wood, M. (1995, July 10-14). A review of tool support for software inspection. *Proceedings of the 7th International Workshop on Computer-Aided Software Engineering* (pp. 340-349). Toronto.

Mashayekhi, V., Feulner, C., & Riedl, J. (1994). CAIS: Collaborative asynchronous inspection of software. *Proceedings of the 2nd ACM SIGSOFT Symposium on Foundations of Software Engineering*, New York, *19*(5), 21-34.

Murphy, P., Ferguson, J. D., & Miller, J. (1999) Groupware support asynchronous document review. *Proceedings of the 17th Annual International Conference on Computer Documentation* (pp. 185-192). New Orleans.

Murphy, P., & Miller, J. (1997). A process for asynchronous software inspection. *Proceedings of the 18th IEEE International Workshop on Software Technology and Engineering* (pp. 96-104).

Perpich, J. M., Perry, E. D., Porter, A. A., Votta, L. G., & Wade, M. W. (1997). Anywhere, anytime code inspections: Using the Web to remove inspection bottlenecks in large-scale software development. *Proceedings of the International Conference on Software Engineering, ICSE* (pp. 14-21).

Perry, D. E., Porter, A., Wade, M. W., Votta, L. G., & Perpich, J. (2002, July). Reducing inspection interval in large-scale software development. *IEEE Transactions on Software Engineering, 28*(7), 695-705.

Stein, M. V., Riedl, J., Harner, S. J., & Mashayekhi, V. (1997). A case study of distributed, asynchronous software inspection, *Proceedings of the 19th International Conference on Software Engineering* (pp. 107-117).

Vitharana, P., & Ramamurthy, K. (2003, February). Computer-mediated group support, anonymity, and the software inspection process: An empirical investigation. *IEEE Transactions on Software Engineering, 29*(2), 167-180.

Yu, W. D. (1994, February), Verifying software requirement: A requirement tracing methodology and its software tools–RADIX. *IEEE Journal on Selected Areas in Communications, 12*(2).

Yu, W. D., Smith, D. P., & Huang, S. T. (1990, May/June). Software productivity measurements. *AT&T Technology Journal, 69*(3), 110-120.

Chapter V

Software Review Inputs, Process, and Performance

Abstract

The literature review in this chapter is aimed to critique the use of inputs and process support strategies in the software review process. This chapter presents the important relationships between the use of inputs, meeting process, and software review process performance. Inputs can be classified into explicit and implicit inputs. Explicit inputs refer to software review artefacts and supporting documents. Implicit inputs refer to a software reviewer's characteristics. A meeting process refers factors that affect meeting process. The software review performance refers the outcomes from the meeting process. Software review performance can be measured by qualitative and/or quantitative methods. The final section presents the limitation of current software review literature.

Use of Inputs

Inputs can be classified into review task, supporting documents, and reviewer characteristics.

Review Task

The nature of the process or task determines the appropriate inputs to the process, as key inputs are easier to identify and analyse through focusing on task characteristics (IEEE Standard 830, 1986; ANSI/IEEE Standard 1028, 1998). For instance, a complex task is difficult, hard to program, and requires diffused skills of individual reviewers (higher knowledge, skills, and effort) to perform the process (Laitenberger & DeBaud, 2000). Thus, it is suggested that the effectiveness of the review process may vary based on the review task (Laitenberger & DeBaud, 2000).

The review task in the software development cycle generally can be categorized into four major artefacts (Kotonya & Sommerville, 1998; Sommerville, 1995, 2001):

- **Requirements Artefact:** This is the initial explicit deliverable of a work product. Data is collected and analysed in the organization to create a specific requirements document (Grunbacher, Halling, Biffl, Kitapci, & Boehm, 2002; Hass, 2001; Hofmann & Lehner, 2001; IEEE Standard 830, 1993; Isazadeh, Macewen, & Malton, 1995; Kantorowitz, Guttman, & Arzi, 1997; Kauppinen & Kujala, 2001; Laitenberger, Beil, & Schwinn, 2002; Mathiassen, 2000; Moynihan, 2000; Pendlebury, 2001; Sandahl et al., 1998). Upon completion of the requirements review, the reviewed requirements document is carried on to the next stage of the development cycle, the design phase.

- **Design Artefact:** This can be viewed as comprising both high and low levels of the design (Parnas & Weiss, 1985). The high level design refers to the functionality of the product, which requires satisfying the requirements and the components of the design. The low level design is divided into data structures and detailed procedures. The goal of review is validation against the requirements and designs (Chechik & Gannon, 2001; Laitenberger & Emam, 2000; Mathiassen & Stage, 1990; Shull, Travassos, & Basili, 1999; Tervonen, 1996; Travassos, Shull, Caver, & Basili, 1999; Travassos, Shull, & Carver, 1999; Travassos, Shull, & Carver, 2001).

- **Code Artefact:** Once a design document is reviewed, the next step is coding. The code artefact should be reviewed to ensure requirements are met before carrying on to the next stage (Chan, 2001; Christenson, Steel, & Lamperez, 1990; Dunsmore, Roper, & Wood, 2002; Host & Johansson, 2000; Kelly & Shepard, 2002; Laitenberger & Atkinson, 1998; Laitenberger & DeBaud, 1997; Linger, Mill, & Witt, 1997; McConnell, 1993; Perpich, Perry, Porter, Votta, & Wade, 1997; Runeson & Wohlin, 1998).

- **Testing Artefact:** The reviews can be performed by using testing artefacts such as a testing plan and cases to ensure requirements are satisfied (Basili & Selby, 1987; Chaar, Halliday, Bhandari, & Chillarege, 1993; Conradi, Marjara, & Skatevik, 1999; Franz & Ship; 1994; Jackson & Hoffman, 1994; Kusumoto, 1993; Panko, 1999; Shirey, 1992).

Supporting Documents

Software review requires a set of a support documents that will facilitate the process (ANSI/IEEE Standard 1028, 1998). The typical supporting documents in software review can be classified as reading technique documents, prescriptive documents, previously reviewed software documents and business reports (ANSI/IEEE Standard 1028, 1998; Kotonya & Sommerville, 1998).

Reading Technique Documents

A reading technique can be regarded as a mechanism for the individual reviewer to detect defects in any software artefact (Basili, Laitenberger, Shull, & Rus, 2000; Dunsmore, Roper, & Wood, 2000, 2001; Emam & Laitenberger, 2000; Linger et al., 1997; Shull, Lanubile, & Biasili, 2000; Thelin, Runeson, & Regnell, 2001; Thelin, Runeson, Wohiln, Olsson, & Andersson, 2002; Thelin, Runeson, & Wohlin, 2003; Travassos, Shull, Fredericks, & Basili, 1999). The expectation of review results depends on the reviewers themselves (Brien, Shaft, & Buckley, 2001) and their strategies for understanding the reviewed artefacts (Rifkin & Deimel, 2000).

A supporting document incorporating particular reading techniques can help a reviewer to find defects and may achieve better performance (Briand & Wust, 2000; Zhang, Basili, & Shneiderman, 1999). A reading technique is defined as a series of procedures a reviewer can use to obtain an understanding of the artefact under review, providing a systematic guideline for finding defects. In practice, Ad-hoc and checklist based reading (CBR) are the most common reading techniques (Basili et al., 1996). Recently, two other types of reading techniques (scenario-based/perspective reading (SBR) and usage-based reading (Basili et al., 1996; Cheng & Jeffery, 1996; Porter, Votta, & Basili, 1995; Thelin, Runeson, & Regnell, 2001; Thelin, Runeson, Wohiln, Olsson, & Andersson, 2002; Thelin, Runeson, & Wohlin, 2003) and stepwise abstraction (Linger et al., 1997; Parnas & Weiss, 1985) have been introduced. Below is a summary of these reading techniques.

Ad-Hoc Approach

The ad-hoc approach as the name implies, provides no explicit instruction for reviewers on how to proceed, or what specifically to look for during the reading activity (Doolan, 1992; Laitenberger & DeBaud, 2000; Shirey, 1992). However, in the ad-hoc approach, the review may examine the reviewed artefact in a systematic way; it depends on the skills, knowledge, and experience of the reviewers to work systematically (Briand, Arisholm, Counsell, Houdek, & Thevenod-Fosse, 1999). Reviewers must rely on their own intuition and experience to determine how to go about finding defects in a software document (Bourgeois, 1996; Miller, 2002). A comprehension training program may help reviewers develop some of these skills to compensate for the lack of reading support (Wong & Wilson, 2003).

Checklist-Based Reading (CBR) Approach

For the checklist-based reading approach, a checklist is used to help reviewers focus on the defects to look for in an artefact and provides categories for classifying defects (Ackerman, Buchwald, & Lewski, 1989; Miller, Wood, & Roper, 1998). In practice, a checklist captures important lessons from previous reviews and is usually no longer then one page (Fagan, 1976; Kelly, Sherif, & Hops, 1992; Porter & Votta, 1994).

Checklists offer support mainly in the form of yes/no questions that reviewers answer while reading a software document (Laitenberger & Emam, 2001). A schema of a checklist consists of two components: the first component is a list of potential problem spots that may appear in the documents (where to look) and the second component is a list of hints on how to identify a defect in the case of each problem spot (what to look for) (Chernak, 1996, Thelin, Runeson, & Wohlin, 2003).

Checklist-based reading has several shortcomings. First, the template of checklist questions from past experience may not apply to the particular problem domain or development environment currently under review (Laitenberger & DeBaud, 2000). The reviewers may not focus on the actual defect types of the current artefact and therefore, there is a high possibility of missing some of the defects which should be looked for. Second, a checklist often contains too many generic questions; it may not be detailed enough and may not provide systematic guidance to locating the defects (Briand & Wieczorek, 2000; Briand & Wust, 2000). Without concrete instructions it is difficult for a reviewer to know how to approach the task.

Finally, how well a checklist will be used depends on the reviewer's experience; it can be very difficult for an inexperienced reviewer to use this technique (Parnas & Weiss, 1987). Thus, the effort required for successful analysis will be dependent on the individual reviewer.

Stepwise Abstraction Approach

Stepwise abstraction provides more structured and precise reading instructions for code documents. This approach was introduced in the late 1970s by the Cleanroom community in a formal review to check for functional correctness (Dyer, 1992). It was also used by Parnas and Weiss in their Active Design review process (1985, 1987).

Reading by Stepwise Abstraction requires a reviewer to read a sequence of statements in the code and to abstract the functions (Parnas & Weiss, 1987). In the first step of code review, each reviewer identifies subprograms and decides the functions for that part. Next, each reviewer decides the function of the whole program and combines sub-functions, as well as constructing specifications for the whole program.

In this defect detection process, a comparison of inconsistencies of the proposed specifications with the official specifications is identified by the reviewers. In the Active Design review, the reviewer is assigned an active role and is required to make assertions about parts of the design artefact.

Scenario-Based Reading (SBR) Approach

The scenario-based reading approach was introduced in mid 1990's (Basili et al., 1996; Briand & Wust, 2000; Porter & Votta, 1994; Thelin et al., 2003). SBR provides systematic guidance for reviewers on what and how to find defects. A scenario may be a set of detailed descriptive questions for a reviewer on how to review an artefact. The rationale behind a scenario reading helps reviewers to concentrate their attention to look for a particular defect.

The effectiveness of the scenario-based reading technique depends heavily on the design and content of the scenario questions. The scenario can be classified into four categories: 1) defect-based scenarios (Porter et al., 1995), 2) function point scenarios (Cheng & Jeffrey, 1996), 3) perspective-based reading scenarios (Basili et al., 1996; Laitenberger & Debaud, 1997), and 4) usage-based reading scenarios (Thelin, Runeson, & Regnell, 2001; Thelin, Runeson, Wohiln, Olsson, & Andersson, 2002; Thelin, Runeson, & Wohlin, 2003).

Porter et al. (1995) describes reading scenarios based on defect classifications (i.e., called defect-based scenarios, DBS) for the review of functional requirements documents. The term "scenario" refers to a collection of detailed procedures for detecting particular classes of defect. These scenarios are derived from defect classes and consist of a specific set of questions a reviewer answers while reading a document (Porter et al., 1995). Porter et al. (1995) claim that DBS use yields better results than checklist-based and ad-hoc approaches.

A function point scenario (FPS) is another type of SBR, which was introduced by Cheng and Jeffery in 1996. The idea of FPS is to develop a set of scenarios based on function point analysis (FPA). The FPA technique defines a software system in terms of specific function point elements, such as inputs, files, inquiries, and outputs (Cheng & Jeffery, 1996). It allows reviewers to systematically detect defects from a functional viewpoint. Biffl and Halling (2002) believe that both function point and defect-based scenario reading techniques improve the average review effectiveness by up to one third.

The basic idea of the perspective-based reading (PBR) approach is to review a document from the perspective of its individual stakeholders (Basili et al., 1996; Laitenberger & Atkinson, 1998; Laitenberger & Emam, 2000, 2001; Shull, Rus, & Basili, 2000; Zhang et al., 1999). In principle, there is little agreement about how to define any of the key quality properties (e.g., correctness) of this approach (Laitenberger & Debaud, 1997). Different stakeholders are interested in different quality factors (Shull, Rus, & Basili, 2000). Hence, reviewers should check the software quality of an artefact from different stakeholders' perspectives. The design of a perspective-based reading depends upon the roles within the development environment. It consists of activities a reviewer performs during defect detection to extract or use the information for specific purposes. The PBR and SBR approaches both use scenarios that contain algorithmic guidelines as to how a reviewer ought to proceed while reading the software documentation (Laitenberger & Atkinson, 1998).

Studies show that the perspective-based review catches 35% more defects than an ad-hoc approach (Boehm & Basili, 2001). However, reading techniques for each perspective or scenario are often very detailed. This requires comprehensive training for each type of reading technique (Porter & Votta, 1997). Given that most project managers face time and costs constraints, these tailored reading techniques may become too onerous and impractical to follow (Zhang et al., 1999).

The usage-based reading (UBR) scenario is aimed at finding defects that have the most negative impact on the users' perception on the software quality (Thelin, Runeson, & Wohlin, 2003). It is very similar to perspective reading except the reading effort is guided by a prioritised, requirements-level use case model during the individual preparation of the software review. The reading method is defined as 1) rank-based reading and 2) time controlled reading (Thelin et al., 2003). Thelin et al. (2003) found that usage-based scenarios increase efficiency and effectiveness in detecting the most critical defects with consistent results from two laboratory experiments.

Comparison of Reading Techniques

Traditional reading techniques, such as the ad-hoc and checklist-based approaches, lack systematic defect reading procedures and this results in a low coverage of the defects (Basili et al, 1996; Laitenberger & Emam, 2000, 2001). The introduction of explicit systematic procedures increases the reading coverage and hence the defect defection performance (Porter & Votta, 1997). As a result, all systematic reading techniques (i.e., scenarios-based and stepwise abstract) contribute significantly to the software review literature.

The scenarios-based reading approach detects more defects than applying either ad-hoc or CBR by up to 35% (Porter et al., 1995). The scenarios-based reading approach is more effective because it helps reviewers focus on specific defect classes (Porter et al., 1995). It has been demonstrated that the use of a checklist-based approach can result in better performance than the ad hoc approach (Porter et al., 1995). They also found that reviewers with more experience do not perform better than reviewers with less experience. By comparison, the results from Cheng and Jeffery (1996) are dramatically different to Porter's study (1995). On average, subjects using the function point scenario approach found more defects than subjects using the ad-hoc approach. In addition, Cheng and Jeffery (1996) argued that experience is a factor that could have biased the results of their experiment, which directly contradicts the study by Porter and his team (Porter et al., 1996). The nature or variation in the reviewers' experience was not explained or elaborated in any of the studies.

Prescriptive Documents

Prescriptive documents describe how a software review should proceed. Below are the procedures in a typical software review process (ANSI/IEEE Standard 1028, 1998; Gilb & Graham, 1993; Reeve, 1991):

1. **Planning:** Define objectives, schedule time, and organise resources such as funding, meeting place, and facilities required for the review (Ackerman et al., 1989; Fagan, 1986). Prepare all necessary supporting documents such as defect standards, checklists and prescriptive documents, reviewers' criteria, assigning roles, arrange and decide the size of teams and total

number of review teams, organise training for the reviewers if required and distribute materials to the participants (Gray & Van Slack, 1994).

2. **Overview:** Procedures for overviewing the software artefacts by the author or technical leader to the reviewers (Fagan, 1986; Gilb & Graham, 1993).

3. **Preparation:** Description of how each reviewer should study and familiarise themselves with the artefacts (Fagan, 1976). In many cases, individual reviewers are required to examine the artefact before meetings are held (Johnson, 1998; Porter & Votta, 1997; Porter, Mockus, & Votta, 1998).

4. **Examination:** This often refers to detection and collection of defects (Johnson, 1999; Porter et al., 1997). The prescriptive documents cover the detail of how the examination should be performed, such as the defect recording procedures, use of supporting documents and decision-making methods (ANSI/IEEE standard 1028, 1998). In practice, the examination step often refers to the interactive review meetings (Porter & Votta, 1998).

5. **Rework:** Details the procedures on how rework should be done. This includes review correction and modification of the artefact (Fagan, 1986; Gilb & Graham, 1993; Gray & Van Slack, 1994).

6. **Follow-Up:** Prescriptive documents may describe an evaluation matrix to determine whether the reviews have been completed (Briand, Freimut & Volle, 1999b, 2000; Chillarge et al., 1992; Offen & Jeffery, 1997; Runeson & Wohlin, 1998).

Generally, common pre-review activities include planning, overview, and the preparation that takes place before the review meeting (Laitenberger & DeBaud, 2000). The post-review activities such as follow-up and rework take place before the exit criteria are checked. The artefact is re-reviewed if the rework is not satisfactory (Gilb & Graham, 1993).

Previously Reviewed Software Documents

The term *previously reviewed software documents* refers to the supporting documents related to a particular software artefact being reviewed (Gilb & Graham, 1993; Kotonya & Sommerville, 1998; Sommerville, 2001). For example, 1) a related document for a design review may be a requirements document and 2) related documents for a code review may be previously reviewed requirement and design documents.

One often-cited factor in project failure is missing requirements in the later stages of software development (Davis, 1993; Fazlollahi & Tanniru, 1991;

Linberg, 1999; Sarrinen & Vepsalainen, 1993; Schulmeyer & Mcmanus, 1999). Practitioners' reports (Davis, 1982; Pendlebury, 2001) already show that requirement documents are often lacking or missing during later stages of software development. Further, Leffingwell and Widrig (2000) suggested that errors occurred when the developers created a technical design from an incomplete or inaccurate set of requirements or defects that should have been detected in requirements earlier in the process. Humphrey, Snyder, & Willis, (1991) found that 4% of the requirements are missed at the preliminary or high-level design phase of a project and that 7% are missed as the project moves further into detailed design. Given requirement uncertainty and complexity, rework costs to fix possible defects consume 30–50% of the total budget of the project (Boehm & Papaccio, 1988). As a result, the availability of previously reviewed documents is vital in the software review process.

Reports

The term *reports* refers to supporting documents adopted by the software organization that describe the application domain, for example organisational review standards, business reports or other business information that supports the system being built (ANSI/IEEE Standard 1028, 1998).

The objective of using business reports and review standards is to allow the review teams to achieve an effectiveness and efficiency in the review process that is suited to their development environments (Wiegers, 2002). The review standards can be obtained from organisations like the American National Standard Institution or the IEEE Computer Society.

Reviewer Characteristics

Ability and Skills

Past studies have suggested that the ability and skills of the reviewers in a review team are important for the effectiveness of the review (Aurum, 2003; Fagan, 1986; Sauer et al., 2000; Strauss & Ebenau, 1994). Ability and skills are often measured by years of experience (Aurum, 2003; Fagan, 1986; Ginac, 2000).

It has been suggested that an effective review requires different levels of software development experience and software review (role) experience based on the type of the artefact being reviewed and the corresponding life cycle state (Ginac, 2000; Mithas, Subramanyam, & Krishnan, 2001). A field study of 93 reviewers in a company indicated that in the early stages of software development, there is a positive relationship between reviewers' experiences and the number of defects found (Mithas et al., 2001).

Further, researchers found that software development experience has some influence on the review performance in checklist-based, function point scenarios and defect-based scenarios reading techniques (Basili, Shull, & Lanubile, 1999). In particular, software review (role) experience has a very strong impact on the software review performance in the checklist-based reading technique (at the 95% level) (Biffl & Halling, 2002). The expected results proved that checklist-based reading provides less guidance (compared to scenario reading techniques) to the reviewer and therefore depends more on the reviewers' individual characteristics, such as relevant experience (Basili & Selby, 1997; Basili et al., 1996; Basili, Laitenberger, Shull, & Rus, 2000; Porter & Votta, 1998; Shull, Travassos, & Basili, 1999; Shull, Rus, & Basili, 2000; Travassos, Shull, Caver, & Basili, 1999; Travassos, Shull, Fredericks, & Basili, 1999).

It is suggested that selection of reviewers is one of the most critical factors since this can reduce the uncertainty surrounding review outcomes and increase the effectiveness of a review (Laitenberger & DeBaud, 2000; Sauer et al., 2000).

Motivation

Another critical factor related to software review is the reviewers' own motivation (Kingston, Webby, & Jeffery, 1999; Kingston Jeffery, & Huang, 2000). Software review is driven by the members of the reviewer team. The success or failure of software review depends on their motivation and effort (Humphrey, 2002; Isazadeh et al., 1995). If the reviewers are unwilling to perform the software review, all efforts could fail. Franz and Ship (1994) indicated that the attitude to defects is the key to effective software review.

Further, Boehm and Basili (2001) strongly believed that increasing the amount of effort leads to higher performance in the review process. This statement is consistent with a number of studies showing that the more effort a reviewer contributes to the defect detection process, the higher the defect detection rate is likely to be (Shull, Lanubile, & Biasili, 2000; Travassos, Shull, Fredericks, & Basili, 1999; Wiegers, 2002).

However, motivation is one variable that is overlooked in the software review literature. At the time of writing no empirical studies have been identified in this important area for research. In a number of studies, other researchers have mentioned that reviewer's motivation is important to review performance (Boehm & Basili, 2001; Fagan, 1986; Franz & Ship, 1994; Kelly & Shepard, 2000; Wiegers, 2002), but there has been no empirical investigation of this in the software review literature. Software review is a human-based activity that is heavily based on a reviewer's individual characteristics such as motivation. The review of the software review literature found only one behavioural paper (Sauer et al., 2000) that discussed review performance, and it completely ignored the factor of motivation.

It is important to note that while motivation is often discussed as an aspect of organizational behaviour, and does demonstrate a significant affect on task performance, the importance of this has not been investigated thoroughly within software review.

Sauer et al. (2000) have pointed out that task expertise is the key driver in group review performance but does not investigate motivation. Is it the case that motivation of reviewers is not important to review performance? The behavioural literature suggests that motivation is an important factor that may improve the review performance and this must be modeled and investigated.

Review Process

Typical support techniques (Powell, 1998) for the review process include determining the size of the review team (Fagan, 1976; Madachy, Little, & Fan, 1993; Weller, 1993), role assignments (D'Astous & Robillard, 2001; Dunsmore et al., 2000; Grady & Van Slack, 1994;), computer support tools, and decision-making methods.

Team Size

The literature suggests that a small team performs better than a large team (Fagan, 1976; Madachy et al., 1993; Porter & Votta, 1997; Weller, 1993). However, no-one has yet defined the perfect team size. One reason for recommending smaller team sizes is that it is more cost effective to run a small team software review than reviews by large teams (Porter & Votta, 1997). Fagan (1976) suggests that four people in a software review team is a good size. This number is also supported by Weller (1993), who showed that four in a team will perform better than three in a team. Madachy et al. (1993) described the optimal team size as three to five people. IEEE Standard 1028 (1997) recommends a team size of between four and six people (IEEE, 1998). Wheeler et al. (1996) reported that team sizes of three to four people are common in practice. However, Porter found that a team of two people performed better than teams of four people (1995).

Roles

Fagan (1986) introduced the idea of role assignment, the assigning of specific responsibilities to team members, to support the review process. He argued that assigning specific roles to team members would achieve better review performance. These role responsibilities can be classified into 1) moderator, 2) author, 3) reader, and 4) tester (Fagan, 1986). Later empirical research has found that adding the roles of organizer, recorder and collector (Ackerman et al., 1989; D'Astous & Robillard, 2000, 2001; Russell, 1991) helps to facilitate the software review process. The important thing is that each assigned role should bring with it the specific skills and knowledge of that domain area (D'Astous & Robillard, 2001; Halling & Biffl, 2002; Johnson & Tjahjono, 1997; Seaman & Basili, 1998). Below are the descriptions for each role.

- **Moderator:** The objective of moderator role is to *"increase the integrity"* (Fagan, 1976) of the review process. The moderator ensures that procedures flow and operate smoothly through each stage of the review process. The moderator effectively coaches the review team and provides the team with strong leadership and direction (Fagan, 1986). Duties include scheduling meetings, reporting review results, coordinating follow-up and rework. This is a key role in the review team and should be supported by special training.

- **Author:** The author is the person who developed the software artefact. It is the responsibility of an author to correct the software artefact after the review.

- **Reader:** The reader describes the software artefact to the review team by explaining and interpreting the material (in detail) so that objectives will be understood by all team members (Fagan, 1986).

- **Reviewer:** Reviews the software artefact. Basili et al. (1996) showed that reviews can be approached from different perspectives or roles, for example, it is not uncommon to see testers, users or designers undertaking the role of software reviewer.

- **Organizer:** The organizer is responsible for process improvement and coordinates overall review activities across the whole project, such as checklist updating and standards development (Laitenberger & DeBaud, 2000).

- **Recorder:** The duty of the recorder is to log all identified defects discovered during the review meeting (Gray & Van Slack, 1994).

- **Collector:** The collector is responsible for collecting all records of defects from individual reviewers on completion of the review activity (Laitenberger & Emam, 2000; Porter & Votta, 1998).

Fagan (1986) suggested that people assigned roles in the software review process should come from the product (software artefact) development team. Assigning reviewers with particular expertise, whether they come from within or outside the development team can be of value and improve review performance (National Aeronautics and Space Administration (NASA), 1993). It is evident that a major concern when preparing for software review is to make sure that the right members are selected for review teams (Laitenberger & DeBaud, 1997). The selection of reviewers should be according to the experience and knowledge each member will bring to a particular role and they should be working on a product (software artefact) with which they are familiar (Fagan, 1986; Strauss & Ebenau, 1994; Vliet, 2000).

Decision-Making Methods

The software review process involves human actors and this raises the potential for subjectivity and inter-personal conflict that may impact on review performance (Sauer et al., 2001). Conflicts of interest may occur when an author is confronted with the defects they have created. Personal conflicts may also occur in review meetings where the competitive nature and strict hierarchies of an organisational environment may compromise communications (Johnson & Tjahjono, 1998; Votta, 1993).

It is important to consider the kinds of decision making strategies involved in review meetings and to anticipate and minimise the potential for conflict among team members (Sauer et al., 2001). This is particularly so in cases of when a software review involves subgroups working on one project, as competition and conflict may arise between the subgroups. It has been demonstrated (Johnson, 1998, 1999; Littlepage, Robison, & Reddington, 1997; Macmillan & Kaplan, 1985; Morris, 1966; Tyran & George, 2002) that competition and personal conflict between team members can result in de-motivation and this negatively influences overall performance.

Process Gains and Losses

The effectiveness of process performance is measured by the difference between process gains and losses (Johnson & Tjahjono, 1998; Porter & Votta,

1994). A typical review meeting lasts between two and three hours (Fagan, 1986; Gilb & Graham, 1993). The process gains of software reviews are defects first found during the group meeting while process losses are measured by the defects found during individual preparation, but not reported in the group meeting (Laitenberger & DeBaud, 2000). The characteristics of the process can seriously impact on this software review performance measure (Miller, 2000; Parnas & Lawford, 2003a, 2003b; Votta, 1993). For instance, Votta (1993) observed a series of review meetings and found that on average only 4% of the defects were found in the review meetings, whereas Miller and Macdonald (1998) reported that experienced review groups produced an average meeting gain of 9% when compared to novice reviewers.

However, determining the factors associated with gains and losses of the meeting process is often difficult as these measures tend to treat the process as a "black box" and do not report on the underlying causes. There is empirical evidence identifying the critical factors that affect review meeting performance in this literature. It is argued here that it is important to investigate what are the meeting process factors that affect the process gains and losses.

Software Review Performance

To measure software review performance, two types of measurement can be applied: qualitative measurement and quantitative assessments (Alshayeb & Li, 2003; Garrity & Sanders, 1998; Jeffery, Ruhe, & Wieczorek, 2001; Pfleeger, Jeffery, & Kitchenham, 1997; Pfleeger, 1998, 1999). Qualitative measurement is based on the subjective opinions of review participants (Gough, Fodemski, Higgins, Ray, 1995) whereas quantitative measurement is based on empirical data collected during defect detection activities such as the number of defects found (Miller, 2000; Wohlin & Runeson, 1998).

Qualitative Measurement

Qualitative measurement emphasises experts' opinions and judgement about the benefits of a review rather than investigation of quantitative data (Brynjolfsson, 1993; Kelly & Shepard, 2000, 2002).

It is generally recognised that qualitative measurements provide a deep understanding of the software development process and provide a good basis for improving teamwork and social integration (Crossman, 1991; Humphrey, 2002; Svendsen, 1992). However, despite this, qualitative measurement is not widely used in practice. The major limitation of a qualitative approach is that it is difficult to provide an evaluative metric that demonstrates the benefits of the software review for the organisations (Brynjolfsson, 1994; Jeffery et al., 2001; Offen & Jeffery, 1997; Pfleeger, 1999).

Quantitative Measurement

Quantitative measurement is the most commonly used method for collecting empirical data from a review process (Jalote & Saxena, 2002; Laitenberger & DeBaud, 2000; Lott & Rombach, 1996). Empirical studies usually require an evaluation model and/or measurement matrix (Briand, Arisholm, Counsell, Houdek, & Thevenod-Fosse, 1999) as a yardstick for assessment. The two most common models used are quality and cost models (Chatzigeorgiou & Antoniadis, 2003; Collofello & Woodfield, 1989; Jones, 1996; Raz & Yaung, 1997; Remus, 1984; Slaughter, Harter, & Krishnan, 1998). The quality model relates to an assessment of quality that is based on the determination of the number of defects found in a software artefact during the review process (Biffl & Halling, 2003; Briand, Freimut, & Vollei, 1999), while cost models are concerned with cost effectiveness in conducting software reviews (Grady & Van Slack, 1994; Kusumoto, 1993). In practice, the majority of measurements of review performance are quality-based, (i.e., they compare the number of defects found by a reviewer with the number of defects found by other team members) (Brohl & Droschel, 1995; Calvin, 1983; Fowler, 1986).

Limitations of the Current
Software Review Literature

One of the most challenging issues for practitioners is assuring that high software quality is achieved at the lowest development cost while still meeting project deadlines (Cadle & Yeates, 2001; DeMarco, 1982; Garden, Horsley, & Pingel, 1986; Gless, 1999; Hofmann & Lehner, 2001; Linberg, 1999; Moynihan, 2000). Software reviews are considered to be one of the most cost-effective techniques for identifying and removing defects in the early stages of the system life cycle (Parnas & Lawford, 2003a, 2003b). The focus of recent empirical research has been on the defect detection process (Basili et al, 2000; Mithas et al., 2001; Porter et al., 1994).

As part of research experiments have mostly aimed to manipulate the following factors:

- **Process Structures:** How the review process should be organized and conducted (Bisant & Lyle, 1989; Fagan, 1976; Knight & Myers, 1993; Martin & Tsai, 1992; Parnas & Weiss, 1985).

- **Use of Review Meeting:** This refers to the controversy regarding the need for review group meetings for all types of review (Johnson & Tjahjono, 1998; Porter et al., 1995; Votta, 1993).

- **Reading Techniques:** These techniques allow reviewers (inspectors) to follow the review aid in maximizing defect detection (e.g., checklist) (Basili et al., 1996; Fagan, 1976; Gilb & Graham, 1993; Porter & Votta, 1994).

- **Use of Roles in Meeting Support:** Review team members can be assigned to different roles (e.g., moderator, author, reader, inspector, etc.) (Ackerman et al., 1989; Fagan, 1976; Russell, 1991).

- **Team Size:** (Bisant & Lyle, 1989; Fagan, 1976; Kelly & Shepard, 1992; Owen, 1997; Porter & Votta, 1997).

- **Computer Support Tools:** Computer-supported defect detection (Johnson & Tjahjono, 1997; Mashayekhi et al., 1993; Murphy & Miller, 1997; Vermunt, Smits, & Van Der Pijl, 1998).

- **Re-Review:** Techniques to capture remaining defects (Biffl et al., 2001; Eick et al., 1992; Emam & Laitenberger, 2001; Strauss & Ebenau, 1994; Votta, 1993).

However, the current literature exhibits a lack of empirical data to support what are the most critical factors influencing software review performance. There is no published evidence on what review inputs are used during defect detection. Neither are there consistent prescriptions of what inputs are necessary for the effective review of different software artefacts. What types of supporting documents are the most critical to the software review performance?

For example, in a code review, are the requirements and design documents both necessary during defect detection? Is review performance (i.e., number of defects found) affected if only one of these documents is present or available? Are different inputs optimal for the review of different software artefacts?

When the explicit inputs (e.g., reading technique documents) are manipulated, the results are conflicting and inconsistent (Basili et al., 1996; Biffl, 2001; Cheng & Jeffery, 1996; Porter & Votta, 1998). For instance, Cheng and Jeffery (1996) found that the average net meeting gain is greater than the average net meeting loss (i.e., the net gain of the group meeting is approximately 12%) while Porter and Votta (1998) found that the net meeting gain rates are not much different from zero (i.e., average net meeting gain is $-0.9 \pm 2.2\%$). Most of the empirical data obtained from the laboratory experiments were uncertain because the small number of defects found in the software review process may be partially due to a lack of reviewers' expertise and/or the use of student subjects (Basili & Selby, 1987; Basili et al., 1996; Bisant et al., 1989; Doolan, 1992; Fagan, 1976; Johnson & Tjahjono, 1998;). Hence what inputs are used in software review is still an open question.

Practitioners' reports (Davis, 1982; Mathiassen, 2000; Pendlebury, 2001; Zhu, Jin, Diaper, & Ganghong, 2002) already show that requirements documents are often missing during later stages of software development. Different input requirements directly affect how the software review is organized. Thus the study of software review inputs is interesting and important for both researchers and practitioners.

Although the above questions provide a rich area for future review research, it is required to undertake the research in the context of a theoretical framework. Therefore, the underlying research goal is to provide guidance for both researchers and practitioners on the most successful review approach in the development process.

The most successful review approach should produce a defect-free work product, achieve optimal cost benefits, and reduce the development time (Franch, 1995; Franch et al., 2003; Kauppinen & Kujala, 2001; Rainer & Hall, 2002; Rifkin & Deimel, 2000). Without a theoretical framework, it is difficult to understand and predict review performance. Transforming software review technique into the software development process and bridging the gap between the theory and practice requires intensive efforts by both researchers and practitioners. However, experimentation tests theories or models to understand and predict the critical factors influencing on review performance. Current software review literature focuses on a small set of variables and often lacks generalisation ability or consistent results (e.g., Chernak, 1996; Miller et al, 1998; Shull, Lanubile, & Biasili, 2000; Thelin, Runeson, & Wohlin, 2003).

As a result, it is important to develop and validate a theoretical model. Theories of modeling (Blakely & Boles, 1991) point out that models provide generalisation ability (Ackoff, 1953; Alreck, 1995; Babbie, 2000) and also provide systematic accumulating of knowledge in a field (Baker & Schuck, 1975; Baker, 1999; Bogdan & Biklen, 1992; Bordens & Abbott, 2002; Boudreau, Gefen, & Straub, 2001; Cohen, 1988; Wold, 1980, 1982).

There are three contributions of a theoretical model. First, it helps researchers and practitioners understand the key factors influencing software review performance. Second, it offers the broader context of theory and emphasizes empirical methodological contributions in a systematic manner. Finally, knowledge accumulation from the theoretical model can contribute to better review approaches and improvements in software quality.

In other words, researchers and practitioners can understand the cause-effect relationships between the factors, and investigate interactions among the factors and refine the model if needed (Denzin, 1987; Denzin & Lincoln, 1995).

A theoretical model, the Explicit and Implicit Inputs-process-Outputs model (EIIO) is developed in the rest of this study to analyse and predict the performance of software reviews. The model consists of three major components: inputs, process, and outputs. The inputs and process factors can be applied in causal and predictive modelling to theory construction (Chin, Gopal, & Salisbury, 1997; Geisser, 1975; Wold, 1980). For each dimension, the model presents a graphical representation in the form of a diagram describing the relationships between the inputs, process factors and performance constructs driven by the theories (Chin, 1998a, 1998b, 2003).

The inputs dimension considers which inputs may influence software review performance. Behavioural literature has linked task outcomes with task inputs (Baker & Schuck; 1975; Davis, 1973; Ericsson & Delaney, 1999; Harmon, Schneer, & Hoffman, 1995; Korman, 1977; Sgobbi, 2002; Steers & Birdsall, 1976; Swets & Birdsall, 1967) (i.e., inputs are used to explain process outcomes in other tasks). Hence this notion of using inputs to explain software review performance is not altogether new (ANSI/IEEE Standard 1028, 1998).

However, within this task domain, the literature review did not find any empirical investigation being undertaken to link software review inputs to process and performance. Given the general consensus for the need to improve software quality (Grunbacher et al., 2002; Kan, 1995; Kettinger, William, Lee, Choong, & Lee, & Sunro, 1995; Kitchenham, Pfleeger, & Fenton, 1995; Philp & Garner, 2001), and the common software engineering problems directly related to software inputs, such as the lack of complete requirements for all stages of software development and the proliferation of software development standards (Easterbrook, 1999; Hofmann & Lehner, 2001; Kauppinen & Kujala, 2001; Leffingwell & Widrig, 2000; Sandahl et al., 1998), there is a strong motivation to examine whether review inputs do in fact affect software review performance.

In addition, it would be interesting for both researchers and practitioners to understand how process gains and losses occur and which of the key process factors affect the software review outcomes. This study is intended to elaborate the meeting process black box.

Summary

In summary, this chapter presents the use of inputs, process, and measurement performance in the software review literature. The chapter concludes with a summary of gaps and limitations of the literature. A theoretical model (i.e., important relationships between inputs, process and performance) will be discussed next chapter.

References

Ackerman, F. A., Buchwald, L.S., & Lewski F. H. (1989, May). Software inspection: An effective verification process. *IEEE Software*, 31-36.

Ackoff, R. L. (1953). *The design of social research*. Chicago: The University of Chicago Press.

Alreck, P. L., & Settle, R. B. (1995). *The survey research handbook*. Chicago: Irwin.

Alshayeb, M., & Li, W. (2003, November). An empirical validation of object-oriented metrics in two different iterative software processes. *IEEE Transaction on Software Engineering, 29*(11), 1043-1049.

ANSI/IEEE. (1989). An American national standard. *IEEE Standards for Software Reviews and Audits, ANSI/IEEE Standard 1028-1998*.

Aurum, A. (2003). Supporting structures for managing software engineering knowledge. In A. Aurum, R. Jeffery, R. Wohlin, & M. Handzic (Eds.), *Managing software engineering knowledge*. Springer, Berling, Heidelberg, New York.

Babbie, E. R. (1973). *Survey research methods*. CA: Wadsworth.

Baker, E. M., & Schuck, J. R. (1975). Theoretical note: Use of signal detection theory to clarify problems of evaluating performance in industry. *Organisational Behaviour and Human Performance*, (13), 307-317.

Baker, T. L. (1999). *Doing social research* (3rd ed.). Boston: McGraw-Hall.

Basili, V. R., Green, S., Laitenberger, O., Lanubile, F., Sorumgard, S., & Zelkowitz, M. (1996). The empirical investigation of perspective-based reading. *International Journal on Empirical Software Engineering, 1*(12), 133-144.

Basili, V. R., Laitenberger, O., Shull, F., & Rus, I., (2000). Improving software inspections by using reading techniques. *Proceedings of International Conference on Software Engineering* (pp. 727-836).

Basili, V. R., & Selby, R. W. (1987). Comparing the effectiveness of software testing strategy. *IEEE Transaction on Software Engineering, 13*(12), 1278-1296.

Basili, V. R., Shull, F., & Lanubile, F. (1999). Building knowledge through families of experiments. *IEEE Transactions on Software Engineering, 25*(4).

Biffl, S. (2001). *Software inspection techniques to support project and quality management: Lessons learned from a large-scale controlled experiment with two inspection cycles on the effect defect detection and defect estimation techniques*. PhD Thesis. Department of Software Engineering, Vienna University of Technology, Australia.

Biffl, S., Freimut, B., & Laitenberger, O. (2001). Investigating the cost-effectiveness of reinspection in software development. *Proceedings of Australian Conference on Software Engineering* (pp. 155-164).

Biffl, S., & Halling, M. (2002). Investigating the influence of inspector capability factors with four inspection techniques on inspection performance. *Proceedings of IEEE Symposium on Software Metrics, Metrics'02*.

Biffl, S., & Halling, M. (2003, May). Investigating the defect detection effectiveness and cost benefit of nominal inspection team. *IEEE Transaction on Software Engineering, 29*(5), 385-397.

Bisant, D. B., & Lyle, J. R. (1989). A two person inspection method to improve programming productivity. *IEEE Transactions on Software Engineering, 15*(10), 1294-1304.

Blakely & Boles. (1991). *Theory construction*. Englewood, Cliffs, NJ: Prentice-Hall.

Boehm, B. W., & Basili, B. R. (2001, January). Software defect reduction top 10 list. *IEEE Computer, 34*(1).

Boehm, B. W., & Papaccio, P. H. (1988). Understanding and controlling software costs. *IEEE Transaction on Software Engineering, 14*(10), 1462-1473.

Bogdan, R. C., & Biklen, S. K. (1992). *Qualitative research for education: An introduction to theory and methods*. Boston: Allyn & Bacon.

Bordens, K. S., & Abbott, B. B. (2002). *Research design and methods: A process approach* (5th ed.). Boston: McGraw Hill.

Boudreau, M. C., Gefen, D., & Straub, D. W. (2001). Validation in information systems research: A state-of-the-art assessment. *MIS Quarterly, 25*(1), 1-16.

Bourgeois, K. V. (1996). Process insights from a large-scale software inspections data analysis, cross talk. *Journal of Defense Software Engineering,* 17-23.

Briand, L. C., Arisholm, E., Counsell, S., Houdek, F., & Thevenod-Fosse, P. (1999). *Empirical studies of object-oriented artefacts, methods, and processes: State of the art and future direction, ISERN Report No. 037-99/E.* International Software Engineering Software Research Network, Fraunhofer Instituted for Empirical Software Engineering, Germany.

Briand, L. C., Freimut B., & Vollei, F. (1999). *Assessing the cost-effectiveness of inspections by combining project data and expert opinion, ISERN Report No. 070-99/E.* International Software Engineering Software Research Network, Fraunhofer Instituted for Empirical Software Engineering, Germany.

Briand, L. C., Freimut, B., & Vollei, F. (2000). *Using multiple adaptive regression splines to understand trends in inspection data and identify optimal inspection rates ISERN Tr 00-07.* International Software Engineering Software Research Network, Fraunhofer Instituted for Empirical Software Engineering, Germany.

Briand, L. C., & Wieczorek, I. (2000). *Resources estimation in software engineering ISERN 00-05.* International Software Engineering Software Research Network, Fraunhofer Instituted for Empirical Software Engineering, Germany.

Briand, L. C., & Wust, J. (2000). *Integrating scenario-based and measurement-based software product assessment, report No. 042-00/E.*, International Software Engineering Software Research Network, Fraunhofer Instituted for Empirical Software Engineering, Germany, ISERN.

Brien, M. P., Shaft, T. M., & Buckley, J. (2001, April). An open-source analysis schema for identifying software comprehension process. *Proceedings of 13th Workshop of the Psychology of Programming Interest Group* (pp. 129-146). Bournemouth.

Brohl, A.P., & Droschel, W. (1995). *Das V-Model.* Munich: Oldenburg.

Brynjolfsson, E. (1993). The productivity paradox of information technology. *Communications of the ACM, 36*(12), 67-77.

Cadle, J., & Yeates, D. (2001). *Project management for information systems* (3rd ed.). Harlow, UK: Prentice Hall.

Calvin, T. W. (1983, September). Quality control techniques for "zero defects". *IEEE Transactions on Components, Hybrids, and Manufactory Technology, 6*(3), 323-328.

Chaar, J. K., Halliday, M. J., Bhandari, I. S., & Chillarege, R. (1993, October 17-21). On the evaluation of software inspections and test. *Proceedings of the International Conference on Test Conference* (pp. 180-189).

Chan, K. (2001, August 27-28). An agent-based approach to computer assisted code inspections. *Proceedings of the Australian Software Engineering Conference* (pp. 147-152).

Chatzigeorgiou, A., & Antoniadis, G. (2003). *Efficient Management of Inspection in Software Development Project,* 45(10).

Chechik, M., & Gannon, J. (2001, July). Automatic analysis of consistency between requirement and design. *IEEE Transaction on Software Engineering, 27*(7), 651-672.

Cheng, B., & Jeffery, R. (1996). Comparing inspection strategic for software requirement specifications. *Proceedings of the 1996 Australian Software Engineering Conference* (pp. 203-211).

Chernak, Y. (1996, December). A statistical approach to the inspection checklist formal syntheses and improvement. *IEEE Transactions on Software Engineering, 22*(12).

Chillarge, R., Bhandari, I. S., Chaar, J. K., Halliday, M. J., Moebus, D. S., Ray, B. K., & Wong, M. Y. (1992). Orthogonal defect classification: A concept for in-process measurements. *IEEE Transaction on Software Engineering, 18*(11), 943-965.

Chin, W. W. (1998a, March). Issues and opinion on structural equation modeling. *MIS Quarterly, 22*(1), Commentary.

Chin, W. W. (1998b). The partial least square approach for structural equation modeling. In G. A. Marcoulides (Eds.), *Modern methods for business research* (pp. 295-336). Mahwah, NJ: Erlbaum.

Chin, W. W. (2003). A permutation procedure for multi-group comparison of pls models. *Proceedings of the PLS'03 International Symposium* (pp. 33-43).

Chin, W. W., Gopal, A., & Salisbury, W. D. (1997). Advancing the theory of adaptive structuring: The development of a scale to measure faithfulness of appropriation. *Information Systems Research,* (8), 342-367.

Christenson, D. A., Steel, H. T., & Lamperez, A. J. (1990). Statistical quality control applied to code inspections. *IEEE Journal, Selected Area Communications, 8*(2), 196-200.

Cohen, J. (1988). *Statistical power analysis for the behaviour sciences* (2nd ed.). Hillsdale, NJ: Lawrence Erlbaum.

Collofello, J. S., & Woodfield, S. N. (1989). Evaluating the effectiveness of reliability-assurance techniques. *Journal of Systems and Software,* (9), 191-195.

Conradi, R., Marjara, A. S., & Skatevik, B. (1999, December). Empirical Study of Inspection and Testing Data at Ericsson, Norway. *Proceedings of the 24th Annual Software Engineering Workshop,* Maryland.

Crossman, T. D. (1991). A method of controlling quality of applications software. *South African Computing Journal,* (5), 70-85.

D'Astous, P., & Robillard, P. N. (2000). Characterizing implicit information during peer review meeting. *Proceedings of the International Conference on Software Engineering* (pp. 460-466).

D'Astous, P., & Robillard, P. N. (2001). Quantitative measurements of the influence of participant roles during peer review meeting. *Journal of Empirical Software Engineering*, (6), 143-159.

Davis, A. M. (1993). *Software requirement: Objectives, functions, and states*. Englewood Cliffs, NJ: Prentice-Hall.

Davis, G. B. (1982). Strategies for information requirements determination. *IBM System Journal, 21*(1), 3-30.

Davis, J. H. (1973). Group decision and social interaction: A theory of social decision schemes. *Psychological Review, 80*, 97-125.

DeMarco, T. (1982). *Controlling software projects*. New York: Yourdon Press.

Denzin, N. K. (1978). *The Research Act: A theoretical introduction to sociological methods* (2nd ed.). New York: McGraw-Hill.

Denzin, N. K., & Lincoln, Y. S. (1995). *Handbook of qualitative research*. Thousand Oaks, CA: Sage.

Doolan, E. P. (1992). Experience with Fagan's Inspection Method. *Software-Practice Experience, 22*(3), 173-182.

Dunsmore, A., Roper, M., & Wood, M. (2000). The role of comprehension in software inspection. *The Journal of Systems and Software, 52*, 121-129.

Dunsmore, A., Roper, M., & Wood, M. (2001). Systematic object-oriented inspection: An empirical study. *Proceedings of the Australian Conference on Software Engineering* (pp. 135-144).

Dunsmore, A., Roper, M., & Wood, M. (2002, May 19-25). Further investigation into the development and evaluation of reading techniques for object-oriented code inspection. *International Conference on Software Engineering* (pp. 47-57).

Dyer, M. (1992). Verification-based inspection. *Proceedings of the 26th Annual Hawaii Proceedings of International Conference on Systems Sciences* (pp. 418-427).

Easterbrook, S. (1999). Verification and validation of requirements for mission critical systems. *Proceedings of the International Conference on Software Engineering* (pp. 673-674). Los Angeles.

Eick, S. G., Loader, C. R., Long, M. D., Votta, L. G., & Vander, Wiel, S. (1992). Estimating software fault content before coding. *Proceedings of the 14th International Conference on Software Engineering* (pp. 49-65).

Emam, K. E., & Laitenberger, O. (2000). The application of subjective estimates of effectiveness to controlling software inspection. *The Journal of Systems and Software, 52*, 199-136.

Emam, K. E., & Laitenberger, O. (2001). Evaluating capture-recapture models with two inspectors. *IEEE Transaction on Software Engineering, 27*(9), 851-864.

Ericsson, K. A., & Delaney, P. F. (1999). Long-term working memory as an alternative to capacity models of working memory in everyday skilled performance, In A. Miyake, & P. Shah (Eds.), *Models of working memory: Mechanisms of active maintenance and executive control* (pp. 157-297). Cambridge: Cambridge University Press.

Fagan, M. E. (1976). Design and code inspections to reduce errors in program development. *IBM System Journal, 15*(3), 182-211.

Fagan, M. E. (1986, July). Advances in software inspections. *IEEE Transaction on Software Engineering, 12*(7).

Fazlollahi, B., & Tanniru, M. R. (1991). Selecting a requirement determination methodology: Contingency approach revisited. *Information and Management,* (21), 291-303.

Fowler, P. J. (1986). In-process inspection software products at AT&T. *AT&T Technical Journal, 65*(2), 744-751.

Franch, V. A. (1995, October 17-20). Applying software engineering and process improvement to legacy defence system maintenance: An experience report. *Proceedings of the International Conference on Software Maintenance* (pp. 337-343).

Franz, L. A., & Ship, J. C. (1994). Estimating the value of inspections and early testing for software project. *Hewlett-Packard Journal*, CS-TR-6.

Garden, M. E., Horsley, P. S., & Pingel, T. C. (1986). The effects of software inspections on a major telecommunication-project. *AT&T Technical Journal, 65*(3), 32-40.

Garrity, E. J. ,& Sanders, L. (1998). *Information system success measurement.* Hershey, PA: Idea Group Publishing.

Geisser, S. (1975). The predictive sample reuse method with applications. *Journal of the American Statistical Association, 70*, 320-328.

Gilb, T., & Graham, D. (1993). *Software inspection.* Harlow, UK: Addison-Wesley.

Ginac, F. P. (2000). *Creating high performance software development teams.* London: Prentice Hall.

Gless, R. L. (1999). Evolving a new theory of project success. *Communications of the ACM, 45*(11), 7.

Gough, P. A., Fodemski, F. T., Higgins, S. A., & Ray, S. J. (1995). Scenarios: An industrial case study and hypermedia enhancements. *Proceedings of the 2ⁿᵈ IEEE International Symposium on Requirements Engineering* (pp. 10-17).

Gray, & Van Slack, T. (1994). Key lessons in achieving widespread inspection use. *IEEE Software, 11*(4), 46-47.

Grunbacher, P., Halling, M., Biffl, S., Kitapci, H., & Boehm, B. W. (2002). Repeatable quality assurance techniques for requirements negotiations. *Proceedings of the 36ᵗʰ Hawaii International Conference on System Sciences (HICSS'03).*

Halling, M., & Biffl, S. (2002, October). Investigating the influence of software inspection process parameters on inspection meeting performance. *IEEE Proc-Software, 149*(5), 115-121.

Harmon, J., Schneer, J. A., & Hoffman, L. R. (1995). Electronic meeting and established decision groups: Audio conferencing effects on performance and structural stability. *Organizational Behaviour and Human Decision Processes, 61*(2), 138-147.

Hass, A. M. (2001, July). Creating requirements from test specifications. *ASIASTAR 2001: Software Testing Analysis and Review.*

Hofmann, H. F., & Lehner, F. (2001, July/August). Requirements engineering as a success factor in software project. *IEEE Software*, 58-66.

Host, M., & Johansson, C. (2000). Evaluation of code review methods through interviews and experimentation. *The Journal of Systems and Software, 52*, 113-120.

Humphrey, W. S. (2002). *Introduction to personal software process.* Boston: Addison-Wesley.

Humphrey, W. S., Snyder, T. R., & Willis, R. R. (1991). Software process improvement at Hughes Aircraft. *IEEE Software, 18*(4), 11-23.

IEEE Standard 830. (1993). *IEEE Recommended Practice for Software Requirements Specifications, IEEE Standard 830*, Institute of Electrical and Electronics Engineers Inc., New York.

IEEE Standard 1028. (1998). *Software Engineering Standard Committee of the IEEE Computer Society, IEEE Standard 1028.* IEEE Standard for Software Review, Institute of Electrical and Electronics Engineers Inc., New York.

Isazadeh, A., Macewen, G., & Malton, A. (1995). Behavioural patterns for software requirement engineering. *Proceedings of the 1995 Conference of the Centre for Advanced Studies on Collaborative Research,* Toronto.

Jackson, A., & Hoffman, D. (1994). Inspecting module interface specifications. Software Testing, *Verification Reliability, 4*(2), 110-117.

Jalote, P., & Saxena, A. (2002, December). Optimum control limits for employing statistical process control in software process. *IEEE Transaction on Software Engineering, 28*(12), 1126-1134.

Jeffery, J., Ruhe, M., & Wieczorek, I. (2001, June 4-6). *Using public domain metrics to estimate software development effort,* 16-17.

Johnson, P. M. (1998). Reengineering inspection. *Communication of ACM, 41*(2), 49-52, February.

Johnson, P. M. (1999a). A critical analysis of PSP data quality: Result from a case study. *Journal of Empirical Software Engineering,* February.

Johnson, P. M. (1999b). Leap: A personal information environment for software engineers. *International Conference on Software Engineering* (pp. 654-657).

Johnson, P. M., & Tjahjono, D. (1997). Assessing software review meetings: A controlled experimental study using CSRS. *ACM Press,* 118-127.

Johnson, P. M., & Tjahjono, D. (1998). Does every inspection really need a meeting? *Empirical Software Engineering,* (3), 3-35.

Jones, C. (1995). Patterns of large software systems: Failure and success. *IEEE Computer, 28*(3), 86-87.

Kan, S. H. (1995). *Metrics and models in software quality engineering.* Boston: Addison-Wesley.

Kantorowitz, E., Guttman, A., & Arzi, L. (1997). The performance of The N-Fold Requirements Inspection Method. *Requirements Engineering Journal, 2,* 152-164.

Kauppinen, M., & Kujala, S. (2001, September). Starting improvement of requirement engineering processes: An experience report. *3rd International Conference on Product Focused Software Process Improvement (PROFES)* (pp. 197-209). Germany.

Kelly, D., & Shepard T. (2000). Task-directed software inspection technique: An experiment and case study. *Proceedings of the 2000 Conference of the Centre for Advanced Studies,* Mississauga, Canada.

Kelly, D., & Shepard, T. (2002). Qualitative observations from software code inspection experiments. *Proceedings of the 2002 Conference of the Centre for Advanced Studies,* Toronto, Canada.

Kelly, J. C., Sherif, J. S., & Hops, J. (1992). An analysis of defect densities found during software inspection. *Journal on Systems Software,* (17), 111-117.

Kettinger, William, J., Lee, Choong, C., Lee, & Sunro. (1995, September/October). Global measures of information service quality: A cross-national study. *Decision Sciences*, *26*(5), 569-588.

Kingston, G., Jeffery, R., & Huang, W. (2000). An explanatory study on the goal alignment in Joint *Software R*eviews, April. Canberra, 63-72.

Kingston, G., Webby, R., & Jeffery, R. (1999, June 23-25). Different and conflicting goals in software reviews. *Proceedings of the 7ᵗʰ European Conference on Information Systems* (pp. 420-435).

Kitchenham, B., Pfleeger, S. L., & Fenton N. (1995). Toward a framework for measurement validation. *IEEE Transaction on Software Engineering*, *21*(12), 929-944.

Knight, J. C., & Myers A. E. (1993, November). An improved inspection technique. *Communications of ACM*, *36*(11), 50-69.

Korman, A. K. (1977). *Organizational behaviour*. Englewood Cliffs, NJ: Prentice Hall.

Kotonya, G., & Sommerville, I. (1998). *Requirements engineering*. UK: Wiley.

Kusumoto, S. (1993). *Quantitative evaluations of software reviews and testing process*. PhD Thesis, Faculty of the Engineering Science of Osaka University.

Laitenberger, O., & Atkinson, C. (1998). Generalizing perspective-based inspection to handle object-oriented development artefacts. *Proceedings of the International Conference on Software Engineering* (pp. 494-503). Los Angeles.

Laitenberger, O., Beil, T., & Schwinn, T. (2002). An industrial case study to examine a non-traditional inspection implementation for requirement specifications. *Proceedings of the 8ᵗʰ IEEE Symposium on Software Metrics (Metrics'02)*.

Laitenberger, O., & Debaud, J. M. (1997). Perspective-based reading of code documents at Robert Bosch GMBH. *Information and Software Technology*, *39*, 781-791.

Laitenberger, O., & Debaud, J. M. (2000). An encompassing life cycle centric survey of software inspection. *The Journal of Software and Systems*, *50*(1), 5-31.

Laitenberger, O., & Emam, K. E. (2000). Experimental comparison of reading techniques for defect detection in UML design documents. *The Journal of Systems and Software*, (53), 183-204.

Laitenberger, O., & Emam, K. E. (2001). An internally replicated quasi-experimental comparison of checklist and perspective-based reading of code documents. *IEEE Transactions of Software Engineering, 27*(5), 378-421.

Leffingwell, D., & Widrig, D. (2000). *Managing software requirements: A unified approach.* NJ: Addison Wesley.

Linberg, K. R. (1999, December). Software developer perceptions about software project failure: A study. *The Journal of Systems and Software, 49*(2/3), 177-192.

Linger, R. C., Mill, H. D., & Witt, B. I. (1997). Perspective-based reading of code documents at Robert Bosch GMBH. *Information and Software Technology, 39,* 781-791.

Littlepage, G., Robison, W., & Reddington, K. (1997). Effects of task experience and group experience on group performance, member ability, and recognition of expertise. *Organizational Behavior and Human Decision Processes, 69*(2), 133-147.

Lott, C. M., & Rombach, H. D. (1996). Repeatable software engineering experiments for comparing defect-detection techniques. *Empirical Software Engineering,* (1), 241-277.

Macmillan, N. A., & Kaplan, H. L. (1985). Detection theory analysis of group data: Estimating sensitivity from average hit and false-alarm rates. *Psychological Bulletin, 98*(1), 185-199.

Madachy, R., Little L., & Fan, S. (1993). Analysis of a successful inspection program. *Proceeding of the 18th Annual NASA Software Engineering Laboratory Workshop* (pp. 176-198).

Martin, J., & Tsai, W. T. (1992, February). N-Fold inspection: A requirements analysis technique. *Communications of ACM, 33*(2), 225-232.

Mashayekhi, V., Drake, J. W. T., & Riedl, J., (1993, September). Distributed collaborative software inspection. *IEEE Software,* 66-75.

Mathiassen, L. (2000). Requirement uncertainty: Should it be latent, aggregate or profile construct? *IEEE Software,* 181-188.

Mathiassen, L., & Stage, J. (1990). Complexity and uncertainty in software design. *Proceedings of the 1990 IEEE Conference on Computer Systems and Software Engineering* (pp. 482-489). IEEE Computer Society Press.

McConnell, S. (1993). *Code complete: A practical handbook of software construction.* Redmond, WA: Microsoft.

Miller, J. (2000). Applying mate-analytical procedures to software engineering experiments. *The Journal of Systems and Software, 54,* 29-39.

Miller, J. (2002). The independence of software inspectors. *The Journal of Systems and Systems, 60,* 5-10.

Miller, J., & Macdonald, F. (1998, October 13-16). Assisting exit decision in software inspection. *Proceedings of the 13ᵗʰ IEEE International Conference on Automated Software Engineering* (pp. 281-284).

Miller, J., Wood, M., & Roper, M. (1998). Further experiences with scenarios and checklists. *Empirical Software Engineering, 3*, 37-64.

Mithas, S., Subramanyam, R., & Krishnan, M. S. (2001). Determinants of inspection effectiveness in software development: An empirical analysis. *The 22ⁿᵈ International Conference on Information Systems* (pp. 437-442).

Morris, C. G. (1966). Task effects on group interaction. *Journal of Personality and Social Psychology, 4*(5), 545-554.

Moynihan, T. (2000). Coping with "requirement-uncertainty": The theories-of-action of experienced is/software project managers. *The Journal of Systems and Software, 53*, 99-109.

Murphy, P., & Miller, J. (1997). A process for asynchronous software inspection. *Proceedings of the 18ᵗʰ IEEE International Workshop on Software Technology and Engineering* (pp. 96-104).

National Aeronautics and Space Administration (NASA) (1993). *Software Formal Inspection Guidebook, NASA-GB-A302.*

Offen, R., & Jeffery, R. (1997, March/April). Establishing software measurement programs. *IEEE Software*, 45-53.

Owen, K. (1997). Software detailed technical reviews: findings and using defects. *Wescon'97 Conference Proceedings* (pp. 128-133).

Panko, R. R. (1999). Applying code inspection to spreadsheet testing. *Journal of Management of Information Systems, 16*(2), 159-176.

Parnas, D. L., & Lawford, M. (2003a). Inspection's role in software quality assurance. *IEEE Software*, 16-20.

Parnas, D. L., & Lawford, M. (2003b, August). The role of inspection in software quality assurance. *IEEE Transaction on Software Engineering, 29*(8), 674-675.

Parnas, D. L., & Weiss, D. M. (1985, August 28-30). Active design reviews: principles and practices. *Proceeding of ICSE '85* (pp. 132-136). London: IEEE Computer Society.

Parnas, D. L., & Weiss, D. M. (1987). Active design review: principles and practices. *The Journal of Systems and Software, 7*, 259-265.

Pendlebury, J. A. (2001, July). Successful testing with limited requirements. *ASIASTER 2001: Software Testing Analysis and Review.*

Perpich, J. M., Perry, E. D., Porter, A. A., Votta, L. G., & Wade, M. W. (1997). Anywhere, anytime code inspections: Using the Web to remove inspection bottlenecks in large-scale software development. *Proceedings of the International Conference on Software Engineering, ICSE* (pp. 14-21).

Pfleeger, S. L. (1998). *Software engineering: Theory and practice*. Upper Saddle River, NJ: Prentice-Hall.

Pfleeger, S. L. (1999). Albert Einstein and empirical software engineering. *IEEE Computer*, 32-37.

Pfleeger, S. L., Jeffery, R., & Kitchenham, B. (1997, March/April). Status report on software measurement. *IEEE Software*, 33-43.

Philp, B. A., & Garner, B. J. (2001, August 27-28). Knowledge mediation in software quality engineering. *Proceedings of the Australian Software Engineering Conference* (pp. 153-159).

Porter, A. A., Mockus, A., & Votta, L. (1998, 41-79, January). Understanding the sources of variation in software inspections. *ACM Transactions on Software Engineering and Methodology*, 7(1).

Porter, A. A., Siy, H. P., Toman, C. A., & Votta, L. G. (1997). An experiment to assess the cost-benefits of code inspections in large scale software development. *IEEE Transaction on Software Engineering*, 23(6), 329-346.

Porter, A. A., & Votta, L. G. (1994). An experiment to assess different defect detection methods for software requirements inspections. *Proceedings of the 16th International Conference on Software Engineering, ICSE'16* (pp. 103-112).

Porter, A. A., & Votta, L. G. (1997, November/December). What makes inspections work? *IEEE Software*, 99-102.

Porter, A. A., & Votta, L. (1998). Comparing defection methods for software requirements inspection: A replication using professional subjects: *Journal of Empirical Software Engineering*, 3, 355-379.

Porter, A. A., Votta, L. G., & Basili, B. (1995). Comparing detection methods for software requirements inspection: A replicated experiment. *IEEE Transaction on Software Engineering*, 21(6), 563-575.

Powell, D. (1998). Deriving verification conditions and program assertions to support software inspection. *Proceedings of the Ninth Asia-Pacific Software Engineering Conference (APSEC'02)* (pp. 447-456).

Rainer, A., & Hall T. (2002). Key success factors for implementing software process improvement: A maturity-based analysis. *The Journal of Systems and Software*, 62, 71-84.

Raz, T., & Yaung, A. T. (1997). Factors affecting design inspection effectiveness in software development. *Information Software Technology*, 39, 297-305.

Reeve, J. T. (1991, March). Applying the Fagan inspection technique. *Quality Forum, 17*(1).

Remus, H. (1984). *Integrated software validation in the view of inspections/ reviews, software validation.* 57-65.

Rifkin, S., & Deimel, L. (2000, November.). Program comprehension techniques improve software inspections: A case study: *Proceedings of the 8th International Workshop on Program Comprehension* (pp. 131-138). Limerick

Runeson, R., & Wohlin, C. (1998). An experimental evaluation of an experience-based capture-recapture method in software code inspection. *Journal of Empirical Software Engineering, 3*, 381-406.

Russell, G. W. (1991, January). Experience with inspection in ultralarge-scale development. *IEEE Software, 8*(1).

Sandahl, K., Blomkvist, O., Karlsson, J., Krysander, C., Lindvall, M., & Ohlsson, N. (1998). An extended replication of experiment for assessing methods for software requirements inspections. *Journal of Empirical Software Engineering, 3*, 327-354.

Sarrinen, T., & Vepsalainen. (1993). Managing the risks of information systems implementation. *European Journal of Information Systems, 2*(4), 283-295.

Schulmeyer, G. G., & Mcmanus, J. I. (1999). *Handbook of software quality assurance* (3rd ed.). Upper Saddle River, NJ: Prentice Hall.

Seaman, C. B., & Basili, V. R. (1998, July). Communication and organization: An empirical study of discussion in inspection meetings. *IEEE Transaction on Software Engineering, 24*(6), 559-572.

Sgobbi, F. (2002). Web design skills and competencies: An empirical analysis. *Human Systems Management, 21*(2), 115-136.

Shirey, G. C. (1992). How inspections fail? *Proceeding of the 9th International Conference on Testing Computer Software* (pp. 151-159).

Shull, F., Lanubile, F., & Biasili, V. (2000). Investigating reading techniques for object-oriented framework learning. *IEEE Transaction on Software Engineering, 26*(11).

Shull, F., Rus, I., & Basili, V. (2000, July 3). How perspective-based reading can improve requirements inspection? *IEEE Computer*, 73-79.

Shull, F., Travassos, G., & Basili, V. (1999, June). Towards techniques for improved design inspection. *Proceeding of the Workshop on Quantitative Approaches in Object-Oriented Software Engineering.* (In Association with the 13th European Conference on Object-Oriented Programming), Lisbon, Portugal.

Slaughter, S. A., Harter, D. E., & Krishnan, M. S. (1998). Evaluating the cost of software quality. *Communication of the ACM, 41*(8), 67-73, August.

Sommerville, I. (1995). *Software engineering* (5th ed.). UK: Addison-Wesley.

Sommerville, I. (2001). *Software engineering* (6th ed.). UK: Addison-Wesley.

Steers, R., & Braunstein, D. (1976). A behaviourally based measure of manifest needs in work setting. *Journal of Vocational Behaviour, 9*(2), 251-266.

Strauss, S. H., & Ebenau, R. G. (1994). *Software inspection process.* McGraw-Hill.

Svendsen, F. N. (1992). Experience with inspection in the maintenance of software. *Proceedings of the 2nd European Conference on Software Quality Assurance.*

Swets, J. A., & Birdsall, T. G. (1967). Deferred decision in human signal detection: A preliminary experiment. *Perception and Psychophysics, 2,* 15-28.

Tervonen, I. (1996). Support for quality-based design and inspection. *IEEE Software, 13*(1), 44-45.

Thelin, T., Runeson, R., & Regnell, B. (2001). Usage-based reading: An experiment to guide reviewers with use cases. *Information and Software Technology, 43,* 925-938.

Thelin, T., Runeson, P., & Wohlin, C. (2003, August). An experimental comparison of usage-based and checklist-based reading. *IEEE Transaction on Software Engineering, 29*(8), 687-704.

Thelin, T., Runeson, P., Wohiln, C., Olsson, T., & Andersson, C. (2002). How much information is needed for usage-based reading? A series of experiments. *Proceedings of the 2002 International Symposium on Empirical Software Engineering (ISESE'02).*

Travassos, G. H., Shull, F., & Carver, J. (1999). Evolving a process for inspection OO design. *Proceedings of the Workshop on Software Quality, Xiii Brazilian Symposium on Software Engineering,* Brazil.

Travassos, G. H., Shull, F., & Carver, J. (2001). Working with UML: A software design process based on inspections for the unified modelling language. Working with UML: A software design process based on inspections for the unified modeling language. *Advances in Computers Book Series, 54,* 35-97, Academic Press.

Travassos, G. H., Shull. F., Caver. J., & Basili, V. R. (1999). Reading techniques for OO design inspections. *Proceedings of the 24th Annual Software Engineering Workshop,* Goddard Space Flight Centre, MD.

Travassos, G. H., Shull, F., Fredericks, M., & Basili, V. R. (1999, November). Detecting defects in object oriented design: Using readying techniques to increase software quality. *The Conference on Object-Oriented Programming, Systems, Languages, and Applications (OOPSLA)*. Denver, Colorado.

Tyran, C. K., & George J. F. (2002). Improving software inspection with group process support. *Communication of the ACM, 45*(9), 97-92.

Vermunt, A., Smits, M., & Van Der Pijl, G. (1998). Using GSS to support error detection in software specifications. *IEEE Proceedings of the 31st Annual Hawaii International Conference on System Sciences* (pp. 566-574).

Vliet, H. V. (2000). *Software engineering*. Chester, UK: Wiley.

Votta, L. G. (1993). Does every inspection need a meeting? *ACM Software Engineering, 18*(5), 107-114.

Weller, E. F. (1993). Lessons from three years of inspection data. *IEEE Software, 10*(5), 38-45.

Wheeler, D. A., Brykczynski, B., & Meeson, R. N. (1996). *Software inspection: An industry best practice*. Los Alamitos, CA: IEEE Computer Society Press.

Wiegers, K. E. (2002). *Peer reviews in software: A practical guide*. Boston: Addison-Wesley.

Wohlin, C., & Runeson, P. (1998). Defect content estimation from review data. *Proceedings of the 20th International Conference on Software Engineering* (pp. 400-409).

Wold, H. (1980). Model construction and evaluation when theoretical knowledge is scarce: Theory and application of partial least squares. In J. Kmenta & J. B. Ramsey (Eds.), *Evaluation of econometric models*. New York: Academic Press.

Wold, H. (1982). Soft modeling: The basic design and some extensions. In K. G. Joreskog & H. Wold (Eds.), *Systems under indirect observations: Causality, structure, prediction, Part* 2 (pp. 1-54). Amsterdam: North-Holland.

Wong, Y. K., & Wilson, D. (2003, November 3-5). Do Individuals' experience and task training really affect software review performance? *Proceedings of the 7th IASTED International Conference on Software Engineering and Applications*. Maria Del Ray, Los Angeles: ACTA Press Publisher. (Nominated best paper award.)

Zhang, Z., Basili, V., & Shneiderman, B. (1999, March). Perspective-based usability inspection: An empirical validation of efficacy. *An International Journal of Software, 4*(1).

Zhu, H., Jin, L., Diaper, D., & Ganghong, B. (2002). Software requirements validation via task analysis. *The Journal of Systems and Software.*

Chapter VI

A Theoretical Model for Analysis of Software Review Performance

Abstract

The aim of this chapter is to develop a theoretical model to assist in the analysis of critical inputs to software reviews and to identify process factors that might impact positively on software review performance. The Explicit, Implicit Input-process-Output (EIIO) model provides a sound theory to drive empirical research in software review and a different perspective to the existing literature that helps to facilitate understanding of the input-process-output relationship in software review process. An overall objective of the EIIO model is to identify what the key inputs are and process factor(s) that significantly influence review outcome(s). Five propositions, ten research questions, and 14 hypotheses are formulated to validate the important relationships between software inputs, processes, and performance.

Theoretical Model for Analysis
Software Review Performance

This chapter presents a theoretical model for analysis and prediction of software review performance. The motivation is to use existing theories in the behavioural literature (e.g., motivation theory and expert theory) to explain software review performance expressed in terms of the following question: What are the critical factors affecting software review performance?

This model presents three major contributions. First, the traditional IPO model is used to develop a conceptual EIIO model for software review. This approach allows the understanding of the important relationships between input, process and output. Second, by emphasizing the conceptual EIIO model, types of inputs (i.e., explicit and implicit) are further identified from the software review literature, as well as group process factors that may affect review performance. Third, a program is developed to formulate and validate the underlying theory so that the conceptual model can drive further empirical research.

Input-process-output models may be represented by the traditional symbol system hypothesis (Newell & Simon, 1976) or the semiotic system hypothesis (Fetzer, 1990) in information systems research. Marr (1982) originated the symbol system hypothesis of "information-processing-outputs" analysis as a way of conceptually separating the essential elements of a theory from its implementation; however, such analysis requires a distinction to be made between explicit inputs (observable signs such as collected data and documents) and implicit inputs (contextual conditions such as reviewer abilities, attitudes, capabilities, motivation, etc.). The semiotic systems hypothesis uses a cognitive approach (Will, 2004; Will & Whobrey, 2003), the "theory of sign focuses on information from user points of view and implies that information be designed knowledge and action support system" (Will, 2004). It differs from mathematics and mathematical logic by its close attention to operation of symbol grounding (Meystel, 1999; Zadeh, 1987). In particular, Will (2004) suggested that:

Semeiotic information systems can meet requirements because they are designed with the users in mind and extend the I-P-O dichotomy into a cognitive tracheotomy: A user of information (or information systems), understood as signs, is aware of them by perception, recognizes them as standing for something else that they represent, and is free to interpret them in the context of his knowledge and intended (or necessary) actions. In order to be assured, every sign user requires evidence that the sign is syntactically correct, semantically true, and pragmatically useful.

For this reason, it has been widely used in information systems, particularly in artificial intelligence systems (Andersen, 1990; Fetzer, 1988, 1990; Meystel, 1999; Newell & Simon, 1976; Simon, 1977) where the technique of protocol analysis (Ericsson & Simon, 1980) often informs system design. Typically, a subject would be given a "puzzle" to solve and would talk through the decision (solution) process out loud into a tape recorder. The protocols thus collected would be analyzed to determine the terms and steps of a successful solution strategy, and a computer would then be programmed to solve similar types of problems using a formally similar strategy. It was clearly intended that the computational symbols should be taken as modeling the conscious contents in the human solver's mind and that actual mental contents in humans were to be understood as computational symbols.

Researchers tend to study social interaction through participant observation (e.g., laboratory studies) rather then survey and interview. It is arguable that close contact in the everyday lives of the participants is necessary for understanding the *meaning of actions*, the definition of the situation itself, and the process by which "actors construct the situation through their interaction" (Popper, 1961). As a result, the research methodology design becomes critical. The semiotics model hypothesis provides a useful dimension for system modeling design, particularly in artificial intelligence. It is useful that this "querying or exploring of the environment as the performance of measurements or tests, and to think of the sensory organs, the transducers, as instruments used to perform them" (Fetzer, 1990). In fact, in the social sciences (particularly in behavioral research), models consist of symbols that are the characteristics of some empirical phenomenon, including its components and relationships between the components. Popper (Popper, 1961) suggests five-stage research processes as one of the most systematic strategies (Popper, 1961). These five-stages are (Frankfort-Nachmias & Nachmias, 1996):

1. Construct an explicit theory or model.

2. Select a proposition derived from the theory or model for empirical investigation.

3. Design a research project to test the proposition (hypothesis).

4. If the proposition (hypothesis) derived from the theory is rejected by the empirical data, make changes in the theory or the research project.

5. If the proposition is not rejected, select other propositions for testing for attempt to improve the theory (or model).

As a result, the EIIO model is used to explain phenomena and to make accurate prediction (Frankfort-Nachmias & Nachmias, 1996) given the traditional scientific method (Popper, 1961). Details of the EIIO model will be discussed in the following sections.

Input-Process-Output

The traditional input-process-output (IPO) model of group performance consists of three major components: inputs, process, and outputs (see Figure 1) (Bushnell, 1990; Homans, 1950; Mecklenbrauker, 1995). The "inputs" component refers to any resources from the environments that are input to the "process" (Zmud, 1983). The "process" refers a set of procedures that transform "inputs" to "outputs". "Outputs" are the outcomes of the process (Zmud, 1983).

The theoretical EIIO (Explicit and Implicit Inputs-process-Outputs) model (see Figure 2) proposed in this work is an expansion of the traditional IPO model for software review. This theoretical EIIO model helps to better conceptualise software review performance in the form of the relationship between input, process, and output. The transformation process from inputs into outputs is shown in the EIIO model. The inputs can be classified into explicit and implicit (Nonaka & Takeuchi, 1995) based on knowledge management theory.

Inputs

The sequences of input-process-output can affect interactions amongst groups of reviewers in performing the process (e.g., decomposition of group members, interaction patterns, content of communication) (Brodbeck & Greitemeyer,

Figure 1. The traditional IPO model

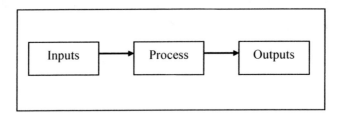

Figure 2. Explicit and implicit inputs-process-outputs (EIIO) model

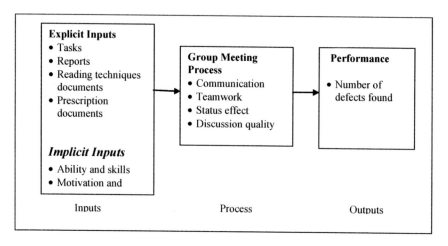

2000; Kerr, 1979; Yetton & Bottger, 1983). Inputs can be classified into explicit and implicit inputs (Engelkamp & Wippich, 1995; Mecklenbrauker, 1995; Nonaka & Takeuchi, 1995; Nyberg & Nilsson, 1995). Explicit inputs include task characteristics and supporting documents while implicit inputs include reviewers' abilities and skills as well as motivation and effort (Ericsson & Delaney, 1999; Yetton & Bottger, 1983).

Explicit Inputs

Review Task (Artefact) Characteristics

In the context of software review, a review task refers to an artefact, which is presented for review. Generally, artefacts can be classified into requirements, design, code, test cases, and any artefacts that related to the work product such as system build procedures or maintenance manuals (IEEE Standard 1028, 1998). The characteristics of an artefact include (Laitenberger & DeBaud, 2000):

•   Complexity of the work product — the more complex the work product, potentially the more defects are likely to be detected.

- Size of the work product — the larger the work product, potentially the more defects are likely to be detected.
- Initial quality of the work product — the higher the initial quality of the work product, potentially the fewer defects are likely to be detected.

Supporting Documents

In relation to the supporting documents, four major types of supporting documents are summarized as following:

- Reports, supporting documents in the domain application and standards adopted by the software organization (ANSI/IEEE, 1989; Kotonya & Sommerville, 1998). These include business reports, which provide domain business information supporting the system being built.
- Reading techniques, including checklists (Ackerman, Buchwald, & Lewski, 1989; Chernak, 1996; Fagan, 1976; Gilb & Graham, 1993; NASA, 1993) and scenarios-based reading technique documents (Basili et al., 1996; Fusaro, Lanubile, & Visaggio, 1997; Gough, Fodemski, Higgins, & Ray, 1995; Laitenberger & Emam, 2001; Porter & Votta, 1994; Porter, Votta, & Basili, 1995; Shull, Lanubile, & Biasili, 2000; Shull, F., Rus, I., & Basili, 2000).
- Prescriptions for organising and conducting reviews, including instruments used during review (e.g., review procedure and structure (Gilb & Graham, 1993; Porter & Votta, 1998; Strauss & Ebenau, 1995), and time review forms (Freedman & Weinberg, 1990)).
- Previously reviewed software documents relating to the software artefact (e.g., a related document for a design review may be a reviewed requirements document) (ANSI/IEEE, 1989; Vliet, 2000).

Each supporting document selection should be determined by the type and characteristics of the artefact.

Implicit Inputs

Ability and Skills

Reviewer characteristics are one of the major factors of review performance and are difficult to articulate with formal language or notation (D'Astous &

Robillard, 2000; Petersson, 2001; Nonaka & Takeuchi, 1995; Roediger, 1990). Reviewer characteristics include reviewers' personal knowledge and expertise as well as behavioural aspects (norms, beliefs, values, etc.) of reviewers (Crutcher & Ericssion, 2000; Nelson & Xu, 1995; Nyberg & Nilsson, 1995; Polanyi, 1966).

Individual performance is determined by two major types of characteristics of a reviewer that include task-relevant abilities and skills (i.e., Can I do it?), and motivation and effort (i.e., Will I do it?) (Herold, 1979; Engelkamp & Wippich, 1995; Roediger & McDermott, 1993;). "When capacity, interest and effort are present; the best performance is likely to result" (Simonton, 1988; Vecchio, Hearn, & Southey, 1992). Individual abilities refer to the knowledge of a specific task and skills refer to specific competencies required to complete the task: to achieve the highest performance in a technical task, it is important to employ expertise (Biederman & Shffrar, 1983; Charness, Krampe & Mayr, 1993; Ericsson & Lehmann, 1996). Experts are those who can achieve outstanding performance by balancing between experience and training (Adam, 1965; Hultman, 1988; Kirkpatrick, 1967; London, 1989), with an innate capability and talent (Bloom, 1985; Galton, 1969).

The foundation of expert theory was introduced by De Groot (1946) in a study of world-class chess players based on "pattern-based retrieval from memory". Further studies show that expertise can be attained from experience of the domain, large amounts of knowledge and the ability of pattern-based retrieval from memory (Chase & Simon, 1973; Chi, Glaser, & Rees, 1982; Cooke, 1994; Hoffman, 1987, 1995). This is consistent with the skill and knowledge acquisition theories (Dick & Hearn, 1988; Fitts & Poser, 1967; Nelson, 1991; Nonaka & Takeuchi, 1995) in which individuals can gain knowledge from pattern-based retrieval. Further, Ericsson and Lehmann (1996) used more than 250 published papers to develop a scope of expert performance theory that consists of:

- Age associated with peak performance — the age at which experts attain their highest level of performance is closely related to their domain of expertise (Ericsson, 1994). Most experts attain their highest achievements in their thirties and forties (Charness et al., 1993).

- Ten years of necessary preparation — preparation is essential in most domains in order to achieve the highest performance (Bloom, 1985; Galton, 1969). In other words, the ten years experience rule is necessary even for a talented individual (Dick & Hearn, 1988). Researchers also found that early young-age training and practice can achieve the highest performance (Ericsson, 1994; Ericsson & Smith, 1991; Ericsson, Krampe, & Tesch-Tomer, 1993). These studies have consistently confirmed the superior knowledge and performance of experts.

- Role of deliberate practice — domain knowledge often draws from effective training and qualification with significant feedback and improvement to achieve the highest performance (Charness et al., 1993; Ericsson & Lehmann, 1996). "Individualized training activities especially designed by a coach or teacher to improve specific aspects of an individual's performance through repetition and successive refinement" (Bushnell, 1990; Ericsson & Lehmann, 1996; Hultman, 1988).

Though Ericsson and Lehmann (1996) did not use any software review studies for outlining the scope of expert performance, these theories might be applied to software review.

In the context of software review, reviewer characteristics refer to reviewers' expertise, and behavioural aspects such as norms, beliefs, and values of reviewers (Nonaka & Takeuchi, 1995; Nyberg & Nilsson, 1995). Sauer, Jeffery, Land, and Yetton (2000) stated that "expertise is a key driver in review performance" and review performance is "dominated by the available task expertise". Task expertise is the superior knowledge and experience needed to perform a particular task. By using individuals' expertise for different aspects of a task, it is possible to construct group expertise (Laitenberger & DeBaud, 2000). In human performance theory, Campell's theory (1976, 1990) suggests that experience, knowledge, and effort could affect error detection performance (see Equation 1):

Equation 1. Determine of individual task performance

Performance =

  f(declarative knowledge, procedural knowledge and skills, motivation)

In particular, Campell (1990) proposed that performance is a function of the individual's declarative knowledge, procedural knowledge and skill, and motivation. Declarative knowledge is defined as knowledge required to complete a task. Procedural knowledge refers to skill-based knowledge about how effectively to perform a task. Declarative knowledge and procedural knowledge are based on eduction, training, experience, and motivation. Motivation refers to a function of three choices: the choice to expend effort, the choice of the degree of effort to expend, and the choice to persist in task performance. Campell's theory (1976, 1990) suggests that motivational influence and experience can affect job performance through changes in declarative knowledge, procedural knowledge, and skill, and/or the three choices.

In fact, Sauer et al. (2000) theorize that expertise is a key driver of software review performance. It was suggested that experience (i.e., knowledge and skills) is the most significant input influencing software review performance. However, some studies have shown that individuals who have experience do not necessarily perform better than in-experienced individuals (Porter & Votta, 1998).

On the other hand, the expectancy theory suggests that highly motivated individuals will exert higher effort levels than less-motivated individuals (Baker, Ravichandran, & Randall, 1989; Butler & Womer, 1985; Harrel & Stahl, 1984; Harrel, Caldwell, & Duty, 1985, Mitchell & Beach, 1977; Snead & Narrell, 1990; Vroom, 1964).

Equation 2. Individual performance

Performance $= f$ (effort, ability and role perception)

As shown in Equation 2, performance can be comprised as a function of individuals' effort, ability, and role perception (Ferris, 1977). Equation 2 hypothesizes that individuals apply different levels of effort, possess different ability levels, and have different role perceptions, so will have different levels of performance. Ability refers to factors such as the person's native intellectual capabilities and the quality of formal education and/or training. Role refers to how well individuals understand their role in a particular task. Effort refers to the function of choices. The foundation of expectancy theory is more or less the same as Campell's theory. In Ferris's study (1977), interesting results show that after considering individual differences in ability and role, the level of effort has no significant impact on the task performance.

In practice, it has been suggested that the IT developers' knowledge and skills are basically classified into four types (Lee, Trauth, & Farwell, 1995):

- **Technology Management:** The general knowledge of the technology environment with which development is concerned, and how to effectively manage the technology to meet the business requirements and objectives (Humphrey, 2002; Vliet, 2000).

- **Business Functions:** As the dynamics of the business process change, the increasing emphasis on applying technological knowledge to meet business reengineering process and business requirements is extremely important (Davenport & Short, 1990). Evidence shows that IT developers require in-depth business functional knowledge and skills before performing a task (Hammer, 1980).

- **Technical Experience:** This refers to experience in the particular domain area that can effectively complete a task (Laitenberger, Beil, & Schwinn, 2002; Wiegers, 2002). In the context of software review, technical experience can be generalized into technical review experience and/or error detection skills.

Motivation

Software review is driven by human factors, that is, reviewers' motivation. The success of a software review depends heavily on reviewers' contributions. To achieve better review performance, it is suggested that a review should not include a management member in a review team (Franz and Ship, 1994; Kelly, Sherif, & Hops, 1992; Venkatesh & Smith, 1999). This will avoid any status effects in which the bias of decision-making methods (e.g., status power), motivation of reviewers' participations (Deci, 1975, Deci, Koestner, & Ryan, 1999a, 1999b; Igbaria, Parasuraman, & Baroudi, 1996; Kreps, 1997; Venkatesh & Smith, 1999; Wild, Enzle, Nix, & Deci, 1997) or misconception about the review results are used in annual appraisals (Pate, 1978; Russell, 1991; Wiley, 1997; Wilkinson, Orth, & Benfari, 1986). From the psychological approach, individual performance is measured on the four Cs (4Cs) of input, as shown in Table 1.

They can be classified as (Kreps, 1997; Maslow, 1943; Pate, 1978; Plant & Ryan, 1985; Shamir, 1991; Vellerand, 1997):

- **Commitment:** The individual is willing to handle the task. (Is it important to me?)
- **Confidence:** The individual has the self-confidence to deal with the task. (Can I do it?)
- **Competence:** Whether the individual has the actual capability to perform a task. (How can I do it?)
- **Contingencies Frustration:** Whether the individual has support from others. (Do I have support?)

Each input is measured by attributes that include values, belief, competence, and favour. Behavioural outputs can be classified into positive and negative behaviours. Individuals with positive behaviour will attain better performance (Wilkinson et al., 1986). On the other hand, individuals with negative behaviour will achieve lower performance (Hultman, 1988).

Table 1. Inputs and outputs of performance (Hultman, 1988)

| Inputs | Attributes | Behavioural Outputs | |
		Positive Aspects	*Negative Aspects*
Commitment	Values	Motivated to pursue success (drives past fear, deciding, choosing, embracing, persevering, initiating, affirming)	Motivated to avoid failure (succumbs to fear by running away)
Confidence	Beliefs	Rational, logical, reasonable (positive self-talk, thinks of reasons to try)	Irrational, illogical (unreasonable, negative self-talk, thinks of reason to not try or to give up)
Competence	Present/ Absent	Successful (performs effectively, keeps trying)	Unsuccessful (performs ineffectively, gives up or doesn't try)
Contingency	Favour	Supportive (cooperating, sharing, forgiving, helping accepting, forgiving)	Divisive (gets even by arguing, blaming, criticizing, condemning, retaliating, sabotaging)

"Lack of commitment is caused by subconscious value conflicts or problems in sorting out what one really considers to be important. Similarly the reasons for lack of confidence often are deeply rooted, and counseling may be needed to help people turn irrational fears into rational beliefs" (Kreps, 1997). Unfavorable contingencies are a reflection of company values that should be reassessed or policies modified (Kreps, 1997; Igbaria et al, 1996; Wiley, 1997).

Studies of behavioral outputs have generally theorized two mechanisms, extrinsic and intrinsic motivation (Deci, 1975; Venkatesh & Smith, 1999; Vellerand et al., 1992). The extrinsic supports (e.g., rewards) enhance feelings of individuals' competence or self-efficacy; this may increase intrinsic motivation (Vellerand, 1997). Further, when extrinsic supports cause individuals to attribute their behaviour to external rather than internal sources, rewards may possibly decrease intrinsic motivation (Deci, 1975; Deci et al., 1999a, 1999b). Previous studies have considered intervening motivation, perceived competence, commitment, contingency and confidence as causes of performance (Deci, 1975; Hultman, 1988; Venkatesh & Smith, 1999).

In fact, Rotter (1966) generalized that expectations regarding internal or external locus of control may influence process attributes that affect task performance. Locus of control suggests the extent to which individuals believe that their fate is controlled by external factors or by themselves. Individuals with a strong external locus of control (they believe their fate is controlled by others) exert less effort and achieve lower performance than those with strong internal locus of control (i.e., they believe they control their own fate) (Anderson, 1977).

Mitchell (1974, 1979, 1982) also indicated that the need for individual achievements is associated with task performance. The need for individual achievements is the extent to which the individual values success (McClelland, 1961; Mitchell, 1974, 1979, 1982; Porter & Lawler, 1968).

Meeting Process Factors

Meeting process has been treated as a black box in the software review literature. Factors impacting on review performance are still open to question. Since no empirical study was found in the software literature and the meeting process involves a small group (review) meeting, this section will employ small group literature to elaborate the software review meeting process.

In the small group literature, it is suggested that an effective group should have common goals, share time amongst group members, share group influence evenly, be willing to disagree and let each member have a personal say, and listen and build on ideas (Dick & Hearn, 1988; Hare, 1962; Huang, 2003; Huang & Wei, 2000; Huang, Wei, & Lin, 2003; Huang, Wei, Watson, & Tan, 2003; Jessup & Valacich, 1993; Littlepage, Robison, & Reddington, 1997; Worchel, Wood, & Simpson, 1992). The critical factors that affect group-meeting performance in the small group literature can be classified into communication, teamwork, status effects and discussion quality (Davison, 1997; Huang, 1999; Huang & Li, 1999; Huang, Raman, & Wei, 1993a, 1993b; Huang, Teo, Tan, & Wei, 1994; Huang, Wei, & Xi, 1997; Huang, Wei, & Tan, 1997; 2001; Morris, 1966; Preston, 1983; Shaw, 1932; Terry, Callan, & Sartori, 1996; Tyran & George, 2002; Worchel et al., 1992).

Communications

Different communication mediums have different levels of richness of information transfer (Harmon, Schneer, & Hoffman, 1995; Huang, 1998; Huang, 2003; Huang & Lai, 2001; Huang, Watson, & Wei, 1998; Huang, Wei, Watson, & Lim, 1998; Jonassen, 2001; Trevino, Daft, & Lengel, 1990). For instance, face-to-face communication has the highest richness of information transfer of any communication medium (Trevino et al., 1990; Vitharana & Ramamurthy, 2003). On the other hand, noise can reduce the effectiveness and efficiency of communication, resulting in decreases in-group performance. Such noise includes physical distractions (e.g., physical distance), absence of feedback, semantic problems (i.e., decoding and encoding errors) and status effects (i.e., power and status of different group members) (Davison, 1997; Simon, 1973; Tyran & George, 2002; Vroom, 1964).

Further, "languages used in the meeting, ease of understanding and self-expression; and willingness to communicate ideas to others" (Davison, 1997; Jonassen, 2001) are indicators that help to evaluate the effectiveness of communication. Effective communications can achieve better group performance (Seaman & Basili, 1998).

Teamwork

Teamwork refers to the ability and willingness to work with others, information sharing and conflict resolution (Davison, 1997; Huang & Li, 1999; Huang, Wei, Bostrom, Lim, & Watson, 1998; Sauer et al., 2000). Vroom (1964) claimed that the higher the support from group members, the higher the performance of the group. Cohesiveness is an important factor influencing group members' support. Cohesiveness means members are "involved in a group" and have the "desire to remain in it" (Vecchio et al., 1992). Since this creates a sense of belonging to the group and strong attraction, it has been suggested that high cohesion can attain better group member support and higher performance (Homans, 1950).

Further, Yatts and Hyten (1998) reported that "trust" among group members can increase group members' support. They defined trust as "the belief that even though you have no control over another person's behaviour toward you, that person will behave in a way that benefits you" (Diehl & Stroebe, 1987). On the other hand, group support might diminish when competitive conflicts occur, where competitive conflict refers to the disagreement among group members vigorously defending their respective positions and attempting to win over others (Diehl & Stroebe, 1987).

Status Effect

Status effect refers to "attempts by some participants to intimidate others either verbally or non-verbally, use of influence, status or power to force views on others, to inhibit others from participating in the meeting through their behaviour, and pressuring others to conform to a particular view" (Davison, 1997). One of the major reasons for poor process performance is the status effect. The lower-status members are unwilling to criticise the higher-status member because of:

- "A fear of negative evaluation and reprisals, resulting in evaluation apprehension" (Diehl & Stroebe, 1987).

- Plurality effect, when the high status members make a decision not agreed among the group. The result of agreement, usually based on majority, would be identified and accepted.

The status effect results in intimidation, which can diminish the group members' performance. Intimidation can be measured by apprehension (Diehl & Stroebe, 1987) and conformance (Davison, 1997).

Discussion Quality

Discussion quality is affected by the meaningfulness, appropriateness, openness, and creativity of the meeting (Davison, 1997; Nemeth & Wachtler, 1983). The notion of perception is important in discussion quality. If group members do not perceive a high quality of discussion, then poor outcomes (outputs) are likely to result. Davison (1997) suggested the "generation of novel, creative solutions or ideas is vital because it promotes a reappraisal of the situation. Creative ideas do not come only from individuals; small team of individuals may form to suggest, or at least support, the creation of ideas" (Davison, 1997; Worchel et al., 1992).

Review Performance

Measurement of review performance can be based on quality, (i.e. number of defects found) (Basili, et al., 1996; Fagan, 1976, 1986; Perry, Porter, Wade, Votta, & Perpich, 2002; Porter & Votta, 1998; Shull, Lanubile, & Biasili, 2000). Task performance is determined by the combined ability and skills of individuals that comprise the group. There are four possible outcomes of defect (error) detection as shown in Figure 3. These include (Anderson & Gerbing, 1984; Fagan, 1976; Klein, Goodhue, & Davis, 1997; Rizzo, 1968; Swets, Tanner, & Birdsall, 1961):

- hit (defect exists and is successfully detected),
- miss (defect exists but is not detected),
- false positive (defect does not exist but is wrongly identified),
-   correct rejection (defect does not exist and is not identified),

Figure 3. Possible outcomes of defect detection

Behaviour

		Defect detected	Defect not detected
Defect	Defect exist	Hit	Missed
	Defect does not exist	False positive	Correct rejection

The probability of results in each of these cells is determined by the performance of individuals and the interaction between those individuals in a group (Baker & Schuck, 1975; Klein et al., 1997; Swets & Birdsall, 1967).

Campbell's theory shows an important relationship between data and human behaviour on defect detection. The group performance is measured by the productivity, minus the losses from group processes, plus the gains from group processes (see Equation 3) (Campell, 1990; Swets & Birdsall, 1967).

Equation 3. Group performance

Group performance =

productivity – losses due to group process + gains from group process

Process gain in the context of software reviews refers to defects first found during the group (review) meeting while process loss refers to defects found during individual preparation, but not reported in the group (review) meeting. The effectiveness of group review performance is measured by the differences between process gain and process loss (Porter & Votta, 1994).

Propositions and Hypotheses

This section presents a number of research hypotheses developed from the EIIO model.

Explicit Inputs

Task Characteristics

The behavioural literature strongly supports the notion of task characteristics determining process and performance. Laitenberger and DeBaud's study (2000) found that the life-cycle of the artefact (product), the size of the product, the complexity of the product and the initial qualities of the artefact affected the number of defects detected. The EIIO model also suggests that task (software artefact) characteristics affect the use of inputs and how software reviews should be organized and conducted.

The current software review literature lacks evidence of how the effectiveness of inputs used (e.g., supporting documents) is affected by software artefact characteristics. Therefore, the following is formally proposed:

Proposition 1a: Task characteristics affect review performance.

Proposition 1b: Task characteristics affect review process.

Proposition 1c: Task characteristics affect the use of inputs.

Supporting Documents

The supporting documents constructs include four major categories: reading technique documents, prescription documents, previously reviewed software documents, and reports. Reading technique documents are currently considered one of the most effective ways to improve software review performance (Basili, Laitenberger, Shull, & Rus, 2000). The basic objective of reading techniques is to help reviewers systematically look for defects in a software artefact (Dunsmore, Roper, & Wood, 2003).

Such techniques include checklists, stepwise-based reading and scenarios-based (or perspectives-based) reading approach and are common in practice and important to review performance (Basili et al., 1996; Basili, Shull, & Lanubile, 1999; Biffl & Halling, 2003; Parnas & Weiss, 1985; Wiegers, 2002). Prescriptions documents are a set of documents that are used in a software review process. These often include guidelines, defect types standards, templates, time record logs, and review training material (IEEE Standard 1028, 1998). In relation to previously reviewed software documents, it has been suggested that previously reviewed software documents are critical to a project's success (Chechik & Gannon, 2001; Hofmann & Lehner, 2001; Xu, 2003; Zhu, Jin, Diaper, & Ganghong, 2002).

Reports and standards are often required in a review process, especially in the planning, organizing and preparation stages (IEEE Standard 1028, 1998). These documents often give a broad idea of the review objectives as well as the business functions and requirements (Wiegers, 2002).

The behavioural literature does not present explicit evidence that supporting documents can improve review performance. However, software review studies have empirically proved that the lack of supporting documents will decrease group performance (Basili, 1997; Laitenberger & Emam, 2001; Porter & Votta, 1994). For instance, practitioners reported (Davis, 1982) that the problem of the absence of requirement documents in the later stages of software development could result in project failure. Further, behavioural literature places a high value on implicit inputs (e.g., motivation). However, the current software review literature does not address the relationships between supporting documents and individual characteristics (i.e., experience and motivation). For instance, what types of supporting documents can improve individual motivation to achieve better review process and performance? As a result, the following is proposed:

Proposition 2a: Supporting documents affect review performance.

Proposition 2b: Supporting documents affect review process.

Proposition 2c: Implicit inputs (individual characteristics) affect the use of supporting documents.

Implicit Inputs

Individual Abilities and Skills

In relation to implicit inputs (individual characteristics), two types of individual characteristics are classified in the EIIO model — abilities and skills, and motivation and effort.

Sauer et al. (2000) claim that "expertise" is a key driver of group performance in software reviews. Improved defect detection performance can be achieved by increasing individual members' task experience, the size of the group, appropriate training and/or varying member selection (Sauer et al., 2000).

Further, Laitenberger and DeBaud's causal model (2000) also confirms that employing an experienced and skilled reviewer can increase the number of defects detected. Many studies emphasize that reviewers should have domain knowledge (e.g., reviewers should have knowledge of fuzzy logic in data modeling when they review fuzzy logic data modeling design documents) (Chen, Yan, & Kerre, 2003; 2002; Chen, Ying, & Cai, 1999; Chen, Kerre, & Vandenbulcke, 1994, 1995, 1996) and experience (e.g., experience of software review (role experience)) (Fagan, 1986). Task expertise is the key driver for achieving the highest performance (Laitenberger & Debaud, 2000). Researchers suggest that experience is critical to review performance (Basili, Shull, & Lanubile, 1999; Kauppinen & Kujala, 2001; Nelson & Cooprider, 2001; Philp & Garner, 2001). Experience in the context of software review can be classified into 1) role experience and 2) working experience in the software industry.

Role experience is defined as the experience gained by performing a similar task (i.e., software review), as long as the experience is relevant to the task. Working experience is defined as any experience gained in the software industry.

The EIIO model theorizes that inputs not only affect the review performance, but also affect review process. Based on this assumption of an important relationship between input-process and outcome, the following is proposed:

Proposition 3a: Reviewers experience affects review performance.

Proposition 3b: Reviewers experience affects review process.

Motivation

To assess an individual's abilities, a simple question can be asked: are you able to do it? Past experience is a good indicator of future behaviour (Alavi & Leidner, 2001; Campell, 1990; Deci, 1975; Deci, Koestner, & Ryan, 1999b). Most companies employ competent individuals with tangible evidence of success and competencies (Ashkanasy, Widerom, & Peterson, 2000; Ericsson, 1994; Ericsson & Delaney, 1999). Competent performance can produce positive working attitudes, reinforcing commitment and confidence (Arnold, 1985; Igbaria et al., 1996; Pate, 1978). The behavioural literature states that a competent person is able to perform a task in an effective way and is able to do it well (Campell & Pritchard 1976; Charness et al., 1993; Littlepage et al., 1997). On the other hand, confidence affects individual behaviour in performing a task (Deci & Ryan, 1987; Venkatesh & Smith, 1999). Lack of confidence leads to task avoidance as individuals seek to protect their self-esteem and this results in decreased individual performance (Hoffman, 1995).

Psychological theory also suggests that commitment is directly related to individuals' values, where the process of choosing among alternatives and consequences affects every action (Chi et al., 1982; Ericsson & Lehmann, 1996; Venkatesh & Smith, 1999). When individuals perceive a task is important to them, they will be willing to increase their effort to attain better performance (Kreps, 1997; Maslow, 1943; McAuley, Duncan, & Tammen, 1987).

Another motivation factor is company support, also known as contingency. Contingency is concerned largely with individuals' perception of company support (Cadle & Yeates, 2001; Kreps, 1997; Shamir, 1991; Vellerand, 1997; Vroom, 1964). Availability and location of material and human resources, such as money, time, equipment, supplies, and training are important to the individuals' perceived support (Bushnell, 1990; Gless, 1999; Humphrey, 2000; Vellerand, 1992). High contingency leads to positive behaviour and a resulting higher performance (Wilkinson, 1986).

In the context of software review, it has been suggested that reviewers increasing their level of effort results in higher performance (Boehm & Basili, 2001). This statement is consistent with Porter and Votta's (1994) contention that the more effort a reviewer is willing to expend on finding defects, the higher the defect detection rate that can be achieved.

Empirical studies in behavioural literature show that motivation and effort affects performance (Campell, 1990; Venkatesh & Smith, 1999). Boehm and Basili (2001) support the notion that motivation and effort can improve individual performance as well as review process. Therefore, propositions 4a and 4b:

Proposition 4a: Motivation affects review performance.

Proposition 4b: Motivation affects review process.

Process

In relation to software review meeting process, though there are no published empirical studies investigating how the defect detection process affects performance, process gains and process losses do occur during the group (review) meeting; however, how or why they occur is often treated as a "black box". Major factors such as communication, teamwork, quality of discussions, and status effect are important in software review performance (Davison, 1997; Dick & Hearn, 1988; Ginac, 2000; Hollenbeck, Ilgen, Lepine, Colquitt, & Hedlund, 1998; Huang, 2001; Huang & Wei, 1997; Humphrey, 2000; Petersson, 2001).

Communication is the major element of group interaction. Without good communication skills, process loss is likely to occur (Jonassen, 2001; Vitharana & Ramamurthy, 2003). In any meeting, communication is an important factor for an effective team meeting process (D'Astous & Robillard, 2002; Huang & Lai, 2001; Huang et al., 1996; 1997; 2001; Seaman & Basili, 1998; Trevino et al., 1990). Evidence suggests that effectively communicating teams can achieve higher team outcomes (Crowther, 2001; Gless, 1999; Williams & Kessler, 2000). Communication is a two way process between team members (i.e., a sender sends a message or idea to a receiver and the receiver(s) reply with an acknowledgment or provide feedback to the sender) (Huang, 1998; Jonassen, 2001; Macdonald, 1999). This process could be one to one, one to many, or many to many (Crowther, 2001). A successful communication team should be: understanding of the use of language, able to express and understand the ideas or concepts being used, and willing to communicate with other team members (Davison, 1997; Jonassen, 2001). As a result, the composite measures of the communication construct include: the language used in the meeting; ease of understanding and self-expression; and willingness to communicate ideas to others (Anderson et al., 2003; Davison, 1997).

The status effect is another factor in the group (review) meeting process, which can affect group performance (Diehl & Stroebe, 1987; Greenbaum, Kaplan, & Metlay, 1988; Worchel et al., 1992). The status effect is defined as some team members using their power or status to influence and/ or pressure others to agree or behave in such ways as they want. This is also called influence behaviour (Cronbach, 1970; Huang & Wei, 2000; Huang et al., 1993a; Yetton et al., 1983). Process loss often occurs when this influence behaviour takes place in a meeting discussion (Ashkanasy et al., 2000; Bushnell, 1990).

Several authors have stated that process losses are due to (Davison, 1997):

- The unwillingness of a lower-status member to criticize the opinions of a high-status member, due to a fear of negative evaluation and reprisals, resulting in evaluation apprehension (Diehl & Stroebe, 1987; Shamir, 1991).
- The tendency of lower-status members to conform to an expected standard or to the standard of higher-status members (Mitchell, 1982; Shaw, 1932).
- The low participation of low-status group members in the discussion process, resulting in 'cognitive inertia' where the line of argument taken by the group will probably adhere to that which the high-status members wish (Ashkanasy et al., 2000; Baker et al., 1975).

In a meeting process, intimidation is the most closely related factor to evaluation apprehension and conformance (Davison, 1997; Mitchell, 1982; Shaw, 1932).

Such influence behaviours may be associated with high-status influence. Intimidation results in the reluctance of team members to participate effectively in meetings (Davison, 1997; Dick & Hearn, 1988). Higher-status members may use their powers to influence the lower-status members participating during the discussions. The notion of perception is vital. If individuals perceive themselves as high-status, then they would expect to exert related influence (Ashkanasy et al., 2000; Cronbach & Show, 1977; Hare, 1962). This is also known as inhibitive behaviour. To be considered a successful team, the key element is the interaction among the team members (Dick & Hearn, 1988; Ginac, 2000; Huang et al., 2001; Humphrey, 2002). Such interactions are discussed in terms of the underlying meeting process (e.g., willingness to work in a team rather than independently, working alone without any interaction, and working with other members) (Cronbach & Show, 1977; Kreps, 1997; Morris, 1966).

The notion of willingness refers to members being able to access information during meeting discussions when they need to (Davison, 1997; Humphrey, 2002). Willingness also involves the responsiveness level of team members (Humphrey, 2000; Yatts & Hyten, 1998). It is suggested that the better the communication of a team, the more likely it is that successful teamwork can be achieved (Dick & Hearn, 1988; Ginac, 2000; Humphrey, 2002). If members are able to communicate in an effective way this also creates a sense of belonging and provides a positive atmosphere for the working environment (Humphrey, 2000; Jonassen, 2001; Seaman & Basili, 1998). This also creates process gains as time during meeting discussions is used in an effective and efficient way (Boomsma, 1983; Porter & Votta, 1998; Yetton et al., 1983). The willingness of participants to respond to questions and to share information can also provide process gains (Harmon et al., 1995).

As a result, the ability to work in a team results in higher performance being achieved (Hacker & Kleiner, 1999; Humphrey, 2002). Group members' perception of the quality of discussions results in higher performance being achieved (Littlepage et al., 1997; Yetton & Bottger, 1983).

Successful meeting process requires openness and a familiar atmosphere and a meaningful and appropriate manner of discussion (Davison, 1997). Meaningful discussion is important, since it promotes a reappraisal of the situation (Nemeth & Wachtler, 1983). Also, openness of communication and a familiar atmosphere allow team members to generate high quality and meaningful comments during the meeting process (Nemeth & Wachtler, 1983; Pressman, 1996). Therefore, proposition 5 is formulated:

Proposition 5: Meeting process affects review performance.

Discussions of the
Theoretical EIIO Model

The purpose of the EIIO model is to describe the important relationships between input, process, and output in the software review process. From the current software review literature, the strong evidence has been presented supporting the theoretical EIIO model.

Task characteristics are the primary focus before other input selection. Hence the nature of different software artefacts may require different inputs for successful defect detection. Laitenburger and Debaud (2000) showed that task characteristics affect how software reviews should be organized.

National Aeronautics and Space Administration (NASA, 1993) and Gilb and Graham (1993) also documented how to organize a review using supporting documents. Recent studies in software review mainly focus on reading techniques. The studies found that reading techniques can improve the number of defects found significantly (Basili et al., 1996; Porter & Votta, 1994).

Some studies also indicate that reviewers' ability and skills could be critical inputs affecting review performance. For instance, Sauer et al. (2000) noted that task expertise affects review performance. Although there is no empirical evidence to support that reviewer effort affects review performance, a number of researchers in software review believe that increasing the amount of effort would increase the defects found (Boehm & Basili, 2001; Laitenberger & DeBaud, 2000; Yetton & Bottger, 1983). Software review process is mostly treated as a black box. Whether software review meeting processes affect output is still an open question.

The behavioural literature explicitly supports process factors affecting outputs. Such factors (i.e., communication, teamwork, discussion quality, and status effect) may potentially affect the number of defects found.

Figure 4 shows the relationship of the research propositions in the theoretical EIIO model. Note that the relationship of input selection is task-determined (i.e., the characteristics of the software artefact affect what inputs should be used).

Supporting Documents: Reports, Prescription
Documents and Reading Technique Documents

The outputs may best be understood through the impact of individuals' ability and skills, motivation and effort, explicit inputs, and meeting process factors. The analysis of explicit and implicit inputs provides additional diagnostic help when

Figure 4. Relationships of propositions in the EIIO model

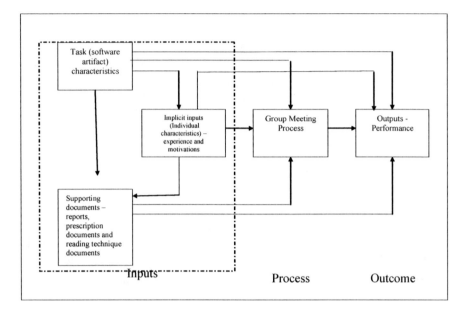

analysing review performance. For example, it is possible to look for difficulties associated with group member's motivation and effort, and to also consider whether the inputs of members with different skills equally impact outputs.

In addition, the proposal is made that task characteristics may influence communication, teamwork, discussion quality, and status effect, and may determine capabilities individual required. Group members' experience affects individual members' motivation levels by influencing beliefs about the outputs. The quality of interaction experiences may change the perception of group success.

The theoretical EIIO model is derived from the IPO model from the behavioural literature. It serves to guide the development of a set of hypotheses to advance our understanding of review performance, i.e. the input-process-output relationship. It is suggested that future research in software review could move in three possible directions, to empirically validate the following. First, given the importance of the reviewers' characteristics, the important elements of selecting reviewers can be identified. For instance, studies should identify reviewers' skills and ability vs. quantitative outcomes (defects found).

Second, further studies should examine reviewer motivation. For example, it is possible to identify the important factors affecting reviewers' motivation and effort by conducting empirical studies. Third, further investigation into how the group processes affect software review performance should be undertaken.

The importance of the EIIO model resides in providing a broader view of software review performance than those provided in the existing review literature. The EIIO model provides a good framework for developing a sound theory to drive empirical research in software review. It also provides a different perspective to the existing literature and helps to facilitate understanding of the input-process-output relationship in software review.

To date, there has been no published empirical evidence regarding the relationships between explicit and implicit inputs and how these inputs affect review outcomes. Laboratory studies have mainly manipulated a small number of inputs that are an incomplete representation of the various inputs necessary for the effective review of a software artefact. As a result, the need to understand how these inputs affect process and outputs is important.

The traditional input-process-output (IPO) model of group performance was used to develop a conceptual EIIO model, which helped to gain a better understanding of the relationships between inputs, process and outputs. From the EIIO model, a series of hypotheses relating to the EIIO model were designed. Possible further research directions of software review will be discussed in the next section. However, one of the limitations of current empirical studies is that they are only focused on outcomes (i.e., review performance). The relationship between inputs and process are critical. Hence, selection of inputs directly affects the process gains and losses, which also influence outcomes. It is interesting and important to understand the relationships between inputs and process. As a result, hypothesis formulation has considered the relationship between inputs and process.

In summary, this study is especially concerned to determine *what* the key inputs are and process factor(s) that significantly influence review outcome(s) in a typical software review. The objectives of this research are as follows:

1.   To validate the important relationships between implicit and explicit inputs.
2.   To validate the important relationships between inputs and process.
3.   To validate the important relationships between process and outcomes.
4.   To validate the important relationships between input, process and outcomes.

Figure 5. Hypotheses summary in the EIIO model

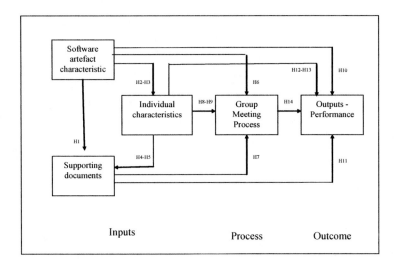

Table 2. Research questions and hypotheses

Questions	Hypotheses
Effect on inputs	
1. Do software artifact characteristics affect the use of supporting documents?	H1 Software artefact characteristics have an effect on the use of supporting documents.
2. Do software artifact characteristics affect implicit inputs?	H2 Software artefact characteristics have an effect on reviewer experience required.
	H3 Software artefact characteristics have an effect on motivation.
3. Do implicit inputs affect the use of supporting documents?	H4 Experience has an effect on the use of supporting documents.
	H5 Motivation has an effect on the use of supporting documents.
Effect on meeting process	
4. Do software artifact characteristics affect meeting process?	H6 Software artefact characteristics have an effect on meeting process (i.e., communication, discussion quality, status effect and teamwork).
5. Does the use of supporting documents affect meeting process?	H7 Use of supporting documents has an effect on meeting process.
6. Do implicit inputs affect meeting process?	H8 Experience has an effect on meeting process
	H9 Motivation has an effect on meeting process

continued on following page

Table 2. cont.

Questions	Hypotheses
Effect on review performance	
7. Do software artifact characteristics affect review performance?	H10 Software artefact characteristics have an effect on software review performance
8. Does the use of supporting documents affect review outcomes?	H11 Use of supporting documents has an effect on software review performance
9. Do implicit inputs affect review performance?	H12 Experience has an effect on software review performance
	H13 Motivation has an effect on software review performance
10. Do meeting process factors affect review performance?	H14 Meeting process has an effect on software review performance

Figure 5 and Table 2 illustrate the 14 hypotheses from the extended propositions of the EIIO model.

Summary

In this chapter, a theoretical Explicit and Implicit Input-process-Output (EIIO) model was developed for analysing software review performance. The chapter also defines the constructs the three concepts of inputs, process, and outcomes, a set of hypotheses positing the nature of the relationships among the model constructs was proposed. An industry survey plan will be developed and discussed in next chapter.

References

Ackerman, F. A., Buchwald, L. S., & Lewski F. H. (1989, May). Software inspection: An effective verification process. *IEEE Software*, 31-36.

Adam, J. S. (1965). Injustice in social exchange. In Berkowitz (Ed.), *Advances in experimental social psychology* (No. 2). New York: Academic Press.

Alavi, M., & Leidner, D. E. (2001). Review: Knowledge management and knowledge management systems: Conceptual foundations and research issues. *MIS Quarterly, 25*(1), 107-136.

Anderson, C. (1977, February). Locus of control, coping behaviours, and performance in stress setting. *Journal of Applied Psychology, 62*(1), 446-451.

Andersen, P. B. (1990). *A theory of computer semiotics: Semiotic approaches to construction and assessment of computer systems.* Cambridge, UK: Cambridge University Press.

Anderson, J. C., & Gerbing, D. W. (1984). The effect of sampling error on convergence, improper solutions, and goodness-of-fit indices for maximum likelihood confirmatory factory analyses. *Psychometrician, 49*, 155-173.

Anderson, P., Reps, T., & Teitelbaum, T. (2003). Design and implementation of a fine-grained software inspection tool. *IEEE Transaction on Software Engineering*, 721-733.

ANSI/IEEE. (1989). An American national standard. *IEEE Standards for Software Reviews and Audits, ANSI/IEEE Standard, 1028-1998.*

Arnold, H. (1985). Task performance, perceived competence, and attributed causes of performance as determinants of intrinsic motivation. *Academy of Management Journal, 28*(4), 876-888.

Ashkanasy, N. M., Widerom, C. P. M., & Peterson, M. F. (2000). *Handbook of organisational culture and climate.* CA: Saga.

Baker, D., Ravichandran, R., & Randall, D. (1989, Winter). Exploring contrasting formulations of expectancy theory. *Decision Sciences, 20*(1), 1-13.

Baker, E. M., & Schuck, J. R. (1975). Theoretical note: Use of signal detection theory to clarify problems of evaluating performance in industry. *Organisational Behaviour and Human Performance*, (13), 307-317.

Basili, V. R. (1997). Evolving and packaging reading technologies (Special Issue). *The Journal of Systems and Software, 38*(1), 3-12.

Basili, V. R., Green, S., Laitenberger, O., Lanubile, F., Sorumgard, S., & Zelkowitz, M. (1996). The empirical investigation of perspective-based reading. *International Journal on Empirical Software Engineering, 1*(12), 133-144.

Basili, V. R., Laitenberger, O., Shull, F., & Rus, I. (2000). Improving software inspections by using reading techniques. *Proceedings of the International Conference on Software Engineering* (pp. 836-727).

Basili, V. R., Shull, F., & Lanubile, F. (1999). Building knowledge through families of experiments. *IEEE Transactions on Software Engineering, 25*(4).

Biederman, I., & Shffrar, M. M. (1983). Sexing day-old chicks: A case study and expert systems analysis of a difficult perceptual-learning task. *Journal of Expert Psychology Learning Memory Cogn.,* (13), 640-45.

Biffl, S., & Halling, M. (2003, May). Investigating the defect detection effectiveness and cost benefit of nominal inspection team. *IEEE Transaction on Software Engineering, 29*(5), 385-397.

Bloom, B. S. (1985). Generalizations about talent development. In B. S. Bloom (Ed.), *Developing talent in young people* (pp. 507-549). New York: Plenum.

Boehm, B. W., & Basili, B. R. (2001, January). Software defect reduction top 10 list. *IEEE Computer, 34*(1).

Boomsma, A. (1983). On the robustness of LISREL (Maximum Likelihood Estimation) against small sample size and non-normality. *Socio-Metric Research Foundation,* Amsterdam.

Brodbeck, F. C., & Greitemeyer, T. (2000). Effects of individual vs. mixed individual and group experience in rule induction on group member learning and group performance. *Journal of Experimental Social Psychology, 36*(6), 621-648.

Bushnell, D. S. (1990, March). Input, process, output: A model for evaluating training. *Training and Development Journal,* 41-43.

Butler, J., & Womer, K. (1985, July). Hierarchical vs. non-nested tests for contracting expectancy-valance models: Some effects of cognitive characteristics. *Multivariate Behavioural Research, 20*(3), 335-352.

Cadle, J., & Yeates, D. (2001). *Project management for information systems* (3rd ed.). Harlow,UK: Prentice Hall.

Campell, J. P. (1990). Modeling the performance prediction problem in industrial and organizational psychology. In M. D. Dunnette & L. M. Hough (Eds.), *Handbook of industrial and organizational psychology* (pp. 687-732) (2nd ed.) Palo Alto, CA: Consulting Psychologists Press Inc.

Campell, J. P., & Pritchard, R. D. (1976). Motivation theory in industrial and organizational psychology. In M .D. Dunnette (Ed.), *Handbook of industrial and organizational psychology* (pp. 63-130) (2nd ed.). Chicago: Rand Mcnally College Publishing Company.

Charness, N., Krampe R. T., & Mayr, U. (1993). The importance of coaching in *entrepreneurial skill domains:* An international comparison of life-span chess skill acquisition. Presented at *Conference Acquisition Expert Performance,* Wakulla Springs, FL.

Chase, W. G., & Simon, H. A. (1973). The mind's eye in chess. In W. G. Chase (Ed.), *Visual information processing* (pp. 215-281). New York: Academic.

Chechik, M., & Gannon, J. (2001, July). Automatic analysis of consistency between requirement and design. *IEEE Transaction on Software Engineering, 27*(7), 651-672.

Chen, G. Q., Kerre, E. E., & Vandenbulcke, J. (1994). A computational algorithm for the FFD closure and a complete axiomatization of Fuzzy Functional Dependency (FFD). *International Journal of Intelligent Systems, 9*, 421-439.

Chen, G. Q., Kerre, E. E., & Vandenbulcke, J. (1995). The dependency-preserving decomposition and a testing algorithm in a fuzzy relational data model. *Fuzzy Sets and Systems, 72*, 27-37.

Chen, G. Q., Kerre, E. E., & Vandenbulcke, J. (1996). Normalization based on fuzzy functional dependency in a fuzzy relational data model. *Information Systems, 21*(3), 299-310.

Chen, G. Q., Yan, P., & Kerre, E. E. (2003). Mining fuzzy implication-based association rules in quantitative databases. *International Journal of General Systems*.

Chen, G. Q., Ying, M. S., & Cai, K. Y. (1999, September). Fuzzy logic and software computing. *The Kluwer International Series on Asian Studies in Computer and Information Science, 6*, 321.

Chernak, Y. (1996, December). A statistical approach to the inspection checklist formal syntheses and improvement. *IEEE Transactions on Software Engineering, 22*(12).

Chi, M. T. H., Glaser, R., & Rees, E. (1982). Expertise in problem solving. In R. S. Steinberg (Ed.), *Advances in the psychology of human intelligence, 1*(75). Hillsdale, NJ: Erlbaum.

Cooke. (1994). Varieties of knowledge elicitation techniques. *International Journal Jum-Computer Study, 41*, 801-49.

Cronbach, L. J. (1970). *Essentials of psychological testing* (3rd ed.). New York: Irvington.

Cronbach, L. J., & Show R. E. (1977). *Aptitudes and instructional methods: A handbook for research on interactions*. New York: Irvington.

Crowther, G. (2001). Face-to-face or e-mail: The medium makes a difference. *Communication World, 18*(5), 23-27.

Crutcher, R. J., & Ericssion, K. A. (2000). The role of mediators in memory retrieval as a function of practice: Controlled mediation to direct access. *Journal of Experimental Psychology, Learning, Memory and Cognition*.

D'Astous, P., & Robillard, P. N. (2000). Characterizing implicit information during peer review meeting. *Proceedings of the International Conference on Software Engineering* (pp. 460-466).

Davenport, T. H., & Short, J. E. (1990). The new industrial engineering: Information technology and business process redesign. *Sloan Management Review, 31*(4), 11-27.

Davis, G. B. (1982). Strategies for information requirements determination. *IBM System Journal, 21*(1), 3-30.

Davison, R. (1997). Instrument for measuring meeting success. *Information and Management, 32*, 163-176.

De Groot, A. D. (1946). *Thought and choice and chess*. Mouton, The Netherlands: The Hague.

Deci, E. L. (1975). *Intrinsic motivation*. New York: Plenum Press.

Deci, E. L., Koestner, R., & Ryan, R. M. (1999a). A meta-analytic review of experiment examining the effect of extrinsic reviewed on intrinsic motivation. *Psychological Bulletin, 125*, 627-668.

Deci, E. L., Koestner, R., & Ryan, R. M. (1999b). The undermining effect is reality after all: Extrinsic rewards, task interest, and self-determination. *Psychological Bulletin, 125*, 629-700.

Deci, E. L., & Ryan, R. M. (1987). The support of autonomy and control of behaviour. *Journal of Personality and Social Psychology, 53*(6), 1024-1037.

Dick, R., & Hearn, G. (1988). Enjoying effective teamwork. Brisbane: *QIT and Interchange*.

Diehl, M., & Stroebe, W. (1987). Productivity loss in brainstorming groups: Towards the solution of a riddle. *Journal of Personality and Social Psychology, 53*, 497-509.

Dunsmore, A., Roper, M., & Wood, M. (2003). The development and evaluation of three diverse techniques for object-oriented code inspection. *IEEE Transactions on Software Engineering, 29*(8).

Engelkamp, J., & Wippich, W. (1995). Current issues in implicit and explicit memory. *The International Journal of Perception, Cognition, and Action, 57*(3-4), 143-155.

Ericsson, K. A. (1994). Analysis of memory performance in terms of memory skill advances. In R. J. Sternberg (Ed.), *The Psychology of Human Intelligence* (pp. 137-179). Hillsdale, NJ: Erlbaum.

Ericsson, K. A., & Delaney, P. F. (1999). Long-term working memory as an alternative to capacity models of working memory in everyday skilled performance. In A. Miyake & P. Shah, (Eds.), *Models of working memory: Mechanisms of active maintenance and executive control* (pp. 157-297). Cambridge: Cambridge University Press.

Ericsson, K. A., Krampe, R. T., & Tesch-Tomer, C. (1993). The role of deliberate practice in the acquisition of expert performance. *Psychology Review, 100*(3), 363-406.

Ericsson, K. A., & Lehmann, A. C. (1996). Expert and exceptional performance: Evidence of maximal adaptation to task constraints. *Psychology Review, 47*, 273-305.

Ericsson, K. A., & Smith, J. (1991). *Toward a general theory of expertise: Prospects and limits.* New York: Cambridge.

Fagan, M. E. (1976). Design and code inspections to reduce errors in program development. *IBM System Journal, 15*(3), 182-211.

Fagan, M. E. (1986, July). Advances in software inspections. *IEEE Transaction on Software Engineering, 12*(7).

Ferris, K. R. (1977, July). A test of the expectancy theory of motivation in an accounting environment. *The Accounting Review, 52*(3), 605-615.

Fetzer, J. H. (1988). Aspects of artificial intelligence. *Studies in Cognitive Systems, 1*, 385.

Fetzer, J. H. (1990). Artificial intelligence: Its scope and limits. *Studies in Cognitive Systems, 4*, 338.

Fitts, P., & Poser, M. I. (1967). The cognition of discovery: Defining a historical problem. *College Computing Communication, 31*, 21-32

Frankfort-Nachmias, C., & Nachmias, D. (1996). *Research methods in the social sciences* (5th ed.). New York: St. Martin's.

Franz, L. A., & Ship, J. C. (1994). Estimating the value of inspections and early testing for software project. *Hewlett-Packard Journal*, CS-TR-6.

Freedman, D. P., & Weinberg, G. M. (1990). *Handbook of walkthroughs, inspections, and technical review: Evaluating programs, projects, and products* (3rd ed.). Dorest House Publishing.

Fusaro, P., Lanubile, F., & Visaggio, G. (1997). A replicated experiment to assess requirements inspection techniques. *International Journal on Empirical Software Engineering, 2*(1), 39-58.

Galton, F. (1969). *Hereditary genius: An inquiry into its laws and consequences.* London: Friedman.

Gilb, T., & Graham, D. (1993). *Software inspection.* Harlow, UK: Addison-Wesley.

Ginac, F. P. (2000). *Creating high performance software development teams*. London: Prentice Hall.

Gless, R. L. (1999). Evolving a new theory of project success. *Communications of the ACM, 45*(11), 7.

Gough, P. A, Fodemski, F. T., Higgins, S. A., & Ray, S. J. (1995). Scenarios: An industrial case study and hypermedia enhancements. *Proceedings of the 2nd IEEE International Symposium on Requirements Engineering* (pp. 10-17).

Greenbaum, H. H., Kaplan, I. T., & Metlay, W. (1988). Evaluation of problem-solving groups: the case of quality circle program. *Group and Organization Studies, 13*(2), 133-147.

Hacker, M. E., & Kleiner, B. M. (1999). A study of the effects of procedural structure and anonymity on process improvement work groups. *Engineering Management Journal, 11*(4), 26-30.

Hammer, M. (1980, July-August). Reengineering work: Don't automate, obliterate. *Harvard Business Review,* 104-112.

Harmon, J., Schneer, J. A., & Hoffman, L. R. (1995). Electronic meeting and established decision groups: audio conferencing effects on performance and structural stability. *Organizational Behaviour and Human Decision Processes, 61*(2), 138-147.

Hare, A. P. (1962). *Handbook of small group research*. New York: Free Press of Glencoe.

Harrell, A. M., Caldwell, C., & Duty, E. (1985, October). Within-person expectancy theory predictions of accounting students' motivation to achieve academic success. The *Accounting Review, 60*(4), 724-735.

Harrell, A. M., & Stahl, M. J. (1984, Winter). Modeling managers' effort-level decisions for a within-persons examination of expectancy theory in a budget setting. *Decision Sciences, 15*(1), 52-73.

Herold, D. M. (1979). Group effectiveness of work groups. In S. Kerr (Ed.), *Organizational behaviour*. Columbus, OH: Grid Publishing.

Hoffman, R. R. (1987). The problem of extracting the knowledge of experts. *The Perspective of Experimental Psychology, 8*(2), 53-67.

Hoffman, R. R. (1995). Eliciting knowledge from experts: a methodological analysis, organisational behaviour. *Human Decision Process, 62,* 129-58.

Hofmann, H. F., & Lehner, F. (2001, July/August). Requirements engineering as a success factor in software project. *IEEE Software,* 58-66.

Hollenbeck, J. R., Ilgen, D. R., Lepine, J. A., Colquitt, J. A., & Hedlund, J. (1998). Extending the multilevel theory of team decision making: Effects of feedback and experience in hierarchical teams. *Academy of Management Journal, 41*(3), 269-282.

Homans, G. C. (1950). *The human group. Brace and World*. New York: Harcourt.

Huang, W. (1998, July). Re-examination of media richness theory: A case of using a lean email medium for rich communication. *Proceedings of the 3rd International Conference on Management,* Shanghai, China.

Huang, W. (1999, June 23-25). Exploring the fit between GSS generic structures and task types in small group decision making meetings. *Proceedings of the 7th European Conference on Information Systems (ECIS'99),* Denmark (pp. 330-347).

Huang, W. (2001, June). An empirical investigation of effects of GSS and goal-setting on virtual teams. *Proceedings of the 2001 International Group Decision & Negotiation Conference,* France.

Huang, W. (2003). Impacts of GSS generic structures and task types on group communication process and outcome: Some expected and unexpected research findings. *Behaviour and Information Technology, 22,* 17-29.

Huang, W., & Lai, V. (2001, January). Can GSS groups make better decisions and feel good at the same time? A longitudinal study of asynchronous GSS groups. *Proceedings of the 34th Hawaii International Conference on System Sciences*

Huang, W., & Li, X. (1999, June 9-12). A conceptual design of a GSS virtual environment for team-building. *Proceedings of Asia Pacific Decision Sciences Institute Conferences* (pp. 392-394). Shanghai, China.

Huang, W., Raman, K. S., & Wei, K. K. (1993a). A process study of the effects of GSS and task type on small groups. In D. R. Vogel, P. H. Marshall, B. C. Classon, & A. A. Verrijn-Stuart (Eds.), *Local area network applications: Leveraging the LAN*. Amsterdam: North-Holland.

Huang, W., Raman, K. S., & Wei, K. K. (1993b). A process study of the effects of GSS and task type on informational and normative influence in small groups. *Proceedings of the 14th International Conference on Information Systems, (ICIS'93)* (pp. 91-101). Florida.

Huang, W., Raman, K. S., & Wei, K. K. (1997, September). Impact of GSS and task type on social influence in small groups. *IEEE Transactions on Systems, Man, and Cybernetics, 27*(5), 578-587.

Huang, W., Teo, H. H., Tan, B., & Wei, K. K. (1994, July 19-22.). Group Support Systems (GSS): History, theories and applications. *Proceedings of the 1st Conference on Management Science for Domestic and Overseas Young Scientists* (pp. 188-195). Beijing, P.R. China.

Huang, W., Tan, C. Y. B., & Wei, K. K. (2001, June). Opening up the black box in GSS research: Explaining group decision outcomes with group processes. *Proceedings of the 2001 International Group Decision & Negotiation Conference,* France.

Huang, W., Watson, R. T., & Wei, K. K. (1998). Can a lean email medium be used for rich communication? A psychological perspective. *European Journal of Information Systems, 7,* 269-274.

Huang, W., & Wei, K. K. (1997). Task as a moderator for the effects of group support systems on group influence processes. *European Journal of Information Systems,* (6), 208-217.

Huang, W., & Wei, K. K. (2000, Fall). An empirical investigation of effects of GSS and task type on social interactions from an influence perspective. *Journal of Management Information Systems (JMIS), 17*(2), 181-206.

Huang, W., Wei, K. K., Bostrom, B., Lim, L. H., & Watson, R. T. (1998, January). Support distributed team-building using GSS: A dialogue theory-based framework. *The Proceedings of 31ˢᵗ Hawaii International Conference on System Sciences (HICSS-98)* (pp. 98-107).

Huang, W., Wei, K. K., & Lin, J. (2003, January-March). Using GSS to support global virtual team-building: A theoretical framework. *International Journal of Global Information Management 11*(1), 72-89.

Huang, W., Wei, K. K., & Tan, B. (1997, January). Why does GSS fail to enhance consensus and satisfaction: An investigation from an influence process perspective? *The Proceedings of the 30ᵗʰ Hawaii International Conference on System Sciences (HICSS'97).*

Huang, W., Wei, K. K., Watson, R. T., & Lim, L. H. (1998, October). Using a GSS to support virtual team-building: An empirical study. *The Proceedings of the Decision Sciences Institute Annual Meeting (DSI'98).* Las Vegas.

Huang, W., Wei, K. K., Watson, R. T., & Tan, C. Y. (2003). Supporting virtual team-building with a GSS: An empirical investigation. *Decision Support Systems, 34*(4), 359-367.

Huang, W., Wei, K. K., Watson, R. T., Bostrom, B., & Lim, L. H. (1996, December). Transforming a lean CMC medium into a rich one: An empirical investigation in small groups. *The Proceedings of the 17ᵗʰ International Conference on Information Systems (ICIS'96)* (pp. 265-277).

Huang, W., Wei, K. K., & Xi, Y. M. (1997, April). An investigation of the effects of GSS and task on group influence behavior. *Proceedings of the Pacific Asia Conference on Information Systems (PACIS'97)* (pp. 203-212).

Hultman, K. E. (1988, July). *The Psychology of Performance Management Training and Development Journal, 121*, 34-39.

Humphrey, W. S. (2000). *Introduction to the team software process*. Boston: Addison-Wesley.

Humphrey, W. S. (2002). *Winning with software: An executive strategy, How to transform your software group into a competitive asset*. Boston: Addison-Wesley.

IEEE Standard 1028. (1998). Software Engineering Standard Committee of the IEEE Computer Society, *IEEE Standard 1028*. IEEE Standard for Software Review, Institute of Electrical and Electronics Engineers Inc., New York.

Igbaria, M., Parasuraman, S., & Baroudi, J. J. (1996). A motivational model of microcomputer usage. *Journal of Management Information Systems, 13*(1), 127-143.

Jessup, L. M., & Valacich, J. S. (1993). *Group support systems: New perspectives*. New York: Macmillan.

Jonassen, D. H. (2001). Communication patterns in computer mediated vs. face-to-face group problem solving. *Educational Technology Research and Development, 49*(1), 35.

Kauppinen, M., & Kujala, S. (2001, September). Starting improvement of requirement engineering processes: An experience report. 3rd *International Conference on Product Focused Software Process Improvement (PROFES)* (pp. 197-209). Germany.

Kelly, J. C., Sherif, J. S., & Hops, J. (1992). An analysis of defect densities found during software inspection. *Journal on Systems Software*, (17), 111-117.

Kerr, S. (1979). *Organizational behaviour*. OH: Grid Publishing.

Kirkpatrick, D. L. (1967). Evaluation of training. In R. L. Craig & L. R. Bittel (Eds.), *Training and development handbook* (pp. 87-112). New York: McGraw-Hall.

Klein, B. D., Goodhue, D. L., & Davis, G. B. (1997, June). Can human detect errors in data? Impact of base rates, incentives, and goals. *MIS Quarterly*, 169-194.

Kotonya, G., & Sommerville, I. (1998). *Requirements engineering*. UK: Wiley.

Kreps, D. M. (1997, May). Intrinsic motivation and extrinsic incentives. *The Interaction Between Norms and Economic Incentives*, 359-364.

Laitenberger, O., Beil, T., & Schwinn, T. (2002). An industrial case study to examine a non-traditional inspection implementation for requirement specifications. *Proceedings of the 8th IEEE Symposium on Software Metrics (Metrics '02)*.

Laitenberger, O., & Debaud, J. M. (2000). An encompassing life cycle centric survey of software inspection. *The Journal of Software and Systems, 50*(1), 5-31.

Laitenberger, O., & Emam, K. E. (2001). An Internally replicated quasi-experimental comparison of checklist and perspective-based reading of code documents. *IEEE Transactions of Software Engineering, 27*(5), 378-421.

Lee, D. M. S., Trauth, E. M., & Farwell, D. (1995, September). Critical skills and knowledge requirements of professionals: A joint academic/industry investigation. *MIS Quarterly,* 313-340.

Littlepage, G., Robison, W., & Reddington, K. (1997). Effects of task experience and group experience on group performance, member ability, and recognition of expertise. *Organizational Behaviour and Human Decision Processes, 69*(2), 133-147.

London, M. (1989). *Managing the training enterprise: High-quality, cost-effective employee training in organizations.* San Francisco: Jossey-Bass.

Marr, D. (1982). *Vision.* Freeman and Co.

Maslow, G. S. (1943). Theory of human motivation. *Psychological Review, 50,* 370-96.

McAuley, E., Duncan, T., & Tammen, V. V. (1987). Psychometric properties of the intrinsic motivation inventory in a competitive sport setting: A confirmatory factor analysis. *Research Quarterly for Exercise and Sport, 60,* 48-58.

McClelland, D. (1961). *The achieving society.* New York: Van Nostrand.

Mecklenbrauker, S. (1995). Input- and output-monitoring in implicit and explicit memory. *The International Journal of Perception, Cognition, and Action, 57*(3-4), 179-191.

Meystel, A. (1999, September 15-17). Multiresolutional semeiotic systems. *Proceedings of the IEEE International Symposium on Intelligent Control/Intelligent Systems and Semiotics.* Cambridge, MA.

Mitchell, T. (1974, December). Expectancy models of job satisfaction, occupational preference and effort: A theoretical, methodological, and empirical appraisal. *Psychological Bulletin, 81*(12), 1053-1077.

Mitchell, T. (1979). Organizational behaviour. *Annual Review of Psychology,* (30), 243-281.

Mitchell, T. (1982). Expectancy-value models in organizational psychology. In N. Feather (Ed.), *Expectations and actions: Expectancy-value models in psychology.* Hillsdale, NJ: Lawrence Erlbaum Associates.

Mitchell, T., & Beach, L. (1977). Expectancy theory, decision theory, and occupational preference and choice. In M. F. Kaplan & S. Schwartz (Eds.), *Human judgment and decision processes in applied settings* (pp. 203-226). New York: Academic Press.

Morris, C. G. (1966). Task effects on group interaction. *Journal of Personality and Social Psychology, 4*(5), 545-554.

National Aeronautics and Space Administration (NASA) (1993). *Software Formal Inspection Guidebook, NASA-GB-A302.*

Nelson, D. L., & Xu, J. (1995). Effects of implicit memory on explicit recall: Set size and word-frequency effects. *An International Journal of Perception, Cognition, and Action, 57*(3-4), 215-219.

Nelson, K. R., & Cooprider, J. G. (2001). The relationship of software system flexibility to software system and team performance. *The 22nd International Conference on Information Systems* (pp. 23-32).

Nelson, R. R. (1991, December). Educational needs as perceived by is and end-user personnel: A survey of knowledge and skill requirements. *MIS Quarterly, 15*(4), 502-525.

Nemeth, C. J., & Wachtler, J. (1983). Creative problem solving as a result of majority vs. minority influence. *European Journal of Social Psychology, 13*, 45-55.

Newell, A., & Simon, H. A. (1976). Computer science as empirical inquiry: Symbols and search. *Communications of the ACM, 19*(3), 113-126.

Nonaka, I., & Takeuchi, H. (1995). *The knowledge-creating company: How Japanese companies create the dynamics of innovation.* Oxford: Oxford University Press.

Nyberg, L., & Nilsson, L. G. (1995). The role of enactment in implicit and explicit memory. *An International Journal of Perception, Cognition, and Action, 57*(3-4), 203-214.

Parnas, D. L., & Weiss, D. M. (1985, August 28-30). Active design reviews: Principles and practices. *Proceeding of ICSE'85* (pp. 132-136). London: IEEE Computer Society.

Pate, L. E. (1978, July). Cognitive Vs. reinforcement views of intrinsic motivation. *Academy of Management Review,* 505-514.

Perry, D. E., Porter, A., Wade, M. W., Votta, L. G., & Perpich, J. (2002). Reducing inspection interval in large-scale software development. *IEEE Transaction on Software Engineering, 28*(7), 695-705.

Petersson, H., (2001, August 27-28). Individual reviewer contribution to the effectiveness of software inspection teams. *Proceedings of Australian Software Engineering Conference* (pp. 160-168).

Philp, B. A., & Garner, B. J. (2001, August 27-28). Knowledge mediation in software quality engineering. *Proceedings of Australian Software Engineering Conference* (pp. 153-159).

Plant, R. W., & Ryan, R. M. (1985). Intrinsic motivation and the effects of self-consciousness, self-awareness, and ego-involvement: An investigation of internally-controlling styles. *Journal of Personality, 53*, 435-449.

Polanyi, M. (1966). The logic of tacit inference. *The Journal of the Royal Institute of Philosophy,* XLI (155), 1-18.

Popper, K.R. (1961). *The logic of scientific discovery.* New York: Science Editions, p. 106.

Porter, A. A., & Votta, L. G. (1994). An experiment to asses different defect detection methods for software requirements inspections. *Proceedings of the 16th International Conference on Software Engineering, Icse-16* (pp. 103-112).

Porter, A. A., & Votta, L. (1998). Comparing defection methods for software requirements inspection: A replication using professional subjects. *Journal of Empirical Software Engineering, 3*, 355-379.

Porter, A. A., Votta, L. G., & Basili, B. (1995). Comparing detection ,methods for software requirements inspection: A replicated experiment. *IEEE Transaction on Software Engineering, 21*(6), 563-575.

Porter, L., & Lawler, E. (1968). *Managerial attitude and performance.* Homewood, IL: Irwin-Dorsey.

Pressman, R. (1996). *Software engineering: A practitioners approach.* McGraw Hill.

Preston, M. G. (1983). Note on the reliability and validity of the group judgement. *Journal of Experimental Psychology, 22*, 462-471.

Rizzo, A. (1968). Human error detection process. In E. Hollnagel, G. Mancini, & D. D Wood (Eds.), *Cognitive engineering in complex dynamic worlds* (pp. 99-114). London: Academic Press.

Roediger, H. L. (1990). Implicit memory: Retention without remembering. *American Psychologist, 45*, 1043-1056.

Roediger, H. L., & Mcdermott, K. B. (1993). Implicit memory in normal human subjects. In F. Boller & J. Grafman (Eds.), *Handbook of neurophysiology* (pp. 63-131). Amsterdam: Elsevier.

Rotter, J. (1966). Generalized expectancies for internal vs. external control of reinforcement. *Psychological Monographs, 80*(1), 1-27.

Russell, G. W. (1991, January). Experience with inspection in ultralarge-scale development. *IEEE Software, 8*(1).

Sauer, C., Jeffery, R., Land, L., & Yetton, P. (2000). Understanding and improving the effectiveness of software development technical reviews: A behaviourally motivated programme of research. *IEEE Transactions on Software Engineering, 26*(1), 1-14.

Seaman, C. B., & Basili, V. R. (1998, July). Communication and organization: An empirical study of discussion in inspection meetings. *IEEE Transaction on Software Engineering, 24*(6), 559-572.

Shamir, B. (1991). Meaning, self and motivation in organizations. *Organisation Studies, 12*(3), 405-424.

Shaw, M. E. (1932). A comparison of individuals and small groups in the rational solution of complex problems. *American Journal of Psychology, 44*, 491-504.

Shull, F., Lanubile, F., & Biasili, V. (2000, November). Investigating reading techniques for object-oriented framework learning. *IEEE Transaction on Software Engineering, 26*(11).

Shull, F., Rus, I., & Basili, V. (2000, July). How perspective-based reading can improve requirements inspection? *IEEE Computer*, 73-79.

Simon, H. A. (1977). Artificial intelligence systems that understand. *Proceedings of the 5th International Joint Conference on Artificial Intelligence, 2* (pp. 1059-1073).

Simon, H. A., & Chase, W. G. (1973). Skill in chess. *American Society, 61*, 394-403.

Simonton, D. K. (1988). *Scientific genius: A psychology of science.* Cambridge: Cambridge University Press.

Snead, K., Jr., & Narrell, A. M. (1990). *An application of expectancy theory to examine managers' motivation to utilize a decision support system.* Unpublished working paper.

Strauss, S. H., & Ebenau, R. G. (1994). *Software inspection process.* McGraw-Hill.

Swets, J. A., & Birdsall, T. G. (1967). Deferred decision in human signal detection: A preliminary experiment. *Perception and Psychophysics, 2*, 15-28.

Swets, J. A, Tanner, W. P., & Birdsall T. G. (1961). Decision processes in perception. *Psychological Review, 68*, 301-340.

Terry, D. J., Callan, V. J., & Sartori, G. (1996). Employee adjustment to an organisational merger: Stress, coping and inter group differences. *Stress Medicine, 12*, 105-122.

Trevino, L., Daft, & Lengel (1990). Understanding managers' media choice. In J. Fulk & C. Steinfield (Eds.), *Organizational and communication technology*. Newbury Park, CA: Sage.

Tyran, C. K., & George J. F. (2002). Improving software inspection with group process support. *Communication of the ACM, 45*(9), 97-92.

Yatts, D. E., & Hyten, C. (1998). *High-performance self-managed work team*. Thousand Oaks, CA: Saga.

Vecchio, R. P., Hearn, G., & Southey, G. (1992). *Organizational behaviour: Lift at work in Australia* (1ˢᵗ Australian ed.) Sydney: HBJ.

Vellerand, R. J. (1997). Toward a hierarchical model of intrinsic and extrinsic motivation. *Advances in Experimental Social Psychology*, (27), 271-360.

Venkatesh, V., & Smith, R. (1999). Creation of favorable user perceptions: Exploring the role of intrinsic motivation. *MIS Quarterly*.

Vitharana, P., & Ramamurthy, K. (2003, February). Computer-mediated group support, anonymity, and the software inspection process: An empirical investigation. *IEEE Transactions on Software Engineering, 29*(2), 167-180.

Vliet, H. V. (2000). *Software engineering*. Chester: Wiley.

Vroom, V. (1964). *Work & motivation*. New York: Wiley.

Wiegers, K. E. (2002). *Peer reviews in software: A practical guide*. Boston: Addison-Wesley.

Wild, T. C., Enzle, M. E., Nix, G., & Deci, E. L. (1997). Perceiving others as intrinsically or extrinsically motivated: Effects on expectancy formation and task engagement. *Advances in Experimental Social Psychology, 23*(8), 837-848.

Wiley, C. (1997). What motivates employees according to over 40 years of motivation surveys. *The International Journal of Manpower, 18*(3), 263-280.

Wilkinson, H. E., Orth, C. D., & Benfari, R. C. (1986). Motivation theories: An integrated operational model. *Advanced Management Journal, 51*(4), 24-31.

Will, H. (2004, July 19-20). Semiotic information systems: Cognitive, methdological, organizational, and technological criteria. *The 7ᵗʰ International Workshop on Organizational Semiotics*. Setúbal, Portugal.

Will, H., & Whobrey, D. (2003). The assurance paradigm and organisational semiotics: A new application domain. *Proceedings of IWOS Conference*.

Williams, L. A., & Kessler, R. R. (2000). All i really need to know about pair programming I learned in kindergarten. *Communication of the ACM, 43*(5), 108-114.

Worchel, S., Wood, W., & Simpson, J. A. (1992). *Group process and productivity*. Newbury Park, CA: Sage.

Yetton, P. W., & Bottger, P. C. (1983). The relationship among group size, member ability, social decision schemes, and performance. *Organizational Behaviour and Human Performance, 32*, 145-159.

Xu, J. (2003, August). On inspection and verification of software with timing requirement. *IEEE Transaction on Software Engineering, 29*(8), 705-720.

Zadeh, L. A. (1987). *Fuzzy sets and applications*. John Wiley & Son.

Zhu, H., Jin, L., Diaper, D., & Ganghong, B. (2002). Software requirements validation via task analysis. *The Journal of Systems and Software, 61*, 145-169.

Zmud, R. W. (1983). *Information systems in organisations*. Tucker, GA: Scott, Foresman and Company.

Chapter VII

Industry Software Reviews Survey Design

Abstract

Chapters five and six described the theoretical EIIO model; this chapter mainly focuses on industry survey design. The first section describes the research methodology and survey used to gather, collate, and analyse data for the study. After presenting the rationale for the research design, including the questionnaire design, measurement scales, and models. The chapter explores issues of validation and reliability, such as cross sectional research and construct operationalisation. The chapter concludes with a discussion of the data collection method and the analytical procedures used in the study.

Industry Survey of Software Reviews

This chapter presents the empirical research method for validating the EIIO model. The details of research method, survey design, measurements (constructs) developments, data collection and data analysis procedures are discussed in details in the following sections.

Research Method

The research method employed is a quantitative survey method. Quantitative surveys attempt to achieve a representative sample and to estimate from the data the characteristics exhibited by the general population (Babbie, 2000; Churchill, 1991; Hancock & Flowers, 2001; Hartog & Herbert, 1986; Judd, Smith, & Kidder, 1991; Pinsonneault & Kraemer, 1993; Salant & Dillman, 1994).

Questionnaire-based surveys for quantitative hypothesis testing are widely used (Babbie, 1973; Babbie, 2000; Creswell, 1994; Newman, 1994). The most common form of survey research method is cross-sectional survey design (Alreck & Settle, 1995; Barker, 1999; De Vaus, 2001). This approach involves observation taken from cross sectional samples of the target population (Australian Bureau of Statistics, 1999; Hyman, 1955; Lazar & Preece, 1999). This survey data can then be used to describe sub-populations of the survey frame and predict patterns for the general population (Fink, 1995a; Hammersley, 1992; Salant & Dillman, 1994).

The survey methodology employed in this study seeks to quantify the data and applies statistical analysis (Bagozzi, 1994a; Barker, 1999; Frankfort-Nachmias & Nachmias, 1996; McNeil, 2001). Quantification of the data in this way will provide a large representative sample, with results that should accurately reflect the characteristics of the population being surveyed (allowing for a margin of error) (Light, 1971; Malhotra, Hall, Shaw, & Crisp, 1996). This analysis should reveal whether apparent differences are statistically significant (McNeil, 2001; Tull & Hawkins, 1990).

The nature of the data observed can be assessed appropriately through measurement with relations between dependent and independent variables made explicit (Kelloway, 1995; Naylor & Enticknap, 1981). Analytical procedures designed to assess the significance of variance in the survey data can be employed to establish tests for reliability and validity (Keesling, 1972; Lyttkens, 1973; Preston, 1983). The study will use principal component factor analysis, convergent, and discriminant analysis for this purpose.

Evidence has shown that the use of self-reporting surveys is predominant in cross-sectional survey research (Coakes & Steed, 2001; Joreskog, 1989; Lyttkens, 1966; Rahim, Antonioni, & Psenicka, 2001). This represents a common approach to correlation research (Areskoug, 1982; Ozer, 1985). Correlation and regression methods to examine the predictive relationships between dependent and independent variables will also be investigated (Fink, 1995a; Judd et al., 1991; Ozer, 1985).

In an attempt to identify the critical factors that affect software review performance in practice, the most appropriate research method is the cross-sectional survey (Alreck & Settle, 1995; Churchill, 1979; Ferber, 1974). There are several benefits of using a survey method in this study. First, it provides an exploratory view (Brown, 1980; Fink, 1995a) that allows the identification of software inputs commonly used by software practitioners.

Though many researchers have identified the possible explicit inputs (e.g., checklists) that should be used in software review, the question of what are the most critical inputs and/or factors affecting software review performance is still open. This study will identify the common types of software review inputs adopted by the software industry. Second, this also helps practitioners and researchers have a better understanding of the key process factors that affect software review in *practice*. This survey presents an overview of the current use of software review and investigates relationships between input, process, and outcome of software review.

Survey Design

The most important considerations affecting survey design are the time issue and resource availability (Forrest, 1999; Furrer & Sudharshan, 2001; McCullough, 1998). There is always a trade-off between these two factors and the amount of data collection (Hancock & Flowers, 2001; Sheatsley, 1974; Sudman, 1994). One of the objectives of cross-sectional design is to explain industry character-istics (e.g., estimate certain numbers of people in a population who behave in certain way) (Australian Bureau of Statistics, 1999; De Vaus, 2001; Ferber, 1974; Malhotra et al., 1996; Sheatsley, 1974).

To ensure sufficient variance in the data (Fink, 1995a), a random sample was selected from Business Who's Who of Australia (2001) that includes companies from six states and two territories in Australia (i.e., New South Wales (NSW), Victoria (VIC), Queensland (QLD), South Australia (SA), Western Australia (WA), Tasmania (TAS), Australia Capital Territory (ACT), and Northern Territory (NT)). The data collected from the heterogeneous sample will not only incorporate the required variance for testing the hypothesised relationships, but also capture the diversity in the software review inputs, processes, and outcome, thereby enhancing the generalisability of the findings.

Questionnaire Design

Questionnaire design is based on the results of hypothesis design (Brog, Gall, & Gall, 1993; Denzin & Lincoln, 1995; Fink, 1995b; Hyman, 1955). The questionnaire design was adopted from several materials (instruments) (e.g., Australian Bureau of Statistics, 2000; Australian Computer Society, 2003; Davison, 1997; Deci, 2000; Lee, Forthofer, & Lorimor, 1989) with some modifications and pretests. There are mainly close-ended questions such as multiple choice and scaling questions in the final questionnaire (Bordens & Abbott, 2002; Creswell, 1994; Fink, 1995b, 1995c, 1995d). In order to increase the response rate and collect reliable factual data, several critical design issues were incorporated in the questionnaire survey (Bagozzi, 1994b; De Vaus, 2002; Fink, 1995c; Kish, 1965; Salant & Dillman).

The questionnaire was presented in the form of a four-page booklet and was printed on both sides to make it less bulky (Kinnear & James, 1996). The first page of the questionnaire included a cover letter to the respondents explaining the nature of the survey (Fink, 1995c). The 19 questions in the questionnaire were evenly distributed over seven pages and one page of instruction so that the questionnaire had a lot of blank space, did not appear too dense, and appealed to the respondents (Bagozzi, 1994a; Fink, 1995c).

All questions were easy to answer, with the multiple-choice questions that required a respondent to choose among a few categories (Bagozzi, 1994a; Kraemer, 1991; McCullough, 1998; Smith, 1998). In the instruction to the respondents it was clearly stated (Fink, 1995c) that any publication of the study results would present information in aggregate form and such information would be anonymous and un-attributable to individual organisations or individual respondents (Kanuk & Berenson, 1975; Kinnear & James, 1996). A copy of the questionnaire is included in Appendix 1.

Measurements

In the software review literature, there is no study that tests the proposed model using multiple indicators (items) to measure constructs. To adequately measure these constructs, new indicators were developed using the literature to develop a theoretical model and modified from four stages of pre-tests (e.g., pilot studies) (Barker, 1999; Bordens & Abbott, 2002; Boudreau, Gefen, & Straub, 2001).

Details of the measures used to operationalize the constructs in the proposed model and the measurement scales will be discussed in the following sections.

Reflective vs. Formative Measures

The measurement design uses multiple indicators (items) to attain higher reliability and validity for each theoretical construct. One of the underlying assumptions in the Structural Equation Modeling (SEM) analysis is that the indicators used to measure a construct (or latent variable (LV)) can be reflective or formative based (Areskoug, 1982; Chin, 1998a, 1998b; Joreskog, 1973; Rahim et al., 2001; Wert, Linn, & Joreskog, 1974) (see Figure 1).

Reflective measures reflect an existing latent variable (or unobservable construct) (Chin, 1998b; Chin, 2003). These measures are also known as effect indicators since they show the effects of the latent variable (Chin, Gopal, & Salisbury, 1997). On the other hand, formative measures examine factors that cause the creation of or change in a latent variable (Bollen, 1984, 1989). Formative indicators form or create an emergent latent (or unobservable) construct (also known as cause measures in the SEM analysis) (Bollen, 1984). As shown in Figure 1, for the formative indicators (F1, F2, F3, and F4), the arrows point in the opposite direction, whereas in the case of reflective indicator (R1, R2, R3, and R4), the arrows point from the existing latent construct to the observed indicators.

The decision to design the model indicators as formative is based on two important criteria (Chin & Newsted, 1996). First, the indicators of a construct should not be highly correlated with each other in theoretical or empirical ways (Bollen, 1989; Chin & Gopal, 1995; Kelloway, 1995; Wiley, 1973).

Figure 1. Reflective vs. formative indicators

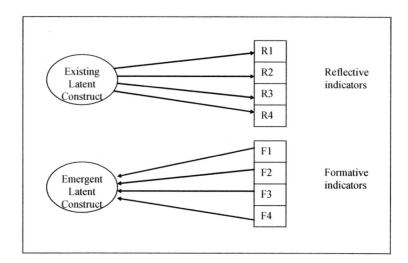

Second, formative indicators are viewed as the cause variables that provide the condition under which the construct they connote may be formed (Chin, 1998a; Rahim et al., 2001). It should be conceptually argued that the measures do not reflect the latent construct (Chin, 2003; Kelloway, 1995). If these two conditions are met, it will be more appropriate to model the indicator as formative (Chin, 1998b).

However, Chin (1998b) suggested that if the indicators are modeled as formative, it is important that "the indicators are relatively independent of one another, that is, there are no multi-collinearity problems, and the sample size is large enough". Moreover, "the formative modeling option may be moot if the estimates are not stable, and the lack of multi-collinearity is important if the researcher is concerned with understanding the formative process of the latent variable" (Chin, 1988b). Because the observed formative indicators cause the latent construct, examination of internal consistency is considered to be inappropriate (Bollen, 1984). This is because that there is no internal consistency measure required for formative measures, however, it is important to have a large number of formative measures to ensure that the domain of the construct being measured is adequately tapped (Bollen, 1989).

The rationale for measuring the constructs in this study with reflective or formative indicators is discussed in next section.

Explicit Inputs

From the theoretical aspect, all explicit input constructs (software artefact characteristics, supporting documents, (reading technique documents, prescription documents, previously reviewed software documents, and reports)) are regarded as measured with formative indicators, since the indicators are not theoretically correlated (Basili et al., 1996; Gilb & Graham, 1993; IEEE Standard 1028, 1998; Laitenberger & Debaud, 2000; Porter & Votta, 1994; Thelin, Runeson, & Regnell, 2001; Wiegers, 2002).

An example of the observed indicators is provided in Table 2 — complexity, size, and initial quality are examples of valid and reliable indictors of artefact characteristics. In this case, the characteristics of the artefacts represent a construct that emerges from these indicators. The complexity of software artefacts is not necessarily correlated to the initial quality or/and size of the artefact. A similar situation applies with all supporting documents; formative indicators are also used accordingly.

Table 1 shows that a total of 16 indicators are measured for the explicit input constructs which include:

Table 1. Formative indicators-explicit inputs

Constructs	Indicators/items	Questions	Scales	Reflective (R)/ Formative (F)
Software artefact characteristics (SAC)	Complexity (CX)	On average, the artefact that I review are complex	Disagree vs. agree	F
	Size (SZ)	On average, the size of the artefacts that I review is large		F
	Initial quality (IQ)	On average, the initial quality of the artefacts that I review is poor		F
Reading technique documents (RTD)	Checklist (CK)	What are the common supporting documents you used in software review?	Not common at all vs. very common	F
	Stepwise reading (ST)			F
	Scenarios/ perspective reading technique (SR)			F

Constructs	Indicators/ items	Questions	Scales	Reflective (R)/ Formative (F)
Prescription documents (PSD)	Procedure guidelines (PG)	What are the common supporting documents you used in software review?	Not common at all vs very common	F
	Template (TE)			F
	Time record form (RF)			F
	Training material (TA)			F
	Defect form (FR)			F
Previously reviewed software documents (PRD)	Design (DE)	What are the common supporting documents you used in software review?	Not common at all vs very common	F
	Requirement (RQ)			F
	Code (CD)			F
Reports (RPO)	Business report (BR)	What are the common supporting documents you used in software review?	Not common at all vs very common	F
	Standards (SS)			F

- Software artefact characteristics — complexity, size, and initial quality
- Reading technique documents — checklist, stepwise, and scenarios
- Prescription documents — procedure guidelines, templates, time record forms, training materials, and defect forms
- Previously reviewed software documents — requirements, design, and code
- Reports — business reports and standards within the domain application

Implicit Inputs

In relation to implicit inputs, the experience construct does satisfy the two important criteria for formative indicators, in that: 1) the measures are causes of the latent constructs and 2) the measures are not correlated (Chin, 1998b, 2003). The experience construct is also operationalised as formative and is measured with the indicators described in Table 2. Two indicators were used for the experience construct: role experience and working experience in the software industry (Sauer, Jeffery, Land, & Yetton, 2000).

On the other hand, the four motivation constructs (commitment, confidence, competence, and contingency) are regarded as measured with reflective indicators, since these indicators are likely to be highly inter-correlated, according to Deci et al. (1999a, 1999b, 1994, 1987, 1980, 1975). Each construct encompasses two or three indicators.

As shown in Table 2, the 14 measurement indicators of five implicit constructs are:

Table 2. Formative vs. reflective indicators-implicit inputs

Constructs	Indicators/items	Questions	Scales	Reflective (R)/ Formative (F)
Experience (EXP)	Role experience (software review experience) (RE)	How many years do you have in the following items?	None, 1–10, 11–20, 21–30, 31 or more years	F
	Working experience in software industry (IND)			F
Competency (CPT)	Effective approach (ET)	I can find defects in an effective way	Disagree vs agree	R
	Do things well (DW)	I do well in software reviews		R
	Perceived capability (CA)	I believe I can find all the defects		R

continued on following page

Table 2. cont.

Constructs	Indicators/Items	Questions	Scales	Reflective (R)/ Formative (F)
Commitment (CMM)	Willingness (WL)	I am willing to participate in software reviews	Disagree vs agree	R
	Motivation (MT)	I am motivated to participate in software reviews		R
	Effort (EF)	I put a lot of effort into finding defects		R
Confidence (CFD)	Confident in capability (CP)	I am confident that I am capable of finding defects	Disagree vs agree	R
	Confident in doing better (CB)	I am confident that I can find more defects than other team members		R
	Confident in teaching (CT)	I am confident that I can teach my defect detection skills to others		R
Contingency (CTG)	Agree (AR)	I agree with the way my company conducts software reviews	Disagree vs agree	R
	Support (SP)	I participate in software reviews because I have support from my company		R
	Encouragement (EC)	I participate in software reviews because my company encourages us to do so		R

- Experience — role experience and working experience
- Competency — effective approach, do things well and perceived capability
- Commitment — willingness, motivation and effort
- Confidence — confident in capability, confident in to teach others, and perform better than others
- Contingency — agreement, support, and encouragement

Process

The meeting process is measured in the questionnaire with four constructs (discussion quality, communication, status effect, and teamwork) in which the questionnaire design was adopted from Davison (1997) with some modifications. As shown in Table 3, each construct is measured with three to four indicators.

A total of fifteen indicators were measured for four meeting process constructs. Since all the indicator levels and the construct level measures can theoretically and empirically have high positive inter-correlations, all constructs are considered to be reflective indicators (Davison, 1997).

Table 3. Reflective indicators-process

Constructs	Indicators/ items	Questions	Scales	Reflective (R)/ Formative (F)
Communication (CMU)	Language (LA)	The language of the meetings prevents me from participating	Disagree vs. agree	R
	Expression (EP)	I experience problems expressing myself		R
	Understanding (UD)	I find it hard to understand other group members when they talk in the meetings		R
	Putting ideas forward (RF)	I feel reluctant to put forward my own ideas		R
Status effects (STE)	Power (SE)	Some group members try to use their influence, status or power to force their opinions on the other group members	Disagree vs. agree	R
	Pressure (PR)	I experience pressure, either to conform to a particular viewpoint or not to contradict others		R
	Intimidation (ID)	Some group members try to intimidate others, e.g. by talking loudly, using aggressive gestures, making threats, etc.		R
	Inhibition (IB)	I feel inhibited from participating in decision-making because of the behaviour of other meeting members		R

continued on following page

According to Table 3, the measurement indicators of the four meeting process constructs include:

- Discussion quality — meaningless vs. meaningful; inappropriate vs. appropriate; closed vs. open environment setting; familiarity vs. creativity
- Communication — language, putting ideas forward, expression, and understanding
- Status effects — power, pressure, intimidation, and inhibition
- Teamwork — working together, sharing information, and willingness

Table 3. cont.

Constructs	Indicators/ items	Questions	Scales	Reflective (R)/ Formative (F)
Teamwork (TEA)	Team (TM)	Members work together as a team	Disagree vs. agree	R
	Sharing (SH)	Members have sufficient access to the information they need to participate actively in and fully understand the meeting		R
	Willingness to participate (WP)	Other members appear willing to answer questions when asked		R
Discussion quality (DSQ)	Meaning (ME)	On average, considering all meeting members as a whole, how would you rate the discussions in the review meetings in terms of the following scales?	totally meaningless vs. very meaningful	R
	Appropriate (AP)		Totally Inappropriate vs. very appropriate	R
	Close (CO)		Totally closed/ restricted vs. very open	R
	Familiar (FI)		Familiar approaches used vs. creative approaches used	R

Performance

Designing the measurement of the performance construct in the EIIO model involves three important issues: primary vs. secondary measures, objective vs. subjective measures, and absolute vs. relative measures (Ackoff, 1953; Babbie, 2000; Creswell, 1994; De Vaus, 2001; Neuman, 2000; Newsted, Huff, & Munro, 1998).

First, secondary sources such as company annual reports and published directories do not contain information on software review performance in the software industry. The unit of analysis in this study is the individual unit;

performance has to be measured with primary data on the basis of self-reports by respondents (Fink, 1995e, 1995f; Tull & Hawkins, 1990). Notwithstanding potential respondent bias, evidence in the literature indicates that self-reported performance measures obtained from primary data are generally reliable (Babbie, 2000; Bagozzi, 1994a; Brown, 1980; Churchill, 1979, 1991; Ferber, 1974; Fink 1995a, 1995c, 1995d; Fornell, 1987; Hartog & Herbert, 1986, Hyman, 1955; Kanuk & Berenson, 1975; Smith, 1998).

Second, it is argued that most software companies do not have measurement matrices in practice (Briand & Wust, 2000; Chillarge et al., 1992). As a result, they are unlikely to have secondary sources available. Even though some of the companies might have objective empirical data collected from their development environment, different companies may have different measurement matrices. Therefore, it is almost impossible for researchers to standardise their measurements matrices objectively across all companies (Sheatsley, 1974; Smith, 1998; Tull & Hawkins, 1990; Zikmund, 2000).

Despite subjective performance measures' lack of precision, subjective performance measures are found to be reasonably reliable, and widely used in survey research (Babbie, 2000; Fink, 1995c; Hancock & Flowers, 2001; Hyman, 1955; Kiesler & Sproull, 1998; Lazar et al., 1999; Lyytinen & Hirschheim, 1987; Newsted, Munro, & Huff, 1991). Considering all the issues and taking advantage of the strengths of the subjective measures, it was more appropriate to use subjective measurement in this study.

The final issue in performance measurement is that the use of absolute vs. relative measures of performance (Judd et al., 1991). There are several reasons why relative rather than absolute measures of performance are more appropriate for this study (Anastasi, 1982).

First, as stated earlier, differences in absolute software review performance may arise due to differences in the measurement practices of different companies, and may not necessarily reflect actual differences in their software review performance. Second, it may be more appropriate to judge the success or failure of an individual on the basis of an individual performance relative to his/her team members, rather than against some arbitrary absolute standard. Hence, a meaningful performance evaluation of a reviewer is against his/her team members in which the reviewer operates.

Third, most software companies do not measure software review performance in practice, and it may be very difficult to expect all respondents to provide absolute measures on their performance (Aurum, Petersson, & Wohlin, 2003). Therefore, to control the effects of software review performance, software review performance was measured relative to individual team's members in their company.

The construct design is measured by the number of defects found with four formative indicators according to the two criteria. The measurement of performance is based on the average number of defects found by an individual respondent compared with the average number of defects found by other team members. The respondents were asked to rate themselves in comparison to their group members.

According to the Table 4, the measurements of review performance often refers to number of defects found which can be classified into true defects, false positives, net defects, and total issues and they are considered formative indicators. For instance, the number of true defects found is not necessarily correlated to false positives and as a result, it is not necessarily correlated to net defects and total issues.

The review performance construct can be classified into (Fagan, 1986; Gilb & Graham, 1993; Shull, Lanubile, & Biasili, 2000; Tervonen, 1996):

- **True Defects (TR):** Defects that actually exist and have been success-fully detected.

Table 4. Formative vs. reflective indicators-performance

Construct	Indicator	Question/ item	Scale	Reflective (R)/ Formative (F)
Performance/ Number of defects found (DEF)	True defects (TR)	On average, I find more defects that actually exist and have been successfully detected than my team members	Disagree vs. agree	F
	False positives (FA)	On average, I find more defects that do not exist but were wrongly identified than my team members.		F
	Net defects (NE)	On average, I find more net defects (defects that actually exist and have been successfully detected **minus** defects that do not exist but were wrongly identified) than my team members.		F
	Total issues (TL)	On average, I find more total defects (defects that actually exist and have been successfully detected **plus** defects that do not exist but were wrongly identified) than my team members		F

- **False Positive (FA):** Defects that do not exist but were wrongly identified.
- **Net Defects (NE):** True defects minus false positive.
- **Total Issues (TL):** True defects plus false positive.

Control Variables

To achieve reliability and validity (i.e., reduce bias) of the results, control variables are necessary. Control variables can be classified based on the demographics as well as the software review process structure. These include process structures (i.e., size of team, type of group (review) meeting), company demographics (i.e., businesses types, number of employees, certificates held by company) and individual demographics (i.e., position, professional qualification membership holders, education).

The questionnaire design used multiple-choice for the control variables. This additional data helped in understanding the profile of the sample and in interpreting the results. The following section discusses the measurement scales of all constructs, and the multiple indicators used to measure these constructs.

Measurement Scales

To adequately tap the broad domain of these constructs, a large number of indicators are used to measure each construct. The questionnaire for the EIIO model contains 49 indicators (items) for measuring the constructs in the proposed model. There are 30 items measuring the input constructs (16 for explicit and 14 for implicit), 15 items measuring process constructs and four items measuring the outcome construct. All questions are closed-ended questions. The above 49 items plus eight for respondent demographics are measured on a five-point rating scale and an additional eight items to record respondent demographics have an ordinal multiple-choice format.

Sampling

An issue in survey design is the size, nature, and method of the sample selection (Australian Bureau of Statistics, 1999, 2001; Azar, 1999; Boomsma, 1983; Sudman, 1994). The sample should be representative of the target population

(Fink, 1995a). When designing a survey, the type of sample drawn from the population of interest is an important factor in determining the type of statistical analyses, which can be performed on the data (Fink, 1995f; Cook & Campbell, 1979). Statistical analysis can provide an estimation of sampling error for various sample sizes. This estimation is based on probability theory, which assumes random sampling (McNeil, 2001; Naylor & Enticknap, 1981). To minimize the sampling error, random sampling procedures should be carefully addressed (Anderson & Gerbing, 1984; Bagozzi, 1994a; Bordens & Abbott, 2002; Fink et al., 1995a). The target population must be able to achieve the research objective in the sense of solving the research problem (Zikmund, 2000; Zmud & Boynton, 1991).

The goal of this study is to identify the characteristics of software review in practice. Thus, the most appropriate target population in the study was Australian software firms as provided by the Australian Bureau of Statistics (2000, 2001).

Sample Size

The next stage is to determine an appropriate sample size. This study is a cross-sectional study. In the context of this study, the sample is identified in two stages. In the first stage, a list of 14,731 software companies in Australia was obtained from the Australian Bureau of Statistics (2000)–this constitutes the target population.

In the second stage, a random sample of 1,380 companies (sample units) from the target population was selected. According to Alreck and Settle (1995), there should be approximately the greater of 100 or 10% of the total target population, sample units to be considered significant (Alreck & Settle, 1995). Table 5 contains the state-by-state distributions of the sample.

On the other hand, the response rate is an important issue for sampling because it creates a response bias (Anderson et al., 1984; Kanuk & Berenson, 1975; Lee et al., 1989). The response bias occurs when some subjects are more likely to provide responses than others (Hartog & Herbert, 1986). For example, a systematic sampling error could occur when subjects refused to fill out questionnaires because the language used in the questionnaires was difficult to understand (Fink et al., 1995a; Lazar et al., 1999). In data collection, the aim of sampling is to have a random sample of the target population (Judd et al., 1991; Neuman, 2000).

Comparing and analyzing the samples to the target population on a range of characteristics is a standard means of assessing representativeness. Such analyses are used to confirm the sample used in the present research.

Table 5. Distributions of the sample

States	Number of the companies retrieved
NSW	621
VIC	374
QLD	144
WA	141
SA	67
ACT	26
TAS	6
NT	1
Total	**1380**

To adequately test the hypothesised relationships and to achieve high reliability of the findings, the sample was selected in such a way as to encompass a large range of variables included in the research hypotheses.

Validation of Questionnaire

To achieve high quality survey results, a critical component is validating the instrument (questionnaire) reliability and validity (Boudreau et al., 2001; Litwin, 1995; Mabe & West, 1982; Newsted, Munro, & Huff, 1991; Newsted, Huff, & Munro, 1998). The validity of the questionnaire is assessed by three components: 1) content validity, 2) sampling validity, 3) empirical validity (Boudreau et al., 2001; Litwin, 1995; Stone, 1974; Straub, 1989). These validation techniques are in accordance with generally accepted procedures and specific tests (Frankfort-Nachmias & Nachmias, 1996; Judd et al., 1991; Miles & Huberman, 1984).

Content validation often refers to face validity (De Vaus, 2001; Judd et al., 1991; Miles & Huberman, 1984). Face validity is determined by comparing the questionnaire with other similar questionnaire surveys (Zikmund, 2000; Zmud & Boynton, 1991). Face validity was also determined through pre-testing such as the initial pilot study (see Section 4.6.1) (Kettinger, William, Lee, Choong, Lee, & Sunro, 1995; Stone, 1974; Straub, 1989).

Sampling validity is another component of validation. A large sample size (i.e., 1380 companies) can ensure low sampling errors and high sampling validity (Australian Bureau of Statistics, 1999; Boomsma, 1983; Boudreau et al., 2001).

Empirical validity examines the survey results by comparison with others studies. The aim is to check consistency with previous results. Empirical validation of the questionnaire reliability often involves two techniques 1) test-retest techniques, determines stability of measured indicators (items) (Frankfort-Nachmias & Nachmias, 1996; Hammersley, 1992; Judd et al., 1991) and 2) construct validity, a score to determine internal consistency-reliability, measured by the Cronbach alpha (Cronbach, 1970; Cronbach & Show, 1977; Litwin, 1995; Preston, 1983).

In the case of this research, the test-retest technique was used in three focus groups (Judd et al., 1991; Rossi & Anderson, 1982). One of the major issues associated with the test-retest technique is that the respondents' answers provided in the first survey can influence those in the second survey because they can remember the answer in the first survey (Frankfort-Nachmias & Nachmias, 1996; Yin, 1994). Because the draft questionnaire was lengthy and with sufficient details, it is argued that the respondents would be unlikely to remember their answers for previous drafts. There is reasonable support for employing the test-retest technique (Judd et al., 1991). This ensures the questionnaire is reliable and there is minimal noise in the measurement process. In terms of measuring internal consistency, the Cronbach alpha is the most common used for construct measurement in questionnaire surveys (Cronbach, 1970; Judd et al., 1991). The results of the internal consistency test are discussed in chapter five.

Overall, validation of the survey questionnaire in the context of this study was undertaken at six checkpoints:

1. At the completion of the preliminary development of the questionnaire.

2. At the completion of the expert opinions but before the focus groups.

3. At the completion of the focus groups but before the industry pilot study.

4. At the completion of the re-confirming tests but before the industry pilot study.

5. After the industry pilot study but before the formal data collections.

6. For confirmation of results, after the final data collection and cross. validation (in-depth interviews).

Four Stages of Pre-Tests

There are four stages of the pre-tests: 1) experts' opinions (Zikmund, 2000), 2) focus groups (Alreck & Settle, 1995; Fuller, Edwards, Vorakitphokatorn, &

Sermsri, 1993; Malhotra et al., 1996; Morgan & Krueger, 1993), 3) re-confirming test, and 4) an industry pilot study, for the validation of the instrument (questionnaire) design (De Vaus, 2002; Frankfort-Nachmias & Nachmias, 1996; Morgan, 1998; Neuman, 2000; Sekran, 1992; Yin, 1994; Zikmund, 2000).

Experts' Opinions

In stage one, five academic experts reviewed the questionnaire. There were three Information Systems lecturers with extensive industry experience (i.e., between ten to twenty years experience working in the software industry and over three years experience in software reviews) and two senior Professors from the Faculty of Business who had twenty years experience in survey research and questionnaire design. Based on their recommendations, a few items were added, deleted, and modified in the initial questionnaire.

Focus Groups

In stage two, the revised questionnaire was tested in three focus groups. The purpose of the focus group meetings was to ensure the quality of the questionnaire (i.e., to make sure it is understandable and readable). The focus group is a common research approach in qualitative research (Morgan, 1998; Morgan & Krueger, 1993). The focus group method is considered a cost effective method to ensure the quality of a questionnaire (Albrecht, Johnson, & Walther, 1993; Marriam, 1988; Neuman, 2000; O'Brien, 1993; Wolff, Knodel, Sittitrai, 1993). In particular, Barker (1999) suggested that the major advantages of focus groups for researchers include:

1. **Scientific Scrutiny:** A range of researchers can observe the group and/or tape recordings or videotape the discussion (Albrecht et al., 1993). This helps foster consistent interpretations (O'Brien, 1993).

2. **Serendipity:** Focus groups bring forth unexpected "out of the blue" ideas (Crabtree, Yanoshi, Miller, & O'Connor, 1993).

3. **Specialization:** This reduces the cost since a group of people can be interviewed together (Knodel, 1993; Morgan & Krueger, 1993; Neuman, 2000).

4. **Speed:** Reduce the time required since a group of people can respond simultaneously (Frey & Fontana, 1993; Zikmund, 2000).

5. **Structure:** The moderator can control the order and times spent on various topics and re-visit topics (Knodel, 1993; Krueger, 1993).

Table 6. Focus group 1 (correlation is significant at the .01 level [2 tailed])

Participants	Correlation coefficient
Participant 1	.81
Participant 2	.90
Participant 3	.89
Participant 4	.89
Participant 5	.85
Participant 6	.85

Table 7. Focus group 2 (correlation is significant at the .01 level [2 tailed])

Participants	Correlation coefficient
Participant 7	.85
Participant 8	.71
Participant 9	.71
Participant 10	.77

Table 8. Focus group 3 (correlation is significant at the .01 level [2 tailed])

Participants	Correlation coefficient
Participant 11	.85
Participant 12	.88
Participant 13	.88
Participant 14	.82
Participant 15	.85
Participant 16	.80

In addition, there are several benefits of focus group for respondents (Barker, 1999):

1. **Security:** Individuals may feel less exposed and more comfortable in expressing views that may be shared (Fuller et al., 1993).

2. **Snowballing:** Comments from one person elicit comments from others (Frey & Fontana, 1993; Morgan, 1998).

3. **Spontaneity:** Since each person is not asked to answer a specific question, respondents may "jump in" with ideas and pick up what interests them. They are not required to answer questions they have no interest in (Frey & Fontana, 1993).

4. **Synergy:** More ideas and information will flow out from this combined interview environment (Knodel, 1993).

The aim of the focus groups in this study is to identify and understand critical factors for organising and conducting software reviews (Neuman, 2000; Yin, 1994). The focus groups sought to validate a questionnaire and required subjects to express their opinions on the nature of their industry experiences in software development/software review and/or questionnaire design (Knodel, 1993; Neuman, 2000).

In designing the focus group, 6-10 subjects were employed in a group (Baker, 1999). This is because a small number will be unable to generate ideas whereas a large number may make it difficult for the moderator to control the meeting discussion and be cost ineffective (i.e. some of the subjects may be unable to participate during the discussion) (Knodel, 1993; Morgan, 1998). Further, in order to ensure the questionnaire design is understandable and easy to fill selected groups will be a mixture of people who are expert and non-expert in the area (Crabtree et al., 1993). Another advantage is that face-to-face is considered the most effective communication medium (Jonassen, 2001; Kanuk & Berenson, 1975). The setting of the focus meetings was a university classroom environment.

The procedure of the focus groups consists of five steps (Knodel, 1993) (see Appendix 2):

1.   Overview of the purpose of the meeting.
2.   A self-administered questionnaire.
3.   Focus group meeting led by a moderator.
4.   General feedback on the overall process.
5.   Post meeting questionnaire.

Two academics in Information Systems, two PhD students in Software Engineering, five honours students in Information Systems and eleven undergraduate students in Information Technology Management were randomly assigned in groups of size four, ten, and six. They all have software industry experience.

All meeting processes were taped by a video camera and recorders. As a result of the focus groups, the suggestion to improve the wording of several items and the questionnaire appearance were implemented.

In order to ensure the reliability of the questionnaire, the test-retest method of testing the reliability of indicators was also employed in the three focus groups (Neuman, 2000). A copy of the invitation letter and a reminder asking the respondents to undertake this task are shown in Appendix 3.

The focus groups provided useful feedback about the perceived length of the questionnaire, the time required to complete the questionnaire, scaling design and the content of the questions. The following Tables 6, 7 and 8 show the test-retest correlation results of the three focus groups. The high correlations shown in Tables 6-8 and the high degree of significance give considerable support for the questionnaire being a reliable measure (De Vaus, 2001; Straub, 1989). However, the correlations were below 0.8 in the results of Table 7. One possible explanation is that three participants' had no software review experience in the industry in which respect they were not reflecting the target sample (Crabtree et al., 1993; Morgan, 1993). The results collected from three participants in Focus Group 2 were not represented in our study (see Table 7).

Re-Confirming Test

After completion of the three focus group studies, another two experienced academics in software review, one experienced professor in survey design and two final year PhD Information Systems candidates evaluated the revised the questionnaire before the industry pilot study. From the feedback and comments, a few wordings of a few items were changed or deleted.

Industry Pilot Study

In the final stage of the pre-test, the industry pilot study was conducted. Sixteen completed questionnaires were received. Based on the comments and feedback from the pilot study, a few questions on company demographics that were not strictly relevant for testing the model were deleted. Altogether, the focus groups and the pilot study provided 35 observations. Since the pre-test sample size was small, the model could not be tested with these data. However, frequency and descriptive analysis indicated that all measures have reasonable variance and range. The correlations among its measures were found to be higher than with the measures of others constructs for each construct (Judd et al., 1991). This indicates a preliminary adequate convergence of discriminant validity (Chin, 1998b; McNeil, 2001).

In summary, pre-testing the survey questionnaire in four stages provided useful guidelines for designing the final survey questionnaires that were simple, well-presented, and had high content validity (Ackoff, 1953; Aron & Aron, 1957; Babbie, 2000; Barker, 1999; De Vaus, 2002; Sheatsley, 1974; Sudman, 1994; Tull & Hawkins, 1990; Zikmund, 2000).

Data Collection

The mail survey is considered the most feasible survey method for large data collection (Fink, 1995c; Zikmund, 2000). Data gathering via mail questionnaire survey remains more reliable than any other type of survey method even web-survey (Bagozzi, 1994a; Schmidt, 1997). The major advantages of mail surveys include:

1. Wider distribution — there is no difficulty in reaching people scattered all over the country (Brown, 1980; Kish, 1965)

2. Less distribution bias — it shows no favouritism for a certain individual (Ferber, 1974)

3. No interview bias — this avoids the bias attributable to the interviewer and also inhibiting factors (Fink, 1995c)

4. Better likelihood of a thoughtful reply — if a person decides to answer a mail questionnaire, he will do it at his leisure and not when the interview happens

5. Time-saving — time saving compared with conducting personal interviews (Fink, 1995d)

6. Centralised control — it is easier to control than personal interviews because a mail survey can be conducted from one office, with built-in checks and controls for every phase of the operation (Kinnear & James, 1996)

7. Cost saving — it is cheaper than the interview method, for which the training, briefing, supervision, and checking cost more than for mail surveys (Frey & Fontana, 1993)

The appropriateness of using a mail survey method for data gathering depends on two main considerations: 1) the availability of a mailing list and 2) the prospects of an adequate response (Crowther, 2001; Fink, 1995c; Hancock & Flowers, 2001; Kanuk & Berenson, 1975).

The major weakness of a mail questionnaire survey is that it does not produce a high response rate in comparison with other methods such as personal interviews (Babbie, 2000; Kraemer, 1991; Litwin, 1995; Sekran, 1992). However, response rates of mail surveys can be improved by a number of techniques. For instance, a cover letter from a prestigious individual or organization urging participation, assurances of anonymity and a clear statement of the purpose of the questionnaire survey (Babbie, 2000).

A mail survey typically requires a couple of mailed letters or a few telephone calls in the follow-up stage (Neuman, 2000). It is recommended that at least two follow-up letters should be addressed to non-respondents at suitable intervals, stressing the importance of their participation, and some tangible inducement may be offered as a reward (Bagozzi, 1994b; Barker, 1999; Kanuk & Berenson, 1975; Kiesler & Sproull, 1999).

When the response rate remains low, intensive efforts such as personal phone calls or e-mail usually produce a sizeable response rate. The great advantage of a mail questionnaire survey is that it is a cost effective formal approach for large coverage of a target population (Fink, 1995c; Frankfort-Nachmias & Nachmias, 1996). The response rate is higher when the cover letter is personalised to respondents (Salant & Dillman, 1994).

The mail questionnaire survey in this study required four months and involved several rounds of reminders and questionnaires. The extensive data gathering effort resulted in a satisfactory response rate and a reasonable sample size.

The data collection used mail survey. The mailing list was obtained from The Business Who's Who Of Australia (2001) and The Dun and Bradstreet Marketing Pty Ltd (2002) (with an access fee), which contains the names of company directors. However, not all of the entries contain the information technology manager, project manager, or software developers who are the desired subjects.

In this situation, two approaches can be used. The first approach is to send a personalised letter to the managers with a request to agree to participate in the research project. Next, copies of questionnaires are sent to the managers to be forwarded to the software developers for their completion. The second approach is to mail a non-personalised letter addressed to the "Information Technology Manager" with a request to agree participating in the research project. In this case, then copies of the questionnaires are sent to the software developers for completion. In the context of this research, both approaches were employed.

In the beginning of the questionnaire survey, both personalised and non-personalised cover letters were addressed to the Information Technology Manager with a request for agreement to participate in the survey research project. An example cover letter is included in Appendix 4. Upon the agreements, copies of the questionnaire were mailed to the companies. With each question-naire, a return envelope was also enclosed to help the respondents in returning the completed questionnaire. To improve the involvement of the companies participating in this research, a copy of the future survey findings was offered to all participants as an incentive.

Following the suggestions in the literature for increasing the response rate (e.g., Salant & Dillman, 1994), three follow-up letters were sent after the questionnaire was mailed. The copies of the initial cover letter and the three reminder letters mailed to the companies are attached in Appendix 5. To improve the response rate, additional copies of the questionnaires were mailed to all the non-responding companies (Zikmund, 2000). Personal telephone calls and e-mail follow-up helped additional non-responding companies to reply (Barker, 1999; De Vaus, 2001).

Analytical Methodology

Data analysis made use of the three-step approach, which was recommended by Anderson and Gerbing (1988):

1. Preliminary data analysis — this includes missing value analysis and descriptive data analysis (Fink, 1995a; Judd et al., 1991).
2. Exploratory data analysis — this includes principal component factor analysis (PCA) and reliability analysis (RA) (Coakes & Steed, 2001).
3. Hypotheses tests — Structural Equation Modeling (SEM) using Partial Least Squares (PLS).

The three-step approach is particularly advantageous for this study where the EIIO model and measures are of an exploratory nature and the theory is not well developed in the context of the software review literature.

Preliminary Data Analysis

The first step in the analytical methodology is preliminary data analysis. Missing value analysis and descriptive data analysis were conducted (Ruyter & Scholl, 1998). Missing value analysis creates a clean set of observation data, which is substantively free from missing values (Alreck & Settle, 1995; Chin, 1998b). It allows an adequate variance for testing the proposed hypotheses. On the other hand descriptive data analysis provides a measurement of the characteristics of the data. This is also called Central Tendency data analysis (Ackoff, 1953). The mean and medium are useful statistics for summarising data measured on an interval or continuous scale (McNeil, 2001). They should be central, that is they should be close to the middle of the distribution. If a measure of spread is required as well, the inter-quartile range and/or the standard deviation (SD) are used to describe the variability in a set of numerical data (Fink, 1995f).

Both the mean and standard deviation are quite sensitive to outliers in the data. Outliers do not affect the medium and inter-quartile range (Fink, 1995f). Therefore, the medium and the inter-quartile range should be used in preference to the mean and the standard deviation (Frankfort-Nachmias & Nachmias, 1996).

Exploratory Data Analysis

In the second step, exploratory principal components analysis (PCA) and reliability analysis (RA) were carried out using the SPSS software package to assess the validity of the measures and constructs (Coakes & Steed, 2001). The ultimate aim of the exploratory analysis is to specify valid and reliable measurement constructs and indicators. Specifying and estimating the constructs in conjunction with a prior valid and reliable measurement model is extremely useful for theory testing and development (Anderson & Gerbing, 1988; Lee et al., 1989; Litwin, 1995). Principal components factor analysis is a data reduction technique to reduce a large number of variables or indicators to a smaller set of underlying constructs or factors (Anderson & Gerbing, 1988). Often, principal components factor analysis is an exploratory technique when a researcher wishes to summarise a set of variables. The objective of principal components factor analysis is to confirm the reliability of the measurement and discriminatory validation (Cohen, 1988; Naylor & Enticknap, 1981). Items within a construct are highly correlated and are an additional measurement for determining whether indicators or variables are tapping into the same construct (Churchill, 1979; McNeil, 2001).

Cronbach's alpha is most commonly used for reliability analysis (Cronbach, 1970). It is based on the average correlation of indicators within a test if the indicators are standardised. If the indicators are not standardised, it is based on the average covariance among all items. Cronbach's alpha also can be interpreted as the correlation coefficient — it lies between values 0 and 1 (Cronbach & Show, 1977). The output of the SPSS software package provides a standardised item alpha and a comparable variance and there is little difference between these two alphas (Coakes & Steed, 2001). Appendix 6 discusses what procedures and formulas are used for the exploratory data analysis.

Hypotheses Tests-Structural Equation Modeling (SEM) Using Partial Least Squares (PLS)

The final step involves hypotheses testing via Structural Equation Modeling (SEM) using Partial Least Square (PLS). The model of software review proposed in the study posits relationships among a set of latent constructs/unobservable theoretical constructs measured with multiple manifest/observed variables (Chin, 1998a; Joreskog, 1973; Kelloway, 1995; Rahim et al., 2001; Wiley, 1973). Since the model posits multilevel relationships among several latent predictor and criterion constructs measured with multiple indicators, Structural Equation Modeling is the most appropriate approach for comprehensively testing the proposed model (Bollen, 1989; Chin et al., 1997; Joreskog, 1989).

The Structural Equation Modeling (SEM) methodology and the Partial Least Squares (PLS) approach are discussed in several books and articles that deal with the theoretical and application issues and advantages in SEM and PLS (Bollen, 1989; Boomsma, 1983; Chin, 1998a, 2003; Chin et al., 1997; Chin & Gopal, 1995; Fornell, 1987; Geisser, 1975; Hui, 1982, 1987; Joreskog, 1973, 1989; Kelloway, 1995; Lohmoller, 1989; Lyttkens, 1973; Rahim et al., 2001; Stone, 1974; Wiley, 1973; Wold, 1985, 1988).

The advantages of using SEM and why it is more appropriate to use the PLS methodology in this study will be discussed in the following sections. To simplify the exposition and to avoid repeatedly citing the sources that discuss the same fundamental issues in SEM, all the references cited above are acknowledged as the sources of ideas presented here.

Structural Equation Modeling combines the econometric perspective focusing on prediction and the psychometric perspective focusing on measuring latent, unobserved concepts with multiple observed indicators. This allows the simultaneous addressing of the issues of construct measurement, and the structural relationships among the constructs (Geisser, 1975; Joreskog, 1989; Rahim et al., 2001; Stone, 1974; Wold, 1988).

The SEM approach offers the flexibility to perform the following (Chin, 1998a, 2003):

- Model the relationships among multiple predictor variables.
- Construct unobservable latent variables.
- Model errors in measurements for observed variables.
- Statistically test a priori substantive/theoretical and measurement assumptions against empirical data.

However, the issue of simultaneity is important. The traditional two-stage approach of first-generation analysis (i.e., factor analysis for the measurement model followed by regression or path analysis for the structural model) can potentially produce an invalid estimation, since it assumes that the relationship among the indicators of a construct is independent of the theoretical context within which the indicators are embedded (Fornell, 1987; Lyytinen & Hirschheim, 1987).

By comparison the SEM offers greater flexibility in testing theoretical models with empirical data, as it allows the handling of latent constructs, models relationships among several latent predictor and criterion constructs, and incorporates errors in measurement. Because of its advantages, Fornell (1987, p. 408) regards SEM as "a second generation of multivariate analysis" in contrast with first-generation techniques such as multiple regression or principle components analysis (Chin, 1998a; Frankfort-Nachmias & Nachmias, 1996).

The two common approaches for SEM are the covariance-based approach, which dates back to the original development by Joreskog (1973) and Wiley (1973) used in LISREL, and the component-based approach, which is developed by Wold (1985; 1988) used in PLS-PC and PLS-Graph (Chin, 1998c; 2003). In the covariance-based LISREL, the objective is to estimate the model parameters so that the difference between the sample covariance matrix and the model-based covariance matrix is minimised (Boomsma, 1983; Joreskog, 1989). On the other hand, the objective in the component-based PLS is to estimate the model parameters "based on the ability to minimise the residual variances of dependent variables (both latent and observed)" (Chin, 1998a).

PLS (component-based approach) is more predictive-oriented (Chin, 1998b) while LISREL is more for theory testing (confirmation) (Wert et al., 1974). PLS is considered to be the most appropriate in the initial exploratory stages of theory development, when the conceptual model and the indicators are not well-developed (Chin, 1998a, 1998b, 2003). On the other hand, if the theory is strong and the measures are well developed, LISREL and other covariance-based software packages such as AMOS, SEPATH, RAMONA, MX, CALIS, and EQS are more appropriate (Chin, 1988b).

Barclay, Higgins, & Thompson, (1995) recommend PLS "for predictive research models where the emphasis may be more on theory development", whereas "LISREL is more suited for testing, in a confirmatory sense, how well a theoretical model fits observed data, generally requiring much stronger theory than PLS."

The component-based PLS offers several advantages over the covariance-based methods such as LISREL. For example, PLS can estimate complex models with small sample sizes, can model both formative (cause) and reflective (effect) indicators, provides determinate values for the latent constructs, and does not make any distributional assumptions about the data used for modeling (Chin, 1998b; Hui, 1982, 1987). Due to factor determinacy, interactions between constructs can be more easily incorporated in models estimated with PLS as compared with LISREL (Boomsma, 1983). Another important advantage of PLS is that the graphical user interface-based PLS-Graph package develop by Chin

(1988b) is relatively easy to use, provides output that is simple to interpret, and alternative models can be quickly estimated and compared with the baseline model. The package also includes the Bootstrap option for significance testing. In addition to the R-square statistic similar to that used in multiple regression, the program can also compute the Q-square statistic proposed by Stone (1974) and Geisser (1975), where Q-square represents a measure of how well the observed values are reconstructed by the model and its parameter estimates (Chin, 1988b).

Overall, the PLS methodology is considered to be more appropriate in this study for the following reasons. First, the PLS component-based approach focuses on building models that are meant to explain the covariances of all the observed indicators and the objective of PLS is prediction (Chin, 2003). In particular, the constructs are defined as the sum of their respective items or indicators and the PLS algorithm attempts to obtain the best weight estimates for each block of indicators corresponding to each latent construct (Chin, 1998b; Kelloway, 1995; Rahim et al., 2001).

Second, the theoretical models and indicators in software review are not well developed. It is therefore more useful to use the PLS methodology in this study since it will help in both developing and testing more robust indicators and models of software review (Chin, 1998b). In addition, PLS can be used for theory confirmation in which it can suggest where relationships might exist and suggest propositions for later testing (Chin, 2003; Hui, 1987).

Third, the measurement model in PLS for both reflective and formative indicators is optimised in conjunction with the structural model (Chin, 2003; Hui, 1982). As a result, the formative indicators in PLS explain the highest amount of variance for the emergent construct as well as for the criterion construct of the predictor emergent construct. Since one of the strengths of SEM lies in simultaneously estimating the measurement and structural models, using externally estimated construct scores reduces this advantage of SEM when using covariance-based SEM method with formative indicators (Chin, 2003, 1998; Hui, 1982, 1987; Rahim et al., 2001).

Fourth, the data may not have a multivariate normal distribution, and this violates an important assumption in the maximum likelihood estimation method in covariance-based SEM methods such as LISREL (Boomsma, 1983; Chin, 1998b; Rahim et al., 2001). The proposed EIIO model includes an interaction between inputs, process and output constructs. Such multiplicative interactions can be more easily incorporated in a model produced with PLS.

Fifth, PLS allows more flexibility in measurement scales (e.g., ratio, multiple choice), allows a smaller sample size (the minimal sample size is 200 for LISREL and 30 for PLS) (Chin, 1998a, 1998b), and works with residual distributions (Wold, 1985). Table 9 provides a summary of the key differences between PLS and covariance-based approaches.

Table 9. Comparison of partial least squares and covariance-based structural equation modeling; source (adopted from Chin & Newsted, 1996, p. 314

Criterion	PLS	Covariance-based
Objective	Prediction oriented	Parameter oriented
Approach	Variance-based	Covariance-based
Assumptions	Predictor specification (non parametric)	Typically multivariate normal distribution and independent observations (parametric)
Parameter estimates	Consistent as indicators and sample size increase (i.e., consistency at large)	Consistent
Latent variable score	Explicitly estimated	Indeterminate
Epistemic relationship between construct (latent variable) and indicators (measures)	Can be modelled in either formative or reflective mode	Typically only with reflective indicators
Implications	Optimal for prediction accuracy	Optimal for parameter accuracy
Model complexity	Large complexity (e.g., 100 constructs and 1,000 indicators)	Small to moderate complexity (e.g., less than 100 indicators)
Sample size	Power analysis based on the portion of the model with the largest number of predictors. Minimal recommendation range from 30 to 100.	Ideally based on power analysis of specific model. Minimal recommendation ranges from 200 to 800.

The five rationales of using PLS methodology in this study are summarized as following:

1. The optimal goal is prediction oriented, not parameter accuracy.

2. The phenomenon of the research questions and the theoretical EIIO model and indicators are relatively new and not well developed in the software review literature.

3. The proposed EIIO model consists of formative and reflective indicators in the estimation.

4. The proposed EIIO model is relatively complex with large numbers of constructs and indicators (items).

5. The sample size is small or/and not normally distributed (nonparametric-based).

Table 10. Research plan summary

Steps	Descriptions
1. Research method	Survey
2. Research design	Cross sectional mail survey
3. Questionnaire design	Design the layout, questions structure and sequence. • Self-administered questionnaire • Closed-ended questions. Questionnaire support includes • Instructions • Cover letter, follow up letters
4. Measurement scales	• 19 questions • Total of 65 indicators, 49 indicators for the constructs and 16 indicators for demographic data • 57 of the indicators are measured on five-point rating scales and 8 indicators follow an ordinal multiple-choice format
5. Sampling	• Target population–software firms (categorized size of firms can be based on Australian Bureau of Statistics) listed under the Australian Bureau of Statistics computer services category and the top 500 list of companies listed on the Australian Stock Exchange. According to the Australian Bureau of Statistics (2000), there were 14,731 businesses under the computer services category at the end of June 1999 • Sample Units: 1380 software firms and listed companies were selected in Australia (Australian Bureau Statistics, 2002)
6. Pre-tests	Stage 1–expert opinion Stage 2–three focus groups Stage 3–re-confirming test Stage 4–industry pilot study
7. Data collection	Conduct mail survey • Invitation letters sent to all companies • Questionnaires sent to respondents • Follow up–two reminder letters sent to those companies who did not return the questionnaire
8. Data analysis	Software packages: SPSS and PLS **Preliminary data analysis** • Missing value (Chi-square tests) • Descriptive (Central tendency) **Exploratory Analyses** • Principal component analysis • Reliability and validity analysis **Hypotheses Tests-Structural Equation Modeling Using Partial Least Squares (PLS) methodology** • Outer (measurement) model--Convergent validity, Correlation matrix; Discriminant validity–cross-loading and Square root of average variance extracted (AVE); Composite reliability • Inner (structural) model–Structural Paths (path coefficients), T-tests • (2-tailed), R-square, Q-square, model estimation with data subset

Due to its numerous advantages, PLS is used as the final data analysis technique for estimating the proposed model. However, in the initial exploratory stages of the analysis, first generation technique such as principal component factor analysis and correlation analysis are also used to obtain useful diagnostic information that is not available in the PLS-Graph package (Chin, 1998a, 1998b). Appendix 7 discusses the details of PLS estimation procedures.

A research plan is summarized in Table 10.

Summary

In summary, this chapter discussed the research methodology that was used in the study for research design, questionnaire design, data gathering and the analytical methodology for hypotheses testing and model estimation. The industry survey results will be discussed in next chapter.

References

Ackoff, R. L. (1953). *The design of social research.* Chicago: The University of Chicago Press.

Albrecht, T. L., Johnson, G. M., & Walther J. B. (1993). Understanding communication processes in focus groups. In D. Morgan (Ed.), *Successful focus groups: Advancing the state of art* (pp. 51-64). Newbury Park, CA: Saga.

Alreck, P. L., & Settle, R. B. (1995*). The survey research handbook.* Chicago: Irwin.

Anastasi, A. (1982). *Psychological testing* (5th ed.). New York: Macmillan.

Anderson, J. C., & Gerbing, D. W. (1988). The effect of sampling error on convergence, improper solutions, and goodness-of-fit indices for maximum likelihood confirmatory factory analyses. *Psychometrician, 49,* 155-173.

Areskoug, B. (1982). The first canonical correlation: Theoretical pls analysis and simulation experiments. In K. G. Joreskog & H. Wold (Eds.), *Systems under indirect observation: Causality, structure, prediction* (pp. 95-128). Amsterdam, North-Holland.

Aron, A., & Aron, E. N. (1997). *For the behavioural and social sciences: A brief course.* NJ: Prentice-Hall.

Aurum, A., Petersson, H., & Wohlin, C., (2002). State-of-the-art: Software inspections turning 25 years. *Journal of Software Testing, Verification, and Reliability, 12*(3), 133-154.

Australian Bureau of Statistics (ABS). (1999). *An introduction to sample survey: A user's guide 1299.0,* Commonwealth of Australia, Australian Bureau of Statistics, Canberra.

Australian Bureau of Statistics (ABS). (2000). *Information technology 8126.0 and 8143.0,* Commonwealth of Australia, Australian Bureau of Statistics, Canberra.

Australian Bureau of Statistics (ABS). (2001). *New South Wales Year Book, No. 81,* Commonwealth of Australia, Australian Bureau of Statistics, Canberra.

Australian Computer Society (ACS) Inc. (2003, February 17). Procedures information manual: Skills assessment–information technology (computing) professional. *Australian Computer Society, 2*(2), 1-10.

Azar, B. (1999). APA statistics task force prepares to release recommendations for public comment. *APA Monitor Online,* 30. Retrieved June 14, 2002, from www.apa.org/monitor/may99/task.html

Babbie, E. R. (1973). *Survey research methods.* Wadsworth, CA.

Babbie, E. (2000). *The practice of social research* (9ᵗʰed.). Wadsworth CA: Belmon.

Bagozzi, R. P. (1994a). *Measurement in marketing research: Basic principle of questionnaire design. Principles of Marketing Research.* Cambridge: Basil Blackwell.

Bagozzi, R. P. (1994b). *Advanced methods of marketing research.* Cambridge: Basil Blackwell.

Barclay, D., Higgins, C., & Thompson, R. (1995). The Partial Least Squares (PLS) approach to causal modeling: Personal computer adoption and use as an illustration. *Technology Studies, 2*(2), 285-309.

Barker, T. L. (1999). *Doing social research* (3ʳᵈ ed.). Boston: Mcgraw-Hall.

Basili, V. R., Green, S., Laitenberger, O., Lanubile, F., Sorumgard, S., & Zelkowitz, M. 1996. The empirical investigation of perspective-based reading. *International Journal on Empirical Software Engineering, 1*(12), 133-144.

Bollen, K. A. (1984). Multiple indicators: Internal consistency or no necessary relationship? *Quality and Quantity, 18,* 377-385.

Bollen, K. A. (1989). *Structural equations with latent variables.* New York: Wiley.

Boomsma, A. (1983). The robustness of LISREL (Maximum Likelihood Estimation) against small sample size and non-normality. *Socio-Metric Research Foundation,* Amsterdam.

Bordens, K. S., & Abbott, B. B. (2002). *Research design and methods: A process approach* (5ᵗʰ ed.). Boston: McGraw Hill.

Boudreau, M. C., Gefen, D., & Straub, D. W. (2001). Validation in information systems research: A state-of-the-art assessment. *MIS Quarterly, 25*(1), 1-16.

Briand, L. C., & Wust, J. (2000). *Integrating scenario-based and measure-ment-based software product assessment report No. 042-00/E.*, International Software Engineering Software Research Network, Fraunhofer Instituted for Empirical Software Engineering, Germany, ISERN

Brog, W. R., Gall, J. P., & Gall, M. D. (1993). *Applying educational research: A practical guide.* New York, NY: Longman.

Brown, F. E. (1980). *Marketing research: A structure for decision making.* Boston: Addison-Wesley.

Chillarge, R., Bhandari, I. S., Chaar, J. K., Halliday, M. J., Moebus, D. S., Ray, B. K., & Wong, M. Y. (1992). Orthogonal defect classification–A concept for in-process measurements. *IEEE Transaction on Software Engineering, 18*(11), 943-965.

Chin, W. W. (1998a, March). Issues and opinion on structural equation modeling. *MIS Quarterly, 22*(1), Commentary.

Chin, W. W. (1998b). The partial least square approach for structural equation modeling. In G. A. Marcoulides (Ed.), *Modern methods for business research* (pp. 295-336). Mahwah, NJ: Erlbaum.

Chin, W. W. (2003). A permutation procedure for multi-group comparison of PLS models. *Proceedings of the PLS'03 International Symposium* (pp. 33-43).

Chin, W. W., & Gopal, A. (1995). Adoption intention in GSS: Relative importance of beliefs. *The Data Base for Advances in Information Systems, 26*, 42-46.

Chin, W. W., Gopal, A., & Salisbury, W. D. (1997). Advancing the theory of adaptive structuring: The development of a scale to measure faithfulness of appropriation. *Information Systems Research, 8*, 342-367.

Chin, W. W., & Newsted, P. R. (1996). Structural equation modeling analysis with small samples using partial least squares. *Statistical Strategies for Small-Sample Research*, 321-326.

Churchill, G. A. (1979, February). A paradigm for developing better measures of marketing constructs. *Journal of Marketing Research, 16*, 64-73.

Churchill, G. A. (1991). *Marketing research: Methodological foundations* (5th ed.). Chicago: The Dryden.

Coakes, S. J., & Steed, L. G. (2001). *SPSS: Analysis without anguish: Version 10.0 for Windows.* Brisbane, Australia: John Wiley & Sons.

Cohen, J. (1988). *Statistical power analysis for the behaviour sciences* (2nd ed.). Hillsdale, NJ: Lawrence Erlbaum.

Cook, T. D., & Campell, D. T. (1979). *Quasi-experimentation: Design and analysis issues for field setting*. Boston: Houghton Mifflin.

Crabtree, B. F., Yanoshi, M. K., Miller W. L., & O'Connor, P. J. (1993). Selecting individual or group interviews. In D. Morgan (Ed.), *Successful focus groups: Advancing the state of art* (pp. 137-152). Newbury Park, CA: Saga.

Creswell, J. W. (1994). *Research design: Qualitative and quantitative approaches*. Thousand Oaks, CA: Sage.

Cronbach, L. J. (1970). *Essentials of psychological testing* (3rd ed.). New York: Irvington.

Cronbach, L. J., & Show R. E. (1977). *Aptitudes and instructional methods: A handbook for research on interactions*. New York, NY: Irvington.

Crowther, G. (2001). Face-to-face or e-mail: The medium makes a difference. *Communication World, 18*(5), 23-27.

Davison, R. (1997). Instrument for measuring meeting success. *Information and Management, 32*, 163-176.

Deci, E. L. (1975). *Intrinsic motivation*. New York: Plenum Press.

Deci, E. L., Eghrari, H., Patrick, B. C., & Leone, D. (1994). Facilitating internationalization: The self-determination theory perspective. *Journal of Personality, 62*, 119-142.

Deci, E. L., Koestner, R., & Ryan, R. M. (1999a). A meta-analytic review of experiment examining the effect of extrinsic reviewed on intrinsic motivation. *Psychological Bulletin, 125*, 627-668.

Deci, E. L., Koestner, R., & Ryan, R.M., (1999b). The undermining effect is reality after all: extrinsic rewards, task interest, and self-determination. *Psychological Bulletin, 125*, 629-700.

Deci, E. L., & Ryan, R. M. (1980). The empirical exploration of intrinsic motivational processes. In L. Berkowits (Ed.), *Advanced in experimental social psychology, 13* (pp. 39-80). New York: Academic Press.

Deci, E. L., & Ryan, R. M. (1987). The support of autonomy and control of behaviour. *Journal of Personality and Social Psychology, 53*(6), 1024-1037.

Denzin, N. K.. & Lincoln, Y. S. (1995). *Handbook of qualitative research*. Thousand Oaks, CA: Sage.

De Vaus, D. (2001). *Research design in social research*. London: Sage.

Ferber, R. (1974). *Handbook of marketing research*. New York: McGraw Hill.

Fink, A. (1995a). *How to sampling in surveys*. Thousand Oaks, CA: Sage.

Fink, A. (1995b). *How to ask survey questions*. Thousand Oaks, CA: Sage.

Fink, A. (1995c). *How to conduct self-administered and mail survey*. Thousand Oaks, CA: Sage.

Fink, A. (1995d). *How to conduct interviews by telephone and in person*. Thousand Oaks, CA: Sage.

Fink, A. (1995e). *How to report on surveys*. Thousand Oaks, CA: Sage.

Fink, A. (1995f). *How to analyze survey data*. Thousand Oaks, CA: Sage.

Fornell, C. (1987). A second generation of multivariate analysis: Classification of methods and implications for marketing research. In M. J. Houston (Ed.), *Review of marketing* (pp. 407-450). Chicago: American Marketing Association.

Forrest, E. (1999). *Internet marketing research: Resource and technique*. Sydney, Australia: McGraw Hill.

Frankfort-Nachmias, C. &Nachmias, D. (1996). *Research methods in the social sciences* (5th ed.). New York: St. Martin's.

Frey, J. H., & Fontana, A. (1993). The group interview in social research. In D. Morgan (Ed.), *Successful focus groups: Advancing the state of art* (pp. 20-34). Newbury Park, CA: Saga.

Fuller, T. D., Edwards, J. N., Vorakitphokatorn, S., & Sermsri, S. (1993). Using focus groups to adapt survey instruments to new populations: Experience from a developing country. In D. Morgan (Ed.), *Successful focus groups: Advancing the state of art* (pp. 89-104). Newbury Park, CA: Saga.

Furrer, O., & Sudharshan, D. (2001). Internet marketing research: Opportunities and problems. *An International Journal of Qualitative Market Research, 4*(3), 123-129.

Geisser, S. (1975). The Predictive sample reuse method with applications. *Journal of the American Statistical Association, 70*, 320-328.

Gilb, T., & Graham, D. (1993). *Software inspection*. Harlow, UK: Addison-Wesley.

Hammersley, M. (1992). Deconstructing the qualitative-quantitative divide. In J. Brannen (Ed.), *Mixing methods: Qualitative and quantitative research*. Avebury, Aldershot.

Hancock, D. R., & Flowers, C. P. (2001). Comparing social desirability responding on World Wide Web and paper-administered surveys. *ETR&D, 49*(1), 5-13.

Hartog, C., & Herbert, M. (1986, December). 1985 Opinion Survey of MIS Manager: Key issues. *MIS Quarterly, 10*(4), 64-69.

Hui, B. S. (1982). On building partial least squares models with interdependent inner relations. In K. G. Joreskog & H. Wold (Eds.), *Systems under indirect observation: Causality, structure, prediction* (pp. 249-272). Amsterdam: North-Holland.

Hui, B. S. (1987). *The partial least squares approach to path models of indirectly observed variables with multiple indicators.* Unpublished Doctoral Dissertation, University of Pennsylvania, Philadelphia.

Hyman, H. (1955). *Survey design and analysis: Principles, cases and procedures.* New York: The Free.

IEEE Standard 1028. (1998). Software Engineering Standard Committee of the IEEE Computer Society, 1998. *IEEE Standard for Software Review Standard 1028*, Institute of Electrical and Electronics Engineers Inc., New York.

Jonassen, D. H. (2001). Communication patterns in computer mediated vs. face-to-face group problem solving. *Educational Technology Research and Development, 49*(1), 35.

Joreskog, K. G. (1973). A general method for estimating a linear structural equation system. In A. S. Goldberger & O. D. Duncan (Eds.), *Structural equation models in the social sciences* (pp. 85-122). New York: Academic Press.

Joreskog, K. G. (1989). *LISREL 7: A guide to the program and applications.* Chicago: SPSS.

Judd, C. M., Smith, E. R., & Kidder, L. H. (1991). *Research methods in social relations* (6th ed.). Forth Worth, Tx: Harcourt Brace Jovanovich College.

Kanuk, L., & Berenson, C. (1975). Mail survey and response rates: A literature review. *Journal of Marketing Research*, 440453.

Keesling, J. W. (1972). *Maximum likelihood approaches to causal analysis.* Unpublished Doctoral Dissertation, University of Chicago.

Kelloway, E. K. (1995). Structural equation modelling in perspective. *Journal of Organisational Behaviour,* (16), 215-224.

Kettinger, William, J., Lee, Choong, C., Lee, & Sunro. (1995, September/October). Global measures of information service quality: A cross-national study. *Decision Sciences, 26*(5), 569-588.

Kiesler, S., & Sproull, L. (1998). Response effects in the electronic survey. *Public Opinion Quarterly, 50*(3), 402-413.

Kinnear, H. C., & James R. T. (1996). *Marketing research: An applied approach* (5th ed.). New York: McGraw-Hall.

Kish, L. (1965). *Survey sampling.* New York: Wiley.

Knodel, J. (1993). The design and analysis of focus groups studies: A practical approach. In D. Morgan (Ed.), *Successful focus groups: Advancing the state of art* (pp. 35-50). Newbury Park, CA: Saga.

Kraemer, K. (1991). The information systems research challenge. In K. Kraemer (Ed.), *Survey research methods* (pp. 299-315). Boston: Harvard Business School.

Krueger, R. A. (1993). Quality control in focus group research. In D. Morgan (Ed.), *Successful focus groups: Advancing the state of art* (pp. 65-149). Newbury Park, CA: Saga.

Laitenberger, O., & Debaud, J. M. (2000). An encompassing life cycle centric survey of software inspection. *The Journal of Software and Systems, 50*(1), 5-31.

Lazar, J., & Preece, J. (1999, Summer). Designing and implementing Web-based surveys. *Journal of Computer Information Systems,* 63-67.

Lee, E. S., Forthofer, R. N., & Lorimor, R. J. (1989). *Analyzing complex survey data.* London: Sage.

Light, R. J. (1971). Measures of response agreement for qualitative data: Some generalizations and alternatives. *Psychological Bulletin, 76,* 365-377.

Litwin, M. S. (1995). *How to measure survey reliability and validity.* Thousand Oaks, CA: Sage.

Lohmoller, J. B. (1989). *Latent variable path modeling with partial least squares.* Heidelberg, Germany: Physica-Verlag.

Lyttkens, E. (1966, June 14-19). On the fix-point property of world's interactive estimation method for principal components. In P. R. Krishnaiah (Ed.), *Proceedings of the International Symposium on Multivariate Analysis* (pp. 335-350). Dayton.

Lyttkens, E. (1973). The fixed-point method for estimating interdependent systems with the underlying model specification. *Journal of the Royal Statistical Society, A136,* 353-394.

Lyytinen, K., & Hirschheim, R. (1987). Information systems failure: A survey and classification of the empirical literature. *Oxford Surveys in Information Technology, 4,* 257-309.

Mabe, P., & West, S. (1982, June). Validity of self-evaluation of ability: A review and meta-analysis. *Journal of Applied Psychology, 67*(3), 280-296.

Malhotra, N. K., Hall, J., Shaw, M., & Crisp, M. (1996). *Marketing research: An applied orientation.* Sydney, Australia: Prentice Hall.

Marriam, S. B. (1988). *Case study research in education: A qualitative approach.* San Francisco: Jossey-Bass.

McCullough, D. (1998, October/November). Market research on the Web. *Communication World,* 29-31.

McNeil, D. (2001). *Modern statistics: A graphical introduction.* Marrickville: Southwood Press Pty Ltd.

Miles, M. B., & Huberman, A. M. (1984). *Qualitative data analysis: A sourcebook of new methods.* Beverly Hill, CA: Sage.

Morgan, D. L. (1998). *Focus groups as qualitative research: Qualitative research methods.* Newbury Park, CA: Sage.

Morgan, D. L., & Krueger, R. (1993). When to use focus groups and why. In D. Morgan (Ed.), *Successful focus groups: Advancing the state of art* (pp. 3-19). Newbury Park, CA: Saga.

Naylor, G. F. K., & Enticknap, L. E. (1981). *Statistics simplified: An introduction for social scientists and others.* Sydney, Australia: Harcourt Brace Jovanovich Group.

Neuman, L. W. (2000). *Social research methods: Qualitative and quantitative approaches* (4th ed.). Boston: Allyn & Bacon.

Newman, W. L. (1994). *Social research methods: Qualitative and quantitative approaches.* Boston: Allyn & Bacon.

Newsted P. R., Huff, S. L., & Munro M. C. (1998, December) Survey instruments in information systems. *MIS Quarterly,* 553-554.

Newsted, P. R., Munro, M., & Huff, S. (1991). Data acquisition instruments in management information systems. In K. Kraemer (Ed.), *The information systems research challenge: Survey research methods* (pp. 187-209). Boston: Harvard Business School.

O'Brien, K. (1993). Improving survey questionnaire. In D. Morgan (Ed.). *Successful focus groups: Advancing the state of art* (pp. 105-117). Newbury Park, CA: Saga.

Ozer, D. J. (1985). Correlation and the coefficient of determination. *Psychological Bulletin, 97*(2), 307-315.

Pinsonneault, A., & Kraemer, K. (1993, 75-105 Fall). Survey research methodology in management information systems. *Journal of Management Information Systems.*

Porter, A. A., & Votta, L. G. (1994). An experiment to asses different defect detection methods for software requirements inspections. *Proceedings of*

16ᵗʰ International Conference on Software Engineering, ICSE'16 (pp. 103-112).

Preston, M. G. (1983). Note on the reliability and validity of the group judgement. *Journal of Experimental Psychology, 22*, 462-471.

Rahim, M. A., Antonioni, D., & Psenicka, C. (2001). A structural equations model of learning power, subordinates' styles of handling conflict. *Job Performance, 12*(3), 191-211.

Rossi, P. H., & Anderson, A. B. (1982). The factorial survey approach: An introduction. In P. H. Rossi & L. S. Nock (Eds.), *Measuring social judgements: A factorial survey approach.* London: Sage.

Ruyter, K. D., & Scholl, N. (1998). Positioning qualitative market research: Reflections from theory and practice. *The International Journal of Qualitative Market Research, 1*(1), 7-14.

Salant, P., & Dillman, D. A. (1994). *How to conduct your own survey.* Canada: John Wiley & Sons.

Sauer, C., Jeffery, R., Land, L., & Yetton, P. (2000). Understanding and improving the effectiveness of software development technical reviews: A behaviourally motivated programme of research. *IEEE Transactions on Software Engineering, 26*(1), 1-14.

Schmidt, W. (1997). World wide Web survey research: Benefits, potential problems, and solutions. *Behaviour Research Methods, Instruments, and Computer, 29*(2), 274-279.

Sekran U. (1992). *Research method for business: A skill building approach* (2ⁿᵈ ed.). New York: John Wiley & Sons.

Sheatsley, P. B. (1974). Survey design. In R. Ferber (Ed.), *Handbook of marketing research.* New York: McGraw Hill.

Shull, F., Lanubile, F., & Biasili, V. (2000, November). Investigating reading techniques for object-oriented framework learning. *IEEE Transaction on Software Engineering, 26*(11)

Smith, M. K. (1998, July). Psychological issues in questionnaire-based research. *Journal of the Market Research Society, 40*(3), 223-236.

Stone, M. (1974). Cross-validatory choice and assessment of statistical predictions: *Journal of the Royal Statistical Society, B36*, 111-133.

Straub, D. W. (1989). Validating instruments in MIS research. *MIS Quarterly, 13*, 147-169.

Sudman, S. (1994). Sampling. In R. P. Bagozzi (Ed.), *Principles of marketing research.* Cambridge: Basil Blackwell.

Tervonen, I. (1996). Support for quality-based design and inspection. *IEEE Software, 13*(1), 44-45.

Thelin, T., Runeson, R., & Regnell, B. (2001). Usage-based reading–An experiment to guide reviewers with use cases. *Information and Software Technology, 43*, 925-938.

Tull, D. S., & Hawkins, D. I. (1990). *Marketing research: Measurement and method* (5th ed.). New York: Macmillan.

Wert, C. E., Linn, R. L., & Joreskog, K. G. (1974). Intra-class reliability estimates: Testing structural assumptions. *Educational and Psychological Measurement, 34*, 25-33.

Wiegers, K. E. (2002). *Peer reviews in software: A practical guide.* Boston: Addison-Wesley.

Wiley, D. E. (1973). The Identification problem for structural equation models with unmeasured variables. In A. S. Goldberger & O. D. Duncan (Eds.), *Structural equation models in the social sciences* (pp. 69-83). New York: Academic Press.

Wold, H. (1985). Partial least squares. In S. Kotz & N. L. Johnson (Eds.), *Encyclopedia of statistical sciences, 6* (pp. 581-591). New York: Wiley.

Wold, H. (1988). Specification, predictor. In S. Kotz & N. L. Johnson (Eds.), *Encyclopedia of statistical sciences, 8* (pp. 587-599). New York: Wiley.

Wolff, B., Knodel, J., & Sittitrai, W. (1993). Focus groups and surveys as complementary research methods. In D. Morgan (Ed.), *Successful focus groups: Advancing the state of art* (pp. 136-188). Newbury Park, CA: Saga.

Yin, R. K. (1994). *Case study research: Design and methods* (2nd ed.). Thousand Oaks, CA: Sage.

Zikmund, W. G. (2000). *Exploring marketing research* (7th ed.). Fort Worth, TX: The Dryden.

Zmud, R. W., & Boynton, A. C. (1991). Survey measures and instruments, MIS: Inventory and appraisal. In K. Kraemer (Ed.), *The information systems research challenge: Survey research methods* (pp. 149-180). Boston: Harvard Business School.

Chapter VIII

Industry Software Reviews Survey Results and Findings

Abstract

This chapter describes the industry survey results and findings, which include preliminary data analysis (missing value and descriptive data analyses), exploratory analyses (principal component analysis, and reliability and validity analysis) and hypotheses tests using Structural Equation Modeling Using Partial Least Squares (PLS) methodology. A total of 15 constructs with 48 indicators are used in the model, but only 15 paths are significant. The results of the model, using an inner model path weighting scheme show a substantial R-square of 0.398 for performance, a moderate level of 0.239 for experience and 0.335 for teamwork and a weak level of 0.024 for reports and 0.049 for previously reviewed software.

Industry Survey Findings

Further to the survey design, the aim of this chapter is to report the industry software review survey findings. Starting with the response characteristics, three data analysis procedures (preliminary analysis, exploratory analysis, and hypotheses tests) will be conducted in this chapter.

Response

Response Rate

The main goal of the sampling process chosen was to capture as wide a range of software development companies in the study as possible. Software firms from the computer services category (category of firms was based on Australian Bureau of Statistics) and from the top 500 companies listed in the Australian stock exchange were identified for this survey study. The survey was conducted between March and August, 2003. Despite the reminder letters, the initial response rate was less than 3% in first month. The response rate increased up to 12% after two reminders were sent. Personal telephone calls and e-mail follow-up helped add an additional 6% to the responding companies. After four months of formal survey, 189 completed questionnaires were received from all states.

Although a total of 1380 company's mailing addresses were retrieved, only 1139 letters were successfully delivered — that is, about 241 letters were unable to be delivered. This is due to the companies no longer existing at the current address (either closed down or changed address) (see Table 1). The pilot study

Table 1. Distribution of the six states and two territories mailing list

States	Number of the Companies Retrieved	Undelivered Mails	Number of Mails Sent Minus the Undelivered Mails
NSW	621	120	501
VIC	374	49	325
QLD	144	29	115
WA	141	29	112
SA	67	9	58
ACT	26	3	23
TAS	6	2	4
NT	1	0	1
Total	**1380**	**241**	**1139**

Table 2. Distribution of response rate in each stage

States and Territories	Number of Responses	Percentages of Responses (Percent)
NSW	89[a]	43.4
VIC	59	28.8
QLD	16	7.8
WA	21[b]	10.2
SA	13	6.3
ACT	5	2.4
TAS	2	1.0
NT	0	0.0
Total	205	100.0

questionnaire was nearly indistinguishable from the final questionnaire except for minor differences in the layout, and the wording of a few questions. Since the measures and constructs in the pilot study and the final questionnaire are essentially same, the 16 pilot cases are combined with the formal survey responses, resulting in a reasonable size of 205 cases for further analysis (see Table 2). This makes the total response rate 18%. This response rate compares favourably with the responses rates of between 6% and 16% reported in the literature for mail surveys (Harzing, 1997).

As shown in Table 2, the distribution of companies in the responses sampled from six states and two territories in Australia–New South Wales (NSW) (43%), Western Australian (WA) (10.2%), Victoria (VIC) (28.8%), Queensland (QLD) (7.8%), Northern Territory (NT) (0%), South Australia (SA) (6.3%), Australia Capital Territory (ACT) (2.4%), and Tasmania (TAS) (1%).

Responses Characteristics

The sample contains 205 responses engaging in 13 different industries and nine business categories (the label of both industry and business categories for the questionnaire design were adopted from Australian Bureau Statistics, 2002). Tables 3 and 4 illustrate the demographic information (i.e., distributions of 13 industries and nine business categories).

The mean and median employees in the departments were 10 and 19, and 50 and 99 in the companies. Forty percent of companies held quality certifications and about 31% of companies were following the ISO 9001 standard.

An approximately 74% of the respondents were male and 26% were female (see Figure 1). The respondents were in age groups ranging from 20 to 60 years of

Table 3. Industry categories

Industry Categories	Frequency	Percent
Computer and business machine manufacturing	12	5.9
Telecommunication, broadcasting equipment manufacturing	7	3.4
Electronic equipment manufacturing	11	5.4
Electric cable and wire manufacturing	17	8.3
Computer wholesaling	18	8.8
Business machine wholesaling	1	0.5
Electrical and electronic equipment wholesaling	4	2.0
Telecommunication services	7	3.4
Data processing service	6	2.9
Information storage and retrieval services	22	10.7
Information maintenance services	2	1.0
Computer consultancy services	20	9.8
Other	78	38.0
Total	205	100

Table 4. Main products/services

Main Products/Services	Frequency	Percent
Computer programming service	42	20.5
Pre-packaged software	16	7.8
Computer integrated systems design	13	6.3
Computer processing and data preparation and processing	15	7.3
Information retrieval service	18	8.8
Information facilities management services	3	1.5
Computer rental and leasing	1	0.5
Computer maintenance and repair	18	8.8
Other	75	36.6
Don't know	4	2.0
Total	**205**	**100**

age. The most frequent age range of respondents was 31-40 years old. Figure 2 illustrates the age demographic.

The number of respondents with software industry experience was approximately 93%. About 40% of respondents have participated in either formal or informal software review training.

About 89% had role experience in requirements review; 92% in design review, 91% in code review and about 72% in testing review. All subjects are industry practitioners and currently working in Australia. This indicates that most respondents have a good knowledge of software review and are able to provide satisfactory responses to the software review related issues in the questionnaire.

Figure 1. Gender

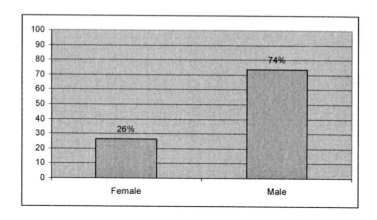

Figure 2. Age

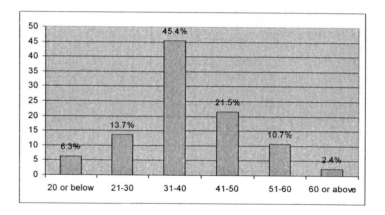

Figure 3 shows that approximately 21% of respondents are Information Technology Managers, 8% are System Analysts, 8% are System Designers, 10% are Software Designers, 23% are Applications and Analyst Programmers, 3% are System Programmers, 1% are Business Analysts, 5% are Testers, and 22% are in software related areas.

For education level, the majority of the respondents have university degrees (see Figure 4). About 77% of respondents held a Bachelor or Master degree with a major in computer sciences or related information technology areas. Also, about 45% of respondents held professional membership of information technology related associations (see Figure 5). This suggests that the respondents are likely

Figure 3. Job positions

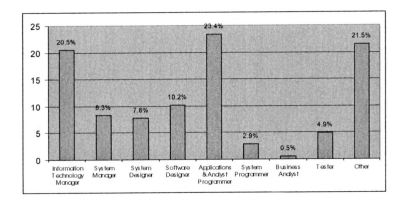

Figure 4. Education

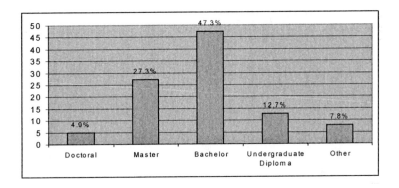

to have a reasonably good education and knowledge about information technology and the software industry, and be able to provide valid and reliable data.

Looking at the software review process, more than 52% of respondents participated in software reviews between 1 and 10 times in last six months, 14% between 11 and 20 times, 10% between 21 and 30 times, 8% between 31 and 40 times, and 16% more than 41 times (see Figure 6).

According to Figure 7, about 30% of respondents have participated in requirement reviews most frequently during the last six months, 33% most frequently in design reviews, 23% most frequently in code reviews, and 14% most frequently in testing reviews.

Figure 5. Professional memberships

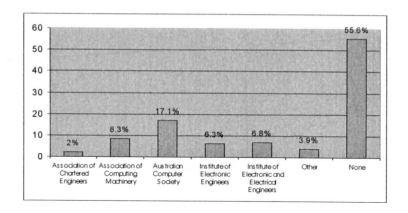

Figure 6. Number of software reviews that respondent participated in software review during last six months

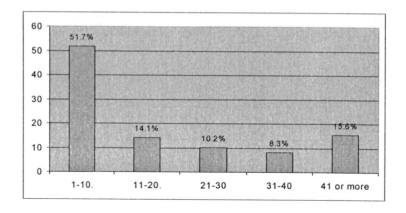

In relation to role assignment, on average the respondents were most frequently involved in the reviewer role 11-20 times during last six months, moderator role 1-10 times, reader role one time, author role 1-10 times, and recorder role one time. The respondents involved in the preparation are 97%, about 90% involved in the individual reviews (individually examine (i.e., identify defects) the arte-fact) and 87% respondents involved in the interactive group meetings (an interactive group meeting for examining the artefact). By far the most frequent size range of group meetings was 3-6 people. Figure 8 summarises the distribution of software review group meeting size.

Figure 7. Number of respondents participated in most frequently during last six months

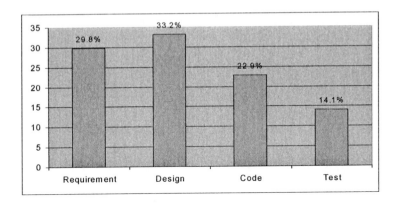

Figure 8. Number of people in a group meeting

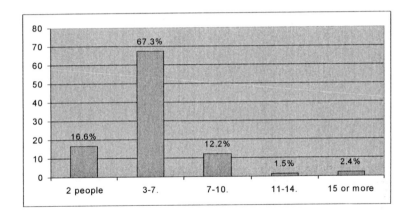

Response Bias

To test if there is a response bias, the survey and response samples were compared on three criteria: total number of respondents, number of respondents from each state, and size of companies (i.e., number of employees).

As mentioned earlier in Table 1, 205 (189 plus 16 respondents from the pilot study) completed questionnaires were received in the survey. Thus, a relatively high 18% of the respondents in the survey sample are represented in the response sample (see Table 5).

Table 5. Response rate

States	Number of The Companies Retrieved	Number of The Companies Retrieved (Percent)	Number of Responses	Number of Responses (Percent)
NSW	621	45	89	43.4
VIC	374	27.1	59	28.8
QLD	144	10.4	16	7.8
WA	141	10.2	21	10.2
SA	67	4.9	13	6.3
ACT	26	1.9	5	2.4
TAS	6	0.4	2	1.0
NT	1	0.1	0	0.0
Total	1380	100	205	100

By state, 7.8% of questionnaires were completed in New South Wales, 1.8% in Western Australian, 5.2% in Victoria, 1.1% in South Australia, 0.2% in Tasmania, 1.4% in Queensland, 0.4% in Australia Capital Territory, and zero in the Northern Territory.

On average, as the percentage of responses per state except Northern Territory (there is only one company in North Territories; since there are about 1138 companies in our samples, the respondent will not affect our sample bias), is in proportion to the percentage of questionnaires sent out by state, there is unlikely to be a bias in the results.

The majority of companies are medium to large size companies — less than 100 employees in their department, and between 20 and 500 employees in Australia. Figure 9 and 10 show the details of the distributions of the employees (the design

Figure 9. Number of employees in the department

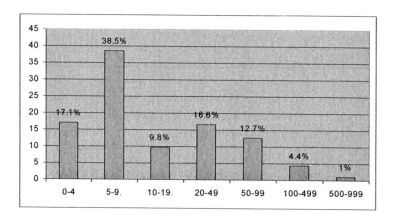

scale of the employee number was adopted from Australian Bureau Statistics, 2002) in the departments and locally (i.e., Australia). The most frequent number of employees in the response sample is between 5 and 9 in department and 50 and 99 employees locally (i.e., Australia only) respectively.

In comparison to the survey and response samples, there are not many differences between the actual responses and survey samples for company size. As a result, this indicates that the responses are representative of the survey sample. In other words, the response samples are representative of the target population of the companies in Australia.

Also, the coverage of software companies in different states and the diverse samples provide sufficient variance to test hypotheses and also increase the generalisation of the results. To our knowledge, there is no other study in the software review literature that has used such a diverse sample for testing the hypotheses.

Preliminary Data Analysis

The preliminary data analysis includes two steps 1) missing value analysis and 2) descriptive analysis. The missing values analysis was carried out to produce a clean data set for hypotheses tests (Coakes & Steed, 2001), whereas the descriptive analysis provided an estimate of the characteristics of the responses such as the mean, variance and standard deviation (De Vaus, 2001).

Figure 10. Number of employees in Australia

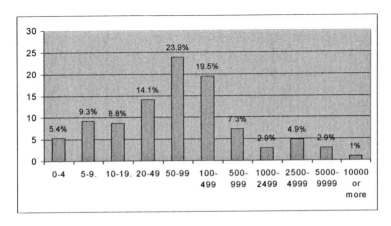

Descriptive Data Analysis

The descriptive analyses of mean, standard deviation, minimum and maximum were computed for each of the 65 items (see Appendix 8) and all measures have reasonable variance, suggesting that the measures are useful for a correlation study. The frequency analysis of the 49 items (indicators) shows that all items have scores spanning the entire range on their respective scales. This indicates that there are no floor or ceiling effects in our measurements (De Vaus, 2001; Zmud & Boynton, 1991).

Missing Value Analysis

The data matrix comprising raw data with 205 cases and 49 indicators has approximately 3% missing values. This is considered a low missing value rate. To verify if the values are missing completely at random, a set of dummy variables was created to indicate the cases with and without missing data.

The Chi-square test was carried out to study the relationship between the cases with and without missing data and cases characteristics both at company level and individual respondent level. Analysing company level includes manufacturing vs. services businesses, size of the department vs. size of the company, and quality certificates companies vs. non quality certificate holders companies.

Analysing individual respondents include managerial vs. non-managerial positions, respondents who held professional memberships vs. those who do not hold any professional memberships. The findings show that there is no significant relationship between the cases with and without missing values. It is suggested that the situations where there are missing values are completely random. This implies replacing the missing values with the series mean would not alter the nature of relationship among the variables, when simultaneously increasing sample size and the power of the statistical tests (Cohen, 1988). Hence, the data can be regarded as having missing values completely at random (Coakes & Steed, 2001). This means that the probability that an observation (X_i) is missing is unrelated to the value of X_i or to the value of any other variables (Cohen & Cohen, 1983; Little & Rubin, 1987; Allison, 2002). For instance, "professional membership" item would not be considered if people who held professional memberships were more likely to report their professional membership than people without professional membership. Similarly, if managerial staff were more likely to omit reporting their positions than non-managerial staff, again, it would not have data that were missing completely at random because missingness would be correlated with background.

Exploratory Analysis

Exploratory analysis is used for reliability testing and also allows examination of the discriminant validity of the item measures for each construct (Chin & Gopal, 1995).

Reliability and Validity

In order to validate the content validity, both primary and secondary sources of data were used during the questionnaire development including questionnaires developed by other researchers (Litwin, 1995). The Explicit and Implicit Input-process-Output (EIIO) model is developed from relevant literature and feedback from pre-test respondents on the representativeness of questions but is independent from earlier instruments (Basili et al., 1996; Boehm & Basili, 2001; Campell, 1990; Campell & Pritchard 1976; Davison, 1997; Deci, Eghrari, Patrick, & Leone, 1994; Deci, Koestner, & Ryan, 1999a, 1999b; Engelkamp & Wippich, 1995; Ericsson, 1994; Ericsson & Lehmann, 1996; Fagan, 1986; Gilb & Graham, 1993; Humphrey, 2000, 2002a, 2002b; IEEE Standard 1028, 1998; Lee, Trauth, & Farwell, 1995; Porter & Votta, 1994; Thelin, Runeson, & Regnell, 2001).

Discriminant validity asks if the items chosen for each construct are truly related to the construct. If constructs are valid, then one can expect that the items underlying each construct will load on different items (Chin, 1998). In addition, in factor analysis, it is generally considered desirable to have a larger number of respondents than constructs (Joreskog, 1989; Kelloway, 1995). Opinion is divided on the extent of the ratio, with some authorities suggesting 1:12 (Davison, 1997) and other suggesting 1:10 (Nunnally, 1976). In this research, a ratio of over 1:12 was achieved. The reliability of a construct can be assessed using Cronbach's alpha. The major function of a reliability test is to assess the internal consistency of the constructs. The reliability level of the input constructs in this study varies from .65 to .93. Tables 6-7 depict the 11 indicators (items) already described according to the four input constructs.

Inputs

The use of common factor analysis and extraction by Principal Component Analysis is an acceptable procedure in attempting data reduction (Babbie, 2000; Lyttkens, 1966; Rossi & Anderson, 1982). As shown in Table 6, the 11 indicators (items) were able to produce four constructs — commitment, contingency,

Table 6. Principal component analysis: Implicit inputs

Indicators/Items	Construct/Components			
	Commitment (CMM)	Contingency (CTG)	Competency (CPT)	Confidence (CFD)
Willingness (WL)	0.907			
Effort (EF)	0.906			
Motivation (MT)	0.894			
Support (SP)		0.910		
Encouragement (EC)		0.910		
Agree (AR)		0.894		
Do things well (DW)			0.904	
Effective approach (ET)			0.902	
Confident in teaching (CT)				0.793
Confident in doing better (CB)				0.775
Confident in capability (CP)				0.669

Extraction Method: Principal Component Analysis.

Table 7. Eigenvalues and reliability test: Implicit inputs

Construct/Component	Total	% of Variance	Cumulative %	Cronbach Alpha
Commitment (CMM)	2.716	24.689	24.689	.9340
Contingency (CTG)	2.593	23.571	48.261	.9058
Competency (CPT)	1.933	17.571	65.832	.9347
Confidence (CFD)	1.746	15.872	81.703	.6460

competency, confidence, with loadings between 0.775 and 0.91 respectively. This also explains 81.7% of the variance (see Table 7). The reliability of constructs, indicated by the Cronbach alpha (1970; Cronbach & Show, 1977), is from 0.646 to 0.935, which can be considered a satisfactory level. It is suggested that below 0.6 is unacceptable, 0.6-0.65 undesirable, 0.65-0.7 minimally acceptable, 0.7-0.8 respectable and 0.8 or above very good (Litwin, 1995). However, one of problematic indicator, capability (from competency construct), has a loading of 0.2, which is below the acceptable level. It is recommended that the indicator should be deleted and it is not suitable and reliable for further data analysis (Litwin, 1995). Therefore, only remaining two indicators of the competency are used for further data analysis.

Process

The Cronbach's alphas of discussion quality, communications, status effects and teamwork are between 0.813 and 0.84 respectively (see Table 8.9), which shows good reliability based on Nunnally's Criteria (1976).

A principal components factor analysis produced four constructs, with loadings between 0.655 and 0.863 (see Table 8) explaining 69.4%of the variance indicates discriminate validity of the instrument (see Table 9).

The strong loadings of the communications construct are between 0.771 and 0.836 (see Table 8). The findings of the factor analysis for the discussion quality construct indicate that the familiar — imaginative indicator, 0.657, does not load

Table 8. Principal component analysis: Process

Indicators/Items	Constructs/Components			
	Communication (CMU)	Discuss Quality (DSQ)	Status Effects (STE)	Teamwork (TEA)
Expression (EP)	0.836			
Language (LA)	0.801			
Putting ideas forward (RF)	0.796			
Understanding (UD)	0.771			
Appropriate (AP)		0.863		
Meaning (ME)		0.824		
Close (CO)		0.818		
Familiar (FI)		0.657		
Power (SE)			0.818	
Intimidation (ID)			0.792	
Inhibition (IB)			0.677	
Pressure (PR)			0.655	
Team (TM)				0.815
Sharing (SH)				0.807
Willingness to participate (WP)				0.745

Table 9. Eigenvalues and reliability test: Process

Constructs/ Component	Total	% of Variance	Cumulative %	Cronbach alpha
Communication (CMU)	2.892	19.278	19.278	.8402
Discussion quality (DSQ)	2.765	18.434	37.712	.8337
Status effects (STE)	2.455	16.367	54.079	.8129
Teamwork (TEA)	2.292	15.28	69.359	.8213

well with the other three indicators (0.818-0.863). These loadings are slightly different to the results from Davison's study (1997), which showed that discussions in the meeting were: open-closed item does not load well with the other three.

One explanation is that the objective of a software review is different to other meetings. Most meetings in organizations aim for novel/new ideas or discussion comments in the meeting whereas software review aims for defect detection.

However, overall the loadings in this context indicate that the discussion construct is considered satisfactory. Three items of the teamwork construct have high loadings, confirming the construct (see Table 8).

Hypotheses Tests: Structural Equation Modelling (SEM) Using Partial Least Squares (PLS)

Since PLS makes no distributional assumptions for parameter estimation, traditional parameter-based techniques for significance testing are inappropriate (Chin, 1998). The evaluation of PLS models is therefore based on prediction-oriented measures that are non-parametric (Chin, 1998).

The PLS measurement (outer) model for reflective constructs is evaluated by examining the convergent and discriminant validity of indicators, and the composite reliability of a block of indicators. On the other hand, the formative indicators are evaluated on the basis of their substantive content, by comparing the relative size of their estimated weights, and by examining the statistical significance of the measure weights (Chin, 1998). Consistent with the distribution free, predictive approach of PLS (Wold, 1980, 1985, 1988), the structural (inner) model is evaluated by assessing the percentage variance, that is, the R-square for the dependent constructs, by using the Stone-Geisser Q-square test for the predictive relevance (Geisser, 1975; Stone, 1974), and by examining the size, t-statistics and significance level of structural path coefficients. Finally, the t-statistics are estimated using the bootstrap re-sampling procedure. Hypothesis tests were carried out with a significance level of 0.05 to test the proposed model in our study.

Table 10. Composite reliability

Construct	Cronbach's Alpha	Internal Consistency (Composite Reliability)
Commitment (CMM)	.934	.802
Contingency (CTG)	.906	.941
Competency (CPT)	.935	.686
Confidence (CFD)	.646	.807
Communication (CMU)	.840	.895
Discussion quality (DSQ)	.834	.890
Status effects (STE)	.813	.875
Teamwork (TEA)	.821	.894

PLS Reliability and Validity Tests

The convergent validity of the measurement model for the reflective indicator is assessed by examining the correlation between the indicators and construct scores computed in PLS. Individual reflective indicators are considered to be reliable if they correlate more than 0.7 with the constructs that they intend to measure. However, in the early stages of instrument development, a loading of 0.5 to 0.6 is considered acceptable if there are additional indicators in the construct for comparison purposes (Chin, 1998). As shown in Table 11 all of the 26 reflective indicators have loadings above 0.631 on their constructs. The composite reliability of a block of indicators measuring a construct is assessed with two measures–the internal consistency measure developed by Wert, Linn, and Joreskog (1974), Joreskog (1973), and Cronbach's alpha (1970; Cronbach & Show, 1977).

According to Chin (1998), "in comparison to Crohbach's alpha, this (the internal consistency) measure does not assume equivalency among the measures with its assumption that all indicators are equally weighted. Therefore, alpha tends to be lower bound estimated of reliability, whereas the internal consistency measure is a closer approximation under the assumption that the parameter estimates are accurate."

As shown in Table 10, the eight constructs measured with multiple reflective indicators have high composite reliability. The internal consistency measure ranges from 0.802 to 0.941 for all constructs, whereas Cronbach's alpha ranges from 0.646 to 0.935. Although the internal consistency measure tends to be higher than Cronbach's alpha (Chin, 1998), especially for constructs measured with few indicators, overall, the composite reliabilities estimated with both the measures are satisfactory.

Table 11 Cross-loadings: Correlations of the constructs (loadings and cross loadings for the measurement (outer) model)

	CMM	CPT	CFD	CTG	CMU	STE	TEA	DSQ
	Pc = .802	Pc = .686	Pc = .807	Pc = .941	Pc = .895	Pc = .875	Pc = .894	Pc = .89
MT	**0.956**	0.626	0.087	-0.116	-0.160	-0.075	0.023	-0.061
WL	**0.907**	0.593	0.119	-0.091	-0.107	-0.020	0.038	-0.034
Effort	**0.852**	0.482	0.190	-0.005	-0.184	-0.039	0.005	-0.040
DW	0.615	**0.631**	0.091	-0.055	-0.137	-0.119	0.047	-0.106
ET	0.514	**0.808**	0.106	0.036	-0.047	-0.058	0.016	-0.098
CB	0.209	0.214	**0.813**	0.274	-0.245	-0.174	0.109	-0.005
CT	0.090	-0.020	**0.818**	0.240	-0.017	0.048	0.193	0.098
CP	0.019	0.048	**0.650**	0.120	0.053	0.043	0.238	0.085
AR	-0.013	0.067	0.189	**0.899**	0.012	-0.203	0.382	0.377
SP	-0.128	-0.029	0.318	**0.933**	0.020	-0.188	0.404	0.390
EC	-0.053	-0.060	0.299	**0.921**	0.018	-0.157	0.358	0.423
LA	-0.153	-0.143	-0.116	-0.018	**0.827**	0.369	0.111	0.137
EP	-0.138	-0.080	-0.107	0.036	**0.855**	0.396	0.033	0.152
UD	-0.117	-0.098	0.005	0.061	**0.803**	0.465	0.125	0.163
RF	-0.196	-0.086	-0.146	-0.001	**0.816**	0.377	0.017	0.165
SE	0.029	-0.057	-0.016	-0.120	0.365	**0.647**	-0.140	-0.118
PR	-0.028	-0.129	-0.087	-0.171	0.400	**0.840**	-0.279	-0.143
ID	-0.027	-0.051	0.047	-0.222	0.422	**0.845**	-0.155	-0.061
IB	-0.168	-0.078	-0.102	-0.172	0.511	**0.845**	-0.124	-0.084
TM	0.017	0.029	0.196	0.371	0.126	-0.158	**0.885**	0.444
WP	0.029	-0.023	0.204	0.393	-0.036	-0.235	**0.863**	0.370
SH	-0.029	0.048	0.192	0.367	0.074	-0.197	**0.828**	0.489
ME	-0.042	-0.065	0.114	0.421	0.155	-0.136	0.443	**0.853**
AP	-0.028	-0.095	0.085	0.264	0.176	0.021	0.424	**0.781**
CO	0.039	-0.120	0.109	0.416	0.112	-0.180	0.459	**0.866**
FI	-0.151	-0.090	-0.009	0.356	0.170	-0.059	0.383	**0.768**

Thus, the constructs are reliably measured by their respective indicators. That is, the reflective indicators are reasonably good measures of their respective constructs. Overall, the SEM using the PLS measurement model for all indicators is satisfactory.

The discriminant validity of the reflective measures is measured by examining the cross-loadings of the indicators and their constructs (Hui, 1982, 1987; Lohmoller, 1989). Exploring the columns in Table 11, the correlations of the constructs with their own indicators are higher than with the measures of any other construct.

This indicates that the constructs predict indicators in their block better than the indicators in any other block. Similarly, looking across the rows in the table, the correlations of the indicators with their construct are higher than with any other construct.

Another method of assessing the discriminant validity is to compare the square root of average variance extracted (AVE) for each construct with the correlation between the construct and other constructs in the model (Chin, 1998).

Table 12. Correlation among construct scores (square root of AVE in diagonal)

	CMM	CPT	CFD	CTG	CMU	STE	TEA	DSQ
CMM	**0.590**							
CPT	0.260	**0.525**						
CFD	0.149	0.110	**0.584**					
CTG	0.065	0.001	0.286	**0.842**				
CMU	0.162	0.102	0.068	0.030	**0.681**			
STE	0.051	0.104	0.012	0.188	0.528	**0.638**		
TEA	0.030	0.038	0.243	0.415	0.087	0.182	**0.738**	
DSQ	0.047	0.104	0.073	0.435	0.197	0.085	0.511	**0.670**

The measures are considered to have adequate discriminant validity if the square root the AVE for each construct is larger than the correlation between the construct and any other construct in the model (Wold, 1980, 1985). As shown in Table 12, all constructs in the estimated model also fulfill this condition of discriminant validity.

There are seven constructs (i.e., experience, software artefact characteristics, reading technique documents, prescription documents, previously reviewed software documents, reports, and performance) with a large number of formative indicators. Since the loadings and cross-loading cannot be used to assess the reliability and validity of formative indicators, their measures are evaluated on the basis of their substantive content, and by comparing the relative size and statistical significance of their estimated weights (Chin, 1998). To evaluate the formative indicators of seven constructs, Table 13 summarises the path weights of the indicators forming the construct, the observed t-values form the bootstrap re-sampling procedures, and the significance level of measure weights.

As shown in Table 13, the significant indicators are: role experience, working experience in software industry, complexity, previously reviewed design documents, business reports, procedure guideline, template, checklist, true defects, and false positives. Table 14 shows the weights and loading of formative indicators.

All measures of the formative indicator constructs (significant and non significant) are retained for estimating the PLS model. The reason being that, unlike the reflective measures whose reliability and validity can be assessed by examining the individual and composite reliability, the reliability of the formative indicators cannot be examined before using PLS.

Further, since all the measures are theoretically grounded, it is interesting to find that the conceptually important facets of all the formative constructs such as training materials, time record form, defect standards, scenarios and stepwise

Table 13. Measurement (outer) model results for formative indicators (n.s. = not significant)

Constructs	Indicators/Items	Path coefficient	T-value	P-value	One-tailed/two- tailed
Experience	Role experience (RE)	0.7905	9.1995	p<.001	two-tailed
	Working experience in software (IND)	0.2581	1.7462	p<.05	one-tailed
Software artefact characteristics (SAC)	Complexity (CX)	1.1562	3.1672	p<.005	two-tailed
	Size (SZ)	0.3996	1.7762	p<.05	one-tailed
	Initial quality (IQ)	0.2503	1.7752	p<.05	one-tailed
Previously reviewed software documents (PRD)	Requirement (RQ)	0.3919	1.7742	p<.05	one-tailed
	Design (DE)	0.7511	2.7017	p<.01	two-tailed
	Code (CD)	0.1676	1.7981	p<.05	one-tailed
Reports (RPO)	Business report (BR)	1.0107	3.9214	p<.001	two-tailed
	Standards (SS)	0.3550	1.7523	p<.05	one-tailed

reading technique documents, net defects are not significant. Overall, the PLS measurement for all indicators achieves satisfactory level. The next step is to test the hypotheses for the structural (inner) model.

Effect on Inputs

The purpose of the study is to predict review performance by looking at the impact of explicit (software artefact characteristics and supporting documents

Table 13. cont.

Constructs	Indicators/Items	Path coefficient	T-value	P-value	One-tailed/ two-tailed
Prescription documents (PSD)	Procedure guidelines (PG)	0.6789	4.4528	p<.001	two-tailed
	Training material (TA)	0.3991	1.6256	n.s.	-
	Time record form (RF)	0.2679	1.3282	n.s.	-
	Defect form (FR)	0.0530	0.3334	n.s.	-
	Template (TE)	0.8579	4.4567	p<.001	two-tailed
Reading technique documents (RTD)	Checklist (CK)	0.9444	2.1683	p<.05	two-tailed
	Scenarios/ perspective reading technique (SR)	0.4643	0.9137	n.s.	-
	Stepwise reading (ST)	0.4103	0.8654	n.s.	-
Performance/ Number of defects found (DEF)	True defects (TR)	0.4694	1.9618	p<.05	two-tailed
	False positives (FA)	0.3590	2.0717	p<.05	two-tailed
	Net defects (NE)	0.0454	0.1994	n.s.	-
	Total issues (TL)	0.2566	1.8497	p<.05	one-tailed

(reading technique documents, prescription documents, previously reviewed software documents, and reports)) and implicit inputs (experience and motivation (commitment, confidence, contingency, and competency)), and process (communication, status effect, teamwork and discussion quality) on review performance (number of defects found).

The structural model results from the PLS analysis of inputs-process-performance (performance is measured by number of defects found) are shown in Tables 15-16 which summarise the proposed research questions and hypotheses

Table 14. Weights and loadings for model using formative indicators

Constructs	Indicators/Items	Weights	Loadings
Experience (EXP)	Role experience (RE)	0.7753	0.8816
	Working experience in software industry (IND)	0.3085	0.5990
Software artefact characteristics (SAC)	Complexity (CX)	1.1044	0.9651
	Size (SZ)	0.2879	0.5912
	Initial quality (IQ)	0.3558	0.6635
Previously reviewed software documents (PRD)	Requirement (RQ)	0.2958	0.8265
	Design (DE)	0.8673	0.3044
	Code (CD	0.2550	0.1367
Reports (RPO)	Business report (BR)	1.0146	0.9969
	Standards (SS)	0.0804	0.1430

Constructs	Indicators/Items	Weights	Loadings
Prescription documents (PSD)	Procedure guidelines (PG)	0.6196	0.2920
	Training material (TA)	0.4316	0.3923
	Time record form (RF)	0.2455	0.4685
	Defect form (FR)	0.1201	0.3045
	Template (TE)	0.8548	0.5829
Reading technique documents (RTD)	Checklist (CK)	1.0940	0.9716
	Scenarios/ perspective reading technique (SR)	0.2815	0.2413
	Stepwise reading (ST)	0.0373	0.2553
Performance/ Number of defects found (DEF)	True defects (TR)	0.6065	0.9329
	False positives (FA)	0.3364	0.8127
	Net defects (NE)	0.1002	0.6632
	Total issues (TL)	0.2499	0.9125

Table 15. The effect of software artefact characteristics on the use of supporting documents and implicit inputs (n.s. = not significant)

Hypotheses	Path Coefficient	T-value	P-value	One-tailed/ two-tailed	Accept /Reject
H1 Software artefacts' characteristics have an effect on use of supporting documents.					
Reading technique documents (RTD)	0.0440	0.4438	n.s.	-	reject
Prescription documents (PSD)	0.3670	4.5992	<.0001	two-tailed	accept
Previously reviewed software documents (PRD)	0.2200	2.0415	<.05	two-tailed	accept
Reports (RPO)	0.1560	2.1613	<.05	two-tailed	accept
H2 Software artefacts' characteristics have an effect on experience required.					
Experience (EXP)	0.2410	3.0217	<.005	Two-tailed	accept
H3 Software artefacts' characteristics have an effect on motivation.					
Commitment (CMM)	0.0390	0.3533	n.s.	-	reject
Competency (CPT)	0.0300	0.2738	n.s.	-	reject
Confidence (CFD)	0.0380	0.4523	n.s.	-	reject
Contingency (CTG)	0.0970	1.0579	n.s.	-	reject

of the effect of artefact characteristics on supporting documents and individual characteristics (implicit inputs), the estimated structural path coefficients, and the observed t-values from the bootstrap re-sampling procedure, and the significance level of the path coefficients based on both one tailed and two-tailed tests.

Table 15 shows that software artefact characteristics have an effect on the use of three supporting documents (prescription document, r = 0.367, p < .0001; previously reviewed software, 0.22, p < .05; reports, r = 0.156, p < .05), but no effect on reading techniques (r = 0.044, not significant (n.s.)). These results indicate that the greater complexity, poorer quality and larger size of the software artefact increases the use of supporting documents.

On the other hand, interesting results show that artefact characteristics have no effect on reviewer motivation (commitment, $r = 0.039$, n.s.; competency, $r = 0.03$, n.s.; confidence, $r = 0.038$, n.s.; contingency, $r = 0.097$, n.s.). However, artefact characteristics have an effect on the reviewer experience ($r = 0.241$, $p < .005$) required. These suggest that the more complex, poorer quality and larger size of the software artefact, the more experienced reviewers are required. As a result, hypotheses 1 and 2 are strongly supported but hypothesis 3 is rejected. In relation to the effect of individual characteristics (implicit inputs) on the use of supporting documents, only experience has a strong negative relationship with the use of prescription documents ($r = -0.417$, $p < .0001$, two-tailed) (see Table 8.16). This suggests that the less experienced reviewers use prescription documents more frequently. In comparison, reviewer experience has no relationship on use of reading technique documents ($r = 0.133$, n.s.), previously reviewed software documents ($r = 0.024$, n.s.) and reports ($r = 0.104$, n.s.).

In addition, perceived contingency has a relationship with use of prescription documents ($r = 0.385$, $< .0001$, two-tailed), but no effect on use of reading technique documents ($r = 0.163$, n.s.). Confidence also has a relationship with use of reading technique documents ($r = 0.23$, $< .05$, two-tailed). The overall results suggest that hypotheses 4 and 5 are weakly accepted.

Table 16. The effect of on implicit inputs supporting documents (n.s. = not significant)

Questions & Hypotheses	Path Coefficient	T-value	P-value	One-tailed/ two-tailed	Accept /Reject
H4 Experience has an effect on use of supporting documents.					
Reading technique documents (RTD)	0.1330	1.6432	n.s.	-	reject
Prescription documents (PSD)	-0.4170	5.0561	<.0001	two-tailed	accept
Previously reviewed software documents (PRD)	0.0240	1.3388	n.s.	-	reject
Reports (RPO)	0.1040	1.5715	n.s.	-	reject

Table 16. cont.

Questions & Hypotheses	Path Coefficient	T-value	P-value	One-tailed/ two- tailed	Accept /Reject
H5 Motivation has an effect on use of supporting documents.					
Effect of commitment (CMM) on reading technique documents	0.1470	1.2348	n.s.	-	reject
Competency (CPT)	0.1280	1.3202	n.s.	-	reject
Confidence (CFD)	0.2300	2.3848	<.05	two-tailed	accept
Contingency (CTG)	0.1630	1.4585	n.s.	-	reject
Effect of commitment (CMM) on prescription documents	0.1460	1.5862	n.s.	-	reject
Competency (CPT)	0.1470	1.5629	n.s.	-	reject
Confidence (CFD)	0.0020	0.0213	n.s.	-	reject
Contingency (CTG)	0.3850	4.1390	<.0001	two-tailed	accept
Effect of commitment (CMM) on previously reviewed software documents	0.0690	0.6978	n.s.	-	reject
Competency (CPT)	0.0700	0.7790	n.s.	-	reject
Confidence (CFD)	0.1360	1.3170	n.s.	-	reject
Contingency (CTG)	0.1410	1.3150	n.s.	-	reject
Effect of commitment on reports	0.0010	0.0134	n.s.	-	reject
Competency (CPT)	0.0220	0.3379	n.s.	-	reject
Confidence (CFD)	0.1180	1.3311	n.s.	-	reject
Contingency (CTG)	0.1250	1.6276	n.s.	-	Reject

Effect on Process

Table 17 shows that artefact characteristics have no impact on communication ($r = 0.12$, n.s.), status effect ($r = -0.035$, n.s.), and discussion quality ($r = 0.102$, n.s.), but significant effect on teamwork ($r = 0.159$, $< .05$, one-tailed). These results suggest hypothesis 6 is weakly accepted.

Further, previously reviewed software documents have a positive effect on communication ($r = 0.163$, $< .05$, one-tailed), teamwork ($r = 0.141$, $< .05$, one-tailed) and discussion quality ($r = 0.23$, $< .05$, two-tailed) and a negative effect on status effect ($r = -0.239$, $< .005$, two-tailed). Reports also have a positive effect on communication ($r = 0.219$, $< .05$, two-tailed), teamwork ($r = 0.154$,

Table 17. The effect of explicit inputs on meeting process (n.s. = not significant)

Questions & Hypotheses	Path Coefficient	T-value	P-value	One- tailed/ two- tailed	Accept /Reject
H6 Software artefacts' characteristics have an effect on meeting process (i.e., communication, discussion quality, status effect and teamwork).					
Communication (CMU)	0.1200	1.2176	n.s.	-	Reject
Status effects (STE)	-0.0350	0.3433	n.s.	-	Reject
Teamwork (TEA)	0.1590	1.9239	<.05	one-tailed	Accept
Discussion quality (DSQ)	0.1020	1.1884	n.s.	-	Reject
Questions & Hypotheses	**Path Coefficient**	**T-value**	**P-value**	**One-tailed/ two-tailed**	**Accept /Reject**
H7 Use of supporting documents has an effect on meeting process.					
Effect of reading technique documents on meeting process – communication	0.1180	1.0247	n.s.	-	Reject
Status effects (STE)	-0.0080	0.0944	n.s.	-	Reject
Teamwork (TEA)	0.0040	0.0607	n.s.	-	Reject
Discussion quality (DSQ)	-0.0380	1.0465	n.s.	-	Reject
Effect of prescription documents on meeting process – communication	0.0250	0.2373	n.s.	-	Reject
Status effects (STE)	-0.0180	0.2086	n.s.	-	Reject
Teamwork (TEA)	0.0440	0.5357	n.s.	-	reject
Discussion quality (DSQ)	0.0510	0.6535	n.s.	-	reject
Effect of previously reviewed software documents on meeting process – communication	0.1630	1.7981	<.05	one-tailed	accept
Status effects (STE)	-0.2390	2.8506	<.005	two-tailed	accept
Teamwork (TEA)	0.1410	1.6772	<.05	one-tailed	accept
Discussion quality (DSQ)	0.2300	1.9984	<.05	two-tailed	accept
Effect of reports on meeting process – communication	0.2190	2.4514	<.05	two-tailed	accept
Status effects (STE)	-0.2040	1.6575	<.05	one-tailed	accept
Teamwork (TEA)	0.1540	2.0168	<.05	two-tailed	accept
Discussion quality (DSQ)	0.0480	0.5035	n.s.	-	reject

< .05, two-tailed) and a negative effect on status effect ($r = -0.204$, < .05, one-tailed). Whereas reading technique documents have no effect on meeting process (communication, $r = 0.118$, n.s.; status effect, $r = -0.008$, n.s.; teamwork, $r = 0.004$, n.s.; discussion quality, $r = 0.038$, n.s.). Prescription documents also have no effect on meeting process (communication, $r = 0.025$, n.s.; status effect, $r = -0.018$, n.s.; teamwork, $r = -0.044$, n.s.; discussion quality, $r = 0.051$, n.s.). Since previously reviewed software documents and reports have effect on meeting process, as a result, hypothesis 6 is weakly supported.

In relation to the effect of implicit inputs (individual characteristics) on meeting process, Table 18 shows that reviewer experience has an effect on communica-

Table 18. The effect of implicit inputs on meeting process (n.s. = not significant)

Questions & Hypotheses	Path Coefficient	T-value	P-value	One-tailed/ two-tailed	Accept /Reject
H8 Experience have an effect on meeting process					
Communication (CMU)	0.1630	1.9285	<.05	one-tailed	accept
Status effects (STE)	0.0110	0.1360	n.s.	-	reject
Teamwork (TEA)	0.0960	1.2526	n.s.	-	reject
Discussion quality (DSQ)	0.2380	2.3603	<.05	two-tailed	accept
H9 Motivation have an effect on meeting process					
Effect of commitment on meeting process – communication	0.0730	0.3249	n.s.	-	reject
Status effects (STE)	0.0040	0.0248	n.s.	-	reject
Teamwork (TEA)	0.0760	0.5427	n.s.	-	reject
Discussion quality (DSQ)	0.0530	0.3141	n.s.	-	reject
Effect of competency on meeting process – communication	-0.2020	0.8940	n.s.	-	reject
Status effects (STE)	-0.0640	0.3698	n.s.	-	reject
Teamwork (TEA)	-0.0960	0.7245	n.s.	-	reject
Discussion quality (DSQ)	-0.0650	0.3768	n.s.	-	reject

continued on following page

Table 18. cont.

Questions & Hypotheses	Path Coefficient	T-value	P-value	One-tailed/ two-tailed	Accept /Reject
Effect of confidence on meeting process – communication	-0.0350	0.3570	n.s.	-	reject
Status effects (STE)	0.0480	0.5994	n.s.	-	reject
Teamwork (TEA)	0.1010	1.0484	n.s.	-	reject
Discussion quality (DSQ)	-0.0840	0.9612	n.s.	-	reject
Effect of contingency on meeting process – communication	-0.0630	0.6689	n.s.	-	reject
Status effects (STE)	-0.2910	3.3794	<.001	two-tailed	accept
Teamwork (TEA)	0.3690	4.5789	<.0001	two-tailed	accept
Discussion quality (DSQ)	0.3360	4.1499	<.0001	two-tailed	accept

tion ($r = 0.163$, $p < .05$, one-tailed) and discussion quality ($r = 0.238$, $p < .05$, two-tailed), but no effect on status effect ($r = 0.011$, n.s.) and teamwork ($r = 0.096$, n.s.).

Effect on Performance

Table 19 shows that only the previously reviewed software documents have a significant effect on the number of defects found ($r = 0.23$, $p < .05$. two-tailed) whereas all other explicit inputs have no effect on the number of defects found (software artefact characteristics, $r = -0.102$, n.s.; reading techniques, $r = 0.038$, n.s.; prescription documents, $r = 0.051$, n.s.; reports, $r = 0.051$, n.s.). In other words, the more reviewers make use of previously reviewed software documents, the more defects can be detected.

Table 19. The effect of explicit inputs on performance (n.s. = not significant)

Questions & Hypotheses	Path coefficient	T-value	P-value	One-tailed/ two-tailed	Accept /reject
H10 Software artefacts' characteristics have an effect on software review performance					
Software artefact characteristics (SAC)	-0.1020	0.9778	n.s.	-	reject
H11 Use of supporting documents have an effect on software review performance					
Reading technique documents (RTD)	0.0380	0.3260	n.s.	-	reject
Prescription documents (PSD)	0.0510	0.6648	n.s.	-	reject
Previously reviewed software documents (PRD)	0.2300	2.1391	<.05	two-tailed	accept
Reports (RPO)	0.0480	0.6334	n.s.	-	reject

However, other explicit inputs such as artefact characteristics and other supporting documents have no significant effect on the number of defects found. Therefore, hypothesis 10 is rejected but hypothesis 11 is weakly accepted.

Table 8.20 shows that interesting results show that only experience ($r = 0.238$, $p < .05$, two-tailed) and perceived contingency ($r = 0.203$, $p < .05$, two-tailed) have a strong effect on the number of defects found. Whereas commitment ($r = 0.241$, n.s.), competency ($r = 0.206$, n.s.) and confidence ($r = 0.075$, n.s.) have no effect on the number of defects found. These results suggest hypothesis 12 is strongly supported and hypothesis 13 weakly supported.

Table 21 shows that only teamwork ($r = 0.172$, $p < .05$, one-tailed) has an effect on the number of defects found while communication ($r = 0.052$, n.s.), status effect ($r = 0.004$, n.s.) and discussion quality ($r = 0.055$, n.s.) have no significant impact on the number of defects found.

Discussions of Survey Results

Inputs

Interestingly, the study shows that the construct of software artefact characteristics that is often discussed in the software review literature (Laitenberger & Debaud, 2000) does not have a significant effect on use of supporting reading

Table 20. The effect of implicit inputs on performance (n.s. = not significant)

Questions & Hypotheses	Path Coefficient	T-value	P-value	One-tailed/ two-tailed	Accept /Reject
H12 Experiences has an effect on software review performance e					
Experience (EXP)	0.2380	2.0747	<.05	two-tailed	accept
H13 Motivation have an effect on software review performance					
Commitment (CMM)	0.2410	1.2092	n.s.	-	reject
Competency (CPT)	0.2060	0.8386	n.s.	-	reject
Confidence (CFD)	0.0750	0.7426	n.s.	-	reject
Contingency (CTG)	0.2030	1.9338	<.05	one-tailed	accept

Table 21. The effect of meeting process on performance (n.s. = not significant)

Questions & Hypotheses	Path Coefficient	T-value	P-value	One-tailed/ two-tailed	Accept /Reject
H14 Meeting process have an effect on software review performance					
Communication (CMU)	0.0520	0.6028	n.s.	-	reject
Status effects (STE)	0.0040	0.0352	n.s.	-	reject
Teamwork (TEA)	0.1720	1.6532	<.05	one-tailed	accept
Discussion quality (DSQ)	0.0550	0.5526	n.s.	-	reject

technique documents (r = 0.0440, not significant (n.s.)) (see Table 15), but has a significant effect on all other three supporting documents (prescription documents, previously reviewed software documents and reports). Observing the formative indicators of software artefact characteristics, complexity is dominant with the strongest weight of 0.9678, whereas initial quality and size have weights of 0.3367 and 0.211 (see Table 23). These results clearly suggest that the more complex the software artefact, the more frequent the use of supporting documents (except reading techniques documents) is required in practice. Although reading techniques are the most commonly discussed supporting documents in the software review literature, surprising results indicate that the characteristics of the software artefact do not have any impact on the use of reading technique documents. One of the possible explanations is that reading techniques documents are not commonly used in practice.

Our results show that only 19.1% of respondents frequently used checklists and figures of 14% for scenarios/perspective-based reading technique documents and 10% for stepwise reading techniques documents. On the other hand, expected results show that the characteristics of the software artefact have the strongest influence on the use of prescription documents (r = 0.3670, p < 0.0001) (see Table 15), whereas the strongest indicator for the prescription document construct is template with a weight of 0.8548, followed by procedure guideline with a weight of 0.6196, training material 0.4316, time record form 0.2455 and defect standards 0.1201 (see Table 14). In other words, the more complex the software artefact, the more frequent the use of templates, procedure guidelines, training materials, time record forms and defect standards are required. In addition, software artefact characteristics also have a moderate impact on the use of previously reviewed software documents and reports (see Table 15).

Looking at the weights of the previously reviewed software documents indicators, previously reviewed design documents has the strongest weight of 0.8673, previously reviewed requirement and code documents have low weights of 0.2958 and 0.255 (see Table 14). This suggests that the characteristics of the artefact are strongly determinant of the use of previously reviewed design documents. In relation to the reports, only business report has a strong weight of 1.0146 whereas ANSI/IEEE standards (1989) have very low weight of 0.0804 (see Table 14).

Additionally, software artefact characteristics also influence the experience of reviewers required (r = 0.241, p < 0.005) (see Table 16) whereas the weight of role experience (review experience) is 0.7753 and working experience in the software industry is 0.3085 (see Table 8.14). In comparison, unexpected results show that the characteristics of software artefact have no significant effect on motivation (commitment, competency, confidence, and contingency). This suggests that for a more complex software artefact, reviewers do not change their motivation and effort in performing a software review task.

In relation to the effect of motivation on use of supporting documents, only confidence has an influence on the use of reading technique documents and perceived contingency has an impact on the use of prescription documents. The strongest formative indicator for reading technique document use is checklist with a weight of 1.094, followed by scenarios 0.0373, and stepwise 0.2815 (see Table 14).

However, all other motivation constructs have no significant effect on the use of supporting documents. Overall results indicate that implicit inputs (both reviewers experience and motivation) have little impact on the use of supporting documents.

Process

Interesting results show that software artefact characteristics do not affect the communication, but do affect status effect, teamwork and discussion quality (see Table 17). The results suggest that the more complex, poor initial quality, larger size of the artefact, the less status and power influence behaviour in the meeting process. However these artefact characteristics increase the collaborative environment and discussion quality between team members. This is not surprising as when reviewers are facing a difficult task, the more support from team members is likely to occur, and also a reduction of the status power in the team. Members are more involved in a team; therefore the better the discussion quality that would be achieved in the meeting discussions. However, artefact characteristics do not affect communication; one of possible explanation is the measurement indicators of communication. The measurement indicators of communication are 1) language, putting ideas forward, 2) expression, and 3) understanding. It is very common that review teams often form from their software project, in which the reviewers should familiar the languages used and would be able to express themselves and putting ideas forward. The results suggest that reading technique documents have no effect on meeting process in practice, but the use of prescription documents has a significant effect on communication ($r = 0.163$, $p < 0.05$). A good use of prescription documents allows team members to follow a systematic process approach. It creates a positive and effective communication environment.

However, the greater the use of previously reviewed software documents, the more negative the communication, and the lower the status effect. On the other hand, the more frequent the use of previously reviewed software documents, the better the discussion quality of review meetings ($r = 0.23$, $p < 0.05$). Through the use of the previous reviewed software documents, the detailed requirements and objectives of the software can be known. Therefore, reviewers perceived better quality of discussions in the review meetings. In fact, the previously reviewed software documents are the most significant influence on the software review meeting process (see Table 17).

Generally, reviewer experience has some effect on meeting process. In particular, experience has impact on discussion quality ($r = 0.238$, $p < 0.05$) and communication ($r = 0.163$, $p < 0.05$). In comparison for motivation, only perceived contingency has a significant influence on review meeting process (see Table 18). In other words, a successful meeting requires perceived strong support and encouragement from the organisation.

Performance

From the PLS analysis tests, interestingly the characteristics of the software artefact have no significant direct influence on performance (i.e., number of defects found) (see Table 19). Laitenberger and Debaud (2000) theorized that artefact characteristics have an effect on the number of defects found. Our results suggest that the more complex, poor initial quality and large size of the artefact, has no direct impact on the number of defects detected. More surprising findings show that none of the supporting documents except previously reviewed software documents have a direct influence on the number of defects found.

Reading technique documents that are the most commonly discussed in the current software review literature (Basili et al., 1996; Basili, Laitenberger, Shull, & Rus, 2000, Chernak, 1996; Laitenberger & Emam, 2001; Linger, Mill, & Witt, 1997; Miller, Wood, & Roper, 1998; Shull, Lanubile, & Biasili, 2000; Shull, Rus, & Basili, 2000; Thelin, Runeson, Wohiln, Olsson, & Andersson, 2002; Thelin, Runeson, & Wohlin, 2003; Travassos, Shull, Caver, & Basili, 1999) do not have a significant direct effect on review performance in practice. The results directly contradict the current software review literature. Reading techniques are considered the most effective technique or strategy for improved software review performance, while our results suggest that previously reviewed software artefacts are the most critical. The results suggest that the current use of reading techniques in practice, are not effective to benefit software review performance. Further tailored reading techniques such as perspective based types of techniques need to be cautiously designed and implemented. Additionally, prescription documents and reports also have similar results; both constructs do not have a significant direct impact on software review performance.

On the other hand, previously reviewed software documents (requirement, design and code) do have a significant effect on software review performance. In particular, previously reviewed design documents have the strongest weight of 0.8673 in their effect on the number of defects found.

As expected, experience is the key driver on software review performance. It has the strongest effect on the number of defects found among all constructs in the EIIO model. It is found that the more role (software review) experience and working experience in the software industry, the better is the software review performance that can be achieved. These results show that a skilful reviewer with good knowledge about business functions and technical experience in software development would provide better performance in the finding of defects. These results suggest that the selection of reviewers should be considered the most critical issue in future research.

To conduct an effective software review, reviewer motivation is also considered an important criterion in the software review process. Our results show that perceived contingency has a significant effect on the number of defects found. If a reviewer agrees with the way the company is conducting the software review and perceives support and encouragement from the company, the better the review performance that can be attained.

In relation to the meeting process, teamwork is the dominant factor. The results show that teamwork is the best indicator of a successfully conducted software review meeting (see Table 21). The more collaborative the review team, the higher the software review outcomes that can be achieved. Precisely, when team members have a high willingness to participate in discussion, are able to share all information and are working closely in a team, the better the software review performance that can be achieved.

The bootstrap re-sampling method was used throughout this study for significance testing of path estimates and the weights for the formative indicators and loadings for reflective indicators. A total of 15 constructs with 48 indicators are used in the model, but only 15 paths are significant. The results of the model, using an inner model path weighting scheme show a substantial R-square of 0.398 for performance, a moderate level of 0.239 for experience and 0.335 for teamwork and a weak level of 0.024 for reports and 0.049 for previously reviewed software.

Summary

In summary, this chapter analysed the data and presented the study's findings. After doing the principal components analysis and reliability analysis, the hypotheses were tested via PLS. The PLS measurement model is satisfactory with high convergent and discriminant validity. A revised EIIO model will be further analysis and validated in next chapter.

References

ANSI/IEEE. (1989). An American National Standard, *ANSI/IEEE Standard 1028*, IEEE Standards for Software Reviews and Audits.

Babbie, E. (2000). *The practice of social research* (9th ed.). Belmon, CA: Wadsworth.

Basili, V. R., Green, S., Laitenberger, O., Lanubile, F., Sorumgard, S., & Zelkowitz, M. (1996). The empirical investigation of perspective-based reading. *International Journal on Empirical Software Engineering, 1*(12), 133-144.

Basili, V. R., Laitenberger, O., Shull, F., & Rus, I. (2000). Improving software inspections by using reading techniques. *Proceedings of International Conference on Software Engineering* (pp. 836-727).

Boehm, B. W., & Basili, B. R. (2001, January). Software defect reduction top 10 list. *IEEE Computer, 34*(1).

Campell, J. P. (1990). Modeling the performance prediction problem in industrial and organizational psychology. In M. D. Dunnette & L. M. Hough (Eds.), *Handbook of industrial and organizational psychology* (2nd ed.) (pp. 687-732). Palo Alto, CA: Consulting Psychologists Press Inc.

Campell, J. P., & Pritchard, R. D. (1976). Motivation theory in industrial and organizational psychology. In M. D. Dunnette (Ed.), *Handbook of industrial and organizational psychology* (2nd ed.) (pp. 63-130). Chicago: Rand McNally College Publishing Company.

Chernak, Y. (1996, December). A statistical approach to the inspection checklist formal syntheses and improvement. *IEEE Transactions on Software Engineering, 22*(12).

Chin, W. W. (1998). The partial least square approach for structural equation modeling. In G. A. Marcoulides (Ed.), *Modern methods for business research* (pp. 295-336). Mahwah, NJ: Erlbaum.

Coakes, S. J., & Steed, L. G. (2001). *SPSS: Analysis without anguish: Version 10.0 for Windows*. Brisbane, Australia: John Wiley & Sons.

Cohen, J. (1988). *Statistical power analysis for the behaviour sciences* (2nd ed.). Hillsdale, NJ: Lawrence Erlbaum.

Cronbach, L. J. (1970). *Essentials of psychological testing* (3rd ed.). New York: Irvington.

Cronbach, L. J., & Show R. E. (1977). *Aptitudes and instructional methods: A handbook for research on interactions*. New York: Irvington.

Davison, R. (1997). Instrument for measuring meeting success. *Information and Management, 32*, 163-176.

Deci, E. L., Eghrari, H., Patrick, B. C., & Leone, D. (1994). Facilitating internationalization: The self-determination theory perspective. *Journal of Personality, 62*, 119-142.

Deci, E. L., Koestner, R., & Ryan, R. M. (1999a). A meta-analytic review of experiment examining the effect of extrinsic reviewed on intrinsic motivation. *Psychological Bulletin, 125*, 627-668.

Deci, E. L., Koestner, R., & Ryan, R.M. (1999b). The undermining effect is reality after all: Extrinsic rewards, task interest, and self-determination. *Psychological Bulletin, 125*, 629-700.

De Vaus, D. (2001). *Research design in social research.* London: Sage.

Engelkamp, J., & Wippich, W. (1995). Current issues in implicit and explicit memory. *International Journal of Perception, Cognition, and Action, 57*(3-4), 143-155.

Ericsson, K. A. (1994). Analysis of memory performance in terms of memory skill. In R. J. Sternberg (Ed.), *Advances in the psychology of human intelligence* (pp. 137-179). Hillsdale, NJ: Erlbaum.

Ericsson, K. A., & Lehmann, A. C. (1996). Expert and exceptional performance: Evidence of maximal adaptation to task constraints. *Psychology Review, 47*, 273-305.

Fagan, M. E. (1986, July). Advances in software inspections. *IEEE Transaction on Software Engineering, 12*(7).

Geisser, S. (1975). The predictive sample reuse method with applications. *Journal of* the *American Statistical Association, 70*, 320-328.

Gilb, T., & Graham, D. (1993). *Software inspection.* Harlow, UK: Addison-Wesley.

Harzing, A.W. (1997, December). Response rates in international mail surveys: Results of a 22-country study. *International Business Review, 6*(6), 641-665.

Hui, B. S. (1982). On building partial least squares models with interdependent inner relations. In K. G. Joreskog & H. Wold (Eds.), *Systems under indirect observation: Causality, structure, prediction* (pp. 249-272). Amsterdam: North-Holland.

Hui, B. S. (1987). *The partial least squares approach to path models of indirectly observed variables with multiple indicators.* Unpublished Doctoral Dissertation, University of Pennsylvania, Philadelphia.

Humphrey, W. S. (2000). *Introduction to the team software process.* Boston:

Addison-Wesley.

Humphrey, W. S. (2002a). *Introduction to personal software process.* Boston: Addison-Wesley.

Humphrey, W. S. (2002b). *Winning with software: An executive strategy, how to transform your software group into a competitive asset.* Boston: Addison-Wesley.

IEEE Standard 1028. (1998). Software Engineering Standard Committee of the IEEE Computer Society, 1998. *IEEE Standard for Software Review, IEEE Standard 1028,* Institute of Electrical and Electronics Engineers Inc., New York.

Joreskog, K. G. (1973). A general method for estimating a linear structural equation system. In A. S. Goldberger & O. D. Duncan (Eds.), *Structural equation models in the social sciences* (pp. 85-122). New York: Academic Press.

Joreskog, K. G. (1989). *LISREL 7: A guide to the program and applications.* Chicago: SPSS.

Kelloway, E. K. (1995). Structural equation modelling in perspective. *Journal of Organisational Behaviour,* (16), 215-224.

Laitenberger, O., & Debaud, J. M. (2000). An encompassing life cycle centric survey of software inspection. *The Journal of Software and Systems, 50*(1), 5-31.

Laitenberger, O., & Emam, K. E. (2001). An internally replicated quasi-experimental comparison of checklist and perspective-based reading of code documents. *IEEE Transactions of Software Engineering, 27*(5), 378-421.

Lee, D. M. S., Trauth, E. M., & Farwell, D. (1995, September). Critical skills and knowledge requirements of is professionals: A joint academic/industry investigation. *MIS Quarterly,* 313-340.

Linger, R. C., Mill, H. D., & Witt, B. I. (1997). Perspective-based reading of code documents at Robert Bosch GMBH. *Information and Software Technology, 39,* 781-791.

Litwin, M. S. (1995). *How to measure survey reliability and validity.* Thousand Oaks, CA: Sage.

Lohmoller, J. B. (1989). *Latent variable path modeling with partial least squares.* Heidelberg, Germany: Physica-Verlag.

Lyttkens, E. (1966, June 14-19). On the fix-point property of world's interactive estimation method for principal components. In P. R. Krishnaiah (Ed.), *Proceedings of the International Symposium on Multivariate Analysis* (pp. 335-350). Dayton.

Miller, J., Wood, M., & Roper, M. (1998). Further experiences with scenarios and checklists. *Empirical Software Engineering 3*, 37-64.

Nunnally, J. C. (1976). *Psychometric theory*. New York: McGraw-Hill.

Porter, A. A., & Votta, L. G. (1994). An experiment to assess different defect detection methods for software requirements inspections. *Proceedings of 16ᵗʰ International Conference on Software Engineering, ICSE'16* (pp. 103-112).

Rossi, P. H., & Anderson, A. B. (1982). The factorial survey approach: An introduction. In P. H. Rossi & L. S. Nock (Eds.), *Measuring social judgements: A factorial survey approach.* London: Sage.

Shull, F., Lanubile, F., & Biasili, V. (2000, November). Investigating reading techniques for object-oriented framework learning. *IEEE Transaction on Software Engineering, 26*(11).

Shull, F., Rus, I., & Basili, V. (2000, July). How perspective-based reading can improve requirements inspection? *IEEE Computer*, 73-79.

Stone, M. (1974). Cross-validatory choice and assessment of statistical predictions. *Journal of the Royal Statistical Society, B36*, 111-133.

Thelin, T., Runeson, R., & Regnell, B. (2001). Usage-based reading–An experiment to guide reviewers with use cases. *Information and Software Technology, 43*, 925-938.

Thelin, T., Runeson, P., & Wohlin, C. (2003, August.). An experimental comparison of usage-based and checklist-based reading. *IEEE Transaction on Software Engineering, 29*(8), 687-704.

Thelin, T., Runeson, P., Wohiln, C., Olsson, T., & Andersson, C. (2002). How much information is needed for usage-based reading? A series of experiments. *Proceedings of the 2002 International Symposium on Empirical Software Engineering (ISESE'02).*

Travassos. G. H., Shull. F., Caver. J., & Basili, V. R. (1999, December). Reading techniques for OO design inspections. *Proceedings of the 24ᵗʰ Annual Software Engineering Workshop,* Goddard Space Flight Centre, MD.

Wert, C. E., Linn, R. L., & Joreskog, K. G. (1974). Intra-class reliability estimates: Testing structural assumptions. *Educational and Psychological Measurement, 34*, 25-33.

Wold, H. (1980). Model construction and evaluation when theoretical knowledge is scarce: Theory and application of partial least squares. In J. Kmenta, & J. B. Ramsey (Eds.), *Evaluation of econometric models.* New York: Academic Press.

Wold, H. (1985). Partial least squares. In S. Kotz & N. L. Johnson (Eds.), *Encyclopedia of statistical sciences, 6* (pp. 581-591). New York: Wiley.

Wold, H. (1988). Specification, predictor. In S. Kotz & N. L. Johnson (Eds.), *Encyclopedia of statistical sciences, 8* (pp. 587-599). New York: Wiley.

Zmud, R. W., & Boynton, A. C. (1991). Survey measures and instruments, MIS: Inventory and appraisal. In K. Kraemer (Ed.), *The information systems research challenge: Survey research methods* (pp. 149-180). Boston: Harvard Business School.

Chapter IX

A Revised EIIO Model and a Simple Software Review Guide

Abstract

This chapter presents the revised EIIO model from the industry survey results. This includes analyzing the structure paths and validation of the final EIIO model. Use of inputs, meeting process, and review performance describes in the final section of the chapter. The chapter also proposes a simple guide for conducting software reviews, which includes: 1) identifying the characteristics of the software artefact, 2) decision of which supporting documents (reports and previously reviewed software documents) to use and reviewers' experience required which are determined by software artefact characteristics, 3) selection of reviewers should be based on their role (review) experience and working experience in the software industry, and how they perceive company support and encouragement, and their acceptance levels of the company that is organising and conducting the software review; and 4) In the review meeting process, the most critical factor is teamwork which can be affected by the characteristics of the software artefact, use of previously reviewed software documents and reports, and perceived contingency (motivation).

A Revised EIIO Model

Further to the hypotheses test using PLS, this chapter aims to discuss the revised EIIO model and the key inputs and process factors that affect software review performance. A set of statistic tests have been conducted to validate the final EIIO model. Discussions of the model also describes is chapter. A software review guide has been proposed for conducting a success software review.

Redundancy Analysis

After eliminating insignificant paths and constructs, the remaining seven constructs with 20 indicators of the final EIIO model was revised and reproduced using PLS. Figure 1 provides the results of the redundancy analysis. All structural paths of the revised model were found to be significant.

Figure 1. Redundancy analysis of the EIIO model

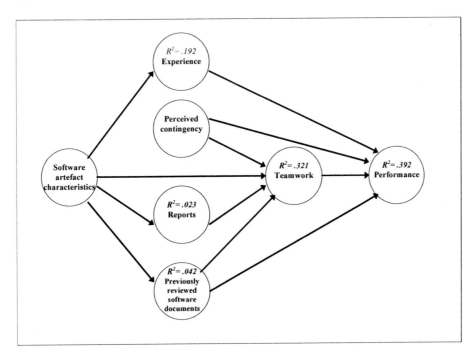

Structural Paths

As shown in Figure 1 and Table 1, the constructs in the model have both small and large effect on inputs, process, and review performance. As expected, implicit inputs have a significant effect on performance. The results demonstrate that experience is the key driver for review performance (r = 0.301, p<.0001).

Table 1. The effect of explicit & implicit and meeting process on performance

Hypotheses	Original path coefficient	Revised model Path coefficient	T-value	P-value	One-tailed/ two- tailed
Effect of software artefact characteristics on:					
Previously reviewed software documents (PRD)	0.22	**0.205**	2.2892	P<.05	two-tailed
Reports (RPO)	0.156	**0.153**	2.0038	P<.05	two-tailed
Experience (EXP)	0.241	**0.438**	6.0355	P<.0001	two-tailed
Effect on teamwork					
Software artefact characteristics (SAC)	0.159	**0.182**	2.5406	P<.05	two-tailed
Previously reviewed software documents (PRD)	0.141	**0.15**	2.147	P<.05	two-tailed
Reports (RPO)	0.154	**0.162**	2.7677	P<.01	two-tailed
Contingency (CTG)	0.369	**0.433**	7.7482	P<.0001	two-tailed
Effect on performance					
Previously reviewed software documents (PRD)	0.23	**0.222**	3.1371	P<.005	two-tailed
Experience (EXP)	0.238	**0.301**	4.3374	P<.0001	two-tailed
Contingency (CTG)	0.203	**0.217**	3.1021	P<.005	two-tailed
Teamwork (TEA)	0.172	**0.204**	2.9496	P<.005	two-tailed

Table 2. Revised model weights and loadings for model using formative indicators

Constructs	Indicators/ items	Weights	Loadings
Experience (EXP)	Role experience (RE)	0.8049	0.9042
	Working experience in software industry (IND)	0.2958	0.5942
Software artefact characteristics (SAC)	Complexity (CX)	0.9678	0.9625
	Size (SZ)	0.2110	0.7323
	Initial quality (IQ)	0.3367	0.6623
Previously reviewed software documents (PRD)	Requirement (RQ)	0.4379	0.7145
	Design (DE)	1.0408	0.9251
	Code (CD)	0.1358	0.1367
Reports (RPO)	Business report (BR)	1.0095	0.9989
	Standards (SS)	0.0479	0.1743
Performance (DEF)	True defects (TR)	0.4996	0.9108
	False positives (FA)	0.3527	0.8317
	Net defects (NE)	0.0991	0.6632
	Total issues (TL)	0.3415	0.9294

Among the formative indicators of experience, role experience has the highest weight of 0.805 and loading of 0.904, whereas working experience in software industry is 0.183 (see Table 2). Substantively, this would suggest that role experience has the strongest impact on review performance. Perceived contingency has a reasonably significant effect on review performance ($r = 0.217$, $p < .005$).

On the other hand, use of previously reviewed software also has an effect on the performance ($r = 0.222$, $p < .005$). The formative indicators of previously reviewed software documents, previously reviewed design documents has the heaviest weight of 1.0408 and loading of 0.9251, whereas previously reviewed requirement documents have a weight of 0.4379 and loading of 0.7145; and previously reviewed code documents have a weight of 0.1358 and loading of 0.1367 (see Table 2).

An unexpected result shows that only teamwork of the review meeting process constructs affects performance ($r = 0.204$, $p < .005$). Looking at the effect on meeting process, software artefact characteristics ($r = 0.182$, $p < .05$), use of previously reviewed software documents ($r = 0.15$, $p < .05$), reports ($r = 0.162$, $p < .05$) and perceived contingency ($r = 0.433$, $p < .0001$) affect teamwork of review meeting process. In particular, perceived contingency is the most important factor and has the strongest influence on teamwork. The results indicate that the more support from the company, the better team process during the meetings. On the other hand, explicit inputs (i.e., characteristics of software artefacts and supporting) have low effect on the teamwork of the meeting process.

According to Table 2, among the formative indicators of software artefact characteristics, complexity has the largest weight of 0.9678 and loading of 0.9625. Initial quality and size of artefacts have low weights (initial quality, 0.3367; size, 0.2110) and loadings (initial quality, 0.6623; size, 0.7323). The weights for the business report and standards related to domain application are 1.0095 and 0.0479, and loadings are 0.9989 and 0.1743 respectively. The weight and loadings show clearly that business report is the strongest indicator for the report construct. The results suggest that more frequent use of the previously reviewed software documents can achieve better teamwork in a review meeting process. In relation to the effect of inputs, Table 1 shows that software artefact characteristics determine the use of both explicit (supporting documents) and implicit (individual characteristics: experience and motivation) inputs.

The results illustrate that software artefact characteristics strongly influence the reviewers experience required ($r = 0.438$, $p < .0001$) and the use of previously reviewed software documents ($r = 0.205$, $p < .05$), but a low impact on the use of reports in a software review process ($r = 0.153$, $p < .05$). This suggests that for larger sizes, more complex with poor initial quality of a software artefact, it requires more experienced reviewers and more frequent use of supporting documents.

The overall structural paths suggest the importance of implicit and explicit inputs as well as process constructs influencing software review performance (i.e., number of defects found). Figure 2 shows the revised model related to formative and reflective indicators (items).

Figure 2. Revised final EIIO model

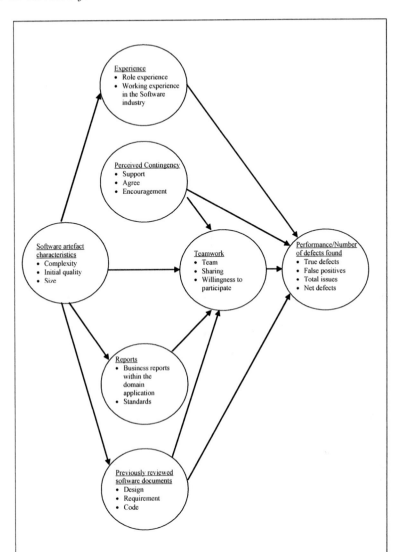

R-Square

The results of the model using an inner model path weighting scheme shows the R-square slightly decrease from 0.398 to 0.392 for performance, 0.239 to 0.192 for experience, 0.335 to 0.321 for teamwork, 0.024 to 0.23 for reports, and 0.049 to 0.042 for previously reviewed software. Overall, all structural paths of the revised model were found to be significant.

The final model has a performance (i.e., number of defects found) R-square of 0.392, whereas the R-square of the teamwork construct is 0.321, experience is 0.328, contingency is 0.162, prescription documents is 0.127, reports is 0.22 and previously reviewed software is 0.044 respectively. The model excluding the teamwork construct has an R-square of 0.364. Thus, the effect size f^2 for the two constructs, teamwork on performance, is 0.2501. The formula of the f-square represents as follow (Equation 1):

Equation 1. Effect size

$$\text{Effect size, } f^2 = \frac{R^2_{included} - R^2_{excluded}}{1 - R^2_{included}},$$

where $R^2_{included}$ and $R^2_{excluded}$ are the R-squares for the dependent latent construct when the additional predictor variable is included in or excluded from the structural equation, respectively.

According to Cohen (1988), when a set of explanatory variables are added to a multiple regression model, the effect size f^2 of 0.02, 0.15 and 0.35 reflects small, medium, and large effect respectively at the structural level (Chin, 1998; Cohen, 1988). Therefore, the effect size can examine the trade-off between model complexity and explanatory power when a new set of explanatory variables is added to the model.

In the final model here, adding the teamwork construct increases performance R-square from 0.364 to 0.392, resulting in an effect size of 0.2501. Since the effect size of 0.2501 is obtained by adding teamwork construct, this may be regarded as having a high effect on performance. Thus, the overall structural model explains a reasonably large variance in the performance construct and an acceptable variance in the teamwork construct.

Q-Square

In addition to the R-square, Q-square also applies the predictive sample reuse techniques (Chin, 1998, p. 317) as introduced by Stone (1974) and Geisser (1975). Q-square technique represents "a synthesis of cross validation and function fitting with the perspective" (Chin, 1998, p. 317) that the "perditions of observables or potential observables is of much greater relevance than the estimation of what are often artificial construct-parameters" (Geisser, 1975, p. 320). Evaluating the model by looking at the Q-square is a measure of how well the observed values are reproduced by the model and its parameter estimates.

The formula of the Q-square represents as follow (Equation 2):

Equation 2. Q-square

$$Q^2 = \frac{Q^2_{\text{included}} - Q^2_{\text{excluded}}}{1 - Q^2_{\text{included}}}.$$

When a Q-square is greater than 0, this implies that the model has predictive relevance, whereas Q-square is less than 0, it suggests that the model lacks predictive relevance (Chin & Gopal, 1995). Two types of Q-squares can be estimated depending on the form of prediction–cross validation communality Q-square and redundancy Q-square (Chin, 2003, 1998).

A cross validation communality Q-square is estimated if prediction of the omitted data points in the blindfolded block of indicators is made by the underlying latent variables. A redundancy Q-square is estimated if prediction of the omitted data points is made by constructs that are predictors of the blindfolded constructs in the PLS model.

The blindfolding results are summarized in Table 3. As shown in the table, using omission distances of 10 and 25 produced similar results, indicating that the estimates are stable. The communality Q-square is greater than 0 for seven

Table 3. Blindfolding results

Constructs	R-square	Omission Distance = 10		Omission Distance =25	
		Communality Q-square	Redundancy Q-square	Communality Q-square	Redundancy Q-square
Previously reviewed software documents (PRD)	0.044	0.4416	0.0501	0.4616	0.0201
Reports (RPO)	0.022	0.5222	0.0326	0.5141	0.0116
Experience (EXP)	0.328	0.4932	0.1644	0.4832	0.1586
Teamwork (TEA)	0.321	0.7444	0.2220	0.7376	0.2370
Performance (DEF)	0.381	0.7012	0.2588	0.7062	0.2688

constructs. This indicates that seven constructs are adequately measured. In relating to the redundancy Q-square for the two constructs of teamwork and number of defect found, it is seen that both constructs have positive redundancy Q-square values. This suggests that the proposed model has good predictive ability for the teamwork and number of defect found constructs. Overall, since the estimated model has satisfactory communality and redundancy Q-squares, the results of the Q-square analysis further confirm that the model indicators are adequate, and that the structural model has satisfactory predictive relevance for input, process, and performance (number of defects found).

Measurement Model Validation

Examining the validity of the measurement (outer) model, the individual loadings and cross-loadings of indicators can be used. Since there are only two constructs with reflective indicators (i.e., contingency and teamwork), the examination of individual loadings is carried out for each construct. In general, the standardised loading should be greater than 0.7. Thus, this condition was met in the study. But the rule of thumb should not be as rigid at early stages of scale development. Loading of 0.5 or 0.6 may still be acceptable if there exists additional indicators in the block for comparison. Once the individual reliabilities are considered, the composite reliability p_c (internal consistency) can be determined. The loadings for the teamwork construct with reflective indicators were uniformly high above 0.8 with a composite reliability (p_c) of 0.941 and an AVE of 0.842 (see Tables 4-5). The loadings for the contingency construct were even higher around 0.9 with a composite reliability (p_c) of 0.894 and an AVE of 0.738. Looking at the columns of Table 4, the loadings for the indicators in each block are higher than any other indicators from other blocks, implying that the construct (component) score does indeed predict each indicator in its block better than indicators in other blocks. Going across the table, each indicator also loads higher with its construct respectively.

Examining discriminant validity requires to calculate the AVE and compare it to the square of the correlations among the constructs. Table 4 provides the results with the AVE given in the diagonals. An indicator of discriminant validity is to have all AVE measures be larger than the square of correlations.

Alternatively, the square root of the AVE can be taken when comparing with the correlations. The results in Table 5 show that square root of the AVE of each construct are greater than the correlations with other constructs. The results indicate that discriminant validity is met.

In summary, this empirical study provides an example of how PLS can be used in a confirmatory sense. An existing theoretical model with established set of

Table 4. Loadings and cross-loadings for the revised model

	Contingency (CTG)	Teamwork (TEA)
	$p_c = 0.941$ AVE = 0.842	$p_c = 0.894$ AVE = 0.738
Support (SP)	**0.9312**	0.4632
Encouragement (EC)	**0.9182**	0.4373
Agree (AR)	**0.9029**	0.4654
Team (TM)	0.4212	**0.8826**
Willingness to participate (WP)	0.4772	**0.8665**
Sharing (SH)	0.3823	**0.8264**

measures was used as the basis for further theoretical and measurement development. Both formative and reflective sets of measures were created to estimate the same underlying construct, which demonstrates the importance of having both sets of indicators.

Without the reflective measures, there would be less evidence as to whether the researcher was successful in estimating the particular construct. With only formative measures, a researcher can demonstrate only the predictive capabilities of the block of measures. But by providing a set of reflective measures, it is demonstrated that both sets converge towards the same construct by measure of redundancy analysis and substitutability in a nomological network. The validity of the indicators can be also examined via the individual loadings, composite reliability, and AVE.

Finally, the use of the cross-validated redundancy measures provides a strong construct to that of the AVE and R-square measures (Chin, 1998, p. 329). The PLS results suggest that the model estimates for both the measurement and structural model are satisfactory. In the case of the measurement model, there is high convergent and discriminant validity. For the structural model, the predictor constructs adequately explain the two constructs of teamwork and performance.

Table 5. Correlation among construct scores (AVE extracted in diagonals)

	Contingency (CTG)	Teamwork (TEA)
Contingency (CTG)	0.842	
Teamwork (TEA)	0.495	0.738

Model Estimation with Data Subsets

After estimating the model with full data, the proposed model was also estimated on several data subsets. The aim is to test the stability of the estimates across the different, smaller data sets. The subsets were created based on the following three categories:

1. Process structures — small size of team vs. large size of team, an interactive group meeting vs. non interactive group meeting.

2. Companies — manufacturing vs. services businesses, employees less than 100 vs. employees over 100, quality certificates vs. non-quality certificates companies.

3. Developers — positions related to information technology vs. positions not related to information technology, professional qualification membership vs. non membership holders, degree vs. non degree educations.

Using the regression heuristic of 10 cases per predictor, the sample size should be at least 10 times the number of paths in the largest regression equation in the PLS estimation (Chin, 1988). If the number of constructs is measured with a maximum of four predictors to properly estimate the model in PLS with degrees of freedom would require a minimum sample size of 40.

The full data with 205 cases exceeds this minimum requirement of 40. Due to the small and potentially inadequate sample size for the subsets, the structural path coefficients estimated with the subset data may not only be insignificant but also may not be very reliable. Thus, whereas broad comparison may be made between the estimates obtained with the full and subset data, it may not be meaningful to statistically test the differences in the size and significance levels of the structural paths estimated with the full data and the different data subsets.

The PLS results from the analysis of the data subsets are summarized in Tables 6a-c. The revised model estimates from the subset data are substantively similar to those from the full data, although there are a few differences in size and/ or significance level of some of the structural path coefficients. However, due to small sample size for most subsets, the R-square may be high due to model over fitting, creating a false sense of achieving a good model fit. For example, there are only 33 cases in the team size over seven people and it resulted in insignificant paths in the model (see Table 6). A similar problem in the non-interactive meeting subset where the number of cases is only 26 which resulted in an invalided model.

In summary, given the reasonably high overall consistency between the model estimates obtained from the full data and all the subset data, it can be concluded that the results presented in the previous sections based on the PLS analysis with full data are reasonably robust, and not biased due to the nature of the sample included in the estimation procedure. However, given the small and maybe even inadequate sample sizes for some subsets, the PLS estimates based on the subsets from the data in Tables 6a-c need to be interpreted with caution. The findings are discussed in the next section.

Table 6a. Comparison of structural (inner) model results for full and sub-sample data: R-square and path coefficients (* = P < .05, ** = P < .01, *** = P < .005, **** = P < .001, two-tailed⁺ = P < .05 one-tailed)

	Full Set	Small Team 6 or Below	Large Team 7 or More	Involved in Interactive Meeting	Non Interactive Meeting
	N = 205	N = 172	N = 33	N = 179	N = 26
Effect on performance (R²)	**0.392**	**0.474**	**0.465**	**0.376**	**0.575**
Previously reviewed software documents	0.222^{***}	0.246^{***}	0.3080	0.214^{***}	0.41
Experience	0.301^{****}	0.401^{****}	0.354	0.327^{****}	0.591
Perceived Contingency	0.217^{***}	0.16*	0.1470	0.186^{*}	0.406
Teamwork	0.204^{***}	0.17*	0.649	0.183^{*}	0.661
Effect on teamwork (R²)	**0.321**	**0.354**	**0.334**	**0.345**	**0.363**
Software artefact characteristics	0.182^{*}	0.175^{*}	0.138	0.253^{***}	0.221
Previously reviewed software documents	0.15*	0.146^{+}	0.367	0.187^{*}	0.442
Reports	0.162^{**}	0.194^{**}	0.082	0.203^{**}	0.03
Perceived Contingency	0.433^{****}	0.439^{****}	0.289^{+}	0.367^{****}	0.273
Effect on experience (R²)	**0.328**	**0.347**	**0.219**	**0.401**	**0.445**
Software artefact characteristics	0.438^{****}	0.363^{****}	0.043	0.302^{****}	0.518
Effect on previously reviewed software documents (R²)	**0.044**	**0.05**	**0.125**	**0.07**	**0.103**
Software artefact characteristics	0.205^{*}	0.223^{*}	0.3530	0.265^{***}	0.321
Effect on reports (R²)	**0.022**	**0.04**	**.026**	**0.027**	**0.108**
Software artefact characteristics	0.153^{*}	0.2^{**}	0.1620	0.165^{*}	0.244

Table 6b. Comparison of structural (inner) model results for full and sub-sample data: R-square and path coefficients* = P < .05, ** = P < .01, *** = P < .005, **** = P < .001, two-tailed ⁺ = P < .05 one-tailed

	Manufactory	Services	Employees <100	Employees >100	Quality Certified	Without Quality Certified
	N = 47	N = 158	N = 126	N = 79	N = 82	N = 123
Effect on performance (R²)	**0.27**	**0.423**	**0.538**	**0.276**	**0.508**	**0.545**
Previously reviewed software documents	0.18^{*}	0.103^{+}	0.191^{*}	0.153^{+}	0.355^{*}	0.184^{*}
Experience	0.169^{*}	0.349^{****}	0.401****	0.178^{*}	0.377^{****}	0.417^{****}
Perceived Contingency	0.114^{+}	0.29^{****}	0.233^{*}	0.336^{**}	0.184^{+}	0.228^{+}
Teamwork	0.501^{+}	0.131^{+}	0.155^{+}	0.165^{*}	0.107^{+}	0.147^{+}
Effect on teamwork (R²)	**0.403**	**0.329**	**0.446**	**0.231**	**0.284**	**0.542**
Software artefact characteristics	0.052	0.196^{**}	0.227^{**}	0.081	0.182^{+}	0.222^{*}
Previously reviewed software documents	0.446^{***}	0.118^{+}	0.159^{+}	0.132^{+}	0.319^{*}	0.135^{+}
Reports	0.127^{+}	0.223^{**}	0.173^{***}	0.29^{**}	0.252^{**}	0.181^{*}
Perceived Contingency	0.257^{*}	0.407^{****}	0.483^{****}	0.349^{**}	0.249^{***}	0.485^{****}
Effect on experience (R²)	**0.386**	**0.297**	**0.412**	**0.267**	**0.419**	**0.49**
Software artefact characteristics	0.182^{+}	0.265^{****}	0.346^{****}	0.256^{*}	0.395^{***}	0.325^{****}
Effect on previously reviewed software documents (R²)	**0.003**	**0.116**	**0.047**	**0.126**	**0.397**	**0.043**
Software artefact characteristics	0.174^{+}	0.341^{****}	0.216^{+}	0.359^{**}	0.63^{****}	0.208^{***}
Effect on reports (R²)	**0.101**	**0.042**	**0.075**	**0.007**	**0.071**	**0.077**
Software artefact characteristics	0.318^{**}	0.206^{*}	0.274^{****}	0.082^{+}	0.266^{*}	0.277^{***}

Discussions

Using the PLS redundancy analysis, a revised EIIO model with seven constructs produced a good R-square of 0.392. The revised model contains all significant paths (see Tables 1-2). However, other possible factors such as role assignments, computer support tools, formal vs. informal review approaches, and decision making methods may influence the software review performance, that were not examined in the proposed EIIO model, because the proposed EIIO model did not capture most variation of software review performance. These possible factors should be investigated in the future studies.

The current empirical software review studies heavily focus on the explicit inputs (supporting documents) rather than implicit inputs (reviewer characteristics)

Table 6c. Comparison of structural (inner) model results for full and sub-sample data: R-square and path coefficients* = P < .05, ** = P < .01, *** = P < .005, **** = P < .001, two-tailed + = P < .05 one-tailed

	I.T. Positions	Non I.T. Positions	Membership	Non Membership	Education - Undergraduates	Education - Postgraduates
	N = 161	N = 44	N = 91	N = 114	N = 139	N = 66
Effect on performance (R^2)	**0.288**	**0.282**	**0.475**	**0.416**	**0.275**	**0.253**
Previously reviewed software documents	0.196^*	0.728^{****}	0.17^+	0.275^+	$0.216*$	0.243^*
Experience	0.175^*	0.209^*	0.499^{****}	0.165^*	0.103^+	0.557^{****}
Perceived Contingency	0.312^{***}	0.24^*	0.181^*	0.3^{**}	0.3^*	0.115^+
Teamwork	0.192^*	0.383^{***}	0.283^*	0.2^*	0.291^*	0.147^+
Effect on teamwork (R^2)	**0.326**	**0.429**	**0.227**	**0.476**	**0.4**	**0.213**
Software artefact characteristics	0.201^*	0.138^+	0.185^+	0.271^{****}	0.143^+	0.251^+
previously reviewed software documents	0.221^*	0.197^+	0.367^{**}	0.185^+	0.213^*	0.194^*
Reports	0.207^{***}	0.614^{****}	0.319^{**}	0.157^*	0.181^*	0.095^+
Perceived Contingency	$.338^{****}$	0.339^{***}	0.205^+	0.508^{****}	0.453^{****}	0.123^+
Effect on experience (R^2)	**0.294**	**0.512**	**0.442**	**0.333**	**0.304**	**0.474**
Software artefact characteristics	0.269^{**}	0.299^*	0.446^{****}	0.126^*	0.284^*	0.371^*
Effect on previously reviewed software documents (R^2)	**0.017**	**0.256**	**0.098**	**0.008**	**0.016**	**0.104**
Software artefact characteristics	0.131^+	0.506^*	0.314^*	0.19^+	0.126^+	0.322^*
Effect on reports (R^2)	**0.024**	**0.074**	**0.01**	**0.035**	**0.012**	**0.101**
Software artefact characteristics	0.154^+	0.272^*	0.19^+	0.187^*	0.107^+	0.319^{****}

(ANSI/IEEE standard 1028, 1989; Basili et al., 1996; Briand & Wust, 2000; Chernak, 1996; Dunsmore, Roper, & Wood, 2002; Laitenberger & Atkinson, 1998; Laitenberger & Debaud, 1997; Laitenberger & Emam, 2001, Miller, Wood, & Roper, 1998; Reeve, 1991; Shull, Lanubile, & Basili, 2000a; Shull, Rus, & Basili, 2000b; Thelin, Runeson, & Regnell, 2001; Thelin, Runeson, Wohiln, Olsson, & Andersson, 2002; Thelin, Runeson, & Wohlin, 2003). However, the survey results in this study suggest that implicit inputs play a dominant role in software review performance. According to Figures 1-2, the key driver to software review performance is reviewers' experience ($r = 0.301$, $p < 0.0001$), followed by previously reviewed software documents ($r = 0.222$, $p < 0.005$), perceived contingency (support, encouragement and agreement from the company) ($r = 0.217$, $p < 0.005$) and teamwork ($r = 0.204$, $p < 0.005$).

To achieve higher performance in the software review process, selection of reviewers becomes the most critical factor. These results also confirm Sauer, Jeffery, Land, and Yetton's theory (2000). In relation to motivation, interesting results suggest that motivation — perceived contingency, is another important factor in the software review process and review performance according to the survey results. However, this variable is often ignored in the empirical software review literature.

Although several researchers have recommended that reviewers' effort and motivation would be important in the software review performance, to our knowledge, no empirical study has been carried out to support this (Humphrey, 2002; Isazadeh, Macewen, & Malton, 1995; Kingston, Webby, & Jeffery, 1999; Kingston, Jeffery, & Huang, 2000). The findings suggest that company support, encouragement and agreement for the way software review is conducted helps to increase reviewers' motivation and effort to attain better review performance.

In regard to supporting documents, the results show that the use of reading techniques, prescription documents and reports have no significant impact on software review performance. This is in direct contradiction to the software review literature (Dunsmore et al., 2002; IEEE standard 1028, 1989; Laitenberger & Atkinson, 1998; Shull et al., 2000b, Thelin et al., 2003; Travassos, Shull. Caver, & Basili, 1999). Our results illustrate that among all supporting documents only previously reviewed software documents are vital to the software review performance in practice. As a result, it is recommended that future empirical studies should consider the use of previously reviewed software documents in laboratory experiments.

Meeting process in the software review literature is often treated as a black box. No theory or studies on this aspect were found in the current literature. Therefore, one of the objectives of this study is to elaborate this black box. Four meeting process factors (communication, status effect, teamwork, and discussion quality) were proposed in the EIIO model, but the survey findings indicate that only teamwork is an important factor in software review meeting process that affects performance. These results suggest a successful review process requires good teamwork with information sharing, willingness to participate in discussions and team members working closely together.

In addition, the findings suggest that inputs that affect teamwork include software artefact characteristics, use of previously reviewed software documents, use of reports, and perceived contingency. Although it seems that explicit inputs are predominant factors (three constructs have an effect on teamwork), the most significant input that has the strongest influence on teamwork is perceived contingency ($r = 0.369$, $p < 0.0001$), followed by software artefact characteristics ($r = 0.159$, $p < 0.05$), use of reports ($r = 0.154$, $p < 0.05$) and previously reviewed software documents ($r = 0.141$, $p < 0.05$).

Again, reviewers' motivation has a positive impact on successful review meeting process and performance. The results suggest that the selection of reviewers should be done cautiously.

In relation to inputs, software artefact characteristics have a significant influence on the use of reports, previously reviewed software documents and experience required. In particular, it has the strongest effect on experience required ($r = 0.241$, $p < 0.0001$), followed by use of previously reviewed software ($r = 0.22$, $p < 0.05$) and reports ($r = 0.156$, $p < 0.05$). The results suggest that correct selection of reviewers is determined by characteristics of software artefacts.

A Simple Review Guide

The overall results indicate that a successful software review should consider the following issues:

1. Identifying the characteristics of the software artefact.

2. Decision of which supporting documents (reports and previously reviewed software documents) to use and reviewers' experience required which are determined by software artefact characteristics.

3. Selection of reviewers should be based on their role (review) experience and working experience in the software industry and how they perceive company support and encouragement, and their acceptance levels of the company that is organising and conducting the software review.

4. In the review meeting process, the most critical factor is teamwork which can be affected by the characteristics of the software artefact, use of previously reviewed software documents and reports, and perceived contingency (motivation).

The four-step guide provides a simple and easy way to conduct software review for industry practitioners. The final EIIO model also provides further details of analysis software review performance. Chapter 11 describes a detailed recommendation of conducting effectiveness software review for both researchers and industry practitioners.

Summary

The structural model also provided reasonable and interesting explanations for software review performance. Finally, the additional analyses with the subset data strongly supported the robustness of the model and findings. Overall, the results provide good indicators for the prediction of software review performance.

The next chapter discusses the cross validations of the research. Case study method has been used in the cross validation.

References

ANSI/IEEE. (1989). An American National Standard, *ANSI/IEEE Standard 1028*, IEEE Standards for Software Reviews and Audits.

Basili, V. R., Green, S., Laitenberger, O., Lanubile, F., Sorumgard, S., & Zelkowitz, M., (1996). The empirical investigation of perspective-based reading. *International Journal on Empirical Software Engineering*, *1*(12), 133-144.

Briand, L. C., & Wust, J. (2000). *Integrating scenario-based and measurement-based software product assessment. ISERN Report No. 042-00/E*, International Software Engineering Software Research Network, Fraunhofer Instituted for Empirical Software Engineering, Germany.

Chernak, Y. (1996, December). A statistical approach to the inspection checklist formal syntheses and improvement. *IEEE Transactions on Software Engineering*, *22*(12).

Chin, W. W. (1998). The partial least square approach for structural equation modeling. In G. A. Marcoulides (Ed.), *Modern methods for business research* (pp. 295-336). Mahwah, NJ: Erlbaum.

Chin, W. W. (2003). A permutation procedure for multi-group comparison of PLS models. *Proceedings of the PLS'03 International Symposium* (pp. 33-43).

Chin, W. W., & Gopal, A. (1995). Adoption intention in GSS: Relative importance of beliefs. *The Data Base for Advances in Information Systems, 26*, 42-46.

Cohen, J. (1988). *Statistical power analysis for the behaviour sciences* (2nd ed.). Hillsdale, NJ: Lawrence Erlbaum.

Dunsmore, A., Roper, M., & Wood, M. (2002, May 19-25). Further investigation into the development and evaluation of reading techniques for object-oriented code inspection. *International Conference on Software Engineering* (pp. 47-57).

Geisser, S. (1975). The predictive sample reuse method with applications. *Journal of the American Statistical Association, 70*, 320-328.

Humphrey, W. S. (2002). *Introduction to personal software process*. Boston: Addison-Wesley.

IEEE Standard 1028. (1998). Software Engineering Standard Committee of The IEEE Computer Society, 1998. *IEEE Standard for Software Review, IEEE Standard 1028*, Institute of Electrical and Electronics Engineers Inc., New York.

Isazadeh, A., Macewen, G., & Malton, A. (1995). Behavioural patterns for software requirement engineering. *Proceedings of the 1995 Conference of the Centre for Advanced Studies on Collaborative Research*, Toronto.

Kingston, G., Jeffery, R., & Huang, W. (2000, April). *An explanatory study on the goal alignment in joint software reviews*. Canberra, 63-72.

Kingston, G., Webby, R., & Jeffery, R. (1999, June 23-25). Different and conflicting goals in software reviews. *Proceedings of the 7th European Conference on Information Systems* (pp. 420-435).

Laitenberger, O., & Atkinson, C. (1998). Generalizing perspective-based inspection to handle object-oriented development artefacts. *Proceedings of the International Conference on Software Engineering* (pp. 494-503). Los Angeles.

Laitenberger, O., & Debaud, J. M. (1997). Perspective-based reading of code documents at Robert Bosch GMBH. *Information and Software Technology, 39*, 781-791.

Laitenberger, O., & Emam, K. E. (2001). An internally replicated quasi-experimental comparison of checklist and perspective-based reading of code documents. *IEEE Transactions of Software Engineering*, *27*(5), 378-421.

Miller, J., Wood, M., & Roper, M., (1998). Further experiences with scenarios and checklists. *Empirical Software Engineering, 3*, 37-64.

Reeve, J. T. (1991, March). Applying the Fagan inspection technique. *Quality Forum, 17*(1).

Sauer, C., Jeffery, R., Land, L., & Yetton, P. (2000). Understanding and improving the effectiveness of software development technical reviews: A behaviourally motivated programme of research. *IEEE Transactions on Software Engineering, 26*(1), 1-14.

Shull, F., Lanubile, F., & Biasili, V. (2000a, November). Investigating reading techniques for object-oriented framework learning. *IEEE Transaction on Software Engineering, 26*(11).

Shull, F., Rus, I., & Basili, V. (2000b, July). How perspective-based reading can improve requirements inspection? *IEEE Computer*, 73-79.

Stone, M. (1974). Cross-validatory choice and assessment of statistical predictions. *Journal of the Royal Statistical Society, B36,* 111-133.

Thelin, T., Runeson, R., & Regnell, B. (2001). Usage-based reading An experiment to guide reviewers with use cases. *Information and Software Technology, 43*, 925-938.

Thelin, T., Runeson, P., & Wohlin, C. (2003, August). An experimental comparison of usage-based and checklist-based reading. *IEEE Transaction on Software Engineering, 29*(8), 687-704.

Thelin, T., Runeson, P., Wohiln, C., Olsson, T., & Andersson, C. (2002). How much information is needed for usage-based reading?–A series of experiments. *Proceedings of the 2002 International Symposium on Empirical Software Engineering (ISESE'02)*.

Travassos, G. H., Shull, F., Caver, J., & Basili, V. R. (1999 December). Reading techniques for OO design inspections. *Proceedings of the 24th Annual Software Engineering Workshop*, Goddard Space Flight Centre, MD.

Chapter X

Case Study of Software Reviews

Abstract

The aim of this chapter is to identify the key software review inputs that significantly affect review performance in practice. A case study research method is employed. Five companies are volunteers participating in the study. In-depth semi-structured interview approach is used for data collection. From the results, the typical issues for conducting software review include 1) selecting right reviewers to perform a defect detection task, 2) the limitation of time and resources for organizing and conducting software review, and 3) no standard and specific guideline to measure an effective review for different types of software artefacts (i.e., requirement, design, code, and test cases). Thus the result shows that the experience (i.e., knowledge and skills) of reviewers is the most significant input influencing software review performance.

Case Study Research

The proposed EIIO model has been empirically validated using questionnaire surveys. However, some important limitations of cross-sectional designs must be recognized, such as internal validity issues in the use of survey results (Ackoff, 1953; Babbie, 2000; De Vaus, 2001). This chapter discusses the case study that was used to further investigate of the survey results.

Case Study: In-Depth Interviews

The research method was used in the case study is in-depth interview. The in-depth interview research method is a useful tool in qualitative research methodology. One of the key advantages of in-depth interviews is that they balance a purely quantitative method by allowing for integration of researchers' and practitioners' perspectives for cross validation in a cost-effective way (Creswell, 1994; Kraemer, 1991; Marriam, 1988). Another advantage of in-depth interviews is that they collect information without losing any significant details (Crabtree, Yanoshi, Miller, & O'Connor, 1993; Fink, 1995; Frey & Fontana, 1993; Light, 1971). As well, in-depth interviews are extremely important to capture rich information, to develop and confirm the context for the theoretical model (Ericsson & Simon, 1980; Marriam, 1988; Zikmund, 2000) and to enhance the validity of a quantitative questionnaire survey method. By combining both qualitative results from the in-depth interviews and quantitative results from the questionnaire survey, a higher quality of findings that reflect the state of software review in practice can be achieved (Malhotra, Hall, Shaw, & Crisp, 1996; Morgan, 1998; Zikmund, 2000).

In this research, several strategies were used to ensure the in-depth interviews addressed the limitations of the questionnaire survey. An experienced interviewer was employed and this enabled a high reliability to be attained. Detailed notes were taken during the interviews and tape recordings and transcripts of each interview were made.

The convergence and divergence in the issues was raised, enabling the constructs of interest to evolve throughout the interview process. The interview process requires openness to new ideas as well as ensuring that all factors are captured (Frey & Fontana, 1993). Data collection provides data useful for generating or confirming theoretical models (Hammersley, 1992; Neuman, 2000). Details of the methodology will be discussed in the following sections.

Case Study:
In-Depth Interview Procedures

The aim of the in-depth interviews is to identify the key software review factors that significantly affect review performance in practice (Yin, 1994). Five in-depth semi-structured interviews were conducted with different information technology organizations. Subjects/Cases are be knowledgeable about the research problem are questioned. Five subjects were interviewed and they all have more than 10 years experience in the software industry, more than 10 years in project development, and between 3 and 22 years experience in software review. The selection criteria were driven by the availability of the subjects and their fit to the following three categories of expertise. The three categories are derived from "scope of expert theories" (Ericsson & Lehmann, 1996):

- **Age and Peak Performance:** The peak age of career achievement often falls during an individual's thirties and forties (Ericsson, 1994; Charness, Krampe Mayr, 1993).

- **The 10-Year Rule:** The ten-year experience rule is considered necessary for all individuals. It has been found that even talented individuals require more than 10 years to achieve international performance (Bloom, 1985; Dick & Hearn, 1988; Ericsson, Krfampe, & Tesch-Tomer, 1993; Galton, 1969).

- **Role of Deliberate Practice:** Domain knowledge develops from training and qualifications with significant feedback and improvement to achieve the highest performance (Charness et al., 1993; Ericsson & Lehmann, 1996).

The communication channel was face-to-face (FtF) interviews. The questionnaire design for the interview was focused on open-ended questions (Crabtree et al., 1993; Fink, 1995; Frey & Fontana, 1993). Three independent reviewers assessed the questionnaire before the interviews. The interviews were approximately two hours each, and they were tape-recorded and transcribed. The analysis of the interviews' transcripts followed Miles and Huberman's recommendation (1984) — a coding scheme based on the theoretical framework was developed, and the transcripts were coded based on the scheme. The study aimed to focus on the interviewees' perception of important software review inputs influence on review performance. A sample questionnaire and a data analysis procedure are included in Appendixes 9 and 10.

Results

As a warm-up, subjects were asked about their companies and their daily roles in general. Upon completion of the warm-up, a serious discussion of the main study was begun. The following descriptions illustrate the interviews. Results are classified into two sections: 1) the common types of inputs and 2) the effect of inputs and process on outcome.

Common Types of Inputs

All subjects indicated that the common type of implicit input is the "experience" of the reviewers. In particular, expertise in domain knowledge is essential.

"On the basis of understanding of the work and experience."

"It's based on experience. Those who have done project management before... which include code review, expert programmers... Intelligent person who has good understanding of the system issues within the business environment ..."

"Someone who has dealt with system development before... operation environment or business production environment ... That's why it is important to have someone who has been exposed to systems ... has been in a production environment and is currently using the system."

"Dealt with whole systems operation in the real business environment over a number of years."

"Perceive a subject as an expert or a stakeholder... If they are being identified as stakeholders in the business requirement proposal or the solutions, then they are required to attend."

Factors that affect selection of software reviewers are costs and experience of the reviewers.

"No other factors such as resources or budget. It is because we prefer to have an expensive person over a short time than an inexpensive person

forever. You need to understand that the job needs to be finished by the deadline."

"They need to have a kind of unique feeling how the system was ....The issues related to why there are system problems such as poorly built components. But if the system goes down the track, they need to know what the problems are if it's designed in a wrong way. They have first-hand experience."

"The reviewers must have a good understanding of the subject areas... what I mean is the experience and the knowledge. Otherwise, the project could easily fall apart."

One subject indicated that the key factors for choosing reviewers are purely based on the organisational structure and the project proposal. Hence their software review team is from the existing project team.

"It is more likely impacted by a proposal. Within the team, they have come down to assessing how important it can be and who will be busy on the day. The team leader will decide what is important, but nothing formally drives the process... The project team is a virtual structure. They formally report to the project manager and are responsible to the team areas. Once we worked it out, what systems would be impacted by the changes, then the representatives of the team to support these systems would be identified to do the work."

In the context of the common types of explicit inputs, four major supporting documents are checklists, standards, guidelines, and templates.

"With a requirements document, there is a template of the requirements documents that people are supposed to follow. We have many templates... We also sometimes use checklists. With design, again the templates, internal developed templates, no checklist. In theory, we should have requirements. Code — they usually use the requirements documents that are available, there are coding standards available. How often they are used probably depends. Because everybody remembers what is in it, nobody needs to have refreshed of course. But if they don't remember, you do go back to check the standard if you have a problem. They should have reviewed the requirements and design documents presented. Most of the time, it will be

the case... but sometimes, if the life cycle overlaps, the review may run out of order... Test — again the templates, guidelines, requirements and design documents as inputs. Test results are also compared with the plan."

"We have client requirements, which are bulleted style... From that we would produce an object diagram. From that point we will often use JAVA... If there is a database, there will be an ER-diagram and then produce tables..."

"We did have guidelines for producing user case documents or guidelines for UML. The QA has guidelines to test the systems. We do not have any supporting documents for the review, but we have guidelines for producing the documents (artefacts) when you look at use cases or UML. We took software development principles, drilled down in a number of guidelines for different types of project. We don't have ISO because it tends to produce lots of documents."

"We have standards, but our standards are oral, I said to them and agree what standard documents we could use — what convention they could follow. Not any formal procedure or guideline. We always sit down — it's part of our engagement."

"We follow ISO requirements; we have a set of templates, guidelines, and checklists for the review process and quality assurance purpose."

In particular, one of the subjects pointed out that the factors for choosing these documents are:

"It is really based on the descriptions and the common sense of the project team. Common sense means that if we review a design document, it will be expected we would have a requirements document present. It should be described as common sense. But some of the people maybe consider that would be unnecessary. There are a couple of reasons; one is I have no time to read the requirements documents; Therefore, I am definitely not going to read the requirement documents... In a few cases, the requirement documents were reviewed recently anyway, so they would remember it. But how valid it is depends."

Inputs Affect Software Review Performance

Overall, none of the respondents believe that the supporting documents (except previously reviewed software documents) they use are significant in helping them to find defects. The results indicate that supporting documents have little impact on the review process and performance.

"No supporting document used to find defects..."

"It heavily depends on the quality of the artefacts. If the requirement is well written, the template and checklist should be effective, but they are not. Primarily it's because people ignore it. Because they think why should I have this imposed on me? Why constrain the way I do my work? I have been doing this for several years; I know what is in it."

An interesting result is that previously reviewed design document may be useful in the review performance. Subjects argued that:

"It will be very helpful if the requirement is well-written and fully inspected before the design review... but most of the cases are not..."

"Most supporting documents are useless however, when a design document is well-written, it definitely helps code review."

All subjects agree that implicit inputs such as the experience of the reviewer are the most significant input affecting review performance.

"Level of experience... We found some people just no good in review or testing. They are just no good. Important is to get someone who is reliable and honest. Often you get someone who just tested once or have done it and said that's enough."

"I think the key factors are experience of the person, either designers or programmers. I define experience as what tasks the person has previously done. I match their previous experience with the task for them. Sometimes, I also asked those questions about how would they do a task, what would they do for particular situation as well."

Further, the interviews also showed that there are a number of problems in conducting software reviews.

"Inability of programmers to conclude satisfactory code (conclude code is satisfactory)."

"It produces an overhead primarily because the activity was not managed and measured and the biggest problem is the people are not reading the materials. The ability to contribute to the process is difficult to control."

"It takes a certain amount of resources. At the start, there is a lot of pressure to drill down, a lot of inspection time, QA (quality assurance) time. Project managers make sure there is a 6 weeks cycle to ensure the deadline is met."

In particular, one of the subjects pointed out that time allocated to software review is often a minimum.

"The reason is that we don't put significant time to do it, so people rush. We have not put enough significant time into the project plan. And more importantly, people take their time off to review somebody's work."

Meeting Process Affects Performance

In relation to the meeting process, all subjects agreed that *teamwork* (information sharing and understanding of the meeting discussions, working together as a team, and willingness of participating in the meeting) is the most critical meeting process factor in a review process.

"The project team is a virtual (team) structure... they formally report to the project manager and are responsible to the team areas."

"... basically communication is through the meeting. Usually, at the initial stage, the team will meet on a weekly basis, to assure everyone can fully understand..."

"Talk about the specification to them, then leave them to go off and cut some code (i.e., no group meeting). I look at the code on screen and sometimes I would get them to print the code and show it to me. I then ask them to explain what the design was... then we have a structured walkthrough of the design discussion. I didn't specify what kind of structured walkthrough, but left them to decide. Usually it's one of them and one of me for the design document (i.e., a pair). It took about a half hour for group discussion and 10-15 minutes for individual review. Because I didn't make them to make a big programme. It is about 10 pages."

"In the case of the design, I would go to the programmer and say, 'Can you understand what is going on here?'... When the designers finish their work, I would have a meeting with the programmers, at that point I say to the person 'Can you follow the designer's work that has been written?' If they can't, the designer needs to explain to the programmer about the work."

Table 1. Summary of the case study, the in-depth interview results

	Interviewee 1	Interviewee 2	Interviewee 3	Interviewee 4	Interviewee 5
Issue of conducting software reviews	Time and resources, no rigorous software mechanisms	Measurement matrix and overhead	Selecting right reviewers, time and costs	Time	Time
Common types of inputs					
Selection of reviewers	Experience	Expert who has domain knowledge	Understanding of the work and experience	Experience	Experience and domain knowledge
Key factors for the use of reviewers	Intelligence, good understanding of the system issues within the business environment	Project proposal, project plan	Resources	Project Manager	Understanding of the subject areas
Common types of supporting documents	Guidelines	Templates and guidelines	Standards	Standards, guidelines and procedures	Guidelines, standards and checklists
Key factors for choosing these documents	Effective to get the job done.	Time, descriptions and the common sense of the project team	Experience of reviewers	ISO standard	ISO standard

continued on following page

Table 1. cont.

	Interviewee 1	Interviewee 2	Interviewee 3	Interviewee 4	Interviewee 5
Inputs affect process and outcomes					
Inputs affect process	Reviewers' motivation and effort	Company support	Encouragement and support from the company	Reviewers' effort	Reviewers' motivation and effort & previously reviewed design documents
Supporting documents that are useful for review performance	None	None. Heavily dependant on the initial quality of the work product	None	Previously reviewed design document	None, but previously reviewed software may be useful
Key factors influencing performance	Experience	Measurement matrix and time	Experience	Experience	Understanding the subject areas
Process affects outcomes					
Meeting process factors affect review performance	Teamwork	Fully participating in the meeting	Information sharing	Working together	Teamwork
Demographics					
Primary function of the business	Education systems	Insurance	Automatic office or commercial systems	Railway systems	Financial web-based systems
Number of employees	12,000	250	500	4,000	50
Years of experience in software development project	16	19	24	12	20
Years of experience in software review	8	19	22	3	10
Age group	41–50	31–40	41–50	31–40	31–40
Position	Quality Assurance Manager	Senior Architect	Group manager	Group IT Manager	Project Manager and Team Leader
Education	BSc	BSc (Computer Science)	MCom (Accounting & Information Systems Management)	BSc (Comp. Sci.), Internal Quality Auditor	PhD (Comp. Sci.)

"We have circulated the requirements... After the submission of BSR, we have a distribution list to the project steering committee and the project working group."

"... all people should fully participate in the meeting..., but sometimes they don't."

"Teams often work in a pair. One person codes the functionality, another will test it... We also have daily and weekly meetings. Once a week, we will get the person who wrote the code, get them up and analyse line by line. What is wrong with it, and how to improve it?"

In particular, subjects pointed out that:

"We are willing to share our work and experience....this improves our teamwork, improves the review performance."

"We are working closely... it usually takes about 1-2 hours per review meeting."

In addition, the results suggest that inputs affect teamwork. Subjects indicated that:

"Our company supports software review...With the team leader's encouragement, the project team generally is quite motivated in the meeting."

"If they are motivated, they are often participating in the meetings... if not, they usually don't turn up..."

"... the design documents are more helpful than requirements in the code review...when the project leader distributed the design documents to the developers who then should be well-prepared before the meeting, the meeting would be much shorter..."

Discussions

The interviews show that experience is the most difficult factor to control in conducting software review activities. Typical issues of organizing and conducting software reviews are: 1) selecting the right reviewers to perform a software review task; 2) limited time and resources to organize and conduct software reviews; 3) no standard or specific guidelines to measure an effective review for different types of software artefacts (i.e., requirements, design, code, and test cases).

As well, the results show that experience (i.e., abilities and skills) of reviewers is the most significant input influencing software review performance (i.e., number of true defects found) and teamwork is the most significant process factor affecting software review performance. Table 1 summarizes the issues identified in the five interviews.

One subject pointed out *"the ability to contribute to the process is difficult to control."* This could indicate a hidden input (i.e., motivation and effort) that most of the subjects might not be aware of. Another interviewee argued that the initial quality of the work product affected reviewers' behaviour.

"If the requirement document is poorly written, more effort is required... this could impact the performance."

With regard to the explicit inputs, no respondents considered supporting documents to have a significant impact on review performance. Two respondents argued that:

"The initial quality is determined by reading techniques...most of the developers will read the documents from page 1 to the last page..."

"It's difficult to control reviewers using the supporting documents, especially experienced reviewers who require less supporting documents than junior reviewers."

Interview results indicated that task characteristics and experience of the reviewers are the key factors influencing the use of supporting documents.

In relation to the process, teamwork is considered the most critical factor in the meeting process.

"If everyone could share their information and experience, working closely, fully participating and engaging in the discussions, meetings would be more important to software review."

On the other hand, motivation and effort were perceived as important factors in the meeting process and review performance.

"With company support, we encourage project teams to participate in the software inspection (review)... One of the issues is that we can't control their level of effort in the review process."

To measure the performance, it is recommended that an appropriate measurement matrix is important. At the moment, there is no formal measurement guideline in place. Many subjects identified the need for improving measurement of the software review process. Subjects recommended that,

"One would be to set objectives for the software review or inspection. The objective should be explicit rather than implicit. The second is the time allocation. People should be allocated the time they need. The third is to look at defect tracking — where is the defect introduced, where has it been removed."

In summary, the aim of these in-depth interviews is to cross-validate the quantitative questionnaire survey and develop an understanding of what software review factors were considered to have a significant affect on performance in practice.

The results elicited various combinations of the experts' views. These results reinforce our contentions that 1) reviewer experience is the most critical factor influencing review performance, 2) supporting documents have a lesser impact on review performance, 3) teamwork is the significant factor in the review meeting process, 4) motivation is the important factor influencing the teamwork in a review process, and 5) selection of inputs is determined by the characteristics of the software artefact that also supports the hypotheses of the EIIO model.

Summary

This chapter discussed case studies and cross validation of the industry survey. The overall results of the case studies confirm the proposed EIIO model and validate the quantitative questionnaire survey results.

The next chapter will discuss the recommendations for conducting software reviews.

References

Ackoff, R. L. (1953). *The design of social research*. Chicago: The University of Chicago Press.

Babbie, E. (2000). *The practice of social research* (9th ed.). Belmon, CA: Wadsworth.

Bloom, B. S. (1985). Generalizations about talent development. In B. S. Bloom (Ed.), *Developing talent in young people* (pp. 507-549). New York: Plenum.

Charness, N., Krampe R. T., & Mayr, U. (1993). The importance of coaching in entrepreneurial skill domains: An international comparison of life-span chess skill acquisition. *Proceedings of Conference Acquisition Expert Performance*, Wakulla Springs, FL.

Crabtree, B. F., Yanoshi, M. K., Miller W.L., & O'Connor, P. J. (1993). Selecting individual or group interviews. In D. Morgan (Ed.), *Successful focus groups: Advancing the state of art* (pp. 137-152). Newbury Park, CA: Saga.

Creswell, J. W. (1994). *Research design: Qualitative and quantitative approaches*. Thousand Oaks: Sage.

De Vaus, D. (2001). *Research design in social research*. London: Sage.

Ericsson, K. A., & Lehmann, A. C. (1996). Expert and exceptional performance: Evidence of maximal adaptation to task constraints. *Psychology Review, 47*, 273-305.

Ericsson, K. A., Krfampe, R. T., & Tesch-Tomer, C. (1993). The role of deliberate practice in the acquisition of expert performance. *Psychology Review, 100*(3), 363-406.

Ericsson, K. A., & Simon, H. A. (1980). Verbal reports as data. *Psychological Review, 87*, 215-251.

Fink, A. (1995). *How to conduct interviews by telephone and in person.* Thousand Oaks, CA: Sage.

Frey, J. H., & Fontana, A. (1993). The group interview in social research. In D. Morgan (Ed.), *Successful focus groups: Advancing the state of art* (pp. 20-34). Newbury Park, CA: Saga.

Galton, F. (1969). *Hereditary genius: An inquiry into its laws and consequences.* London: Friedman.

Hammersley, M. (1992). Deconstructing the qualitative-quantitative divide. In J. Brannen (Ed.), *Mixing methods: Qualitative and quantitative research.* Avebury, Aldershot.

Kraemer, K. (1991). The information systems research challenge. In K. Kraemer (Ed.), *Survey research methods* (pp. 299-315). Boston: Harvard Business School.

Light, R. J. (1971). Measures of response agreement for qualitative data: Some generalizations and alternatives. *Psychological Bulletin, 76,* 365-377.

Malhotra, N. K., Hall, J., Shaw, M., & Crisp, M. (1996). *Marketing research: An applied orientation.* Sydney, Australia: Prentice Hall.

Marriam, S. B. (1988). *Case study research in education: A qualitative approach.* San Francisco: Jossey-Bass.

Miles, M. B., & Huberman, A. M. (1984). *Qualitative data analysis: A sourcebook of new methods.* Beverly Hill, CA: Sage.

Morgan, D. L. (1998). *Focus groups as qualitative research: Qualitative research methods.* Newbury Park, CA: Sage.

Neuman, L. W. (2000). *Social research methods: Qualitative and quantitative approaches* (4th ed.). Boston: Allyn and Bacon.

Yin, R. K. (1994). *Case study research: Design and methods* (2nd ed.). Thousand Oaks: Sage.

Zikmund, W. G. (2000). *Exploring marketing research* (7th ed.). Fort Worth, TX: The Dryden.

Chapter XI

Recommendations for Conducting Software Reviews

Abstract

This chapter provides recommendations for conducting software reviews in software development environments. It is recommended that the software review process planning should consider three issues. These include: 1) decision on the selection of inputs, 2) a determination of the level of review meetings required, and 3) identifying the measurement metrics. For researchers, it is recommended that 1) future research should pay more attention to important relationships between software artefact characteristics and the use of supporting documents, 2) designing and conducting laboratory studies be done more realistically, 3) direct and indirect relationships between the use of inputs as predictors for software review performance, 4) the important relationships between the software artefact characteristics and meeting process factors, 5) meetings should be held when the artefact is complex, of large size and poor initial quality, 6) the use of previously reviewed software documents in relation to meeting process, 7) perceived contingency (motivation) is the most critical factor to meeting process, and 8) future studies should further concentrate on the use of previously reviewed software documents in combination with the implicit inputs, process, and performance.

Introduction

This chapter discusses the theoretical and methodological contributions of the book, the key findings and managerial implications of the studies, the limitations and directions for future research, and the final conclusion of this book.

Recommendations for Conducting Software Reviews

For Practitioners

With rapid changes occurring in business and information technology, practitioners often face pressure to produce high quality software in tight timeframes to satisfy stakeholders and/or users. The discussed benefits of software review to system development indicate that practitioners should pay more attention to achieving an effective review process. The book has developed guidelines to practitioners for organising and conducting their software reviews in an effective way.

Firstly, the use of inputs becomes more important to the organization of their software review process. Next, practitioners should be cautious in selecting the right people to perform software review tasks. Finally, according to the survey and in-depth interview findings, it is recommended that the review process planning should consider three concerns:

1. Decision on the selection of inputs.
2. A determination of the level of review meetings required.
3. Identifying the measurement metrics.

Use of Inputs

The first step is to identify the software artefact characteristics, as they determine the level of reviewer experience required and the types of supporting documents that should be used. Selection of reviewers should be based on the characteristics of the software artefact. When the artefact is more complex, larger, and of poor initial quality, more experienced reviewers are required, particularly those having role (review) experience. The research has not quantified the years of experience required in terms of the software artefact characteristics.

Further, working experience in the software industry is also considered an important factor to improve review performance. However, practitioners should decide what kinds of domain knowledge are required when conducting a software review. For instance, someone who has UML knowledge and design review experience as a reviewer is required when there is a UML design review task.

Also, the use of supporting documents is considered critical to the software review process and performance. Use of supporting documents is based on software artefact characteristics. More complexity, larger size and poorer initial quality increase the need for supporting documents.

The survey results suggest that the use of previously reviewed software documents has the most significant impact on meeting process and performance among the supporting documents, while business reports within the application domain are also important to the software review meeting process and performance.

When a software artefact is more complex, larger and of poor initial quality, the use of previously reviewed software documents and reports becomes vital to review meeting process and performance. Hence, explicit inputs have a strong influence on the meeting process, particularly teamwork. As a result, organising and conducting software review should take software artefact characteristics and supporting documents closely into account.

In the survey study, the findings suggest that both explicit and implicit inputs affect software review performance (i.e., number of defects found). Significant explicit inputs include software artefacts characteristics (complexity, size, and initial quality), previously reviewed software documents (requirements, design, and code), and reports (business reports and standards within the application domain and developments). The significant implicit inputs (individual characteristics) include experience (role experience and working experience in the software industry), perceived contingency (perceived support, encouragement, and acceptance levels of the company conducting the software review).

Overall, it is suggested that practitioners should pay more attention to artefact characteristics, experience and motivation of reviewers, and supporting documents. Experience is the input that has the most significant impact on the software review performance (i.e., number of defects found). Reviewers' perceived contingency also has a strong impact on review performance. Selection of reviewers to perform a software review task is the most critical issue. Thus, practitioners should pay more attention to the skills and experience of the reviewers. Both survey and in-depth interviews validated that experience is the most critical factor in software review performance. Experience such as role experience and software industry experience (in particular domain knowledge) should be considered important attributes when seeking a software reviewer.

The Need for Team Review Meetings

The software review literature has consistently debated the importance of holding team meetings in the review process. The meeting process is often treated as a black box and achieving process gains and losses is often treated as a theoretical question. The empirical results of this study indicate that the decision on the need for review meetings should be based on the characteristics of software artefact to be reviewed. The findings propose that more complex, larger, and poorer initial quality artefacts require better teamwork in review meetings. During the meeting process, practitioners should pay more attention to teamwork. Effective teamwork is the key driver of software review performance. Recalling from Chapter II, teamwork is defined as:

- Members working together as a team.
- Other members appearing willing to answer questions when asked.
- Members having sufficient access to the information they need to participate actively in and fully understand the meeting.

In addition, critical factors affecting teamwork include software artefact characteristics, reports, previously reviewed software documents and perceived contingency. Perceived contingency is the most important factor influencing teamwork in the meeting process. When managers assign a task to a group, they should consider reviewers' perceived contingency, software artefact characteristics and the use of supporting documents. The survey study findings on input-process-performance relationships can also help managers to make a better selection of potential reviewers.

Selection of Measurement Metrics

In addition, selection of measurement metrics of software review outcomes is also important according to the in-depth interview results. To achieve an optimal outcome, it is important for practitioners to decide the measurement model (Jeffery, Ruhe, & Wieczorek, 2001) and objectives (Kingston, Webby, & Jeffery, 1999; Kingston, Jeffery, & Huang, 2000) for the review performance. For instance, this study suggested that measurement performance is based on the number of defects found. Further measurement metrics include the time used for organising and conducting software reviews (Fagan, 1986; Kan, 1995; Votta, 1993; Porter & Votta, 1994) and the number of reviewers used and team size (Biffl & Halling, 2003; Humphrey, 2000; Petersson, 2001). This directly indicates that the objectives of the software review task should be related to the selections of the inputs used and the organization of the review process. With clear objective-based measurement metrics, practitioners should be able to identify the important inputs and the need to hold review meetings.

Summary Key Points for Conducting Software Review

- The first step is to identify the software artefact characteristics, as they determine the level of reviewer experience required and the types of supporting documents that should be used.

- More complexity, larger size, and poorer initial quality increase the need for supporting documents.

- Use of previously reviewed software documents has the most significant impact on meeting process and performance among the supporting documents.

- Business reports within the application domain are also important to the software review meeting process and performance.

- The significant implicit inputs (individual characteristics) include experience (role experience and working experience in the software industry), perceived contingency (perceived support, encouragement and acceptance levels of the company conducting the software review) that affect software review performance.

- Experience is the input that has the most significant impact on the software review performance (i.e., number of defects found).

- When managers assign a task to a group, they should consider reviewers' perceived contingency, software artefact characteristics and the use of supporting documents.

- During the meeting process, practitioners should pay more attention to teamwork. Teamwork is defined as: members working together as a team, other members appearing willing to answer questions when asked, members having sufficient access to the information they need to participate actively in and fully understand the meeting.

- Critical factors affecting teamwork include software artefact characteristics, reports, previously reviewed software documents and perceived contingency.

- Perceived contingency is the most important factor influencing teamwork in the meeting process.

- With clear objective-based measurement metrics, practitioners should be able to identify the important inputs and the need to hold review meetings.

In summary, the critical requirement for successful software review performance is a good fit between explicit inputs, implicit inputs, and teamwork. A review team that has a good fit in terms of the above factors is likely to produce higher review performance. Thus, the results strongly support the behavioural theories, but provide only partial support to the software review literature. For example, reading documents and prescription documents did not have a significant impact on performance. Overall, the findings provide useful guidelines to practitioners for more effectively managing their software reviews.

For Researchers

Use of Inputs

Explicit inputs-software artefact characteristics (complexity, initial quality, and size) and supporting documents (reading technique documents, prescription documents, previously reviewed software documents, and reports)-are the commonly discussed inputs in the software review literature. Current software review literature mainly emphasises the rigorous and formal procedures of conducting software reviews. The strategies or techniques such as reading techniques have been heavily focused on in the last decade.

According to the proposed EIIO model, the questionnaire results show that the software artefact characteristics have a significant effect on the use of previously reviewed software artefacts, prescription documents and reports. To my knowledge, there is no other empirical research that demonstrates the important relationships between characteristics of software artefacts and the use of supporting documents. While most researchers have mainly focused on other supporting documents, particularly reading techniques, (Basili et al., 1996, Dunsmore, Roper, & Wood, 2002; Shull, Lanubile, & Biasili, 2000), the survey results indicate that reading techniques have no significant effect on teamwork and/or review performance. These interesting results indicate that there is a gap between the software review literature and the industry practice.

The findings from the in-depth interviews illustrate that industry practitioners believe the supporting documents (e.g., prescription documents), are not useful and do not help them in finding defects during the software review process. A question is raised that these results are not in line with the emphasis in the current software review literature. One possible explanation is that the supporting documents such as reading techniques are not designed properly and/or not used in an effective way in practice. Future empirical research should consider the important relationships between software artefact characteristics and the use of supporting documents.

In addition, as software review is human-activity based, the use of supporting documents is directly associated with the individual reviewer characteristics such as experience and motivation. The questionnaire survey results show that reviewers' experience affects the use of prescription documents, confidence of reviewers affects use of reading technique documents and perceived contingency has a significant effect on the use of prescription documents.

However, the surprising results demonstrate that both reviewers' experience and motivation have no significant effect on the use of reading technique documents in practice, which differs from the findings of most laboratory studies (Basili, Laitenberger, Shull, & Rus, 2000; Chernak, 1996; Laitenberger & Emam, 2001; Miller, Wood, & Roper, 1998; Thelin, Runeson, & Wohlin, 2003) in the software review literature. One possible reason is that current laboratory studies lack controls on the use of completed supporting documents in relation to reviewers' characteristics. Further, classroom settings, employing students as subjects in laboratory experiments, the selection of software review tasks, use of completed supporting documents and software review procedures do not necessarily reflect industry practice. It is suggested that designing and conducting laboratory studies be done more realistically. The dynamic changes of technologies and business environments add to the challenges of designing laboratory studies.

In comparison, the characteristics of software artefacts affect reviewers' experience required but do not impact on motivation. This implies that software artefact characteristics should dictate the selection of reviewers' experience in practice. The results suggest that reviewer experience should be a significant factor in organising software review teams. To my knowledge, there is a lack of research in this area. No empirical research was found that investigated the important relationships between software artefact characteristics and selection of implicit inputs, which directly and indirectly affect the software review process and performance. In addition, this book provides an understanding of the critical role of implicit with explicit inputs (i.e., software review characteristics and supporting documents). Future research can investigate the direct and indirect relationships between the use of inputs as predictors for software review performance.

Meeting Process

Meeting process is often treated as a black box in the software review literature. This book identifies the meeting process factors as well as empirically validating the important relationships between inputs, process and outcomes. Looking at the relationships between inputs and process, the findings suggest that there is a significant effect of inputs on process.

Software artefact characteristics have direct influence on the review meeting process, and are particularly strongly correlated with the teamwork construct. This is a good indication that when an artefact is complex, of large size and poor initial quality, there will be a potential positive effect on the teamwork in a review meeting. Previous studies recommended that review meetings are not always necessary in all software reviews (Johnson, 1998; Johnson & Tjahjono, 1998; Porter, Mockus, & Votta, 1998; Porter & Votta, 1994), but the question of whether review meetings should be organised is still under debate (Seaman & Basili, 1998; Van Genuchten, Van Dijk Scholten, & Vogel, 1998). The survey findings suggest that meetings should be held when the artefact is complex, of large size and poor initial quality.

These results are definitely interesting for researchers to further explore the important relationships between the software artefact characteristics and meeting process factors.

On the other hand, while reading techniques and prescription documents have no impact on meeting process, previously reviewed software documents and reports have a significant effect on the meeting process. Previously reviewed software documents have the strongest influence on the meeting process. It is quite clear that the use of previously reviewed software documents is a critical factor in the meeting process. The results suggest that a successful meeting can achieve higher review performance. Hence, it is recommended that future research should pay more attention to the use of previously reviewed software documents in relation to meeting process.

In relation to implicit inputs, the survey results suggest that reviewers' experience has a direct effect on communication and discussion quality in the meeting process. Although no previous empirical research has suggested that reviewer experience has an impact on the software review process, the research results suggest that future studies should explore how experience affects the communication and discussion quality. In addition, as expected, the survey results indicate that reviewers' motivation (i.e., perceived contingency) has the strongest impact on the review meeting process among all inputs. These results consistently reinforce the behavioural literature, which has heavily focused on the relationships between motivation, process and performance (Ashkanasy, Widerom, & Peterson, 2000; Campell, 1990; Hare, 1962; Hoffman, 1995; Shaw,

1932). The survey findings proved that among the motivation constructs, only perceived contingency has an influence on the software review meeting process.

According to the original proposed EIIO model, there is no evidence to suggest which inputs are most critical to meeting process. The survey results have proved that perceived contingency is the most critical factor to meeting process.

As a result, further research is required to investigate what types of perceived contingency would motivate reviewers' effort in their group meetings, and how perceived contingency affects the meeting process. Since experience, software artefact characteristics, previously reviewed software documents and reports have a significant effect on meeting process, further investigation of the effect of the above factors on meeting process should be taken into account when designing and formulating empirical research.

Performance

Overall results suggest explicit inputs, implicit inputs and process have a significant impact on software review performance. In particular, the survey results and in-depth interviews with experts have proved that the key driver to software review success is reviewers' experience. The survey results indicate that reviewers' experience is followed by previously reviewed software documents, perceived contingency, and teamwork (see Figure 1 and Table 1 in Chapter IX).

Implicit inputs have very strong direct and indirect effects on software review performance. The results suggest that an experienced reviewer is the key driver for software review performance. This confirms the existing software review literature (Sauer, Jeffery, Land, & Yetton, 2000). Perceived contingency also has a reasonably strong direct and indirect effect on the software review performance. Although motivation of reviewers is often an ignored factor in designing and conducting software review studies, this book provides empirical results suggesting that further research studies need to consider the relationships between reviewers' motivation, especially perceived contingency, and software review process and performance. However, commitment, competency and confidence have no direct impact on software review performance. Future studies should therefore focus on reviewers' experience and perceived contingency. The question of why the other three motivation constructs (commitment, competency, and confidence) did not affect the software review performance needs to be addressed.

Unexpected results were that software artefact characteristics have no direct influence on software review performance, but indirectly affect software review performance via affecting experience, use of reports and teamwork. In contrast, both use of reports and previously reviewed software documents have a direct effect on review performance. In particular, reviewed software documents have the strongest direct impact on teamwork and review performance compared with other supporting documents. This suggests that future studies should further concentrate on the use of previously reviewed software documents in combination with the implicit inputs, process, and performance.

Looking at other supporting documents, the use of reading technique documents and prescription documents has no significant effect on software review performance. The findings exemplify that previously reviewed software documents play a more critical role than other supporting documents (prescription documents and reading technique documents). Although the software review literature has suggested that formal procedures and techniques are important to software review performance, the results indicate that prescription documents do not directly improve software review performance. It is recommended that future empirical studies should analyse how and why these supporting documents do not have an effect on software review performance in practice.

Teamwork, of the meeting process factors, is the only important factor to the review performance. The inputs that affect teamwork in a meeting process are software artefact characteristics, previously reviewed software documents, reports and perceived contingency. This book has explored the meeting process and identified the important factors affecting meeting process and software review performance. This provides a critical path for researchers to in future validate the important relationships between input, process, and outcome.

Key Points for Researchers

- Future research should pay more attention to important relationships between software artefact characteristics and the use of supporting documents.

- Designing and conducting laboratory studies be done more realistically.

- The direct and indirect relationships between the use of inputs as predictors for software review performance.

- The important relationships between the software artefact characteristics and meeting process factors.

- Meetings should be held when the artefact is complex, of large size and poor initial quality.

- The use of previously reviewed software documents in relation to meeting process.

- Perceived contingency (motivation) is the most critical factor to meeting process.
- Further concentrate on the use of previously reviewed software documents in combination with the implicit inputs, process and performance.

Summary

In summary, this chapter provided the recommendations for conducting software reviews. The concerns are the use of the inputs, understanding review team, and designing an objective measurement for review performance. Capstones were also summarised.

References

Ashkanasy, N. M., Widerom, C. P. M., & Peterson, M. F. (2000). *Handbook of organisational culture and climate*. Thousand Oaks, CA: Saga.

Basili, V. R., Green, S., Laitenberger, O., Lanubile, F., Sorumgard, S., & Zelkowitz, M. (1996). The empirical investigation of perspective-based reading. *International Journal on Empirical Software Engineering, 1*(12), 133-144.

Basili, V. R., Laitenberger, O., Shull, F., & Rus, I., (2000). Improving software inspections by using reading techniques. *Proceedings of International Conference on Software Engineering* (pp. 836-727).

Biffl, S., & Halling, M. (2003, May), Investigating the defect detection effectiveness and cost benefit of nominal inspection team. *IEEE Transaction on Software Engineering, 29*(5), 385-397.

Campell, J. P. (1990). Modeling the performance prediction problem in industrial and organizational psychology. In M. D. Dunnette & L. M. Hough (Eds.), *Handbook of industrial and organizational psychology* (2nd ed.) (pp. 687-732). Palo Alto, CA: Consulting Psychologists Press Inc.

Chernak, Y. (1996, December). A statistical approach to the inspection checklist formal syntheses and improvement. *IEEE Transactions on Software Engineering, 22*(12).

Dunsmore, A., Roper, M., & Wood, M. (2002, May 19-25). Further investigation into the development and evaluation of reading techniques for object-oriented code inspection. *International Conference on Software Engineering* (pp. 47-57).

Fagan, M. E. (1986, July). Advances in software inspections. *IEEE Transaction on Software Engineering, 12*(7).

Hare, A. P. (1962). *Handbook of small group research.* New York: Free Press of Glencoe.

Hoffman, R. R. (1995). Eliciting knowledge from experts: A methodological analysis. *Organisational Behaviour Human Decision Process, 62,* 129-58.

Humphrey, W. S. (2000). *Introduction to the team software process.* Boston: Addison-Wesley.

Jeffery, J., Ruhe, M., & Wieczorek, I. (2001, June 4-6). *Using public domain metrics to estimate software development effort.* 16-17.

Johnson, P. M. (1998, February.). Reengineering inspection. *Communication of ACM, 41*(2), 49-52

Johnson, P. M., & Tjahjono, D. (1998). Does every inspection really need a meeting? *Empirical Software Engineering,* (3), 3-35.

Kan, S. H. (1995). *Metrics and models in software quality engineering.* Boston: Addison-Wesley.

Kingston, G., Jeffery, R., & Huang, W. (2000, April). An explanatory study on the goal alignment in joint software reviews. *Proceedings of Australian Conference on Software Engineering* (pp. 63-72), Canberra.

Kingston, G., Webby, R., & Jeffery, R. (1999, June 23-25). Different and conflicting goals in software reviews. *Proceedings of the 7th European Conference on Information Systems* (pp. 420-435).

Laitenberger, O., & Emam, K. E. (2001). An internally replicated quasi-experimental comparison of checklist and perspective-based reading of code documents. *IEEE Transactions of Software Engineering. 27*(5), 378-421.

Miller, J., Wood, M., & Roper, M. (1998). Further experiences with scenarios and checklists. *Empirical Software Engineering 3,* 37-64.

Petersson, H. (2001, August 27-28). Individual reviewer contribution to the effectiveness of software inspection teams. *Proceedings of Australian Software Engineering Conference* (pp. 160-168).

Porter, A. A., Mockus, A., & Votta, L. (1998, January). Understanding the sources of variation in software inspections. *ACM Transactions on Software Engineering and Methodology, 7*(1), 41-79.

Porter, A. A., & Votta, L. G. (1994). An experiment to assess different defect detection methods for software requirements inspections. *Proceedings of the 16ᵗʰ International Conference on Software Engineering, ICSE'16* (pp. 103-112).

Sauer, C., Jeffery, R., Land, L., & Yetton, P. (2000). Understanding and improving the effectiveness of software development technical reviews: A behaviourally motivated programme of research. *IEEE Transactions on Software Engineering, 26*(1), 1-14.

Seaman, C. B., & Basili, V. R. (1998, July). Communication and organization: An empirical study of discussion in inspection meetings. *IEEE Transaction on Software Engineering, 24*(6), 559-572.

Shaw, M. E. (1932). A comparison of individuals and small groups in the rational solution of complex problems. *American Journal of Psychology, 44*, 491-504.

Shull, F., Lanubile, F., & Biasili, V. (2000, November). Investigating reading techniques for object-oriented framework learning. *IEEE Transaction on Software Engineering, 26*(11).

Thelin, T., Runeson, P., & Wohlin, C. (2003, August.). An experimental comparison of usage-based and checklist-based reading. *IEEE Transaction on Software Engineering, 29*(8), 687-704

Van Genuchten M., Van Dijk C., Scholten H., & Vogel D. (2001, May/June). Using group support systems for software inspections. *IEEE Software.*

Votta, L. G. (1993). Does every inspection need a meeting? *ACM Software Engineering, 18*(5), 107-114.

Chapter XII

Contributions and Future Directions of Software Review

Abstract

This chapter presents theoretical and methodological contributions. It also addresses the limitations of the empirical studies (i.e., industry survey and case study). Discussions of future research are presented in the final section of this chapter.

Contributions

This book makes several key theoretical and methodological contributions to the software review literature.

Theoretical Contributions

The book adapted the input-process-output (IPO) approach to develop the Explicit and Implicit Input-process-Output (EIIO) Model. Thus, a richer and more comprehensive model of software review was developed by integrating key conceptual frameworks across multiple disciplines. Advances in software engineering and information systems science are characterised by constructs being conceptualised progressively from simple, one-dimensional phenomena measured with single or multiple items, to complex multidimensional phenomena, with each dimension measured with multiple indicators (items) (Bagozzi, 1994).

In the EIIO model, the concepts of the explicit and implicit inputs, process, and outputs in the proposed model are represented with multiple constructs, with each construct further represented with multiple indicators to encompass the rich and broad domain of the model constructs. Thus, the model proposed and tested here is both theoretically meaningful and managerially useful. This model overcomes specific problems of current models (e.g., Laitenberger & Debaud's model (2000), Sauer's behavioural approach to technical review model (2000)) in the software review literature. The model also expands the concepts of the implicit inputs, meeting process factors, and review performance to increase the importance and value of software reviews in the system development life cycle.

This book developed a systematic model to analyse software review performance (i.e., number of defects found). Due to its comprehensiveness, the revised EIIO model has a significant R-square of 0.392 for the number of defects found. Additionally, the model has reasonable explanatory power for the teamwork, experience, use of reports and previously reviewed software documents constructs, with R-squares of 0.321, 0.192, 0.023, and 0.042 respectively. By identifying the factors that influence software review performance, the findings will help managers to effectively leverage their resources (both explicit and implicit inputs) and improve their software review performance. First, a theoretical EIIO model is used to understand the important relationships between input, process and outputs to analyse software review performance. Second, from the results of the survey study and in-depth interviews with experts, the key software review inputs that influence review performance were identified and validated. Third, the in-depth interview results also identified the issues in organizing and conducting software reviews. Fourth, the research programs (a set of hypotheses), was developed to formulate the underlying theory so that the research program can be empirically tested and validated.

In summary, the theoretical contributions from this work are twofold. Firstly, this work furthers understanding of how to improve the review process by looking at the important relationships between inputs, process, and outcomes. Secondly, from the EIIO model, this work generated practical guidelines for organizing and conducting software review in terms of the use of software review inputs.

Methodological Contributions

Beside the theoretical contributions, this book also makes several important methodological contributions to the software review literature. First, current software review studies often focus on laboratory experiments, as a result reducing external validity (generalisabilty), whereas the survey methodology approach has high external validity. Although surveying has low internal validity, the in-depth interviews with experts have helped to increase internal validity. Second, by combining both quantitative questionnaire survey and qualitative in-depth interview data, the book provides significant and meaningful results to enhance future empirical research and software review development in practice.

In addition, the survey study has used the novel Structural Equation Modelling (SEM) based on Partial Least Squares (PLS) methodology. The proposed measurement (indicators) and structural (paths) models are estimated simultaneously using the SEM-based PLS methodology. This approach allows the analysis of the model as a whole in relation to inputs, process and outcomes respectively. Further, SEM-based procedures have substantial flexibility to "a) model relationships among the multiple predictor and criterion variables, b) statistically test *a priori* substantive/theoretical and measurement assumptions against data (i.e., confirmatory analysis)" (Chin, 1998a).

However, the issue of simultaneity is especially important since the indicators often draw their meaning from the structure within which they are embedded. This is particularly important for constructs measured with formative indicators, such as the software artefact characteristics, use of supporting documents (previously reviewed software documents, reading technique documents, reports and prescription documents) and experience used in this survey study. These measurements cannot be assessed using reliability measures such as Cronbach's alpha (Chin, 1998b).

Another benefit of structural equation modelling is that it forces researchers to think about the measurement issues while developing their conceptual models. The EIIO model was tested with a reasonably large and diverse sample (205 questionnaires) in Australia. The findings from such a diverse sample are not only more generalisable, but also provide a stronger foundation for developing a theory of software review. To test the robustness of the proposed EIIO model estimates, three additional analyses were carried out. The results show that the comprehensive EIIO model explains a significantly larger proportion of variance in software review performance.

The permutation test confirmed that the model largely captures meaningful relationships (significant paths); whereas the structural paths estimated with data subsets are mostly similar to those with the full data. Overall, the additional analyses essentially confirmed the robustness of the proposed EIIO model estimates. In summary, the combination of rigorous quantitative questionnaire survey and qualitative in-depth interviews used in this book has contributed to the software review literature.

Limitations

Although this book makes important theoretical and methodological contributions to the literature and provides guidance for practitioners, it is not without limitations. The following are some of the limitations of the study, and the directions identified for future research.

Since the proposed theoretical model encompasses a large number of constructs, the trade-off between breadth and depth in this study was resolved in favour of testing a broad overall model of software review. Given that the overall model works, future research using action studies may explore the processes used by software companies to achieve better review performance. That is, future studies may address the critical question of how practitioners manage software review inputs and the meeting process of a software review to improve their overall review performance.

Although the PLS methodology used here has several advantages, it also has a few limitations. First, the PLS estimation procedure can result in larger loadings for reflective indicators by up to 10% when compared to their true values (Dijkstra, 1983). Second, since the algorithm tends to keep the model closer to the measures, the structural paths tend to be weaker when compared to a model estimated with LISREL and other covariance-based approaches (Chin, 1998b). Third, since the model is fitted in parts, there is no overall measure of model fit available in PLS (Anderson & Gerbing, 1984).

In future research, it may be useful to re-estimate the model using covariance-based approaches. However, since the proposed model is quite complex, with a large number of constructs and measures, it may be difficult to estimate the full model with the full information-based maximum likelihood estimation (MLE) method used in covariance-based packages (Chin 1998b; Kelloway, 1995).

Also, the MLE procedure may require a much larger sample size as well as multi-normally distributed data to estimate the large number of parameters in the model tested here (Boomsma, 1983; Chin, 1998a, 1998b). To overcome these problems, a number of sub-models may be created from the full model and each estimated separately using the covariance-based algorithm in LISREL (Joreskog, 1989).

As discussed in Chapter VII, the EIIO model posits non-recurves (i.e., two-way arrows) (Chin, 1998a), that is, reciprocal feedback effects, from explicit and implicit inputs, process and outcome. That is, the theories postulate that reviewers not only react to the meeting process but also engage in actively creating, managing and changing their knowledge to their advantage. However, such a non-recursive relationship could not be tested formally due to the cross-sectional nature of the data and PLS software design. Even in the covariance-based software such as LISREL or AMOS, they all have same problem (Richardson & Joshi, 1997). Further, the study ignores the dynamics in the environment and its impact on the organisational structure and other software review outcomes such as time used and satisfaction of reviewers. In future, research longitudinal studies may be carried out to formally test the plausible non-recursive relationships in the model. Also, longitudinal studies can provide meaningful insights about the effect of the changing inputs on meeting process and their impact on software review performance.

Implicit and explicit tests, although heuristically useful at the beginning of a domain investigation, have eventually proved to be too simple (Roediger & McDermott, 1993). Generally, the discriminating properties of both implicit inputs and meeting process, such as data-driven or automatic, could not be operationally defined independently of performance in a particular test. Furthermore, it seems improbable that the different relationships between implicit and explicit inputs are on only one dimension. Finally, it became obvious that factors that were expected to influence performance in the one test did so in the other test also.

Future Directions

In addition to the future research issues identified in the previous paragraph to overcome the research limitations, the following are additional directions for future research that may be explored to further extend the model proposed here.

The EIIO model does not include all aspects of software review currently reported in the literature (e.g., use of computer support tools, organisation structure, decision making methods, and other measures for performance (i.e., in additional to the number of defects, other natures, or characteristics of defects (e.g., type of defect) may be relevant as well) and the model proposed here may be extended in future research. Ultimately, combining the findings from the overall project function-level studies will provide a more comprehensive understanding of the issues of software review. Since the primary goal of software review is to achieve lowest-cost and zero-defect artefacts in the shortest timeframe to satisfy the customer needs (Boehm & Basili, 2001; Calvin, 1983; Ciolkowski, Laitenberger, Rombach, Shull, & Perry, 2002; Ciolkowski, Laitenberger, & Biffl, 2002), the research of software review may be incomplete without a global survey with detailed inclusion of these control variables. In future research, the global research can increase generalisability (Judd, Smith, & Kidder, 1991; Zikmund, 2000) across all countries with a detailed survey of the control variables matrices.

The PLS methodology implicitly assumes linear relationships–in the measurement model between the indicators and constructs, and in the structural model among the constructs (Bollen, 1984; Chin, 1998a; Wiley, 1973). No research could be found in the literature that uses variables with non-linear transformations in structural equation modelling (Chin, 1998b; Joreskog, 1973; Rahim, Antonioni, & Psenicka, 2001; Wiley, 1973). In future research, it would be interesting to explore how measures with non-linear transformations and non-linear structural relationships may be modelled as non-linear (McNeil, 2001; Stone, 1974), either in the full model or in the sub-models derived from the full model. Incorporating non-linear relationships may not only improve the model fit but also provide a richer explanation of the nature of relationships among the model constructs. However, it may increase the model complexity with each transformation represented with an additional construct (Wert, Linn, & Joreskog, 1974).

In summary, the key directions for future research include extending the structural model to include the completed model and other factors (e.g., organisation structure, decision making methods, computer tools support, measurement outcomes metrics (time used, satisfaction)) with alternative analytic methodologies such as stochastic frontier analysis (SFA), and testing smaller sub-models from the completed model using covariance-based approaches such as LISREL and AMOS (Bollen, 1984; Boomsma, 1983; Chin, 1998a; Joreskog, 1989; Wiley, 1973).

Additional, non-linear relationships may be explored to improve the model fit (Chin, 1998a), and longitudinal studies may be conducted to formally test the potentially non-recursive, reciprocal relationships among the input, process and outcome constructs and predictability of reviewer performance.

Finally, empirical laboratory studies may be carried out to understand in a control environment, the inputs-process factors involved in managing software outcomes to increase the internal validity of the model.

Summary

With a growing number of companies in the software industry and increasing globalisation of the world economy, there is competitive pressure on software firms to succeed and survive. At the same time, with greater rationalisation of global industries, existing software artefacts are becoming larger in size and more complex in their organisation. Despite their growing importance, there is little empirical research on how to effectively create, manage and review these large, complex software artefacts. This book will hopefully improve an understanding of the important relationships between input-process-performance in software review.

The objective of this book has been to understand the input and process factors that drive software review performance. To achieve this objective, the book proposed the EIIO model that links the software review literature and related behavioural theories. The EIIO model adopted the traditional input-process-output (IPO) approach, that is, input and process factors are considered determinant of software review performance.

The EIIO model considers explicit and implicit inputs and meeting process factors as the most important influences on software review performance. These factors are the key to improve software review performance and a good fit between software development and review. By representing the concepts of the inputs, process and outcomes with multiple constructs, the EIIO model was developed and empirically tested with data from both quantitative questionnaire surveys and qualitative in-depth interviews with experts.

Based on this research, the three key recommendations for future studies are the following. First, researchers need to develop multidimensional and multilevel models in order to gain a comprehensive understanding of the environmental and organisational factors that affect theoretical concepts and multiple constructs. Multilevel models provide a richer abstraction of reality by incorporating sequential and mediator effects. Additionally, the science of strategy ultimately rests on the art of measurement. Thus, developing and testing multidimensional, multilevel, and multifaceted models will enable the simultaneous achievement of the trinity in software review literature, that is, advance information technology research to make it theoretically meaningful, methodologically robust and managerially useful. Second, the empirical data collected from both the survey research and in-depth interviewers have validated the EIIO model. The model provides a fundamental guideline to understand the important relationships between use of explicit and implicit inputs, meeting process and review performance.

The final point is that the achievement of a good fit between theory and practice is the sine qua non for improving software review performance. That is, practitioners operating in environments characterised by knowledge-based inputs should have a strategic strategy and structure to organise and conduct different types of software reviews (e.g., requirements, design, code, and test cases). For example, selecting the right reviewers with appropriate supports (e.g., use of supporting documents) in conducting software reviews would be considered a critical element in the software review process.

References

Anderson, J. C., & Gerbing, D. W. (1984). *The effect of sampling error on convergence, improper solutions, and goodness-of-fit indices for maximum likelihood confirmatory factory analyses.* Psychometrician, 49, 155-173.

Bagozzi, R. P. (1994). *Measurement in marketing research: basic principle of questionnaire design. Principles of Marketing Research.* Cambridge: Basil Blackwell.

Boehm, B. W., & Basili, B. R. (2001, January). Software defect reduction top 10 list. *IEEE Computer, 34*(1).

Bollen, K. A. (1984). Multiple indicators: Internal consistency or no necessary relationship? *Quality and Quantity, 18*, 377-385.

Boomsma, A. (1983). On The robustness of lisrel (maximum likelihood estimation) against small sample size and non-normality. *Socio-Metric Research Foundation,* Amsterdam.

Calvin, T. W. (1983, September). Quality control techniques for "zero defects". *IEEE Transactions on Components, Hybrids, and Manufactory Technology, 6*(3), 323-328.

Ciolkowski, M., Laitenberger, O., & Biffl, S. (2003). Software reviews: The state-of-the-practice. *IEEE Software,* 46-51.

Ciolkowski, M., Laitenberger, O., Rombach, D., Shull, F., & Perry, D. (2002, May 19-25). Software Inspection, reviews and walkthrough. *International Conference on Software Engineering* (pp. 641-642).

Chin, W. W. (1998a, March), Issues and Opinion on Structural Equation Modeling, *MIS Quarterly, 22*(1), Commentary.

Chin, W. W. (1998b). The partial least square approach for structural equation modeling. In G. A. Marcoulides (Ed.), *Modern methods for business research* (pp. 295-336). Mahwah, NJ: Erlbaum.

Joreskog, K. G. (1973). A general method for estimating a linear structural equation system. In A. S. Goldberger & O. D. Duncan (Eds.), *Structural equation models in the social sciences* (pp. 85-122). New York: Academic Press.

Joreskog, K. G. (1989). *LISREL 7: A guide to the program and applications.* Chicago: SPSS.

Judd, C. M., Smith, E. R., & Kidder, L. H. (1991). *Research methods in social relations* (6th ed.) Fort Worth, TX: Harcourt Brace Jovanovich College.

Kelloway, E. K. (1995). Structural equation modelling in perspective. *Journal of Organisational Behaviour,* (16), 215-224.

Laitenberger, O., & Debaud, J. M. (2000). An encompassing life cycle centric survey of software inspection. *The Journal of Software and Systems, 50*(1), 5-31.

McNeil, D. (2001). *Modern statistics: A graphical introduction.* Marrickville: Southwood Press Pty. Ltd.

Rahim, M. A., Antonioni, D., & Psenicka, C. (2001). A structural equations model of learder power, subordinates' styles of handling conflict. *Job Performance, 12*(3), 191-211.

Richardson, A.J., & Joshi A. (1997, April). Exploring the empirical relationship between legitimacy and efficiency: models and methods. *Proceedings of the Interdisciplinary Perspectives on Accounting Conference,* Manchester, UK.

Roediger, H. L., & Mcdermott, K. B. (1993). Implicit memory in normal human subjects. In F. Boller & J. Grafman (Eds.), *Handbook of Neurophysiology,* (8) (pp. 63-131). Amsterdam: Elsevier.

Sauer, C., Jeffery, R., Land, L., & Yetton, P. (2000). Understanding and improving the effectiveness of software development technical reviews: A behaviourally motivated programme of research. *IEEE Transactions on Software Engineering, 26*(1), 1-14.

Stone, M. (1974). Cross-validatory choice and assessment of statistical predictions. *Journal of the Royal Statistical Society, B36,* 111-133.

Wert, C. E., Linn, R. L., & Joreskog, K. G. (1974). Intra-class reliability estimates: Testing structural assumptions. *Educational and Psychological Measurement, 34,* 25-33.

Wiley, D. E. (1973). The Identification problem for structural equation models with unmeasured variables. In A. S. Goldberger & Duncan (Eds.), *Structural equation models in the social sciences* (pp. 69-83). New York: Academic Press.

Zikmund, W. G. (2000). *Exploring marketing research* (7th ed.). Forth Worth, TX: The Dryden.

Appendix Section

Appendix I

Survey of Software Review

The overall objective of this study is to identify the key factors that affect software defect detection undertaken by both individuals and groups.

- All information given will be treated in the strictest confidence.
- Any publications of this study will present information in aggregate form and such information will be anonymous and un-attributable to individual organisations or individual respondents.
- Participants are expected to answer all the questions.
- The questionnaire takes about 20 minutes to complete.
- Please try to answer as many as you can. If you have any difficulties to answering any questions, please leave them blank.
- If you have any queries, please call or write:

Mobile:

E-mail:

Mailing Address:

- Thank you for dedicating your time to completing this questionnaire

Company Name: _____

SECTION 1. This section is concerned with software review practice.

1. **Please indicate the software review that you have participated in most frequently during last 6 months.**
    (Please tick one box)
    - ❏   Requirement reviews
    - ❏   Design reviews
    - ❏   Code reviews
    - ❏   Test reviews
    - ❏   I never participate in software reviews (go to question 12)

    Please answer the following questions (Q2-Q11) based on *the type of review you selected in*
    question 1.

    2. **How   many   times   have   you   participated   in   software   review   during   last   6   months?**
        (Please tick one box)
        - ❏   1-10 times
        - ❏   11-20 times
        - ❏   21-30 times
        - ❏   31-40 times
        - ❏   41 times or above

    3. **How many times been you been you involved in the following roles?**
        (Please circle one number for each line)

	None	1-10 times	11-20 times	21-30 times	31 times or more
Inspector/ Reviewer (i.e., Identify defects)		1	2	3	4	5
Moderator (Plan and manage meetings for software review process)	1	2	3	4	5
Reader/ Presenter (i.e., Leading review team and paraphrase sections of the work)	1	2	3	4	5
Author (i.e., Responsible for the software elements meeting the review entry criteria and performing any rework)	1	2	3	4	5
Recorder (i.e., Recording defect detection at the meeting, and recording review data required for process analysis)	1	2	3	4	5

    4. **With regard to your own experience of software reviews, please indicate to what extent you agree**
        with the following statements.
        (Please circle one number for each line on a scale of 1 to 5, where 1 means disagree, 5 means agree)

	Disagree				Agree
On average, the artefacts (Examples: Requirement documents, designs, code, test cases) that I review are complex	1	2	3	4	5
On average, the size of the artefacts that I review is large	1	2	3	4	5
On average, the initial quality of the artefacts that I review is poor	1	2	3	4	5

5.   What are the common supporting documents you used in software reviews?
(Please circle one number for each line on a scale of 1 to 5, where 1 means not common at all and 5 means very common)

	Not common at all				Very common
Checklist	1	2	3	4	5
Scenarios/ Perspective reading techniques	1	2	3	4	5
Stepwise reading technique	1	2	3	4	5
ANSI/IEEE (An American National Standard, IEEE Standards for Software Reviews 1028) guideline	1	2	3	4	5
Defect type standards	1	2	3	4	5
Procedure guidelines	1	2	3	4	5
Review training materials	1	2	3	4	5
Time record log	1	2	3	4	5
Previously reviewed requirement document of current work product	1	2	3	4	5
Previously reviewed design document of the current work product	1	2	3	4	5
Previously reviewed code document of the current work product	1	2	3	4	5
Business Reports (Please specify _____)	1	2	3	4	5
Templates	1	2	3	4	5

6.   How many times were you involved in the following activities in the last 6 months?
(Please circle one number for each line)

	Never	1-10 times	11-20 times	21-30 times	31 times or more
Interactive group meeting (i.e., An interactive group meeting for examining the artefact)	1	2	3	4	5

If you circled "1" for interactive group meeting, please go to question 10, otherwise go to next question.

7.   How many people usually attend a software review meeting?
(Please tick one box)
❑   2 people
❑   3-6 people
❑   7-10 people
❑   11-14 people
❑   15 or more people

7. **How many people usually attend a software review meeting?** (Please tick one box)
   - ☐   2 people
   - ☐   3-6 people
   - ☐   7-10 people
   - ☐   11-14 people
   - ☐   15 or more people

8. **With regard to your own experience in software review meetings, how often do the following activities occur in these meetings?**
   (Please circle one number for each line on a scale of 1 to 5, where 1 means never, 5 means always)

	Never				Always
The language of the meetings prevents me from participating	1	2	3	4	5
Some group members try to use their influence, status or power to force their opinions on the other group members	1	2	3	4	5
I experience problems expressing myself	1	2	3	4	5
I find it hard to understand other group members when they talk in the meetings	1	2	3	4	5
I experience pressure, either to conform to a particular viewpoint or not to contradict others	1	2	3	4	5
I feel reluctant to put forward my own ideas	1	2	3	4	5
Members work together as a team	1	2	3	4	5
Other members appear willing to answer questions when asked	1	2	3	4	5
Members have sufficient access to the information they need to participate actively in and fully understand the meeting	1	2	3	4	5
Some group members try to intimidate others (e.g., by talking loudly, using aggressive gestures, making threats, etc.).	1	2	3	4	5
I feel inhibited from participating in decision-making because of the behaviour of other meeting members	1	2	3	4	5

9. **On average, considering all meeting members as a whole, how would you rate the discussions in the review meetings in terms of the following scales?**
   (Please circle one number for each line on a scale of 1 to 5)

Totally meaningless	1	2	3	4	5	Very meaningful
Totally Inappropriate	1	2	3	4	5	Very appropriate
Totally closed/ restricted	1	2	3	4	5	Very open
Familiar/ Unimaginative approaches used	1	2	3	4	5	Creative/Imaginative approaches used

Please answer the following questions (Q10-Q11) based on the type of review you selected in question 1.

10. **Please indicate to what extent you agree with the following statements.**
    (Please circle one number for each line on a scale of 1 to 5, where 1 means disagree, 5 means agree)

	Disagree				Agree
On average, I find more defects that actually exist and have been successfully detected than my team members	1	2	3	4	5
On average, I find more defects that do not exist but were wrongly identified than my team members.	1	2	3	4	5

On average, I find more net defects (defects actually exist and have been successfully detected minus defects do not exist but were wrongly identified) than my team members.	1	2	3	4	5
On average, I find more total defects (defects actually exist and have been successfully detected plus defects do not exist but were wrongly identified) than my team members	1	2	3	4	5

11. Please indicate to what extent you agree with the following statements.

	Disagree				Agree
I am willing to participate in software reviews	1	2	3	4	5
I am motivated to participate in software reviews	1	2	3	4	5
I put a lot of effort into finding defects	1	2	3	4	5
I am confident that I am capable of finding defects	1	2	3	4	5
I am confident that I can find more defects than other team members	1	2	3	4	5
I am confident that I can teach my defect detection skills to others	1	2	3	4	5
I can find defects in an effective way	1	2	3	4	5
I do well in software reviews	1	2	3	4	5
I agree with the way my company conducts software reviews	1	2	3	4	5
I participate in software reviews because I have support from my company	1	2	3	4	5
I participate in software reviews because my company encourages us to do so	1	2	3	4	5
I believe I can find all the defects	1	2	3	4	5

SECTION 2. This section is concerned with demographic information

12. How many years of EXPERIENCE do you have in the software development?
    (Please circle one number for each line)

	None	3 years or less	4-9 years	10-15 years	15 years or more
Software development	1	2	3	4	5
Software Review(s)	1	2	3	4	5

13. What is your POSITION in your company? (Please tick one box)
  ❏ Information Technology Manager
  ❏ Systems Manager
  ❏ System Designer
  ❏ Software Designer
  ❏ Applications & Analyst Programmer
  ❏ Systems Programmer
  ❏ Computer System Auditor
  ❏ Business Analyst
  ❏ Tester
  ❏ Other (please specify_____)

14. What level of EDUCATION have you completed?
(You may tick more than one box; also please specify your majors)
- ❑ Doctoral (please specify your thesis topic_____)
- ❑ Master's degree (please specify your majors_____)
- ❑ Bachelor's degree
  (please specify your majors_____)
- ❑ Undergraduate Diploma (please specify your majors_____)
- ❑ Other (please specify_____)

15. Are you a MEMBER of any of the following professional bodies? (You may tick more than one box)
- ❑ Association of Chartered Engineers
- ❑ Association for Computing Machinery (ACM)
- ❑ Australian Computer Society (ACS)
- ❑ Institute of Electronic Engineers (IEE)
- ❑ Institute of Electronic and Electrical Engineers (IEEE)
- ❑ Other (please specify_____)
- ❑ None of the above

16. Please categorise your company's MAIN products and services? (You may tick more than one box)
- ❑ Computer programming service
- ❑ Pre-packaged software
- ❑ Computer integrated systems design
- ❑ Computer processing and data preparation and processing services
- ❑ Information retrieval service
- ❑ Computer facilities management service
- ❑ Computer rental and leasing
- ❑ Computer maintenance and repair
- ❑ Other (please specify_____)
- ❑ Don't know

17. Please indicate the INDUSTRY of your company: (You may tick more than one box)
- ❑ Computer and business machine manufacturing
- ❑ Telecommunication, broadcasting equipment manufacturing
- ❑ Electronic equipment manufacturing
- ❑ Electric cable and wire manufacturing
- ❑ Computer wholesaling
- ❑ Business machine wholesaling
- ❑ Electrical and electronic equipment wholesaling
- ❑ Telecommunication services
- ❑ Data processing services
- ❑ Information storage and retrieval services
- ❑ Computer maintenance services
- ❑ Computer consultancy services
- ❑ Other (please specify_____)
- ❑ Don't know

18. NUMBER OF EMPLOYEES of your company in Australia: (Please tick one box for each column)
- ❑ 0-4
- ❑ 5-9
- ❑ 10-19
- ❑ 20-49
- ❑ 50-99
- ❑ 100-499
- ❑ 500-999
- ❑ 1,000-2,499
- ❑ 2,500-4,999
- ❑ 5,000-9,999
- ❑ 10,000 or more
- ❑ Don't know

19. **Does your company hold any of the following QUALITY CERTIFICATIONS?**
(You may tick more than one box)
- ☐ ISO 9001
- ☐ ISO 9002
- ☐ ISO 9003
- ☐ Tick IT
- ☐ Other (Please specify_____)
- ☐ Don't Know
- ☐ None of Above

Thank you for taking the time to complete this questionnaire.

Appendix II

Focus Group 1

Date:

Time:

Location:

Instructions to Participants

Title: Survey of Software Review.

Objective:

The aim of this study is to identify and understand the critical factors for organising and conducting software reviews for different types artefacts in practice. The focus group seeks to validate a questionnaire and requires you to express your opinions on the nature of your industry experiences in software development/software review and/or questionnaire design.

Ethics:

The focus group meeting is strictly confidential. Any publications of this study will present information in aggregate form and such information will be anonymous and un-attributable to individual organizations or individual participants. Participants are asked to participate on a voluntary basis. Participants are expected to answer all the questions truthfully. Participants are asked to participate on a voluntary basis without any consequences for participating or not participating.

Focus Group Meeting Procedures:

Steps

1.   Five minutes to overview the purpose of the meeting[2]. Twenty minutes for individuals to review the questionnaire (i.e., individuals will be expected to self-administer the questionnaire, comment on the questionnaire and re-cording them on a comment form, no group discussion).

3.   One minute post online survey investigation.

4.   Thirty minutes group discussion lead by a moderator (i.e., discuss the issues of the questionnaire's questions). The meeting process will recorded on a video-recorder and tape recorders.

5.   Five minutes general feedback on the overall process.

6.   Two minutes post meeting questionnaire.

Thank you for taking time participate this focus group meeting!!

Appendix III

Dear <Participants>

Re: Invitation – A focus group meeting on software review

I should like to invite you to participate in a focus group meeting being undertaken by xxx.

The aim of this study is to identify and understand the critical factors for organising and conducting software reviews for different types artefacts in practice. The focus group seeks to validate a questionnaire and requires you to express your opinions on the nature of your "**industry experiences in software development/software review**". You are welcome to bring your friends who have industry experience in software development and/or software review.

The focus group meeting is strictly confidential. I do not expect to publish material directly based on the focus group. However, any publications of this study will present information in aggregate form and such information will be anonymous and un-attributable to individual organizations or individual participants. Participants are asked to participate on a voluntary basis.

Date:

Time:

Location:

(Drinks and snacks will be provided)

I should be grateful if you could please to reply this mail and provide your contact numbers and number of participants as soon as possible.

If you have any questions about the focus group meeting, please don't hesitate to contact xxx.

I look forward to meeting you next Thursday.

Best regards,

xxx

Dear <participant>

Re: Reminder for the focus group meeting

Thank you for taking time to participate the focus group meeting.

Date:

Time:

Location:

(Drinks and snaps will be provided)

If you have any questions about the focus group meeting, please don't hesitate to contact xxx.

I look forward to meeting you tomorrow.

Best regards,

Appendix IV

Dear «Contact»Information Technology Manager

We should like to invite you to participate in the research project *"xxx"* being conducted by xxx.

The purpose of this study is to investigate the impact of software review inputs on outcomes. An overall objective of this study is to increase understanding of how software review inputs affect software defect detection undertaken by both individuals and groups. We should like to encourage your IT staff and general staff who have experience in software review to participate in this vast project.

If you agree to participate, your staff will be asked to complete a questionnaire that will require 20 minutes of their time. The research data gathered from this project will be published in aggregate form that does not identify you or your organization or individual participants in any way.

If you have any questions about the study, you can contact xxx.

Please complete and return the attached form via e-mail, fax, or mail and we shall send the questionnaire to you. We thank you in anticipation of your agreement to precipitate.

Yours sincerely

Please complete and return this form via the following options.

Attention to: _____

E-mail: _____

Mailing Address: _____

Mobile: _____

Fax: _____

Company Name: _____

Mailing Address: _____

Number of Participants: _____

(i.e., IT staff and general staff who have experience in software review)

Contact Name: _____

Contact Number: _____

Signed: _____

Date _____

«No»

Appendix V

Dear

I sincerely thank you for participating in the research project "*xxx*" being undertaken by xxx.

The questionnaire is easy and requires about 20 minutes to complete. Please try to answer all questions in the survey, as this would helps us in providing you the findings that accurately reflect software review practice in your company. The information provided will be strictly confidential and used only for academic purpose. The views of individuals will not be released to third parties and only aggregate analyses published. Therefore, please feel free to express your opinions. The identification number on the questionnaire is for mailing purpose only, will be used for checking your company name off the mailing list when your completed questionnaire is returned.

I will be grateful if your staff could complete and return the attached questionnaires in the provided envelop soon as possible, preferably within a week.

If you have any queries or suggestions, please write or call xxx.
Thank you again for you participating in this research study.

Yours sincerely

xxx

Dear

I sincerely thank you for participating in the research project "*xxx*" being undertaken by xxx. The purpose of this study is to increase understanding of how software review inputs affect software defect detection undertaken by both individuals and groups.

If your company have returned the completed questionnaires, we would like to convey our sincere thanks for your participation. You will receive a summary of our findings as soon as the completed questionnaires are returned, and the data analysis is completed.

However, if your company has not returned the completed questionnaires, please ask your staff to complete and return them as soon as possible. Your contributions are extremely important in this study. We will grateful if the completed questionnaires are returned promptly as it will help us in quickly analysing the data and sharing our findings with your company.

If you have any queries or suggestions, please write or call xxx.

Thank you very much for your contribution.

Yours sincerely,

Dear IT Manager,

Thank you for your agreement of participating in the research project of "*xxx*" being undertaken by xxx. We sent you the questionnaires a few weeks ago, but we have not yet received your completed questionnaires.

The purpose of this study is to investigate the impact of software review inputs on outcomes. An overall objective of this study is to increase understanding of how software review inputs affect software defect detection undertaken by both individuals and groups. The results of the study will provide practical benchmarks that will help your company to improve the software review performance.

I am writing to you again because of the significance each questionnaire has to the usefulness of this study. We have invited only a small but representative sample of companies to participate in this survey. In order for the findings to be truly representative of the opinions of software practitioners, it is important that the views of your staff members are included in the study. I assure you that the information provided will be strictly confidential, and used only for academic purposes.

I will be grateful if all your staff members in your company can return all completed questionnaires as soon as possible.

If you have any queries, please write or call xxx.

Thank you for your kind cooperation.

Yours sincerely

Dear,

Final Reminder: Research project

About three months ago, we wrote to you seeking your participation in a software review survey being undertaken xxx. We also sent you a few sets of question-naires upon your agreement. However, we are still waiting other sets of questionnaires from your company.

The aim of the survey is to collect the data my doctoral thesis. The purpose of this study is to investigate the impact of software review inputs on outcomes.

We are writing to you again because of your contributions is extremely important to the study. We have invited only a small but representative sample of companies to participate in this survey. In order for the findings to be truly representative of the opinions of software practitioners, it is important that the views of your staff members are included in the study. We guarantee that all information provided will be strictly confidential, and used only for academic purposes.

The study will not be possible without your generous help. We will be grateful if all your staff members can return all completed questionnaires by xxx, as it will help us in quickly analysing the data and sharing our findings with you. Please ask your staff member to contact xxx if they cannot return the questionnaires before the deadline.

If you have any queries, please write or call xxx.

This is a final reminder and we look forward to your early reply. Thank you for your kind cooperation.

Yours sincerely,

Appendix VI

Reliability Tests

Individual reliability for the indicators of the constructs was evaluated by the size of the loadings and communalities (Barclay, Higgins, & Thompson, 1995; Chin, 1998a, 1998b). A loading of 0.7 is considered to be the minimum required for a reliable measure, since it ensures that at least 50% of the variance of the measures is accounted by the construct that the indicators intends to measures (Bagozzi, 1994; Cronbach, 1970; Nunnally, 1976). However, in the initial stages, when the research exploratory and the measures are not well-developed, indicators with smaller loadings of 0.5 and 0.6 can be used, provided the measures are theoretically grounded and there are other indicators of the construct for the comparison purposes (Barclay et al., 1995; Chin, 1998b).

Composite reliability of the constructs was assessed using three criteria: internal consistency, Cronbach alpha and average variance extracted (AVE) (Areskoug, 1982; Chin, 1998b; Cronbach, 1970). Cronbach alpha is estimated using the reliability analysis (RA) procedures in SPSS (Coakes & Steed, 2001), whereas the average variance extracted (AVE) is obtained from principal components analysis (PCA) (Chin, 1998b). Cronbach alpha assumes parallel measures, and represents a lower bound of composite reliability (Chin & Gopal, 1995). In SEM, the indicators/ constructs are weighted unequally based on their reliability, with relatively higher weighs for measures with greater reliability; a better estimate of composite reliability is obtained by using the following internal consistency formula of Wert, Linn, & Joreskog (1974).

Equation 1:

$$\text{Internal consistency } (Pc) = \frac{(\sum \lambda_i)^2 \, \text{var } F}{(\sum \lambda_i)^2 \, \text{var } F + \sum \theta_{ii}}$$

Where λi, F and θii are the factor loading, factor variance and unique/ error variance. The loadings from the PCA are used to calculate the internal consistency measure of composite reliability for both the constructs. Since the variable scores in PCA are implicitly standardized, var F is 1, and θii is $(1 - \lambda_i^2)$. Thus, $\sum \theta_{ii}$ becomes $(k - \sum \lambda_i^2)$, where k is the number of the indicators measuring the construct. Thus, the formula for calculating internal consistency reduce to:

Equation 2:

$$\text{Internal consistency } (Pc) = \frac{(\sum \lambda_i)^2}{(\sum \lambda_i)^2 + k - (\sum \lambda_i^2)}$$

By using the vales from the PCA output in SPSS, the simplified Equation 2 can be used to calculate internal consistency.

References

Areskoug, B. (1982). The first canonical correlation: Theoretical PLS analysis and simulation experiments. In K. G. Joreskog & H. Wold (Eds.), *Systems, under indirect observation: Causality, structure, prediction* (pp. 95-128). Amsterdam, North-Holland.

Bagozzi, R. P. (1994). *Measurement in marketing research: Basic principle of questionnaire design. Principles of Marketing Research.* Cambridge: Basil Blackwell.

Barclay, D., Higgins, C., & Thompson, R. (1995). The Partial Least Squares (PLS) approach to causal modeling: Personal computer adoption and use as an illustration. *Technology Studies, 2*(2), 285-309.

Chin, W. W. (1998a). Issues and opinion on structural equation modeling. *MIS Quarterly, 22*(1), Commentary.

Chin, W. W. (1998b). The partial least square approach for structural equation modeling. In G. A. Marcoulides (Ed.), *Modern methods for business research* (pp. 295-336). Mahwah, NJ: Erlbaum.

Chin, W. W., & Gopal, A. (1995). Adoption intention in GSS: Relative importance of beliefs. *The Data Base for Advances in Information Systems, 26*, 42-46.

Coakes, S. J., & Steed, L. G. (2001). *SPSS: Analysis without anguish: Version 10.0 for Windows.* Brisbane, Australia: John Wiley & Sons.

Cronbach, L. J. (1970). *Essentials of psychological testing* (3rd ed.). New York: Irvington.

Nunnally, J. C. (1976). *Psychometric theory.* New York: McGraw-Hill.

Wert, C. E., Linn, R. L., & Joreskog, K. G. (1974). Intra-Class reliability estimates: Testing structural assumptions. *Educational and Psychological Measurement, 34*, 25-33.

Appendix VII

Structural Equation Modeling (SEM) Methodology: A Formal Specification of the Partial Least Squares (PLS) Model

The following PLS estimation procedures were directly adopted from Chin and Newsted (1996, p.321-326).

The PLS estimation procedures, the model specification that guides the process is presented as following. The path modes in PLS consist of three sets of relations: 1) the inner model, which specified the relationships between latent variables (LVs), 2) outer model, which specifies the relationships between latent variables (LVs) and their associated observed or manifest variables (MVs), and 3) the weight relations upon which case values for the latent variables can be estimated. Without loss of generality, it can assumed that LVs and MVs are scaled to zero means and unit variances so that location parameters (i.e., constant parameter terms) can be eliminated in the following equations.

Inner Model

The inner model (also refereed to as the inner relations, structural model, and substantive theory) depicts the relationship among the constructs based on substantive theory:

Equation 1

$$\eta = \beta 0 + \beta \eta + \Gamma \xi + \zeta$$

Where η represents the vector of the endogenous (i.e., dependent) latent variables, ξ is a vector of the exogenous (i.e., independent) variables, and æ is the vector of residual variables (i.e., unexplained variance). Because the basic PLS design assumes recursive relations (i.e., one-way arrows) among the LVs, each dependent variables η_j in termed 'causal chain system' of constructs can be specified as follows:

Equation 2

$$\eta_j = \Sigma \beta_{ji} \eta_i + \Sigma \lambda_{jh} \xi_h + \zeta_j$$

Where η_{ji} and η_{jh} are the path coefficients linking the prediction for endogenous and exogenous constructs (variables) î and K over the range specified by the indices i and h, and $æ_j$ is the inner residual variable. The inner model (equation 1) is subject to predictor specification (Wold, 1988):

$$E(\eta_j \mid_{\vee} \eta_{j,} \xi_h) = \eta_j = \Sigma\beta_{ji}\eta_i + \Sigma\lambda_{jh}\xi_h$$

Thus, it is assumed that each LV is a linear function of its predictors and that there are no linear relationship between the predictors and the residual:

$$E(\eta_j \mid_{\vee} \eta_{j,} \xi_h) = 0 \quad \text{and} \quad \text{Cov}(\zeta_{j,} \eta_i) = \text{Cov}(\zeta_{j,} \xi_h) = 0$$

For the indices i and h ranging over all predictors.

The structural form of the inner model can be also be written in reduced form by subtracting $\beta\eta$ from both sides of Equation 1 and pre-multiplying by $(1 - \beta)^{-1}$ yielding:

$$\eta = (1 - \beta)^{-1} \Gamma\xi + (1 - \beta)^{-1} \zeta$$
$$= \beta * \xi + \zeta *$$

Where $\beta *$ represents the total effect of the exogenous construct (variable) ξ. To make predictor specification possible for both the structural and the reduced forms, a assumption is made that $E(\zeta_j * \mid_{\vee} \xi_h) = 0$ for all j endogenous LVs as they relate to the exogenous variables impacting in the first j relations given in the structural form given in Equation 2.

Outer Model

The outer model (also referred to as outer relations or measurement model) defines how each block of indicators relates to its latent variable. The MVz are partitioned into non-overlapping blocks. For those blocks with reflective indicators, the relationships can be defined as:

$$x = \Lambda_x \xi + \varepsilon_x$$
$$y = \Lambda_y \eta + \varepsilon_y$$

Where x and y are the variables for the exogenous and endogenous variables ξ and η, respectively. Λ_x and Λ_y are the loadings matrices representing simple regression coefficients connecting the variable and their indicators. The residuals for the indicators ε_x and ε_y, in turn, can be interpreted as measurement errors or noise.

Predictor specification, as in the case for the inner model, is assumed to hold for the outer model in reflective mode as follow:

Equation 3:

$$E\ [x \mid \xi] = \Lambda_x \xi$$
$$E\ [y \mid \eta] = \Lambda_x \eta$$

For those blocks in a formative mode, the relationship is defined as:

$$\xi = \Pi_\xi x + \delta_\xi$$
$$\eta = \Pi_\eta y + \delta_\eta$$

Where ξ, η, x and y are the same as those used in Equation 3. Πx and Πy are the multiple-regression coefficients for the LVs on its block of indicators and δ_ξ and δ_η are the corresponding residuals from the regressions. Predictor specification is also in effect as:

$$E[\xi \mid x] = \Pi_\xi x$$
$$E[\eta \mid y] = \Pi_\eta y$$

As opposed to the weight relations to be discussed next, the formative specification for outer relations refers to the MV and the true LV. This, in turn, provides the basis for the manner in which weights are determined with the PLS estimation algorithm estimating the LV.

Weight Relations

Although the inner the outer models provide the specifications that are followed in the PLS estimation algorithm, the weight relations need to be defined for completeness. The case value for each LV is estimated in PLS as follows:

$$\xi_h = \Sigma_{kh} w_{kh} x_{kh}$$

$$\eta_i = \Sigma^{ki} w_{ki} y_{ki}$$

Where w_{kh} and x_{kh} are the k weights used form the variable estimates of ξ_h and η_i.

Thus, the variables estimates are linear aggregates of their observed indicators whose weights are obtained via the PLS estimation procedure as specified by the inner and outer models where is the η vector of the endogenous (dependent) latent variables, ξ is the vector of the exogenous (independent) latent variables, δ is the vector of residuals, and B and T are the path coefficient matrices.

Predictor Specification

Predictor specification (Presp), therefore, forms the basis for PLS modeling. Whereas the covariance-based estimation rests on the assumptions of a specific joint multivariate distribution and independence of observations, the PLS approach does not make these hard assumptions. Instead, the PLS technique of model building uses very general, software distributional assumptions, which often lead to his approach being termed "software modeling". Thus, as Lohmoller (1989, p. 64) noted, "it is not the concepts nor the models nor the estimation techniques which are 'soft', only the distributional assumptions."

Predictor specification (Presp) "is imposed on relations that the investigator wants to use for prediction, but it in theoretical or estimated form, and predictor specification provides the ensuing prediction" (Wold, 1988, p. 589).

Lohmoller (1989, p. 72) further states that "with the purpose of prediction (not primarily a structural explanation), (and) sets up a system of relations preferably linear, where the structure of the relations must be founded in the substance of the mater, and the predictive purpose should not jeopardize a structural-causal interpretation of the relation (causal-predictive relation)". Predictor specification adopts the statistical assumption for a linear conditional expectation relationship between dependent and independent variables, which can be summarized as:

Equation 4

$$y = \alpha + Bx + v, \qquad\qquad ý \equiv E \,[y \mid x] = \alpha + Bx$$

$$\Rightarrow E \,[v] = 0$$

$$\Rightarrow Cov \,[x, \, v] = Cov \,[ý, \, v] = 0$$

$$\Rightarrow Cov \,[x, \, v] = Cov \,[ý, \, v] = B \, var \,[x]$$

where y and x are m x 1 and n x 1 matrices of dependent and independent variables, v is an m x 1 matrix of residuals, and B the m x n matrix of coefficient relations between y and x. The implications are that, for a given x and y:

1. x is a predictor (cause or stimulus) of y, and not the other way around (i.e. non-reversibility
2. ý is the systematic part of y, with respect to x
3. The systematic part, ý, is a linear function of x

The observational or empirical representation of Equation 4 would follow simply by including the index n for observations 1..., N:

$$y = \alpha + \beta x_n + v_n, \qquad\qquad ý_n \equiv E \,[y_n \mid x_n] = \alpha + \beta x_n$$

$$\Rightarrow E \,[v_n] = 0$$

$$\Rightarrow Cov \,[x_n, \, v_n] = Cov \,[ý_n, \, v_n] = 0$$

$$\Rightarrow Cov \,[x_n, \, v_n] = Cov \,[ý_n, \, v_n] = \beta \, var \,[x_n]$$

Therefore, it should be noted that identical distributions are not assumed. For any two cases, say n and n+1, no assumption is made that the residuals v_n and v_{n+1} have the same distribution. Nor is independence of cases required because no specification was made regarding the correlation between two different cases (i.e., $Cov \,[v_{n,} \, v_{n+1}]$. In general, a sufficient condition for consistency of least squares estimates is that, as the number of observations approaches infinity, the sum of the correlations between cases must stay below infinity (i.e., $\Sigma_i \mid cor(v_{n,} \, v_{n+1}] \mid < \infty$)) (Wold, 1988). Thus, predictor specification can be viewed as a least squares counterpart to the distributional assumption of ML modeling. It avoids the assumptions that observations follow a specific distributed. Therefore, no restriction is made on the structure of the residual covariances and, under least squares modeling; the residual variance terms are minimized.

In summary, Wold (1988) states that predictor specification "provides a general rationale for (i) least squares (LS) specification and (ii) LS estimation, and thereby also for the applications of (iii) the cross-validation test for predictive relevance…and (iv) the assessment of SEs by Tukey's jackknife" (p.587) which are used for model evaluation. Further discussions of the PLS methodology can be found in several articles (e.g., Areskoug, 1982; Barclay, 1985; Chin,1998a, 1998b, 2003; Chin & Gopal, 1995, 1997; Chin & Newsted, 1996; Dihjstram, 1983; Hui, 1987, 1982; Lohmoller, 1989; Wold, 1980, 1982, 1985, 1988).

References

Areskoug, B. (1982). The first canonical correlation: Theoretical PLS analysis and simulation experiments. In K. G. Joreskog & H. Wold (Eds.), *Systems, under indirect observation: Causality, structure, prediction* (pp. 95-128). Amsterdam, North-Holland.

Barclay, D., Higgins, C., & Thompson, R. (1995). The Partial Least Squares (PLS) approach to causal modeling: Personal computer adoption and use as an illustration. *Technology Studies, 2*(2), 285-309.

Chin, W. W. (1998a). Issues and opinion on structural equation modeling. *MIS Quarterly, 22*(1), March, Commentary.

Chin, W. W. (1998b). The partial least square approach for structural equation modeling. In G. A. Marcoulides (Ed.), *Modern methods for business research* (pp. 295-336). Mahwah, NJ: Erlbaum.

Chin, W. W. (2003). A permutation procedure for multi-group comparison of PLS models. *Proceedings of the PLS'03 International Symposium* (pp. 33-43).

Chin, W. W., & Gopal, A. (1995). Adoption intention in GSS: Relative importance of beliefs. *The Data Base for Advances in Information Systems, 26*, 42-46.

Chin, W. W., Gopal, A., & Salisbury, W. D. (1997). Advancing the theory of adaptive structuring: The development of a scale to measure faithfulness of appropriation. *Information Systems Research*, (8), 342-367.

Chin, W. W., & Newsted, P. R. (1996). Structural equation modeling analysis with small samples using partial least squares. *Statistical Strategies for Small-Sample Research*, 321-326.

Dihjstram, T. (1983). Some comments on maximum likelihood and partial least squares methods. *Journal of Econometrics, 22*, 67-90.

Hui, B. S. (1987). *The partial least squares approach to path models of indirectly observed variables with multiple indicators*. Unpublished Doctoral Dissertation, University of Pennsylvania, Philadelphia.

Hui, B. S. (1982). On building partial least squares models with interdependent inner relations. In K. G. Joreskog & H. Wold (Eds.), *Systems under indirect observation: Causality, structure, prediction* (pp. 249-272). Amsterdam: North-Holland.

Lohmoller, J. B. (1989). *Latent variable path modeling with partial least squares*. Heidelberg, Germany: Physica-Verlag.

Wold, H. (1980). Model construction and evaluation when theoretical knowledge is scarce: Theory and application of partial least squares. In J. Kmenta & J. B. Ramsey (Eds.), *Evaluation of econometric models*. New York: Academic Press.

Wold, H. (1982). Soft modeling: The basic design and some extensions. In K. G. Joreskog & H. Wold (Eds.), *Systems under indirect observations: Causality, structure, prediction* (Part 2) (pp. 1-54). North-Holland, Amsterdam.

Wold, H. (1985). Partial least squares. In S. Kotz & N. L. Johnson (Eds.), *Encyclopedia of statistical sciences*, 6 (pp. 587-591). New York: Wiley.

Wold, H. (1988). Specification, predictor. In S. Kotz & N. L. Johnson (Eds.), *Encyclopedia of statistical sciences*, 8 (pp. 587-599). New York: Wiley.

Appendix VIII

Descriptive Analysis

	Mean	Median	Standard Deviation	Variance	Range	Minimum	Maximum
FI	3.40	3.00	1.08	1.17	4.00	1.00	5.00
TR	3.03	3.00	1.27	1.61	4.00	1.00	5.00
FA	3.19	3.00	1.12	1.25	4.00	1.00	5.00
NE	2.95	3.00	1.13	1.28	4.00	1.00	5.00
TL	3.01	3.00	1.14	1.29	4.00	1.00	5.00
DW	3.73	4.00	1.28	1.63	4.00	1.00	5.00
CA	3.30	3.00	1.21	2.10	4.00	1.00	5.00
MT	3.91	4.00	1.07	1.14	4.00	1.00	5.00
WL	3.83	4.00	1.07	1.14	4.00	1.00	5.00
ET	3.47	4.00	1.17	1.36	4.00	1.00	5.00
EF	3.57	4.00	0.99	0.97	4.00	1.00	5.00
CP	3.92	4.00	1.04	1.09	4.00	1.00	5.00
CB	3.35	3.00	1.00	0.99	4.00	1.00	5.00
CT	3.27	3.00	1.04	1.09	4.00	1.00	5.00
AR	3.24	3.00	1.17	1.38	4.00	1.00	5.00
SP	3.60	4.00	1.20	1.44	4.00	1.00	5.00
EC	3.55	4.00	1.28	1.63	4.00	1.00	5.00
Position	4.99	5.00	3.27	10.71	9.00	1.00	10.00
Training	2.46	3.00	0.84	0.70	3.00	1.00	4.00
Education	2.91	3.00	0.95	0.90	4.00	1.00	5.00
Member	5.42	7.00	1.98	3.91	6.00	1.00	7.00
Age	3.24	3.00	1.10	1.20	5.00	1.00	6.00
Gender	1.74	2.00	0.44	0.19	1.00	1.00	2.00
Quality cert.	4.38	6.00	2.56	6.53	6.00	1.00	7.00
States	2.22	2.00	1.58	2.49	7.00	1.00	8.00
Artifact type	2.21	2.00	1.03	1.05	3.00	1.00	4.00
Reviewer	3.00	3.00	1.31	1.71	4.00	1.00	5.00
Moderation	1.98	2.00	1.07	1.15	4.00	1.00	5.00
Reader	1.56	1.00	0.81	0.65	4.00	1.00	5.00
Author	2.22	2.00	1.21	1.46	4.00	1.00	5.00
Record	1.58	1.00	0.90	0.80	4.00	1.00	5.00
Preparation	2.86	2.00	1.19	1.41	4.00	1.00	5.00
Independent	2.81	2.00	1.22	1.49	4.00	1.00	5.00

Descriptive Analysis (cont.)

	Mean	Median	Std. Deviation	Variance	Range	Minimum	Maximum
IND	3.72	4.00	1.30	1.70	4.00	1.00	5.00
RE	2.22	1.00	1.52	2.32	4.00	1.00	5.00
CX	3.26	3.00	1.27	1.60	4.00	1.00	5.00
SZ	3.03	3.00	1.14	1.30	4.00	1.00	5.00
IQ	2.82	3.00	1.14	1.30	4.00	1.00	5.00
CK	2.52	2.00	1.43	2.04	4.00	1.00	5.00
SR	2.34	2.00	1.43	2.04	4.00	1.00	5.00
ST	1.69	1.00	1.07	1.14	4.00	1.00	5.00
FR	1.28	1.00	0.64	0.41	4.00	1.00	4.00
SS	2.10	2.00	1.21	1.47	4.00	1.00	5.00
PG	2.47	2.00	1.36	1.86	4.00	1.00	5.00
TA	2.19	2.00	1.29	1.67	4.00	1.00	5.00
RF	2.45	2.00	1.55	2.40	4.00	1.00	5.00
RQ	3.29	3.00	1.29	1.67	4.00	1.00	5.00
DE	2.96	3.00	1.44	2.09	4.00	1.00	5.00
CD	2.20	2.00	1.32	1.73	4.00	1.00	5.00
BR	1.76	1.00	1.29	1.66	4.00	1.00	5.00
TE	2.45	2.00	1.47	2.15	4.00	1.00	5.00
LA	1.40	1.00	0.66	0.44	2.00	1.00	3.00
SE	2.44	2.00	1.03	1.06	4.00	1.00	5.00
EP	1.82	2.00	0.92	0.84	3.00	1.00	4.00
UD	1.73	1.00	0.89	0.80	4.00	1.00	5.00
PR	2.06	2.00	0.96	0.91	4.00	1.00	5.00
RF	1.67	1.00	0.86	0.74	4.00	1.00	4.00
TM	3.69	4.00	0.89	0.78	4.00	1.00	5.00
WP	4.13	4.00	0.84	0.70	4.00	1.00	5.00
SH	3.54	3.00	0.99	0.99	4.00	1.00	5.00
IB	2.67	1.00	0.94	0.89	4.00	1.00	5.00
ID	2.92	3.00	1.16	1.35	4.00	1.00	5.00
ME	3.68	4.00	0.95	0.91	4.00	1.00	5.00
AP	3.54	4.00	0.93	0.87	4.00	1.00	5.00
CO	3.64	4.00	1.01	1.02	4.00	1.00	5.00

continued on following page

Descriptive Analysis (cont.)

	Mean	Median	Standard Deviation	Variance	Range	Minimum	Maximum
Group meeting	2.49	2.00	1.13	1.27	4.00	1.00	5.00
Number of Meetings	2.06	2.00	0.75	0.57	4.00	1.00	5.00
Main products	5.59	5.00	3.34	11.17	9.00	1.00	10.00
Industry	9.05	10.00	4.26	18.18	12.00	1.00	13.00
Employees Dept.	2.86	2.00	1.51	2.29	6.00	1.00	7.00
Employee Aus.	5.02	5.00	2.20	4.82	10.00	1.00	11.00

Appendix IX

Software Review in Practice

1. Is software review common in practice?
2. How do you conduct software review? (i.e., requirement, design, code, and testing case).
3. What are the key major issues of conducting reviews?

Common Types of Inputs

4. How do you select the reviewers?
5. What are the key factors for the use of reviewers?
6. Why are the key factors influencing select of these reviewers?
7. What are the COMMON types of supporting documents you use in requirements and design review?
8. What are the key factors for choosing these documents?

Usage of the Inputs During the Process

9. How do you assign the roles or task of the reviewers? (Hint: Is there roleassignment?

10. How do you use these documents during the review process?

11. When do you use these documents during the review process?

12. How do you use (read) the documentation (Hint: Do you use a checklist)? Do you take a top-down approach (following instructions in order)? Do you apply (read) different supporting documents at the same time?

13. At what point in the defect detection process do you start to use (read) these documents (Hint: at the beginning, middle and at the end of the process) ?

14. What percentage of the detect defection process does the use of documentation comprise?

Inputs Affect Outcomes

15. What documents are useful helping you to find defects? If yes, which documents are most valuable?

16. What are the key-factors influence your performance?

17. Why do these key factors influencing your performance?

Costs and Benefits

18. How do you evaluate the benefits of these inputs? How do you evaluate these benefits based on the results/ or outcomes from the software review?

19. What are the costs of using these inputs?

20. How do you evaluate these costs of these inputs? How do you evaluate these costs based on the results/ or outcomes from the software review?

Demographic

21. What is the primary function of your business?

22. How many employees are in your company?

23. What is the total asset value of the company?

24. How many years of experience do you have in the software industry (i.e., both the interviewee or the organization)?

25. How many years of experience do you have in software project development (i.e., both the interviewee or the organization)?

26. How many years of experience do you have in software review [i.e., both the interviewee or the organization?]?

27. Have you been trained in software review (i.e., formal and informal training)? How much software review training have you had? (Specify in hrs, weeks, months and years)? What type of training? (i.e., both the interviewee or the organization?)?

28. What is your educational level? (Hint: Doctoral, Master, or Postgraduate Diploma, University Graduate, Undergraduate Diploma, Other tertiary [e.g., College diploma or certificate] High School or Primary)?

29. What is your age group? (Hint: Under 25, 25-30, 31-40, 41-50, 51-60, over 65)

30. What is your position in the organization?

31. Are you male or female?

Appendix X

The 10-steps of data analysis are (Miles & Huberman, 1984):

1. Finding a focus — questionnaire design was based on the EIIO model.

2. Managing data — record answers in electronic form.

3. Reading and annotating — a checklist was developed using EIIO model to guide reading and make comparisons. Annotating data involves making notes about the data (Miles & Huberman, p. 88).

4. Creating categories — grouped data and developed a set of criteria indicating how to distinguish observations as similar or related. This was done by developing a set of categories, with each category expressing a set of criteria for distinguishing some observation from others, as similar or related in some particular respect (Miles & Huberman, p. 96).

5. Assigning categories — if the data are not actually transferred, they are copied, and the copy filed under the appropriate category (Miles & Huberman, p. 113).

6. Splitting and splicing — also known as recontextualization (Tesch, 1990). This splits up the results into a number of subcategories. Splicing is a process of identifying formal connections among categories (Miles & Huberman, p. 151).

7. Linking data and making connections linking the data to the EIIO model (Miles & Huberman, p. 157). Making connection is to connect two categories based on our observation and experience of links and how they operate. So, the links are an empirical basis for connecting categories.

8. Of maps and matrices — The matrices are used for making comparisons across cases, and maps for representing the shape and scope of concepts and connections in the analysis (our computer will help us to do these)

9. Corroborating evidence — collects evidence to check the quality (include validity and reliability) of data (Miles & Huberman, p. 224).

10. Producing an account — The techniques for producing an account are tabulating tables and writing texts. To produce an account, we have to incorporate the disparate elements into a coherent whole. As the ultimate product of the analytic process, it provides the overall framework for our analysis.

Conclusion

This sequence reflects the logical relationships between different phases. But in practice we rarely proceed in a direct line from the first encounters with the data to the conclusions. Because of that, it is more realistic to imagine qualitative data analysis as a series of spirals as we loop back and forth through various phases within the broader progress of the analysis (Miles & Huberman, p.264).

References

Miles, M. B. & Huberman, A. M. (1984). *Qualitative data analysis: A sourcebook of new methods.* Beverly Hill, CA: Sage.

About the Author

Dr. Yuk Kuen Wong holds a PhD in computing sciences from The University of Technology Sydney (UTS). She received a master's degree in advanced information systems and management from The University of New South Wales (UNSW) and a Bachelor of Commerce from The Curtin University of Technology.

Her research expertise includes software review, system and software process improvement, and empirical software engineering. Dr. Wong recently produced high quality publications (book, journals, and referred conference papers) in the past two years.

Dr. Wong is currently teaching at Griffith University. She taught at The UNSW and UTS between 2001 and 2004. Prior to her academic appointments, she worked in the areas of enterprise resources planning systems implementation, systems, and business processes re-engineering consulting, e-commerce solutions, logistics, operations and procurement, sales and marketing, and product development since 1991.

Index

Advances in Software Maintenance Management:
Technologies and Solutions

Macario Polo, Mario Piattini and Francisco Ruiz
University of Castilla La Mancha, Spain

Advances in Software Maintenance Management: Technologies and Solutions is a collection of proposals from some of the best researchers and practitioners in software maintenance, with the goal of exposing recent techniques and methods for helping in software maintenance. The chapters in this book are intended to be useful to a wide audience: project managers and programmers, IT auditors, consultants, as well as professors and students of Software Engineering, where software maintenances is a mandatory matter for study according to the most known manuals - the SWEBOK or the ACM Computer Curricula.

ISBN 1-59140-047-3 (h/c) • US$79.95 • eISBN 1-59140-085-6
• 310 pages • Copyright © 2003

"Software organizations still pay more attention to software development than to maintenance. In fact, most techniques, methods, and methodologies are devoted to the development of new software products, setting aside the maintenance of legacy ones."

Macario Polo, Mario Piattini, and Francisco Ruiz
University of Castilla—La Mancha, Spain

It's Easy to Order! Order online at www.idea-group.com or
call 717/533-8845 x10
Mon-Fri 8:30 am-5:00 pm (est) or fax 24 hours a day 717/533-8661

Idea Group Publishing
Hershey • London • Melbourne • Singapore